The Ethics and Economics of Agrifood Competition

The International Library of Environmental, Agricultural and Food Ethics

VOLUME 20

For further volumes:
http://www.springer.com/series/6215

Harvey S. James, Jr.
Editor

The Ethics and Economics of Agrifood Competition

Editor
Harvey S. James, Jr.
Department of Agricultural and Applied Economics
University of Missouri
Columbia, MO, USA

ISSN 1570-3010
ISBN 978-94-007-6273-2 ISBN 978-94-007-6274-9 (eBook)
DOI 10.1007/978-94-007-6274-9
Springer Dordrecht Heidelberg New York London

Library of Congress Control Number: 2013934952

Printed on acid-free paper

Springer is part of Springer Science+Business Media (www.springer.com)

Acknowledgements

This book would not have been possible without the support and cooperation of a number of people. First, I express appreciation to the authors—a group of outstanding scholars who greatly improved my understanding of the agrifood industry. They made me think about competition in ways that were innovative and insightful. The authors were also helpful in expanding my network of colleagues interested in agrifood competition and derivative issues and problems.

Second, I acknowledge the cooperation of organizing committees for the 2011 annual meetings of the Agriculture, Food and Human Values Society and the Agricultural and Applied Economics Association. Special sessions in each meeting allowed many of the authors to present preliminary versions of their chapters and to receive feedback from a receptive group of colleagues.

Third, because the book was peer reviewed, it benefited from several anonymous scholars who offered comments for improving individual chapters and the book as a whole. There were several necessary "course corrections" that took place because of comments from the reviewers. The book is better because of their constructive feedback.

Fourth, I appreciate the support of the publisher and editorial team, with whom I have worked for a number of years because of my role as editor-in-chief of the academic journal *Agriculture and Human Values*, also published by Springer.

Finally, I am eternally grateful to my wife, Heather, and children, Isaac and Hannah, who continually encourage me to explore, learn and grow, not only as a scholar but also as a human being. This book is evidence of their loving and unqualified support.

Contents

About the Authors

Gilberto Aboites-Manrique, Ph.D., is a researcher at the Centro de Investigaciones Socioeconomicas (Center of Socioeconomic Research), Universidad Autónoma de Coahuila (Autonomus University of Coahuila) and a professor at Universidad Autónoma Agraria Antonio Narro (The Antonio Narro Agrarian Autonomus University), Saltillo, Coahuila, México. Most of his research focuses on the impacts of globalization on the State of Coahuila and Mexico regarding labor, the home, and patterns of food consumption.

Vera Belaya, Ph.D., is a scientific researcher at Institute of Farm Economics of Johann Heinrich von Thünen-Institute (vTI). She completed her Ph.D. at the Department of Agricultural Markets, Marketing and World Agricultural Trade of the Leibniz Institute of Agricultural Development in Central and Eastern Europe (IAMO). Vera received her diploma in Accounting and Auditing from Economic Faculty of Astana Agrarian University (Kazakhstan) and her master's degree in Business Administration in Agriculture from University of Applied Sciences Weihenstephan (Germany). Vera has published in such journals as *Journal of Relationship Marketing, The Marketing Review, Post-Communist Economies* and *Journal for East European Management Studies* and presented several papers at a number of international scientific conferences. Vera's research areas include business to business marketing, strategic management, and economic assessment of food safety, among others.

Alessandro Bonanno, Ph.D., is Texas State University System Regents Professor of Sociology and Scholar in Residence at Sam Houston State University. In recent years, Dr. Bonanno has researched the implications that globalization has for social relations and institutions. In particular and employing the agro-food sector as an empirical area of concentration, he investigated the impact that globalization has on the state, democracy and the emancipatory options of subordinate groups. Dr. Bonanno has written and/or edited 14 books and more than 100 referred publications which appeared in English and other major languages. His work appeared in journals such as *Sociological Quarterly*, *Rural Sociology*, *American Studies*, *Current Perspectives in Sociological Theory*, *Critical Sociology*, *Sociological Spectrum*, *Journal of Rural*

Studies, *Agriculture and Human Values*, *International Journal of Sociology of Agriculture and Food*, *Sociologia Ruralis*, and *Research in Social Movements and Change*. Dr. Bonanno is the current (2011–2013) editor of *Rural Sociology* and the past President (2004–2208) of the International Rural Sociological Association (IRSA).

Douglas H. Constance, Ph.D., is Professor in the Department of Sociology at Sam Houston State University. His research focuses on the community impacts of the globalization of agriculture and sustainable agriculture. Dr. Constance has published several articles, book chapters, and books on this topic. He currently serves a Chair of the Administrative Council for the USDA/Southern SARE program. Dr. Constance is past-President of the Agriculture, Food, and Human Value Society (2007–2008) and the Southern Rural Sociological Association (2002–2003).

Patrick Flanagan, Ph.D., is an assistant professor of Theology and Religious Studies at St. John's University in New York. His primary research area is moral theology with a special interest in its application to information technology and the marketplace, and their convergence with Roman Catholic Social Teaching. Patrick completed his undergraduate work in Biology and Education at Niagara University and has an MDiv degree from the Seminary of the Immaculate Conception in Huntington, New York. He received his doctoral degree in Theological Ethics from Loyola University Chicago, where he wrote his dissertation on the intersection of the common good and information technology.

Xavier Gellynck, Ph.D., is a professor in the Department of Agricultural Economics in the Faculty of Bioscience Engineering at Ghent University (Belgium), where he directs a research group of 10 doctoral researchers. Professor Dr. Gellynck also has an M.S. in Industrial Economics from Ghent University and an MBA in Marketing Management of Service Industries from the Business School IAAE at the University of Aix-Marseille in France. His main fields of research interest are situated in the domain of agribusiness marketing and supply chain and network management. He is also founder and chairman of the board of management of Afoheat NV, a food machinery construction company, as well as a member of the board of management of Landbouwkrediet NV.

Jon H. Hanf, Ph.D., is a professor of International Wine Economics at the University of Geisenheim, where he also coordinates the Wine Business program. His research focuses on strategic marketing and collaboration covering the whole value chain. His work appears in journals such as *Agribusiness: An International Journal*, *Energy Policy*, *Food Economics*, *International Food and Agribusiness Management Review*, *Journal on Chain and Network Science*, and *Journal of Rural Co-operation.*

Aimé Heene, Ph.D., is a professor in the Department of Management, Innovation, and Entrepreneurship at Ghent University (Belgium), where he teaches strategic management for private and public organizations. Professor Dr. Heene holds a doctorate in educational sciences and an MBA from Ghent University. He has published five books on strategic management in private and public organizations and has served as a co-editor of a large number of English volumes on competence-based strategy theory.

Mary K. Hendrickson, Ph.D., is assistant professor in the Department of Rural Sociology at the University of Missouri, where she has spent 15 years providing extension programming on creating community food systems. She serves as the Undergraduate Advisor Chair in Sustainable Agriculture and teaches courses on sustainable food and farming systems. She has a B.S. in Agribusiness from the University of Nebraska, and M.S. and Ph.D. in rural sociology from the University of Missouri. Her research programs focus on understanding the changes taking place in the global food system and help farmers, eaters, and communities create profitable alternatives.

Philip H. Howard, Ph.D., is associate professor in the Department of Community Sustainability at Michigan State University. He has a master of Environmental Studies from The Evergreen State College, and a Ph.D. in Rural Sociology from the University of Missouri. Dr. Howard is a member of the editorial board of the journal *Agriculture and Human Values*. His research emphasizes visualizing structural changes in the food system, and characterizing consumer interests in food ecolabels.

Harvey S. James, Jr., Ph.D., is associate professor of Agribusiness Management in the Department of Agricultural and Applied Economics at the University of Missouri. He has a B.A. in Economics and an M.S. in Sociology from Brigham Young University, and an M.A. and Ph.D. in Economics from Washington University in St. Louis. Dr. James is editor-in-chief of the journal *Agriculture and Human Values* and is a member of the editorial board at *Business Ethics Quarterly*. His research interests are in applied ethics and the economic foundations of trust and ethical behavior.

Ani L. Katchova, Ph.D., is an associate professor in the Department of Agricultural Economics at the University of Kentucky. She has a Ph.D. from The Ohio State University. Dr. Katchova has served as an associate editor for the *American Journal of Agricultural Economics* and is currently on the editorial board for *Agribusiness: An International Journal*. Her research areas are industrial organization, agricultural finance, agribusiness management and marketing, and applied econometrics.

Francisco Martinez-Gomez, Ph.D., is researcher at the Centro de Investigaciones Socioeconomicas (Center of Socioeconomic Research), Universidad Autónoma de Coahuila (Autonomus University of Coahuila) and professor at Universidad Autónoma Agraria Antonio Narro (The Antonio Narro Agrarian Autonomus University), Saltillo, Coahuila, México. Most of his research has focused on the impact of globalization on rural development, in particular international negotiations in plant genetic resources and the social impacts of globalization and industrialization in agro-food systems.

Adrienn Molnár, Ph.D., is a postdoctoral researcher at the Department of Agricultural Economics at the Ghent University, Belgium. She has a degree in Agribusiness from the University of Debrecen, in Hungary, and a doctorate in Applied Biological Sciences from Ghent University. Her dissertation, completed in 2010, is entitled *Supply Chain Performance and Relationships: The European Traditional Food Sector*. Dr. Molnár is currently working on research projects in the field of supply chain management, focusing on performance and relationships in supply chains and networks, and supply chain governance and strategies.

Emelie K. Peine, Ph.D., is assistant professor of International Political Economy at the University of Puget Sound in Tacoma, Washington. Her research focuses on the political economy of international food systems, with emphasis on the role of transnational corporations in constructing systems of governance around global commodity complexes. Her past research has examined transnational capital in the development of the Brazilian soybean export sector. She is a 2012–2013 Fulbright Scholar and is using the award to continue the work presented in this chapter. Her project examines the implications of Chinese investment in the Brazilian soybean industry for both Brazilian soy farmers and Brazilian food sovereignty.

Yasha Rohwer, Ph.D., is the Postdoctoral Fellow for the Mizzou Advantage One Health/One Medicine Initiative at the University of Missouri. He earned his Ph.D. in Philosophy in 2012 from the University of Missouri. He also holds a master's in History and Philosophy of Science from Florida State University and a Maîtrise in Philosophie from the Université de Paris X, Nanterre. His postdoctoral research concerns the ethical implications of cognitive and moral enhancement of humans and animals, using an evolutionary framework. He also has ongoing projects in Philosophy of Biology, Epistemology and Environmental Ethics.

Erik Schweickert, Ph.D., is a Member of the German Parliament and a professor in the Department of Economics at the Geisenheim University. His research focuses on market analysis as well as policy analysis and recommendation. His work appeared in journals such as *Enometrica, Handlexikon der Europäischen Union*, and *International Journal of Cooperative Management*. Since 2009, Dr. Schweickert has also been a member of the German Parliament.

Michael E. Sykuta, Ph.D., is an associate professor in the Department of Agricultural and Applied Economics and Director of the Contracting and Organizations Research Institute at the University of Missouri. He received a B.S. degree in Economics from University of Missouri-St. Louis, and an M.S. and Ph.D. in Economics from Washington University in St. Louis. Dr. Sykuta is co-editor for the Social Science Research Network's *New Institutional Economics Abstracting Journal*. He has published in a variety of journals including *American Journal of Agricultural Economics*, *Journal of Law & Economics*, *Managerial and Decision Economics*, and *Journal of Corporate Finance*. He also co-edited *The Elgar Companion to Transaction Cost Economics*. His research focuses on the organizational structure and performance of agricultural businesses and markets, and on the law, economics and political economy of regulation.

Federico Tarantini, M.A., received his graduate degree in "Economics of European Integration" from Brussels University (ULB) and is currently working as academic assistant at the College of Europe, Department of Economics. He is responsible for the academic program "European Economic Integration and Business," focused on EU (de)regulation and single market, business and corporate strategy, and lobbying activity at European level. Mr. Tarantini's previous research activity concentrates on public finance and corporate governance.

C. Robert Taylor, Ph.D., is the Alfa Eminent Scholar (Distinguished University Professor) in Agricultural Economics and Public Policy in the College of Agriculture at Auburn University. Prior to joining the Auburn faculty in 1988, he held faculty positions at the University of Illinois, Texas A&M University, and Montana State University. He has conducted applied research on a wide variety of topics, including market concentration, conservation, buyer power, bioenergy, and sustainable agriculture. He has authored or coauthored 5 books and over 200 articles and reports. He has testified to Congress on concentration and consolidation of the food system and, in 2010, was invited by the US Department of Justice and USDA to testify at two of their Joint Workshops on Competition Issues in Agriculture.

Paul B. Thompson, Ph.D., holds the W.K. Kellogg Chair in Agricultural, Food and Community Ethics at Michigan State University. His research has traversed a wide array of ethical issues arising in connection with agriculture and food systems. Of late he has been focused on standards for animal welfare in concentrated animal feeding operations (CAFOs) and in the overarching debate between industrial and agrarian philosophies of agriculture. His most recent book, *The Agrarian Vision: Sustainability and Environmental Ethics*, was published by the University Press of Kentucky in 2010.

Katrien Van Lembergen, M.Sc., graduated as a Bioscience Engineer in Agriculture at Ghent University (Belgium) in 2009. In July 2009 she started as an assistant at the Department of Agricultural Economics of Ghent University. Besides academic teaching, she was mainly involved in the research activities of the European project Transparent-Food financed by the European Commission and took part in several research projects on price transparency in the food chain. In October 2010 she became lecturer of Agricultural Economics at the Bio- and Food Sciences Department in the Faculty of Science and Technology at University College Ghent.

Randall Westgren, Ph.D., holds the Al and Mary Agnes McQuinn Chair in Entrepreneurial Leadership in the Division of Applied Social Sciences at the University of Missouri. His research is focused on the evolution of firms and markets driven by product, process, and structural innovation, including the dynamics of supply webs. He holds the Ph.D. in Agricultural Economics from Purdue University and the MBA from the University of Denver.

Timothy A. Woods, Ph.D., is a professor of Agricultural Economics at the University of Kentucky, where he teaches agribusiness management and marketing of horticultural products, and he is a state extension specialist in horticulture, agribusiness marketing, and management, with the responsibility of facilitating the development of small agribusinesses and cooperatives. He recently served as the staff economist in the Kentucky Governor's Office of Ag Policy and Ag Development Board. His work in farm entrepreneurship, business planning, cooperative development, consumer market research for microenterprises, and facilitating value-added enterprises for farmers and agriculture has been presented at international workshops, professional meetings, and state and regional extension programs. Dr. Woods has worked extensively with agriculture in other countries, including programs in India, Ukraine, Romania, Indonesia, Thailand, Ecuador, and France.

Chapter 1
Introduction to the Ethics and Economics of Agrifood Competition: Connotations, Complications and Commentary

Harvey S. James Jr.

A sense of injustice must be examined even if it turns out to be erroneously based, and it must, of course, be thoroughly pursued if it is well founded. And we cannot be sure whether it is erroneous or well founded without some investigation.

– Amartya Sen (2009, pp. 388–389)

Abstract After briefly explaining the context for questioning whether the agrifood industry suffers from a lack of free and fair competition, this introduction has three objectives. First, to assess the meaning of adequate and fair competition. Second, to summarize the contributed essays published in this volume. Third, to comment about what the analyses tell us about the ethics and economics of agrifood competition.

1.1 Introduction

In 2010, the US Departments of Agriculture and Justice held five workshops on the issue of agricultural competition in the United States that allowed participation by farmers and agricultural producers.[1] Speaking in the opening session, US Attorney General Eric Holder said, "Is today's agriculture industry suffering from a lack of free and fair competition in the marketplace? That's the central

---

[1]Transcripts and videos of the sessions are available online at http://www.justice.gov/atr/public/workshops/ag2010/index.html

H.S. James Jr., Ph.D. (✉)
Department of Agricultural & Applied Economics, University of Missouri, Mumford Hall 146, Columbia, MO 65211, USA
e-mail: hjames@missouri.edu

H.S. James Jr. (ed.), *The Ethics and Economics of Agrifood Competition*, The International Library of Environmental, Agricultural and Food Ethics 20,
DOI 10.1007/978-94-007-6274-9_1,

question" (USDOJ-USDA2010, p. 11). The fact that the question is asked suggests a perception exists that too little attention has been given to the question of adequacy and fairness in agrifood competition. Given Sen's (2009) admonition to examine claims of injustice "thoroughly," a careful consideration of competition in the agrifood industry might be warranted. Why? Even a cursory review of the transcripts of the 2010 workshops reveals numerous claims by farmers and ranchers that the current state of competition in the agrifood industry is far from free and fair, especially in the livestock sector. There are also concerns that the economic system and laws governing the activities of participants within the agrifood industry are not only harmful to farmers but also contribute to a deteriorating physical environment and public health condition;[2] that the only way farmers can make a profit is with government support; and that the blame for this rests in large measure with the power and influence of large multinational corporations and policymakers who turn a blind eye to their (anti-)competitive tactics.

Not all farmers feel wronged by their industries, however. Some farmers testified at the workshops that the agrifood system works well for them. Even though farming conditions are different today than they were in previous generations, farms are more productive and farmers can choose the technologies and farming techniques they wish to use. For instance, one farmer stated in the opening session: "Challenging as it is to compete in this global marketplace, I would not choose to live in the past. The challenges are balanced by the opportunities. Life on the farm is better for me and my children. We have access to technologies, tools, and markets our parents could only dream about" (USDOJ-USDA 2010, p. 65).

Most people have an intuitive sense of justice and fair play, even if they can't articulate good reasons for why they believe the way they do.[3] If they lose a game but sense that the competition was fair, then most people are willing to take their loss, if not gracefully then at least not loudly. But if there is a perception that the competition was biased against them from the start, then people are likely to complain, as they should. The charge of inadequate and unfair competition therefore deserves a careful investigation, even if it is eventually found to be unsubstantiated. This book contributes to that effort. Its primary objective is to answer the question of whether there is adequate and fair competition in agriculture through conceptual and detailed studies of specific agrifood sectors. Moreover, agrifood scholars contributing to this effort not only address the question of adequate and fair competition, but also consider the perspective of farmers, since concerns about agrifood competition have generally been asked by or on behalf of them.[4]

---

[2]Quoting one farmer testifying at the meetings: "cheap food is not really cheap" (USDOJ-USDA 2010, p. 330).

[3]Sen (2009, p. 4) quotes an eighteenth century British judge who said the following: "consider what you think justice requires and decide accordingly. But never give your reasons; for your judgment will probably be right, but your reasons will certainly be wrong."

[4]For example, the subtitle of the US Departments of Justice and Agriculture workshops held in 2010 is "A Dialogue on Competition Issues Facing Farmers in Today's Agricultural Marketplace."

The question of whether there is adequate and fair competition in the agrifood sector is related to research on the consolidation and globalization of agrifood markets. Scholars have modeled how and data have confirmed that agrifood markets have become more concentrated over time.[5] For example, in the US the four largest (non poultry) animal slaughtering plants accounted for 26% of the value of shipments in 1967, but within 40 years that share more than doubled to 59%. Similarly, the four largest wet corn milling plants accounted for 68% of the total value of shipments in 1967 and 83% in 2007, while the total value of shipments by the four largest firms in flour milling increased from 30% in 1967 to 55% in 2007.[6]

There are a number of implications that arise from industry concentration, particularly in the agrifood sector. On the positive side, the merging and consolidation of firms and farms could capture economies of scale, resulting in increasing productivity and lower costs to downstream firms and consumers at the retail end (Paul et al. 2004; Nguyen and Ollinger 2006). On the negative side, industrial concentration could shift the locus of decision-making control and balance of economic power away from farmers towards agrifood firms (Hendrickson et al. 2001). Such a change may or may not be a bad thing. It would depend on the type of decisions made by agribusinesses and how they affect other stakeholders. It could also result in a reduction in innovation and R&D activity (Schimmelpfennig et al. 2004). But do data on consolidation and discussions of agrifood globalization tell the whole story about the nature of competition in the agrifood industry? Research presented in this book affirms that consolidation is not *de facto* evidence of inadequate agrifood competition. As demonstrated in several essays published here, the problem is more complicated than what concentration ratios tell us, and concerns about fairness make the question even more difficult to examine.

Having an interest in the question of whether agrifood competition is adequate and fair, I sought answers from the literature but came away disappointed. Few scholars have explored this issue, with the exception of the concentration studies noted above. In short, I have not seen a compelling argument that convinces me one way or the other about the adequacy and fairness of competition in the agrifood industry.

Is the nature of competition in the agrifood industry an important issue? I admit to having two minds on the subject (a typical failing of economists, I might add). On the one hand, it appears that the agrifood industry functions well. The system produces a plentiful supply of relatively inexpensive food and other products to

---

[5]The literature is extensive, but a sampling of studies includes: Drabenstott (1999), Sexton (2000), Hendrickson et al. (2001), Barkema et al. (2001), Reardon et al. (2009), and Howard (2009).

[6]Concentration ratios are reported in 1967 using SIC codes, while in 2007 they are reported using the revised NAICS codes. The bridge between SIC and NAICS codes for the data reported here is as follows: For animal slaughter the SIC code used is 2011 and NAICS used is 311611; for wet corn milling the SIC is 2046 and NAICS is 311221; and for flour milling the SIC is 2041 and NAICS is 311211. Data from US Census Bureau (2012) tables on concentration ratios, share of value of shipments accounted for by the largest companies for industries indicated.

consume – at least in the developed world. On the other hand, there may be serious questions about the state of our agrifood system. A sustainability perspective that takes into account not only the economic viability of farmers and food processors but also the environment and social justice concerns, including how economic benefits and costs are distributed, raises the question of whether there is something different and unique about how we grow and distribute the food we consume. Food is the most basic and essential of all requirements of humans and animals. Therefore, should agriculture and the question of how food is provided deserve *special* consideration relative to concerns about how other products and services are provided?[7]

Given this context, the remainder of this introduction has three objectives. The first is to discuss the meaning of adequate and fair competition. The second is to provide an overview of the contributions published in this volume. The third is to provide a final comment about what the analyses tell us about the ethics and economics of agrifood competition.

1.2 The Meaning of Adequacy

Competition is what happens when two or more rivals struggle to obtain an objective or prize that cannot be shared among them (Stigler 1987). Economic competition is rivalry for economic exchange opportunities and is thus linked to markets. It can be evidenced by the existence of an exchange price accompanying the transfer of goods or services from a producer to a buyer, or by an agreement (either formal or implied) between producer and buyer to exchange at some future date. Whether the exchanges are simultaneous or occur at different points in time, competition among producers implies that there is more than one producer or potential producer. The same is said about buyers; competition among buyers implies that there is more than one consumer or potential buyer of the product.

If competition is a rivalry among potential exchange partners, then when is competition adequate? This question turns out to be difficult to answer, which is one of the reasons why there is disagreement about the adequacy of competition in the agrifood industry.

According to neoclassical economics, competition is adequate when it is perfect or nearly so – that is, when it is easy for potential buyers and sellers to enter the market in order to propose exchanges, when buyers and sellers have sufficient

[7] Vorstenbosch (2000) addresses this issue by considering the question of whether farmers should be entitled to special compensation from public funds and whether such compensation deserves differential treatment (e.g., why not compensate workers or firm owners in other industries with public funds when adverse circumstances arise?). His argument is that compensating agricultural participants with public resources, perhaps justifiable historically, requires today "fundamental rethinking in view of the changing technological, economic, and cultural conditions of agriculture" (p. 81).

knowledge of or can obtain at low cost information about the products or services offered for exchange and their expected prices, when the products or services offered for exchange by different producers are similar, and when there are a large number of buyers and sellers. To the extent that some or all of these conditions are not met, competition will be less than adequate. For example, if exchange prices are not transparent or readily identifiable, then it may be difficult for potential sellers or buyers to determine the appropriateness of entering or exiting a market, the result being a suboptimal number of participants in the market. Similarly, if it is difficult for potential sellers to offer an exchange to potential buyers of a good or service – that is, if there are barriers to entry – then existing producers and sellers will face less competition than when it is easy for potential sellers to propose exchanges.

The extent to which barriers to entry (and exit) exist is the *sine qua non* of competition analysis and market power.[8] When entry and exit barriers are minimal, buyers and sellers will choose to participate in the market based on their assessments of the profitability of potential exchange opportunities. If participants believe they can earn profits by participating in the market, then they will enter it by offering exchange opportunities with other market participants. If they believe that the likelihood of profiting from exchanges is low, however, then they will look elsewhere for profitable exchanges. Expected profitability of exchange opportunities is related to market or exchange prices. Rising prices signal more favorable profit opportunities to sellers, but less favorable ones for buyers.[9] Exchange prices increase as sellers leave or as buyers enter, while exchange prices decline as sellers enter the market or as buyers exit. The result in such cases is that over time there will generally be enough buyers and sellers in the market so that no single participant can unilaterally affect the exchange prices, implying that market power is dispersed among market participants. Adequate competition could also indicate fair competition, if fair is defined by the extent to which market participants cannot influence market conditions. As entry and exit barriers become more prominent, however, the number of buyers and/or sellers in the market will decline, which allows market power to become concentrated into the control of fewer participants. In the case of monopoly (one seller) or monopsony (one buyer), a single participant has strong control over market price. A monopolist seller can reduce the amount of output it offers for sale in order to increase prices, while a monopsonist buyer can restrict the amount it seeks to purchase in order to lower prices offered to sellers. Within this framework, evidence of a declining number of market participants over time could indicate the existence of barriers to entry or exit, thus suggesting that competition is inadequate. For these reasons researchers interested in industry competition have given attention

[8]For a useful though simple discussion, see OECD (2007).

[9]The caveat here is that market prices have the appropriate signaling property when they are rising (or falling) relative to prices in other markets. If there is a general increase in prices characterized by inflation, then rising prices will not signal the potential for more favorable exchange opportunities to sellers.

to studies of concentration and consolidation, raising alarms when measures of industry concentration (e.g., four firm concentration ratios) become "too large."

However, a focus on the number of firms overlooks the fact that that there might be circumstances when competition is effectively adequate even when competition does not meet the technical definition of being perfect. The inverse may also hold: there might be cases in which an industry meets characteristics of perfect or near-perfect competition but other indicators suggest that competition is not adequate. In the case of the former, Baumol et al. (1982) argue that if there are few barriers to entry and any non-recoverable costs incurred to enter a market are low, then the *potential* for entry by new producers could be sufficient to generate competitive prices even in markets with few sellers. In the case of the latter, Diamond (1971) shows that even when there are many sellers marketing a standardized or homogeneous product, if it is difficult for buyers to discover prices and buyers randomly select stores to visit, then the market equilibrium price will be closer to that of monopoly than competition.

Moreover, what constitutes adequate competition differs depending on the theoretical perspective one takes, since not all economists accept the neoclassical framework as an appropriate standard. For example, an Austrian economics perspective on competition emphasizes the process by which competitive activity occurs – for instance, the extent to which entrepreneurs are able to identify and exploit profit-making activities – not necessarily static indicators of numbers of firms or monopolization. To this end, Hayek (1948, p. 105) distinguishes between an "intrenched (sic) monopoly" that aims to keep output low and prices high and a monopolist that "does comparatively little harm" and that acquired its position due to "superior efficiency." Similarly, a Schumpeterian approach distinguishes between competition within a market and competition between markets, arguing that the latter is the more important competition to worry about. In contrast, a Marxian perspective on competition focuses on the goals of firms to grow and to control resources, with emphasis placed on the size of firms, not necessarily on their numbers in a particular industry.

A determination of adequacy is also complicated by the fact that even if everyone agreed to adopt the neoclassical "textbook" definition of "perfect competition" as the appropriate standard and that such market conditions existed, there will still be losers in the economic game. When market competition functions well according to neoclassical principles, market prices will adjust so that buyers and sellers who are willing to exchange at the given market price are able to do so. However, there may (most likely will) be buyers who would be willing to participate in the market, but for the fact that the market price is too high, and there may be sellers who would be willing to participate in the market, but for the fact that the market price is too low. These non-participants might complain about the inadequacy of the market process, although competitors with an appropriate sense of fair play might not be moved to vocalize dissatisfaction with the process or outcome. Nonetheless, if they do, and if others, such as policymakers, listen to and heed their complaints without a careful examination of the market and behavior of other participants, then there may be a temptation to conclude that competitive conditions are not adequate. In other words, just as the state of industry competition cannot be assessed by a simple analysis of industry concentration, adequacy of competition should not be assessed merely from the commentary of participants.

So where does this leave us?

If I understand what farmers who complain about the adequacy of competition in the agrifood industry are saying, it seems that the standard of adequacy ought to be based on the extent to which there is rivalry among sellers from the perspective of buyers, and among buyers from the perspective of sellers. For example, even if there are only two buyers in a market, if they are strenuously engaging in efforts to secure economic exchanges with potential sellers of a product, then from the perspective of the sellers the efforts of the buyers to induce sellers to exchange with them rather than with a rival buyer might be sufficient to give the sellers reason to believe that competition is adequate. A similar assessment can be made (by buyers) if there is rivalry among potential sellers. From the perspective of buyers, any number of sellers could produce a belief or perception among the buyers that competition is adequate, as long as the sellers are strenuously engaging in efforts to attract buyers into exchange relationships with them. It is only when buyers and sellers cease having an incentive to strive for exchange opportunities that competition will be viewed as less than adequate. For this reason, perhaps adequacy is best evaluated by observing how and to what extent sellers seek potential buyers, and how and to what extent buyers seek potential sellers. If sellers are not strenuously striving to win over a potential buyer's business, or if buyers are not strenuously striving to win over a potential seller's business, then we have grounds to wonder "why not?"

As a case in point, one farmer and cattle feeder participating in the US Departments of Justice and Agriculture workshops made this observation: "... in my cattle operation, it's not unusual in a week's time that we're down to 15 and 20 min cash market per week compared to a grain producer maybe has 1,500 min a week in order to make grain sales, and it's because there are only a handful of end users in the cattle market versus ... end users for grain" (USDOJ-USDA 2010, p. 62). Although cattle feeders could enter into contracts with packers as an alternative to cash market sales, the fact that roughly two-thirds of the production value in cattle during the 2006/2007 growing season was *not* under contract (O'Donoghue et al. 2011), suggests that limited efforts as measured by time of buyers seeking exchange opportunities with cattle feeders in competitive bidding could be *prime facie* evidence for a claim of inadequate competition by cattle buyers. If so, then per Sen's (2009) admonition to investigate such claims "thoroughly" deserves attention.

1.3 The Meaning of Fairness

If rivalry is a key aspect in conceptualizing competition, then what is rivalry? A dictionary definition is that it is the struggle "to outdo another for acknowledgment, a prize, supremacy, profit, etc.," and it is synonymous with "opposition, antagonism" and "jealousy."[10] The synonyms suggest that a problem with rivalry is that there exists an incentive for the competing parties to seek ways of altering the competitive conditions in order to give themselves an advantage over others. It is this reason that Marshall, who wrote what is perhaps the first modern economic textbook, asserted that the word "'competition' has gathered about it evil savour, and has come to imply a certain selfishness and indifference to the wellbeing of others" (1920, bk 1, ch 1, sec 4). In other words, the very act of competing raises ethical issues of fairness, justice, propriety and self-restraint. Do economists recognize and account for the ethics of competition? Historically, yes, but most contemporary economic studies do not.

Much has been written about how ethical considerations, especially the role of justice, were necessary components of not only Adam Smith's theory of economics, but also other contributors to the early developments of economic theory and philosophy (see, for instance, Evensky 1993; James and Rassekh 2000; Verburg 2000). For example, Evensky (1992, p. 61) says that "Ethics is the *sine qua non* of the constructive competition envisioned by classical liberalism. Only in a community of ethical individuals can the invisible hand do its job properly, for it is ethics that keeps the hands of individuals from disabling, and thus distorting the actions of, the invisible hand. In the absence of such an ethical community, competition becomes destructive." Marshall (1920, bk 1, ch 1, sec 4) expressed a concern that modern economic conditions created "new openings for dishonesty in trade," in part because the "producer is now far removed from the ultimate consumer."[11] Accordingly, he recognized the importance of market participants who possess "habits of trustworthiness on the one side and a power of resisting temptation to dishonesty on the other." In other words, classical economic theory is built on a moral or ethical foundation, in the sense that the social benefits of individuals engaging in economic activities are maximized only when economic agents do not seek to opportunistically exploit vulnerabilities of their trading or exchange partners.

There are a number of scholars today who lament the fact that contemporary economic theory is devoid of ethical substance and reflection (e.g., Sen 1987), although some economists are attempting to re-emphasize the necessity of considering ethics and morality as the foundation of economic behavior (e.g., Rose 2011). Can one be a good economist without being concerned about ethics? The fact that economists need to be told that they "should care about moral questions," as Hausman and McPherson (1993, p. 673) eloquently argue, suggests that somewhere between the moral philosophy of Adam Smith's classical economics and the highly mathematical and technical approach to economics promulgated in graduate schools

[10]The quote is from the definition of "compete," and the synonyms listed are to the word "rivalry" (see http://dictionary.com, accessed 27 January 2012).

[11]Within agrifood scholarship, the phrase "farm to fork" and the issue of "local foods" reflect a similar concern about the growing distance between farmer and food consumer.

today, economic theory had lost its moorings to ethics.[12] This is no truer than in discussions about the merits and implications of economic competition.

The importance of ethics to economic competition is more than just a concern about the ethical behavior of people who participate in the market, however. A consideration of ethics and competition also reflects two other issues. The first is the appropriateness of market competition as a standard for economic activity, and the second is how competition should be structured and what limitations and oversight should be developed in order to organize and maintain a system of free and fair competition. The first issue is widely debated, with commentary ranging from Milton Friedman's argument that people should be "free to choose" whether and how to enter into market exchanges to Karl Marx's thesis that the inherent class struggle between the small number of capital owners and the majority non-capital owners make capitalistic competition a temporary precursor or step toward socialism.[13] The second issue deserves special attention.

In order to highlight the complexities associated with a study of what constitutes fair competition, I begin with Knight's (1935) extensive treatment of the subject from his book, appropriately titled, *The Ethics of Competition*. In this work, Knight critiques what he calls the "presuppositions [or conditions] of a competitive system,"[14] and he contrasts those conditions with what is necessary to consider the system fair. According to Knight, competition presumes the following: Individuals must be free to contract, while those who do so must "know what they want and [be] guided by their desires," which is to mean that they must also be "perfectly rational."[15] There must be "fluidity" of resources and perfect "mobility of all goods and services entering into exchange." Potential contracting parties must be perfectly able to recognize when there is a beneficial exchange opportunity and be able to access it. Individuals must also "have a rational attitude toward risk and chance," which means that they must be "reasonably fit and competent to take responsibility" (see pp. 41–46 for the full discussion).

Knight's purpose in articulating conditions for adequate competition is not to argue that these rarely hold in reality, nor is it to claim that these conditions are unsound in principle. Importantly, unlike Marx and other critics of capitalism, Knight's purpose is also not to argue that markets ought to (or will) be replaced by

[12]Sen (1977, p. 317) places the blame on Francis Edgeworth, whom Sen quoted as saying in his 1881 book, *Mathematical Psychics*, that "the first principle of Economics is that every agent is actuated only by self-interest."

[13]See, for instance, Friedman (1962), Friedman and Friedman (1980), and Marx (1867).

[14]Hence Knight's book can also be used as a framework for defining the meaning of adequate competition.

[15]However, this desire for individual satisfaction, according to Knight, means that there will be a strong incentive for "deceit and corruption" (pp. 41–42). This concern mirrors that raised by the classical economists about the need for justice in economic exchange.

other systems of organizing economic society.[16] Rather, his purpose is to show that adequate competition *alone* is inadequate as a social objective, because competition "cannot bring about an ideal utilization of social resources" without a concurrent consideration of the "ethics of distribution" (p. 46). In other words,

> a freely competitive organization of society tends to place every productive resource in that position in the productive system where it can make the greatest possible addition to the total social dividend as measured in price terms, and tends to reward every participant in production by giving it the increase in the social dividend which its co-operation makes possible. In the writer's [Knight's] opinion such a proposition is entirely sound; but it is not a statement of a sound ethical social ideal, the specification for a utopia (p. 40).

Simply stated, the conditions that make economic competition adequate are not fully consistent with what is needed for the system to be considered fair. In fact, Knight argued that there is a "deep-seated conflict" between the ideals of adequate competition and ethical concerns of fairness, liberty, and equality.

Does this mean that there is a tradeoff between efficiency and fairness? There has been a growing academic literature on this topic (Rabin 1998). Camerer and Loewenstein (1993) illustrate the problem this way: Economic theory presumes that efficiency is related to the amount of information trading partners have. The more information available, or the more complete information is, the more likely the parties in an exchange will reach efficient outcomes. In their experiments, however, Camerer and Loewenstein demonstrate that increasing the amount of information each party to an exchange has about the other party can increase perceptions of unfairness rather than improve the likelihood of efficient outcomes. For instance, suppose a pair of workers must decide on how to split the surplus from an activity requiring joint effort. If effort is normally difficult to observe or verify, then a worker who knowingly and typically expends less than the average amount of effort may appeal *ex ante* for an equal split of the surplus. But if the other party who typically expends a greater than average amount of effort receives credible information about the expected or actual work effort of her partner, then she may argue that a share proportional to effort is fairer. Thus, instead of improving efficiency, increasing information transparency could reduce it if there is a conflict about how benefits (or costs) are allocated. This suggests that resolving concerns about fairness *ex ante* could have efficiency benefits.

So, what is fair competition? There are two general approaches to answering this question, both of which are based on the idea of equating fairness with justice. One is to assess actual competition relative to an ideal state, and the other is to determine whether some improvements can be made to make it less unfair. The first approach is best illustrated by the work of Rawls (1971), who argues that justice (and thus fairness) should be assessed relative to an ideal state that all participants would agree upon if they did not know what their individual circumstances would be in

[16]For instance, while Knight believed that "There seems to be ground for treating Marx's conclusions seriously," he believed that Marx's "supporting logic" should be "repudiated" (p. 44, footnote).

reality.[17] In this view, fair competition in the agrifood industry would be defined by that institutional arrangement that allows each person an equal opportunity to participate in food production, processing, distribution or consumption. If there are inequities in outcomes – that is, if some participants in the agrifood industry benefit more extensively than others – then such a state is fair only if those individuals least advantaged in society have the greatest benefits relative to those they would have under any other feasible system of producing and distributing food. In this framework, fairness would have to take into consideration a global perspective, meaning that it would have to assess how the agrifood industry affects not only farmers and ranchers, farm input suppliers, food processors and grocery retailers, but also food consumers, noting particularly how the least advantaged are faring. For instance, are the poor and disadvantaged in society consuming more and better quality food in the current agrifood system (characterized by consolidation, global supply chains, and dominance by large multinational agrifood businesses) than they would by a system existing, say, 50 or 100 years ago, where a majority of citizens lived on farms and farm operations were relatively small and localized?

A Rawlsian approach to fairness would also have to assess the extent to which participants in the agrifood industry who assert a claim of injustice had a role in creating the system they may later complain about. For example, Vorstenbosch (2000, p. 93) asserts that although small farmers may not be able to influence the system in which they now find themselves, the

> development of modern farming – with its mechanization, artificial insemination and breeding programmes, its milking machines, its computerized feeding programmes, its genetically modified seeds, its use of pesticides, herbicides and fungicides – cannot be seen as a development that just 'happened' to the farmers or producers, without them having any control over the matter and for which they, therefore, don't bear any responsibility. Most developments are self-initiated and rationally decided on the basis of cost-benefit analysis.

In other words, one could argue that the current plight of farmers expressing concern about the state of agrifood competition reflects in part decisions farmers made regarding how they farm. If farmers don't like the system within which they operate, then they could seek to change it, or to engage in entrepreneurial efforts to create new marketing opportunities. The obvious limitation of the Vorstenbosch thesis, however, is that there is an historical context to the agrifood system. Farmers today are affected by the decisions farmers and other participants in the agrifood system made generations ago.

The second approach is best illustrated by Sen (2009), who argues that the question of what is just or fair can only be answered relative to the existing rather

[17]Rawls introduced the idea of the "veil of ignorance." If all members of society met to decide the rules by which they would live, and if they did so under a "veil of ignorance," not knowing what their circumstances would be in the society (e.g., whether they would be rich or poor, etc.), then what rules would they establish? Rawls argued that under a veil of ignorance people would choose a system of rules that ensured all members of society had access to basic liberties and that the least advantaged members of society received the greatest benefit relative to some other potential system of societal rules.

than ideal state. In his view, justice is not about reaching a hypothetical ideal, as it is for Rawls. Instead, it is about finding an outcome that is less unfair than current conditions. Thus, in the context of assessing the fairness of agrifood competition, Sen would say that the question of whether the agrifood system is fair is the wrong question to ask. For him, the better question is "Can we make the agrifood system less unfair than it currently is?" since it is likely that any analysis will find some elements of unfairness or injustice.

If we consider the perspective of farmers and ranchers, since they seem to be the ones most vocal about alleged injustices within the agrifood industry, then have consolidation, agricultural contracting, globalization and biotechnology made things more or less fair for them? On the one hand, some could argue that the advances in farm production and livestock growing technologies, accompanied by the growth in the scale of farming, have improved the economic well-being of farmers. On the other hand, some might claim that these changes have limited opportunities for farmers and constrained their choices, thus making their positions relatively more unjust over time (see, for instance, Hendrickson and James 2005). Sen acknowledges the fact that there will be conflicts of opinion, observing that "There may not indeed exist any identifiable perfectly just social arrangements on which impartial agreement would emerge" (2009, p. 15). This "inescapable plurality" of perspectives is not a weakness, according to Sen, but rather an opportunity to continually re-examine where we are and where we could go to provide incremental though real improvements in the fairness of the system. To this end, Sen proposes that a standard for deciding among competing claims about fairness is whether participants in the economic system have more *opportunity* to pursue their objectives and whether the *process* of deciding what opportunities to pursue is improved (see p. 228; emphasis in original). Thus, an assessment of the fairness of agrifood competition can build on these concepts.

Although I admit to being partial to Sen's perspective, whether we assess fairness relative to an absolute standard or ideal state, or to an incremental improvement to existing circumstances, we need to assess carefully how things actually are. Such is the objective of this book.

1.4 Analyses of Agrifood Competition

This volume is divided into two sections. In the first part, entitled "conceptualizing agrifood competition," the contributors use ethics and economics to illuminate ideas and perspectives that inform on and improve the way we think about agrifood competition. One important implication arising from this first collection of essays is that *how* we conceptualize competition affects the way we assess adequacy and fairness. In the second part, entitled "assessing agrifood competition," the contributors provide evaluations of competition in specific agricultural contexts.

In his chapter, "Conceptualizing Fairness in the Context of Competition: Philosophical Sources," Paul Thompson reviews four different philosophical approaches to defining and assessing fairness. These perspectives can be summarized as follows: An event is "fair" if (1) people who participate were not compelled to do so; (2) no participant is able to subvert the competitive efforts of others; (3) the outcome does not disadvantage the least well-off individuals relative to some other outcome; and (4) the rules for participation apply the same to everyone. Thompson states that "the plurality of ways in which fair competition might be understood philosophically matches up with the multiple and contrasting opinions on the fairness of competition in contemporary agriculture." This is important because knowing the philosophical essence of the argument commentators make about the nature of competition in the agrifood industry "opens a path to more fruitful analysis and debate over the issues." And a fruitful analysis and debate is precisely what we need.

Chapter three, by Yasha Rohwer and Randall Westren, is entitled "Are Ethics and Efficiency Locked in Antithesis?" The authors argue that it is not appropriate to describe a tradeoff between efficiency and ethics. Rather, efficiency should be assessed only after identifying relevant ethical norms. For instance, a production process could be efficient and ethically desirably, and a second one could be inefficient and ethically undesirable. The evaluation of whether a process is efficient or not must first take into consideration specifically-defined constraints, and ethical standards should be included. Rohwer and Westgren apply this idea to important questions relevant to agrifood production, arguing for a heightened sense of moral obligations "to people, animals, and the environment."

Michael Sykuta's chapter, "The Fallacy of "Competition" in Agriculture," defines free and fair competition, drawing heavily on the economic notion of perfect competition. He then presents evidence that the agrifood industry, particularly from the perspective of individual farmers and ranchers, "remains indisputably competitive." Sykuta states that complaints by farmers about inadequate and unfair competition are an attempt to hide a clear truth: Farmers who do not do well in the current competitive landscape are trying to farm the way they have always been farming, but this approach is contrary to the what competition is about. To remain competitive, farmers need to adapt, as do all producers in a dynamic and changing economic landscape. Sykuta asks: "Why are the interests of a minority of farmers, who are economically unable to compete, of greater value than the economic interest of the remaining farmers who make more effective use of their resources to compete in the market?" Competition should induce participants who want to excel to change their behavior in order to stay ahead of their competitors. Farmers who do not change should not be surprised if they lose. In such cases, complaining about their disadvantage is not fair.

Robert Taylor counters, in his chapter "Efficiency, Power and Freedom," that an economic approach that emphasizes efficiency as the primary justification for allowing competition to remain "free" is not fully compatible with a legal perspective that places an emphasis on normative concepts such as equity and fairness. A legal perspective is important in order to protect farmers, who "are particularly vulnerable to disproportionate economic and political power of large buyers," in part because they market perishable commodities. Unfortunately, Taylor claims, "economists have 'had their way' with interpretation of antitrust laws," so that instead of addressing concerns about unfairness in agrifood competition, policymakers and courts have promoted efficiency, the result of which has been increasing concentration of economic power in the hands of fewer and larger agribusiness firms. Taylor draws on the writings of numerous scholars to argue that a change is needed in how we think about and use the law to promote fair competition within the agrifood industry.

In the sixth chapter entitled "Networks, Power and Dependency in the Agrifood Industry," authors Harvey James, Mary Hendrickson, and Philip Howard state that an assessment of fairness is ultimately an assessment of how power is distributed within the agrifood industry. However, because power is difficult to define and measure, an alternative approach is to consider relative dependencies. When participants in the agrifood industry are equally dependent on each other, power is balanced and we can say the competitive relationships are fair. When some participants are more dependent than others, however, there is a power imbalance that has significant implications for how we think about fairness. James et al. draw on network exchange theory to identify principles relating dependency to the way in which farmers, agribusinesses and consumers are linked to each other. Then they examine the network relationships participants in the broiler, beef and commodity seed sectors to assess relative dependencies. They conclude that network exchange theory can provide a viable means of assessing the effects of competition on power and dependency in the agrifood system.

Patrick Flanagan provides an alternative perspective on agrifood competition in his chapter, entitled "Reaping and Sowing for a Sustainable Future: The Import of Roman Catholic Social Teaching for Agrifood Competition." Flanagan claims that Roman Catholic social teaching provides important insights into how we should think about competition in the agrifood industry, especially from the perspective of farmers. By reviewing letters written by Catholic popes between 1891 and 2009 on topics ranging from land, agriculture, and farmers to the competitive system, Flanagan is able to articulate a framework for evaluating the ethics of agrifood competition. He then argues that if governments and agribusiness firms could answer affirmatively that they promote and follow policies that help people overcome poverty and hunger, provide a sustainable food supply, and ensure a decent life for farmers and other agricultural workers, among other conditions, then "there would not even be a debate about the 'ethics' of agrifood competition." The fact that there is a debate suggests that participants in the agrifood industry could learn much about ethics and fairness from a more careful consideration of Roman Catholic social teaching.

Douglas Constance, Francisco Martinez, Gilberto Aboites, and Alessandro Bonanno review the development of the broiler production system in their chapter, "The Problems with Poultry Production and Processing." This system began as a collection of independent chicken breeders and processors centered in the Northwest US in the 1930s, but it evolved into the tightly controlled, vertically-integrated contract production system that the authors call the "southern model" because of its concentration in the US South. In this system, a broiler processing firm, called an integrator, contracts with growers to raise chicks that are owned by the integrator. The grower provides labor and growout houses while the integrator provides the chicks, feed, veterinary care and collects the broilers at harvest. From the integrator's perspective, the system is flexible because the production contracts allow the firm to control virtually all aspects of the production process without having to own land and buildings or manage workers. However, the authors also identify a number of ethical problems with the system, including how production contracts erode farmer autonomy by creating a cycle of dependency on the integrators. The authors argue that problems with broiler contracting are not unique to the broiler industry because the "southern model of poultry production will likely be the model of agrifood globalization as it spreads into other commodities." For this reason, the authors contend, ethical problems associated with contract broiler production need to be rectified in order to foster a more fair and just agrifood industry.

In chapter nine, "Agricultural Contracting and Agrifood Competition," Ani Katchova examines the increasing use of marketing and production contracts in agriculture and assesses their effects on market prices and the distribution of power in the agrifood industry. She summarizes current trends in agricultural contracting and also identifies benefits and risks associated with them. Katchova then answers the question of whether agricultural contracts restrict competition, increase the power of agribusiness firms or otherwise limit or distort the price mechanism. Although "the bargaining power of farmers will likely continue to weaken as more production shifts to contracting with larger processors," Katchova concludes that "there is limited evidence that processors are exercising market power in terms of offering lower prices to farmers who may not have other marketing options in their areas."

Emelie Peine examines the effect of a global supply chain on agrifood competition in her chapter, entitled "Trading on Pork and Beans: Agribusiness and the Construction of the Brazil-China-Soy-Pork Commodity Complex." She focuses on the trade between Brazil and China in soybeans "as a lens on global agrofood restructuring." In response to a rapidly expanding pork production system in China, Brazil increased its sale of soybeans to China, resulting in a tightly coordinated commodity complex between the two nations. Importantly, this system is not governed by the two governments but rather by the four largest transnational soybean brokers and processors, which Peine labels ABCD (for ADM, Bunge, Cargill and Dreyfus). Peine explains how these firms came to dominate the trade in soybeans between Brazil and China, revealing an increasing ability of global agrifood firms to rival the power of national governments in addition to dominate the soybean growers "for whom the 'free market' is a Smithian fantasy." Peine claims that her analysis reveals "another twist on the question" of agrifood competition by highlighting the fact that an assessment of competition cannot be limited to national boundaries.

In chapter eleven, "Who's Got the Power? An Evaluation of Power Distribution in the German Agribusiness Industry," Jon Hanf, Vera Belaya, and Erik Schweickert review definitions of power in order to assess how power is distributed between large grocery chains and agrifood processing companies in Germany. Using a framework in which power consists of different aspects or types, the authors examine transcripts from a government-sponsored meeting consisting of representatives from food processors, food retailers, farmers, scholars and policymakers (not unlike the workshops held in the US in 2010) in order to assess the extent to which food retailers have power over food processors. The authors find that there is power asymmetry in the German agrifood industry, although "not uniformly and not fully in favor of large retailers." Importantly, the authors argue that a consideration of distinct and specific aspects of power reveals that some food processors, even smaller ones, can maintain a competitive advantage relative to their larger competitors and relative to the largest food retailers. In other words, if we are interested in considering power distribution as a metric for assessing the extent to which agrifood competition is adequate, then it matters how power is defined and measured.

In their chapter, "Local Foods and Food Cooperatives: Ethics, Economics and Competition Issues," Ani Katchova and Timothy Woods explore the ability of local food cooperatives to provide a competitive advantage for agricultural producers relative to traditional retail grocers. Local food cooperatives capitalize on the growing popularity of regional food networks as an alternative to the traditional agribusiness food model. In a local food cooperative, consumers own the business. They emphasize the procurement of local as well as natural and/or organic foods. Generally, only members are able to purchase food from the cooperative. Katchova and Woods survey food cooperative managers in order to assess their ability to compete relative to other grocery retailers and to identify the most effective business practices and strategies for local food cooperatives. They argue that local food systems can be characterized by adequate and fair competition and that local food cooperatives can obtain comparative advantages relative to food retailers because they "will be able to develop better supply chain management and new cooperatives will be better aware of viable business models based on the characteristics of their local food networks." Such strategies also have advantages for local farmers supplying them. The chapter is important because it emphasizes the point that competition in the agrifood sector is not static. If farmers or other participants in the agrifood industry believe that competition from national or global agrifood businesses is inadequate or unfair, then they could consider other options in the development of alternative food systems.

In the final chapter, "Price Transparency as a Prerequisite for Fair Competition: The Case of the European Food Prices Monitoring Tool," Adrienn Molnár, Katrien Van Lembergen, Federico Tarantini, Aimé Heene, and Xavier Gellynck describe a system for tracking and reporting prices in key European agricultural sectors. They argue that a prerequisite to adequate and fair competition is the necessity of having transparency in agrifood prices. To this end, the European Union developed and implemented a system for making agrifood prices more transparent. This system, called the European Food Prices Monitoring Tool, provides aggregate price data in 17 selected food supply chains at three levels within each chain: farmer, food processor and retailer. The authors describe the justification and development of the price monitoring tool, identify its strengths and weaknesses, and explain how it can contribute to debates about fairness in agrifood competition.

1.5 The Lesson

The chapters in this volume represent a wide assortment of perspectives and approaches with respect to the ethics and economics of agrifood competition. Indeed, the collection might appear somewhat eclectic. While I could have solicited contributions with a narrow focus (e.g., livestock) using a single perspective (e.g., economics) targeting a particular audience (e.g., policymakers) considering all aspects, angles and arguments, I rejected this approach. The reason is that while there appears to be considerable interest in the topic of agrifood competition, as evidenced by the desire of the U.S. government to hold workshops on the topic, there has been very little systematic scholarly attention given to the question of agrifood competition. And herein is the strength of this collection of essays. The chapters in this volume paint a broad picture of the scope and complexity of the problem, and of the issues, arguments and perspectives that can and perhaps should be considered in efforts to assess the adequacy and fairness of agrifood competition. Thus, subsequent research can follow a number of different paths, with this book being a starting point.

Is there adequate and fair competition in the agrifood industry? According to the contributing authors of this book, the answers are "yes," "no," and "not sure." I suppose this is not surprising. Contributing authors presented arguments and analyses from different perspectives using different scholarly approaches and analytical styles, so it is not likely that there would be uniform consensus among them. That said, I admit that I had hoped there would be a definitive or emerging consensus so that I could state with confidence a clear answer to the question. Alas, I cannot, or at least will not, right now. There are compelling arguments for both sides. Thus, Sen's (2009) advice, quoted at the beginning of this essay, seems particularly relevant. We need a forum where scholars can respond to concerns expressed about the nature of competition in the agrifood industry through the presentation of careful and well-articulated arguments. I believe the contributing authors to this volume have done just that.

So what can we learn from the studies published here? It is simply that the topic of adequacy and fairness of agrifood competition is important and that significantly more attention is needed in addressing the question directly. If this book stirs the pot and generates an increase in scholarship on the topic, then I will consider it a success.

References

Barkema, A., M. Drabenstott, and N. Novack. 2001. The new U.S. meat industry. Federal Reserve Bank of Kansas City, *Economic Review* Second Quarter, 33–56.

Baumol, W.J., J.C. Panzar, and R.D. Willig. 1982. *Contestable markets and the theory of industry structure*. San Diego: Harcourt Brace Jovanovich.

Camerer, C.F., and G. Loewenstein. 1993. Information, fairness, and efficiency in bargaining. In *Psychological perspectives on justice: Theory and applications*, ed. B.A. Mellers and J. Baron, 155–180. New York: Cambridge University Press.

Diamond, P.A. 1971. A model of price adjustment. *Journal of Economic Theory* 3: 156–168.
Drabenstott, M. 1999. Consolidation in U.S. agriculture: The new rural landscape and public policy. Federal Reserve Bank of Kansas City, *Economic Review* First Quarter, 63–71.
Evensky, J. 1992. Ethics and the classical liberal tradition in economics. *History of Political Economy* 24(1): 61–77.
Evensky, J. 1993. Retrospectives: Ethics and the invisible hand. *Journal of Economic Perspectives* 7(2): 197–205.
Friedman, M. 1962. *Capitalism and freedom*. Chicago: University of Chicago Press.
Friedman, M., and R. Friedman. 1980. *Free to choose: A personal statement*. New York: Harcourt.
Hausman, D.M., and M.S. McPherson. 1993. Taking ethics seriously: Economics and contemporary moral philosophy. *Journal of Economic Literature* 31(June): 671–731.
Hayek, F.A. 1948. The meaning of competition. In *Individualism and economic order*, ed. F.A. Hayek. London: Routledge.
Hendrickson, M.K., and H.S. James Jr. 2005. The ethics of constrained choice: How the industrialization of agriculture impacts farming and farmer behavior. *Journal of Agricultural and Environmental Ethics* 18(3): 269–291.
Hendrickson, M., W. Heffernan, P.H. Howard, and J. Heffernan. 2001. Consolidation in food retailing and dairy. *British Food Journal* 103(10): 715–728.
Howard, P.H. 2009. Visualizing consolidation in the global seed industry: 1996–2008. *Sustainability* 1(4): 1266–1287.
James Jr., H.S., and F. Rassekh. 2000. Smith, Friedman, and self-interest in ethical society. *Business Ethics Quarterly* 10(3): 659–674.
Knight, F.H. 1935/2009. *The ethics of competition*. New Brunswick: Transaction Publishers.
Marshall, A. 1920/1997. *Principles of economics*. Amherst: Prometheus Books.
Marx, K. 1867/1906. *Capital: Critique of political economy*. New York: Random House.
Nguyen, S., and M. Ollinger. 2006. Mergers and acquisitions and productivity in the U.S. meat products industries: Evidence from the micro data. *American Journal of Agricultural Economics* 88(3): 606–616.
O'Donoghue, E.J., R.A. Hoppe, D.E. Banker, R. Ebel, K. Fuglie, P. Korb, M. Livingston, C. Nickerson, and C. Sandretto. 2011. *The changing organization of U.S. farming. Economic research service Electronic Information Bulletin EIB-88*. Washington, DC: US Department of Agriculture, Economic Research Service.
Organization for Economic Co-operation and Development (OECD). 2007. *Policy brief: Competition and barriers to entry*. Paris: OECD. http://www.oecd.org/dataoecd/9/59/37921908.pdf. Accessed 23 Jan 2012.
Paul, C., R. Nehring, D. Banker, and A. Somwaru. 2004. Scale economies and efficiency in U.S. agriculture: Are traditional farms history? *Journal of Productivity Analysis* 22(3): 185–205.
Rabin, M. 1998. Psychology and economics. *Journal of Economic Literature* 36(1): 11–46.
Rawls, J. 1971. *A theory of justice*. Cambridge: Harvard University Press.
Reardon, T., C.B. Barrett, J.A. Berdegué, and J.F.M. Swinnen. 2009. Agrifood industry transformation and small farmers in developing countries. *World Development* 37(11): 1717–1727.
Rose, D.C. 2011. *The moral foundation of economic behavior*. New York: Oxford University Press.
Schimmelpfennig, D.E., C.E. Pray, and M.F. Brennan. 2004. The impact of seed industry concentration on innovation: a study of US biotech market leaders. *Agricultural Economics* 30: 157–167.
Sen, A.K. 1977. Rational fools: A critique of the behavioral foundations of economic theory. *Philosophy & Public Affairs* 6(4): 317–344.
Sen, A.K. 1987. *On ethics & economics*. Malden: Blackwell.
Sen, A.K. 2009. *The idea of justice*. Cambridge, MA: Belknap Harvard.
Sexton, R.J. 2000. Industrialization and consolidation in the U.S. food sector: Implications for competition and welfare. *American Journal of Agricultural Economics* 82(5): 1087–1104.
Stigler, G.J. 1987. Competition. In *The New Palgrave: A dictionary of economics*, ed. J. Eatwell, M. Milgate, and P. Newman, 531–535. New York: The Stockton Press.

US Census Bureau. 2012. *Concentration ratios*. Washington, DC: US Census Bureau. http://www.census.gov/econ/concentration.html. Accessed 25 Jan 2012.

US Department of Justice and U.S. Department of Agriculture (USDOJ-USDA). 2010. *Proceedings, public workshops exploring competition issues in agriculture*. Washington, DC: US Department of Agriculture and Department of Justice. http://www.justice.gov/atr/public/workshops/ag2010/iowa-agworkshop-transcript.pdf. Accessed 16 Jan 2012.

Verburg, R. 2000. Adam Smith's growing concern on the issue of distributive justice. *European Journal of the History of Economic Thought* 7(1): 23–44.

Vorstenbosch, J. 2000. Of firms and farms: Agricultural ethics and the problem of compensation. *Journal of Agricultural and Environmental Ethics* 12: 81–98.

Part I
Conceptualizing Agrifood Competition

Chapter 2
Conceptualizing Fairness in the Context of Competition: Philosophical Sources

Paul B. Thompson

Abstract There are multiple ways of conceptualizing the notion of fairness. After reviewing the basis of fairness in human psychology, I present four different philosophical perspectives about fairness. Each of these perspectives is illustrated by considering well known perspectives from the history of philosophy. I conclude with a discussion of how these four approaches might be brought to bear in contemporary discussions of agrifood competition.

2.1 Introduction

Many current complaints about the competitive conditions that exist in American agriculture are ethical in nature. Their substance turns on a standard of fairness that is putatively not being met. Producers who "win" are believed to have been the beneficiaries of unfair advantages. The game is thought to be rigged so that some producers simply cannot be among the winners, no matter how worthy, efficient and viable their farming operations might be when evaluated objectively. If competition is unfair, those who do well in the current system do not deserve their profits. Those who control or exploit the terms of competition may have acted wrongly first by creating a system that is unfairly biased, by failing to correct the system once the bias has been recognized or by using ill-gotten gains to strengthen their position for future competition. There are thus layers of potential moral culpability that are implied by the idea that competition can be fair or unfair.

However, few analyses of competition in agriculture address it explicitly in ethical terms, and there are good reasons why. The academic and policy-related

P.B. Thompson, Ph.D. (✉)
Department of Philosophy, Michigan State University, 503 S. Kedzie Hall,
East Lansing, MI 48824, USA
e-mail: thomp649@msu.edu

H.S. James Jr. (ed.), *The Ethics and Economics of Agrifood Competition*,
The International Library of Environmental, Agricultural and Food Ethics 20,
DOI 10.1007/978-94-007-6274-9_2,

organizations that do analysis of agricultural issues have never invested in people who are trained in ethics. Rural social scientists often seem loathe to even acknowledge the existence of ethical issues, much less to develop an analysis of competitive conditions that draws explicitly on a normative idea such as fairness. There is also a widespread assumption that since everyone is supposed to act ethically, everyone must already know everything there is to know about ethics. But on the contrary, the idea of fair competition is complex in its own right. There are a number of different things that someone might mean by asserting that a competition is unfair, and it is sometimes difficult to tell what standard of fairness is being applied in any given circumstance.

Given the plurality of meanings, there is a real risk that placing emphasis on the *unfairness* of competition will create misunderstanding. This misunderstanding can lead to recriminations that poison the wells, making a civil and productive evaluation of competitiveness in contemporary agriculture impossible. Thus some of the reasons to be cautious about interjecting a specifically ethical theme into the analysis of agricultural competition are well motivated. Nevertheless, being able to articulate and examine an alleged problem of fairness will eventually bring one to ethics. The purpose of this chapter is to provide an overview of various criteria one might use that would allow a more dispassionate and measured use of ethical ideas in the discussion of competitive conditions in the agrifood industry.

Fairness may have a basis in human psychology that precedes any particular way of describing it or specifying standards for fair practice. It is therefore useful to begin with a brief discussion of the pervasive ways in which people perceive a situation to be fair or unfair, even in the absence of any well-conceptualized theory or view of fairness. Given this background, there are at least four different ways that one might develop and specify a systematic conception of fairness in the context of competition, and each can be illustrated by considering well known perspectives from the history of philosophy. First, when two or more parties form an agreement or contract that specifies future terms of their mutual conduct, the rationality and acceptability of the contract implies a standard of fairness. People would not find an unfair or biased agreement to be attractive or ethically acceptable. The early social contract theories of Thomas Hobbes and John Locke model this conception of fairness. Second, utilitarian philosophy begins with an analysis of the mutual benefits of competition, then defines fairness in terms that specify the conditions under which these benefits can be realized. Third, more recent work on the social contract by John Rawls made fairness into an explicit theme. His approach ties fairness to distributive justice and suggests an analysis that differs markedly from that of Hobbes and Locke. Finally, Robert Nozick's criticism of Rawls provides an alternative conceptualization that emphasizes consistency in application of rules, rather than the distribution of rewards.

After developing each of these conceptualizations, I conclude with a brief discussion of how each of these four approaches might be brought to bear in contemporary discussions of agrifood competition. I do not suggest that the four approaches I describe exhaust the playing field. Other alternatives could certainly be developed, and might well be better adapted to the cases discussed in succeeding chapters. Nor do I think that I have necessarily found the most natural or most consistent way to apply these approaches to ongoing debates about the fairness of competition in U.S. agriculture. One must start a discussion somewhere, and the most that I would claim for this chapter is that it is a place from which future analysts might begin to engage the normative dimension of an ethical problem in a more systematic and explicitly articulated manner.

2.2 Fair Treatment and Fair Play

The ability to perceive a given situation as fair or unfair develops in early childhood. Mainstream opinion in the psychology of moral development has held that "fairness" reflects a fairly complex integration of cognitive information, including semantic perception of factual states and emotive responses. Nevertheless, by 4 years of age children have developed sufficient integrative capacity to achieve a well-developed sense of equity (Anderson and Butzin 1978). Although there is considerable variation in the criteria for fair treatment across cultural groups, the cognitive capacity for experiencing fairness and internalizing a normative structure may be innate in humans (Sripada and Stich 2006). Children who observe a parent's treatment of siblings gauge whether the parental allocation of attention, affection and rewards is equitable according to a standard that comes to reflect a greater number of variables (developmental timing, differential needs, and unique situations, for example) as they mature. However, persistent preferential treatment of siblings is internalized in a variety of ways that are injurious to a child's well-being (Kowal et al. 2002). Developmental psychologists theorize fairness and equity within the context of sibling competition, arguing that parents must structure this competition and balance the relative distribution of their time and resources among siblings. Failure in this parenting task results in dysfunctional personalities and unhappiness (Volling et al. 2010).

The capacity to evaluate the conduct of others according to a norm of fairness may not only be innate, but also not even be unique to the human species. A number of predatory species engage in a form of play behavior that is thought to refine and develop their hunting skills, to prepare them for intra-group tests of dominance and to hone their fighting abilities in defending prey or territory. These play activities are typically initiated by a "bow" that signals mutual agreement to engage in behavior that would otherwise be aggressive. Animals engaged in play hold back on biting or clawing that could inflict real harm (Bekoff 1995). Animals that violate the implicit norms of fair play are subjected to retaliatory punishment. Bekoff and Pierce (2009) have argued that this behavior can be understood as a form of "wild justice", a precursor to the fully moral notions of fair play found in humans.

In these literatures, fairness is a norm reflecting a situation in which two or more individuals' behavior is tested or evaluated for conformity to expectations. These expectations are themselves formed within a context of competition, games and play. The conformity or nonconformity to expectations provides the basis for a moral standard: conduct is morally right or morally wrong according to whether the competition is played or adjudicated in a manner that is expected. However, the competition, game or play is itself structured by variables that determine which elements of situation are salient for the formation of expectations. We may suppose that in the case of play behavior among wolves or coyotes, this structure is a mix of neural architecture and learning by imitation. Among humans, additional variables become salient as individuals learn to evaluate a parent's behavior as a response to both shared and divergent needs of siblings.

The emphasis on adjudication and plays suggests that the relevant expectations have a rule-like structure. Rules create a structure of sameness and difference. Play differs from fighting or hunting, and it is structured by the similarities it bears to these "serious" behaviors as much as by the differences. Once in place, a rule structure reflects a class of cases or situations that can be and should be treated alike. In the case of sibling rivalries, parenting must reflect certain sameness or equality of treatment at the same time that it is capable of reflecting a highly nuanced system of differences. Unfairness is, in this sense, a failure to abide by the rule of treating like circumstances as like. But at the same time, in the complex games that human families play, there may be numerous opportunities to refine and revise the rules that govern sibling expectations. In this process of revision and adjustment, more abstract and principled conceptions of fairness begin to emerge.

Significantly, concepts of fairness, competition and play appear to interpenetrate one another, achieving a form of meaning coherence Wittgenstein analyzed as a "language game" that defies conventional approaches to definition (Wittgenstein 1952). People who share a language can discuss play, fairness and competition in meaningful ways. Although we can exhibit our facility with these concepts, however, we cannot isolate them and offer discrete definitions without engaging in circularity. That is, we find ourselves relying on our ability to *use* a word like "fairness" in our very attempts to *define* it. We may rely on near synonyms (like "equitable" or "unbiased") but our attempts at definition thus fail to explain a concept or provide criteria of meaning that would be useful to someone who did not already have facility with the word in common communicative contexts. There is thus a profound sense in which fairness must be regarded as a primitive: as something *felt* rather than cognized, interpreted or intellectually grasped. At the same time, human beings' seemingly infinite ability to refine and restructure the rules by which we engage one another leaves room for considerable diversity in specific conceptions of fairness, as well as in different cultural or exchange traditions where criteria of fairness and unfairness may be applied.

2.3 Fairness and the Social Contract

Fairness has a close connection to exchange relations, contracts and the governance of such within the written literature of ethics and politics. In a tradition that begins with Thomas Hobbes, a political relationship between two or more people is regarded as ethically legitimate if it reflects the bargain that they might have struck absent of violence and coercion. Fairness is subtly indicated in the idea that the bargain reflects a value for value trade: each party is getting something of equal value. In the case of large bargains among all members of society—the social contract—all parties are presumably benefiting and benefiting equally. At the same time, fairness is also implicated in the idea that a bargain struck under the threat of coercion is no bargain at all. And why not? It would be unfair.

Hobbes and John Locke developed the most influential versions of social contract, and both utilize the constructs of a state of nature and a state of war. For present purposes, these constructs (along with the social contract itself) are regarded as "intuition pumps": metaphors or narratives that invite us to conceptualize and experience competition or fairness in one way rather than another. As such, some liberties are taken with the specific formulations that would be found in definitive textual sources such as Hobbes' *Leviathan* (1761) or Locke's *The Second Treatise of Government* (1793). The treatment offered here is not intended as a historically faithful interpretation of these philosophical works or their authors' intentions.

For both Hobbes and Locke, the state of nature is a situation devoid of civil authorities. People in the state of nature are unbound by civil law and unburdened by the coercive force of the state, embodied in the police power. They are maximally free. For Locke if not Hobbes, the state of nature is portrayed in idyllic terms: People go about their daily affairs quite like they might have done in late seventeenth century England, making trades and conducting business according to the dictates of the natural law. But the moral force of the natural law is weak. Envy and covetousness drive them to theft, extortion and acts of violence. For both Locke and Hobbes, the state of war is characterized by extreme and unregulated competition amongst men, where each is constantly at risk from whatever action seems momentarily advantageous to anyone else.

Whether created by compact (Hobbes) or dictated by God (Locke), morality is a co-operative endeavor that constrains competition. But morality is not enough. The police are needed to constrain the wicked and relieve the fair from the constant burden of self-defense. The authority to implement police power is created by the social contract, where people relinquish their right to retaliate and to punish offenders who violate the moral code, assigning a monopoly on the use of coercive force to the state. The metaphor of a contract suggests both that this transfer of right is done voluntarily, and that it is in the obvious interests of all to do so. Hobbes and Locke thus utilize a value-for-value trade to model the perspective from which the principles of civil society are to be evaluated. Contractors agree amongst themselves to trade the state of nature for the civil society. This bargain is a fair one only if people derive enough benefit to compensate them for the loss of their freedoms.

In common commerce, the test for fairness is that a person would not freely agree to the bargain unless he or she derives benefit sufficient to compensate for what they are giving up. This is why people in the state of nature must be regarded as free to reject the trade-off implied by the social contract. Yet both Hobbes and Locke argue that it would be irrational for them to do so, and presumably this is because it was obvious to them that the risk of devolving into a state of war outweighs the benefits of maximal freedom. Criteria of rationality are thus tightly interwoven with the conceptualization of unforced, voluntary choice, on the one hand, and the value-for-value conceptualization of a "fair bargain", on the other. Readers of their works are being invited to see that it would be crazy to choose the state of nature, and that it is therefore only rational to accept the constraints on personal freedom that go along with civil society. However, the metaphor of the social contract is simultaneously creating normative conditions that *constrain* the power of the state. The terms of the social contract cannot be so onerous that a free person in the state of nature would question whether it is rational to accept them.

2.4 Fairness and Efficient Competition

Although social contract theory promoted intuition pumps that were highly suggestive in the way that they linked bargaining and fairness to a more comprehensive understanding of the social good, the formulations of Hobbes and Locke did not suggest that competitiveness had any redeeming features. The state of war was the natural end point of unconstrained competitive urges, and it produced a quality of life that Hobbes famously characterized as "nasty, brutish and short." The role of morality and the civil society alike was to limit competition, which is portrayed largely as an evil to be avoided. It is true that bargaining itself implies some hint of a competitive situation, as the parties to a bargain each try to strike the terms most beneficial to themselves. The interests of buyer and seller compete in our ordinary conception of exchange. Yet at the magic point of the unforced value-for-value exchange, the competitive situation vanishes and the fair contract emerges in its place. Fairness and competition are not opposites in this picture, but fairness is the moral good that vanquishes the evil of competition through cooperative endeavor.

Needless to say, this is not the picture of competition that is most familiar to twenty first century social scientists. Although his book *The Wealth of Nations* accomplished many things, Adam Smith's (1776) presentation of the invisible hand became a compelling intuition pump that has permanently restored competition to a much more vaunted ethical position. Smith showed how merchants and manufacturers each seeking their own advantage would seek efficiencies that lower their costs. Doing so increases their profit. However, if they are competing with one another in relatively unregulated markets they pass the benefit of these efficiencies on to their customers in order to attract as many buyers as possible. What is more, in seeking efficiencies merchants and manufacturers seek the lowest price from *their* suppliers, so the cost of goods comes down for all. In the present context it is unnecessary to recount Smith's development of the invisible hand or his often misquoted endorsement of greed in greater detail.

It is not that greed is good, as Gordon Gecko (Michael Douglas's character in the 1987 film *Wall Street*) would have had it, but Smith does show that under appropriately competitive circumstances, pursuit of self-interest can result in more effective promotion of social benefit than acts deliberately intended to do so.

Determining what is "appropriately competitive" becomes a problem to which a large body of research in economics has been dedicated. The point to notice is that the criterion of promoting social benefit does not make an obvious appeal to the concept of fairness. Consumers experience benefit from lower prices because they can re-allocate the savings to consumption of other goods. They can satisfy preferences that would have otherwise gone unsatisfied. An approach to the determination of what is "appropriately competitive" that evaluates appropriateness in terms of maximizing social welfare or the satisfaction of consumer preferences need not make strong appeals to the social contract tradition's conception of fairness in bargaining.

However, it is possible to build a bridge between Smith's argument on the social benefits of competition and the utilitarian conception of fairness. Following Jeremy Bentham, a utilitarian identifies the ethically correct act or policy in terms of the net happiness or satisfaction (e.g. utility) it yields for affected parties. But it is crucial that in estimating utility, all affected parties are counted equally: "each person is to count for one and no one for more than one" as Bentham had it Bentham (1789). A policy or social choice is fair when everyone's preferences have been taken into account, and when no one's preferences have priority over those of everyone else. It is a notion of fairness that derives saliency from voting, from the proverbial "show of hands." Of course, the outcome of modern elections can be affected by other factors, and our concept of a fair election has become quite complex. But voting is not limited to elections. Bills and proposals are voted up or down, and friends sometimes vote when deciding where to have dinner. Importantly, competition is not typically salient to such situations. The relevant conception of fairness emphasizes equal consideration of everyone's preferences, but not the aspects of fairness that we derive from bargains or games.

Utilitarian philosophers such as Bentham and John Stuart Mill drew upon this conception of fairness to argue against a system of privilege that favored entrenched interests in eighteenth and nineteenth century England and its colonies. They argued for the *utilitarian maxim:* "the greatest good for the greatest number" would be the decision rule. Whether Smith can be regarded as utilitarian or not, the close historical association between utilitarian ethics and welfare economics suggests that even contemporary analyses of competitiveness may be drawing heavily on a conception of fairness that emphasizes the equal consideration of preferences, rather than the nexus of rationality, competition and bargaining that arises from the social contract. Here, it is systematic distortions that result in some parties' preferences being favored or omitted that makes a situation unfair.

When this tradition is conjoined with Smith's analysis of competition, what ultimately matters is whether the savings from greater efficiencies that are obtained when producers and suppliers compete with one another get passed along to consumers. Monopoly is "unfair" because it allows for outcomes where the interests of certain firms get to count more than the interests of consumers who would ultimately buy their products. On the other hand, there can be circumstances in which concentration in an industry actually leads to efficiencies that can, in turn, be passed on to consumers. If the utilitarian standard of fairness is utilized, a trend to fewer firms competing with one another need *not* be indicative of unfairness, for the test is whether or not the efficiencies that are the *sine qua non* of competitiveness are being achieved, and whether the benefits are being shared by all.

2.5 Fairness and Outcomes

England in the seventeenth and eighteenth centuries was an extremely hierarchical society, with a highly structured set of social classes. The texts of *Leviathan* and *The Second Treatise of Government* make it clear that the social contract applies to property owning males. There is no pretense that this is a "fair deal" for the landless, the commoners or for women, and social theorists of the twentieth century faulted the philosophies of Hobbes and Locke on precisely this point (Pateman 1989). The point to notice is that the absence of coercion implied by the state of nature metaphor establishes the parameters for a conception of fairness *among contracting parties*. They are obligated to comply with the terms of an agreement into which they have voluntarily entered. But this does not imply that the agreement or its outcome is fair to those who are not parties to the contract. One possible response is to just abandon the contract metaphor, and this is what the utilitarians did. But the twentieth century saw a significant revitalization of contract thinking in political ethics, in part because of perceived deficiencies in the utilitarian approach.

If social life is a social contract, it becomes crucial to reconstruct the contract metaphor so that all members of society can see themselves as a contracting party. John Rawls proposed that we should understand social justice as a particular conceptualization of fairness. One synoptic statement of Rawls' view stressed two principles. The *Principle of Liberty* states that all citizens have equal rights to the most extensive liberty compatible with a similar liberty for others, while The *Difference Principle* states that given equal liberty, social policies should benefit to the worst off group. Liberty is here understood to mean the absence of a state-imposed constraint on individual conduct (Rawls 1971). For present purposes, the *Principle of Liberty* can be read as recapitulating elements in the contract theories of Hobbes and Locke, while the *Difference Principle* acknowledges the need to restructure the terms of the bargain in a manner that would make it rational for a materially disadvantaged person to accept it.

Rawls suggested the aphorism "Justice as fairness" to recapitulate his theory. As in traditional social contract theory, the test of a fair bargain lies in whether someone would freely choose to accept it. Rawls did not incorporate a totally equal distribution of social resources into the terms of his bargain because he had read Smith and saw that competition can be socially beneficial. Allowing competition to work means allowing some inequalities to accrue, thus some measure of inequality is beneficial to all. In other words, the worst off in society would be better off in a world where unequal distributions of resources fed processes of economic expansion and wealth creation than they would in a world of total equality. Such a world would meet the test of the *Difference Principle,* hence it would be rational for people who are among the worst off to accept a bargain that involves inequalities. Such a bargain would be "fair," and it would presumably include such redistributive policies as would be needed to forestall the intolerable inequalities of seventeenth century England. But what about the well-off, the white male property owners who benefited handsomely from the old contract of Hobbes and Locke? Why would they accept Rawls' revised bargain?

Rawls did not, in fact, think it rational for someone who knows that they will live handsomely under an unequal system to accept anything else. He thus argues that we need to revise the bargaining situation in order to capture the appropriate standard of fairness. We must imagine that the bargainers know a great deal about what society will look like, but that they do not know whether or not they will be among the advantaged or the disadvantaged groups. It is a choice made from behind this "veil of ignorance" about one's societal prospects that models fairness, rather than the common commerce of everyday life. All parties are equally ignorant in these highly idealized circumstances, which Rawls called "the Original Position" (Rawls 1971). By restructuring the state of nature as the Original Position, Rawls is able to re-unite rationality and voluntary choice, on the one hand, with equality among contractors, on the other. As with Hobbes and Locke, the outcome of the contract is fair because it is the bargain that any rational agent would choose voluntarily under the circumstances. Losers accept that they are less advantaged than winners, but winners accept that fairness requires redistribution to insure that the losers are as well off as they can be.

Although I would not claim that this sketch adequately captures Rawls' intentions in writing *A Theory of Justice,* it suggests several points relevant to the present context. First, against the utilitarians, a society that achieves "the greatest good for the greatest number," but where the disadvantaged lose regularly, will not be considered fair. Second, like the utilitarians, fairness seems to turn on facts about the distribution of wealth (or other social benefits). It is a function of social outcomes. Third, unequal distribution of wealth is ethically just (e.g. fair) *only* to the extent that the inequality actually works to improve the lives of people who are on the short end of distributive inequalities.

2.6 Fairness and Rules

Rawls' great contemporary critic was Robert Nozick, who published *Anarchy, State and Utopia* a few years after *A Theory of Justice.* Nozick's (1974) book came (at least for a time) to be regarded as the most philosophically sophisticated statement of libertarian philosophy. In contrast to Rawls' treatment, Nozick insisted that our ideas of fairness do not really focus on social outcomes. In order to make this point, he offered a thought experiment that emphasized the high income of star basketball player Wilt Chamberlain. Nozick points out that no one who comes to see Chamberlain play basketball is being forced to do so, and all of them can be presumed to feel that they are getting fair value for the price of their ticket.

Otherwise, they would not buy it. But because so many people want to watch Wilt Chamberlain play basketball, he is able to derive an income vastly greater than all but a few of the individuals who pay to watch him play. Nozick says that we perceive nothing unfair about this, because (a) we have not been coerced; and (b) everyone (including Chamberlain) has followed the rules of market exchange in the transactions that bring this result about.

However, this pattern of exchange does not benefit the worst off group. As such, one might argue that it violates Rawls' *Difference Principle*. Now, Rawls never intended for the *Difference Principle* to be applied in such cases. The *Difference Principle* was intended to be applied to what Rawls calls the "basic structure" of society, not to individual cases. It is entirely possible that if the exchange rules leading to this outcome (e.g. Chamberlain's disproportionate wealth) *would in fact* satisfy the *Difference Principle* if it turns out that a society structured in this manner really did tend to provide the greatest benefit to the worst off group. Nozick's point, however, is that this is not, nor should it be, the way that we evaluate cases where wealth distributions become skewed. Rather, we permit skewed distributions because it would be decidedly *unfair* for the government to intervene in this process and prevent the exchanges that result in Chamberlain's great wealth.

According to this argument, fairness is not a concept that applies to outcomes. Fairness concerns *whether* the rules apply to all, and *whether* they have been uniformly applied. Fairness is a matter of establishing rules that *treat* everyone the same, and then *following* those rules. Nozick's solution to the problem of identifying the ethically proper institutions for society was "the minimal state", one where government is sharply constrained. The libertarian rationale of limited government is that personal and commercial freedoms should be as extensive as possible, subject to the requirements of fairness. In this, they appeal to the same *Principle of Liberty* advanced by Rawls. That is, constraints on liberty are justifiable in order to ensure that the same liberties are shared by all. Thus libertarians associate fairness with a principle that might be characterized as "equality under the law" as opposed to fair distribution.

2.7 Assessing Fair Competition

Although these descriptions are caricatures of Rawls and Nozick—not to mention Hobbes, Locke and Smith—in that they do not adequately describe important elements in their respective political philosophies, they are sufficient to illustrate alternative ways the idea of fairness can be interpreted with respect to competition. In the case of early contract theorists, the implicit idea is that a bargain is fair when one gets at least as much value as one has to give up. The social contract is a bargain in which everyone gives up the freedom of the state of nature, and what they get is the security of civil society. But notice that the social contract of Hobbes and Locke is not a situation in which parties are actually bargaining with one another. The implicit notion of fairness here is that people accept the terms of social contract because they believe they are better off to do so. When two or more individuals' interests collide (as in real bargaining) this principle implies that the terms of the bargain will converge on trades in which all parties feel that they have been made better off. Fair bargains are those in which everyone walks away feeling that they have gotten value that adequately compensates for the value they have given up.

Utilitarians are focused on achieving "the greatest good for the greatest number," and would subject any proposed rules for structuring competition to that test. Competition is fair so long as no competitor (or sub-group of competitors) can subvert market forces that yield efficient outcomes. If Rawls' *Difference Principle* is taken as the standard, fairness is a distributive principle. It is motivated by the idea that no rational person would choose to accept social inequalities *unless* these inequalities actually work to the benefit of the worst off group. What is important in drawing the contrast between the libertarian view and the outcome-focused utilitarian and Rawlsian philosophies is simply the point that neither the efficiency nor the distribution of outcomes matters to the libertarian. As long as rules are applied universally, that is, in a consistent manner to all participants, the competition is considered fair, and fairness in this sense is the principal criterion for evaluating a competition in ethical terms.

The last three of these philosophies can potentially reconcile the post-Smithian idea that competition can be good with the earlier social contract thinking that emphasized fairness in ordinary bargaining. None of them suppose that competition is a natural evil. All recognize the potential growth in productivity and wealth can competition can yield. Like the original social contract theorists, the outcome-oriented utilitarian and *Difference Principle* focus on the value-for-value aspect of a fair bargain. The utilitarians want to maximize net social value (utility), and they have taken Smith's point: competition does precisely this. Rawls is concerned that this approach to competitive situations might permit a pattern of outcomes in which one group loses most of the time. And that would not be a bargain that any rational person would accept. The libertarians draw on the idea that a bargain between two parties is fair so long as it is freely chosen, and so long as no hegemonic power has intervened in the bargaining process. They deny Rawls' claim that a pattern of winning or losing has anything to do with fairness.

2.8 Fair Agrifood Competition

Given this population of concepts there are a number of ways in which ethically grounded complaints about competition among agricultural producers can be framed. If we construe the social contract idea as a way of thinking about fairness where people are free to enter the bargain if they believe they are better off doing so, then in the context of agrifood competition, one could ask whether producers are being constrained, or whether they are willing participants in the system. In contrast, the utilitarian tradition will be focused on whether there is *enough* competition to yield the productivity and efficiency returns hypothesized by Adam Smith.

Applying these tests requires a significant amount data and expertise, but the key point to notice from an ethics perspective is there is no *a priori* reason to think that this criterion of fair competition will correspond to the criteria that might be advanced on any of the other grounds. Having an economically competent measure of competitiveness in an economy is *one* approach to determining whether criteria of fairness are being met, but it may not adequately articulate the feelings and opinions of those who complain about a lack of fairness.

The *Difference Principle* is suggestive of several different ways to articulate conceptions of fairness. Most straightforwardly, it suggest that if agricultural markets are structured so that poor, less-well educated or regionally, racially or otherwise marginalized farms continue to be the losers in markets where they must compete with larger or better capitalized farmers, something is amiss. This kind of structural disadvantage is unfair. What is more, this way of conceptualizing fairness could construe such a distribution of the benefits from competition as a *sufficient* condition for unfairness. There would be no need to search more deeply for the underlying cause of persistent losses. This construal of the Rawlsian distributive conception would appear to be very much at odds with economic analyses that probe the question of whether some farming or business methods are simply more efficient than others.

The finding of unfairness, however, does not stipulate what the appropriate remedy would be. Nothing in Rawls' philosophy suggests that anyone is entitled to be successful in his or her chosen pursuits, pecuniary or otherwise. The Rawlsian view is often thought to provide a rationale for redistributive policies effected by government to "even the playing field," but this evening of the field might well involve perennial losers investing in different remunerative pursuits. Here, subsidies, direct payments or special educational and financial assistance programs might be thought to rectify the unfairness, but it would *not* be typical of this approach to propose remedies that call for retributive action from the winners. Although Rawlsian egalitarian notions of fairness provide a philosophical justification for actions that would involve transfers to an economically defined subgroup such as smallholders, this kind of redistributive policy has been rare in the United States.

It may be more plausible to trace feelings of unfairness to libertarian sentiments. Here, several different considerations might be put forward. Indeed, unless I am mistaken, the social contract focus on whether people are free to enter the bargain is, in fact, quite consistent with some versions of libertarianism: if farmers are willing participants in the system, all is fair. But contemporary libertarians are "minimalists" with respect to the role of the state in a way that the original contract theorists were not. Government intervention in agriculture has been extensive for well over a century. It is thus quite plausible to argue that those who have risen to the top in farming have benefited unfairly from government interventions that range from extension services and agricultural research to the subsidy programs. A different approach would hold that rules either unfairly advantage one actor in the supply chain, or that they are not being applied fairly. Finally, a non-state actor can attain such a concentration of power as to trigger libertarian objections on the grounds that freedoms are not being distributed equally. This approach construes hegemonic interference in liberty more broadly than conventional libertarian positions that focus exclusively on state power, but it nonetheless squares with the intuition that fairness is to be understood primarily as a constraint on the use of power constrain bargains that parties would otherwise freely undertake.

Finally, and perhaps most plausibly of all, there are native intuitions or feelings of fairness, feelings that develop at an early age and that may not even be limited to the human species. Such feelings are grounded in the perception that parties to a transaction or situation are not being treated even-handedly, or in the umbrage felt when a party has broken implicit rules in order to secure and advantage. There are, of course, any number of ways that such perceptions could arise in common commerce, and agriculture should not be regarded as an exception.

Succinctly stated, the plurality of ways in which fair competition might be understood philosophically matches up with the multiple and contrasting opinions on the fairness of competition in contemporary agriculture. Philosophers are no better, and are probably worse, at resolving such disputes than others. Sometimes the explicit articulation of a given ethical concept, and its application to a problem at hand, has the effect of coalescing opinion, but this is hardly to be expected in the typical case. Sometimes such an articulation leads to a debate that is conclusive, at least to the majority of listeners. Perhaps the most frequent happy outcome is that the articulation of multiple, principled points of view leads to a practical compromise or agreement among the disputants, not for philosophical reasons, but because no one has the desire to see the controversy continue indefinitely. The last possibility, of course, is that the controversy endures.

An explicit recognition of the ethical dimensions cannot be guaranteed to bring about a happy conclusion to controversies. Nevertheless, it is possible that simply describing ethical perspectives as philosophical alternatives opens a path to more fruitful analysis and debate over the issues. When allegations of unfairness or unethical conduct are closely tied to a particular individual or group, it is not surprising people will shy away from talk of ethics simply to avoid a confrontational situation. These philosophical sources depersonalize the ethical dimension, and they illustrate how multiple ways of conceptualizing the ethical dimension are possible.

References

Anderson, N.H., and C.A. Butzin. 1978. Integration theory applied to children's judgments of equity. *Developmental Psychology* 14(6): 593–605.

Bekoff, M. 1995. Play signals as punctuation: The structure of social play in canids. *Behavior* 132: 419–429.

Bekoff, M., and J. Peirce. 2009. *Wild justice: The moral lives of animals*. Chicago: The University of Chicago Press.

Bentham, J. 1789/1996. *An introduction to the principles of morals and legislation*. New York: Oxford University Press.

Hobbes, T. 1761/1991. *Leviathan*. New York: Cambridge University Press.
Kowal, A., L. Kramer, J.L. Krull, and N.R. Crick. 2002. Children's perceptions of the fairness of parental preferential treatment and their socioemotional well-being. *Journal of Family Psychology* 16(3): 297–306.
Locke, J. 1793/2002. *The second treatise of government*. New York: Oxford University Press.
Nozick, R. 1974. *Anarchy, state and utopia*. New York: Basic Books.
Pateman, C. 1989. *The disorder of women: Democracy, feminism and political theory*. Palo Alto: Stanford University Press.
Rawls, J. 1971. *A theory of justice*. Cambridge, MA: Harvard University Press.
Smith, A. 1776/1991. *Wealth of nations*. Amherst: Prometheus Books.
Sripada, C.S., and S. Stich. 2006. A framework for the psychology of norms. In *The innate mind: Structure and contents: V. 2 Culture and cognition*, 280–301. New York: Oxford University Press.
Volling, B.L., D.E. Kennedy, and L.M.H. Jackey. 2010. The development of sibling jealousy. In *Handbook of jealousy: Theory, research, and multidisciplinary approaches*, ed. S.L. Hart and M. Legerstee. Oxford: Wiley-Blackwell.
Wittgenstein, L. 1952. *Philosophical investigations*. New York: Cambridge University Press.

Chapter 3
Are Ethics and Efficiency Locked in Antithesis?

Yasha Rohwer and Randall Westgren

Abstract We argue that ethics and efficiency are not locked in antitheses; that is, we argue that ethics and efficiency are not related in a fixed way. To do this we first argue that we have obligations to other human beings, animals and the environment. These obligations can be grounded in a number of moral theories that share a common normative outcome. We then explicate two conceptions of how ethics and efficiency may and actually do coexist in the food market. We argue that our moral obligations must be included in analyses of the behavior and performance of agri-food markets and that these duties do not lead to inefficiency, *per se*. At a minimum, they represent a set of constraints on production to which efficient producers adhere. We also note that there are markets for ethically produced foods, ranging from Fair Trade commodities to organic vegetables, wherein producers and consumers discover the prices of ethical attributes in efficient exchange. However, the existence of these markets for ethically produced products does not exhaust our moral obligations. If we have such duties, they must be institutionalized throughout the sector.

3.1 Introduction

We consider whether there is an inherent antagonism between ethics and efficiency, using the modern agrifood sector as the context. We begin with a definition of ethics, leading to the specific choice of normative ethics as the *sine qua non* of

Y. Rohwer, Ph.D.
Department of Philosophy, University of Missouri, 435 Strickland Hall, Columbia, MO 65211, USA

R. Westgren, Ph.D. (✉)
Department of Agricultural & Applied Economics, University of Missouri, 141 Mumford Hall, Columbia, MO 65211, USA
e-mail: westgrenr@missouri.edu

H.S. James Jr. (ed.), *The Ethics and Economics of Agrifood Competition*, The International Library of Environmental, Agricultural and Food Ethics 20, DOI 10.1007/978-94-007-6274-9_3, our argument: do we have ethical obligations? If so, to whom or what? What is the nature and extent of the obligations? After examining multiple theories we conclude that there is good reason to believe that we have ethical obligations to humans (e.g. smallholders and factory workers), animals and the environment. That is, we explicitly endorse animal welfare and sustainability as ethical considerations in the agrifood sector.

We then examine production efficiency. We use Farrell's (1957) characterization of efficiency, which permits us to ask whether any just analysis of smallholders' competitiveness in the sector is possible in the light of the existence of large, industrialized competitors. The latter will have superior positions with respect to both technical efficiency (input/output relationships) and allocative efficiency (relative prices paid for inputs), but these judgments do not take seriously any ethical constraints.

Our analysis considers two alternative conceptions of products and markets for food that incorporate ethical production and consumption in different ways. In the simplest case, we treat ethical considerations (fair wages, animal welfare, sustainability) as constraints on the production function. To the extent that the market is construed to be homogeneous (i.e. a commodity market), the comparison of the efficiency of ethically-constrained producers to those that are unconstrained is unjust and perhaps not informative given the existence of ethical duties. In the second case, we examine the development of markets for product attributes, including ethical attributes, in the light of Kelvin Lancaster's reformulated utility function (1966) and the subsequent development of hedonic pricing of consumer choice. Lastly we consider how these ethical duties can *actually* become institutionalized in the food system via three legitimation processes: cognitive, normative, and regulative (Scott 1995).

As we develop the two conceptions of how ethics and efficiency may coexist in the food market and how compliance to these duties could become more widespread, we show that the conception can exist, and does exist, in the sector. This shows that ethics and efficiency are not locked in antithesis and that economists can incorporate ethical obligations into their models. In fact, doing so can often give one a more thorough and fruitful explanation of production and consumption processes. But our analysis is not purely descriptive; we also argue that economists have an obligation to recognize and represent these obligations and ask whether certain initiatives that address ethical production in the agrifood sector fulfill our obligations. We argue that often these changes do not. Hence, it is important to consider how these unfulfilled duties could become more institutionalized.

3.2 What Is Ethics?

How much am I obligated to pay workers? Is it wrong to keep pigs in pens where it is nearly impossible for them to move? Is it wrong to clear the rainforest to make room for soybeans? These questions are the domain of ethics or moral philosophy. In what follows we briefly define ethics and explicate a few dominant ethical theories. We use three theories to arrive at very similar conclusions regarding the existence of certain obligations. This provides strong evidence that these kinds of obligations exist. Not only do these obligations exist, they have been, can be, and ought to be integrated into efficiency concepts and model equations used by economists. Thus, ethics and efficiency are not locked in antithesis.

Ethics is a broad field, usually composed of three different subfields: value theory, normative ethics and metaethics (Shafer-Landau 2012). Roughly speaking, value theory tries to figure out what, if anything, is intrinsically valuable. Normative ethics is concerned with explaining to whom we have obligations and what the natures of those obligations are. Metaethics deals with the nature of moral claims, examining whether or not they are true and if they are, what makes them true.

When trying to answer a particular, real world question—like the ones above—the field of normative ethics is of particular importance. To answer a question like "is it wrong to keep pigs in pens where it is nearly impossible for them to move?" I need to know whether or not I have an obligation, or duty, to pigs. If I do, then I need to know the extent of that obligation. That is, I need to know what actions fulfill that duty and what actions go above and beyond that duty. But, most importantly, I need to know what grounds that obligation.

Different normative theories will give different answers to these types of questions, and this can be frustrating for a non-philosopher. However, the disagreement between normative ethical theories shouldn't be taken as evidence that there is no correct answer or that the process is futile. In fact, there is a surprising amount of agreement between ethicists, and reasoning with different moral theories will frequently take ethicists to the same conclusions. The great nineteenth century British ethicist John Stuart Mill notes this when he writes, "they recognize also, to a great extent, the same moral laws; but differ as to the evidence, and the source from which they derive their authority" (1993, p. 139).

Their groundings may indeed be different, but what unites every plausible normative ethical theory is the importance that each places on the process of reasoning to arrive at the truth. Good reasons, not popular opinion or strong feeling, are indicators of truth. People clearly disagree on whether or not it is true that "We ought not raise cattle in high-density feed lots," but there certainly is a fact of the matter as to whether or not we ought not raise cattle in high-density feed lots and that fact is independent from people's particular beliefs on the matter. The ethicist is, in this respect, like a scientist. He or she is trying to discover what the ethical facts of the world are just as the scientist is trying to discover facts about the natural world. Believing that the world is flat does not make it so; similarly, believing that animals have no moral status does not make it so. So, if we want to determine what we owe each other, or what we owe cattle, which actions are permissible, which forbidden and which obligatory—we need to examine the reasons given and decide on the basis of the best reasons. Let us now turn to the theories to see how using them we can arrive at similar kinds of duties.

Enlightenment philosopher Immanuel Kant's widely influential moral theory links morality with a standard of rationality that he called the "Categorical

Imperative" (Johnson 2008). For Kant, rationality is linked with morality because when we act immorally we are pursuing impossible or contradictory ends. In one formulation, Kant described the Categorical Imperative this way: "act only in accordance with that maxim through which you can at the same time will that it become a universal law" (Kant 1998, p. 31). Think of a maxim as a plan of action. This formulation of the categorical imperative has been understood as a decision procedure that allows one to figure out if a proposed plan of action is obligatory, forbidden or just permissible (Johnson 2008; Rawls 1989). Understood as a procedure, it has four steps that show how acting immorally is linked to perusing impossible or incoherent ends (Johnson 2008). First, one formulates a plan of action. Second, one universalizes the plan, such that everyone follows it. Third, one asks if there is any contradiction in conceiving of a world where everyone follows the plan. That is, could that world even exist, or would it be as impossible as a square circle? If impossible, then the plan of action is morally wrong and one has a duty to never act on that maxim. If such a world is not impossible, then we go to the last step, which is to ask whether one could coherently will that everyone follows the plan. If so, then acting on that plan is permissible. If not, then the action is wrong and one has a duty to do the opposite, at least some of the time.

Here are two examples: Kant thought lying was always wrong because the plan to lie fails at step three. If everyone lies to get what they want, it would be impossible for me to lie to get what I want because there would be no trust. Hence, we must always tell the truth. Kant also thought we had a duty to help people some of the time. The reason why is that a plan to be selfish fails at step four. Kant believed that everyone wants their own happiness and human happiness depends on others. Hence, while a world where everyone is selfish is possible, if no one helped anyone, then I would never receive help and I would thwart a goal I have and everybody else has by their very nature: happiness.

Kant's moral theory is often criticized for supposing that there are absolute moral rules—e.g. it is always wrong to lie. Certainly sometimes it is permissible to lie. Those who hid Jews in their homes during World War Two surely had no obligation to tell the truth if a Nazi asked them if they were hiding anyone.

Utilitarianism is an ethical theory where it is the *consequences* of an action that really matter when trying to figure out which action is right. Utilitarians believe we have an obligation, when we act, to perform the action that maximizes overall happiness and minimizes overall pain. Happiness or pleasure is not the only thing that has been claimed as valuable for its own sake. Twentieth-century British philosopher G.E. Moore (1903), for example, thought that beauty and truth were also valuable for their own sake. For Moore, when deciding on which action is the right action, beauty and truth as well as pleasure needed to be part of the calculation. Moore was an ideal utilitarian, one of the many different flavors of utilitarianism—but what unites them is the focus on consequences, even if other things besides happiness need to be considered. Utilitarianism is very appealing as a normative theory since consequences certainly matter and are clearly an important factor when thinking about what we ought to do.

A classical objection to utilitarianism comes in the form of a thought experiment. Imagine there is a set of 10 people and two possible actions, each producing different amounts of happiness. Imagine that the first action raises everyone's happiness by, let us say, 10 points but also cause everyone to feel 2 points of pain. So, there is an 80 point increase in overall happiness. The second action raises everyone's happiness by 10 points as well but causes only one individual to feel 15 points of pain. So, there is an 85 point increase in overall happiness. Given these numbers, according to the utilitarian, the right action is the second even though one person has a heavy burden to carry. For some, this doesn't seem fair.

Social contract theory is a third approach to ethics. Morality is, for the social contract theorist, enlightened self-interest. Thomas Hobbes used another kind of thought experiment to try to show this.[1] Imagine there was no society but rather we were in a "state of nature" were everyone was essentially at war with everyone. If this were the case, then life would be "solitary, poor, nasty, brutish, and short" (Hobbes 1651). Morality is the system of rules that allows us to escape this possible scenario. We consent to rules that restrain our own self-interest because they allow us to reap the benefits of social living. Acceptance of these rules is thus like making a contract with each other. The contract benefits the individual, so it is rational to sign on. The rules that constitute morality are mutually beneficial, but they are only so as long as everyone accepts them and follows them. Therefore, for the social contract theorist, "morality consists in the set of rules, governing behavior, that rational people will accept, on the condition that others accept them as well" (Rachels and Rachels 2012, p. 85)

One problem with older social contract theories is that the various parties do not come to the negotiation of the contract from the same place. That is, rational individuals may have very different backgrounds, abilities and access to power and those variables might bias them when it came to accepting a set of rules. Serfdom might be a pretty good social system if you are a landowner . . . or currently a slave. American philosopher John Rawls (1971) wanted to ensure fairness, so he proposed a thought experiment involving the "original position." The central feature of the original position is that when we think about the set of rules that constitute morality we must imagine that we are behind a "veil of ignorance," which makes the thinker ignorant of their own social status, gender, race and other factors that might bias him or her to a particular set of rules. A contract drawn up by parties who do not know their place in society would presumably be fair since no one would want there to be a short end of the stick, lest they end up holding it.

Often social contract theory is criticized for ignoring our obligations to non-human animals, children, and future generations. These individuals cannot be part of any given social contract since they cannot consent to anything. Also, Rawls has been criticized for making certain assumptions about decision procedures for any

[1]Hobbes didn't think this was a thought experiment, but it is best described as such since nothing like the "state of nature" he describes ever existed.

being behind the veil of ignorance (Harsanyi 1975). He assumes that they would use a risk-averse decision procedure, but it is unclear why this must be so.

We have explicated, albeit very quickly, three different moral theories. Reasoning with any of the three theories, we would arrive at the general conclusion that we have obligations to other human beings. For example, each theory would claim that we have an obligation to pay workers a livable wage. However, exactly how much this is will differ from thinker to thinker. From a utilitarian perspective, given that there are far more workers and that one's happiness plateaus at a certain level of income, the action that would maximize happiness and minimize pain might be to pay the workers a substantially greater wage than the industry norm. Further, doing so would presumably mean that the owner of the company would have to make less. From the perspective of Social Contract Theory and Kant's moral philosophy, a perhaps less equal distribution of wealth might be morally permissible. Rawls (1971) certainly did not think that behind the veil of ignorance we would necessarily choose a society where goods where distributed equally. According to Rawls, it is possible that we would agree that there be disparate incomes between workers and owners. For any ethicist, the devil is in the details: exactly how much should workers be paid to meet one's duty to them?

Do we have an obligation to animals? Kant, interestingly, thought that we had no obligations *strictly speaking* to animals. But he did believe that we should avoid harming them, because when we harm animals we desensitize ourselves to pain and suffering and this puts us at risk of harming other humans to which we have a clear duty (Kant 1971). So, while we may have no direct duty to treat animals humanly, we do have an *indirect* duty to do so given our duties to humans. Kant thought animals had no moral status, but some more modern ethicists who follow Kant reject this (e.g., Korsgaard 1996).

Utilitarianism has a very different position when it comes to animals. Animals have moral status, because they, like humans, also feel pain and pleasure. In so far as we have an obligation to maximize overall happiness and minimize overall pain, clearly how we treat animals is important. How you treat an animal will affect the overall amount of pleasure in the world. If a farmer can raise a pig in conditions that don't hurt or discomfort the pig, then according to utilitarianism, they have an obligation to do so. Indeed, some of the most famous arguments that demonstrate that we have obligations to animals are championed by the utilitarian Peter Singer (1975).

Obligations to animals are different for a social contract theorist, and some have criticized this theory precisely because it seems to only include rational thinkers. Rational thinkers—humans—are the only ones who can participate in the contract, so they are the only ones to whom I have obligations. However, that might not be so. We might have indirect duties to animals. Here, we have duties to humans and insofar as their interests concern animals, as in the case of a pet owner who loves his dog, we have duties to the animals as well. But all these duties are grounded in our duties to other humans in the contract. Even when using this indirect grounding, the very same rules that a rational person would accept (given that others also accept) could also govern our interactions with animals.

While most theories would surely say we have duties of some sort or another to animals, the hard question is what do those duties entail and what is the nature of those duties? Is it always wrong to eat meat or only meat that comes from farms where animals are unhappy?

Establishing an obligation to the environment might seem more difficult, but if it is true that we have obligations to humans (which all plausible ethical theories assert) and that we have obligations to non-human animals, then we will clearly have at least indirect duties to the environment since both humans and animals depend on it to live. So, on utilitarian grounds, contractarian grounds and even Kantian grounds, we do have a duty of some sort to be good stewards of the environment.

Here, we have only talked about three main theories of ethics; there are many who think that the environment is intrinsically valuable and needs no work-around to ground our duty to it. Whether one grounds an environmental ethic in this "bio-centric" way, or whether one grounds it in "anthropocentric" or "zoocentric" indirect duties, determining what one's obligations are to an ecosystem is often less clear than determining one's obligation to an individual organism. But once the obligation is established, the hard question again remains: what is the extent of that duty?

3.3 What Is Efficiency?

Efficiency is a term, like many others in the social sciences, that carries several meanings that are tied to the context of use. It can be as imprecise as minimizing the effort required to complete a task and as precise as the ratio of output (energy) produced in a physical system to the energy used as inputs. In economics, the term has two primary meanings: *production efficiency* and *exchange efficiency*. The latter term is the stuff of welfare economics, wherein one seeks to allocate goods or resources among competing uses and efficiency is obtained when no individual can be made better off without making another individual worse off. This is the Pareto Principle. The problem, of course, is that as the economic system under study becomes more complex—the number (and heterogeneity) of goods and individuals increases beyond a Robinson Crusoe economy—the more difficult are the measurement issues and the more intractable are the calculations of gains and losses.

In this chapter we will consider economic efficiency as production efficiency, following Farrell (1957). Farrell begins with the set of technical possibilities for producing a given level of output using the available and known combinations of inputs. For a simplistic model with two productive inputs and one output, Farrell disaggegrates production efficiency into two components: *technical efficiency* and *allocative efficiency*. Technical efficiency is the input/output relationship inherent in the production technology, as in "what are the minimal inputs needed to produce a given quantity of the output?" Allocative efficiency measures how close the prevailing relative prices for production inputs in the market are to the values of the inputs actually used in the firm.

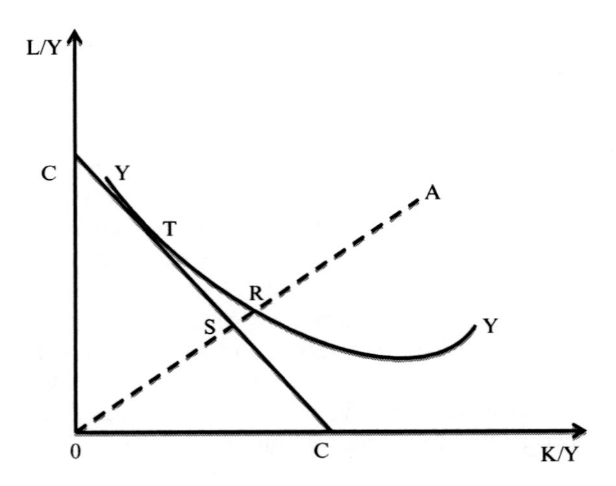

Fig. 3.1 Demonstration of Farrell's (1957) distinction between allocative and technical efficiency (Source: Farrell 1957)

These measures of efficiency are depicted in Fig. 3.1. The production possibilities set is shown as the isoquant YY, defined as the minimal quantities of combinations of two inputs, K (capital) and L (labor), required to produce the common level of output. As students in the principles of microeconomics will know, each point on an isoquant is a unique combination of K and L that can be combined to produce the quantity represented by YY. Let us call a specific quantity Y*. Thus, any point on YY is technically efficient, as each combination yields Y*. The relative prevailing market prices for K and L are reflected in the slope of the isocost line CC. The isoquant and the isocost line are tangent at point T. At this point, production is technically efficient and allocatively efficient. The firm is minimizing its inputs and its costs at that point—uniquely. If labor costs per hour increase, the firm should use less labor and more capital to remain allocatively efficient—moving toward point R.

Consider point A in Fig. 3.1. It is the combination of K and L that is being used to create Y* in a manner that is not efficient. It uses much more of both inputs to produce the given level of output (Y*) than any point along YY. Farrell decomposes the total inefficiency of point A into technical inefficiency, measured by the distance between point A and point R, and allocative inefficiency, measured by the gap between point R and point S. The former represents a failure to use efficient production technology (attaining a minimal input combination implied by the isoquant YY). The latter is the efficiency penalty for using too much capital (relatively costly) and too little labor.

Murillo-Zamorano (2004) shows how this original formulation has been exploited in empirical analyses of economic efficiency through the 1990s by using a variety of techniques, including data envelopment analyses (e.g., Charnes et al. 1994). He also notes that there have been a number of studies that have incorporated multiple outputs and alternative objective functions to cost minimization or profit maximization. It is in this spirit that we would like to first take our analysis of ethics and efficiency.

3.4 The Relation Between Ethics and Efficiency

3.4.1 Ethical Duties as a Constraint on Production

Murillo-Zamorano (2004) alludes to the necessity of including additional constraints to any model of efficiency to account for regulation and other technical parameters that are beyond the control of the decision-maker. If the arguments in the ethics sections are successful, then it is a fact that producers, like the rest of us, have duties to workers, animals and the environment. Having these duties is beyond the control of the decision-maker because they are a fact of our world, even if we can control whether or not we fulfill them. The fact that these duties exist allows us to consider the explicit inclusion of ethical elements to the simple cost minimization problem that is inherent in the Farrell approach to efficiency, wherein we have a production function (F) with a vector of inputs as arguments that constrains the minimization of the cost function (C).

$$\text{Min } C(x_1, x_2, x_3, \ldots, x_n; p_1, p_2, p_3, \ldots, p_n) = C(p_1x_1 + p_2x_2 + \ldots + p_nx_n)$$

$$\text{s.t. } F(x_1, x_2, x_3, \ldots x_n) \geq 0$$

The arguments x_i are the physical quantities of the production inputs and the arguments p_i are the prices for those inputs. One can add any number of additional constraints beyond this (relatively) flexible production function. A lower limit can be placed on the wages earned by production workers (p_i). A lower limit can be placed on the price paid for a raw material (p_j), as is done within fair trade programs. This may also engender a fee for certification or other costs. Technical constraints may be added, as a limitation to purchased inputs, as a consequence of specifying sustainability schemes (shade-grown, free-range, integrated pest management, etc.). Recalling the simple depiction of Fig. 3.1, these additional constraints may (a) alter the shape of the production isoquants, (b) change the slope of the isocost line, or (c) force the isoquant farther from the origin. Thus, both the technical efficiency and the allocative efficiency of the altered model will be different from the unconstrained model.

To be clear, economic efficiency is measured against the constrained production function and the relevant input prices of the constrained set of inputs. For example, the technical and allocative efficiency measurements for a smallholder who practices shade-grown coffee production with specified *Arabica* varieties are meaningful only when compared to other producers subject to the same production function and constraints. To compare technical efficiency (for example, per 60 kg bag) between the smallholder producing shade-grown coffee and a plantation growing coffee conventionally on 450 ha can be justified if and only if the outputs are indistinguishable in the market; coffee is coffee. But clearly, this is not the case. One coffee, presumably, is being produced in accordance with our moral obligations, and the other is not. While it is difficult to agree on the extent of our obligations, the shade grown coffee is, at the very least, closer to that obligation than the standard coffee. Hence, while both are physically equivalent, morally they are not. We will return to this issue in more detail later, but for now, let us examine the ethical consequences of this kind of comparison.

If coffee is coffee, and there is one common exchange for coffee between producers and consumers without quality (ethical) dimensions tied to production practices, then we may measure the economic efficiency of the smallholder and the plantation (per 60 kg bag) relative to a common production function and a common set of input prices. We might reasonably assume that the plantation's scale and its access to lower prices for labor and other purchased inputs will result in superior allocative efficiency. Moreover, the additional production constraints on the smallholder will drive its technical efficiency down relative to the plantation. The plantation's production point might lie on the isoquant YY (efficient frontier), whereas the smallholder will be well above the isoquant, resulting in a significant measure of technical inefficiency. The plantation will have a small wedge between the prevailing market prices for inputs and what they pay; they are allocatively efficient (close to point T on Fig. 3.1). The smallholder's cost function will be different from the plantation's, resulting in large discrepancy from the efficient norm. In summary, the smallholder's operation will be judged inefficient compared to the plantation's operation.

But this comparison omits important details. It ignores the fact that the smallholder's operations are fulfilling their ethical obligations or are, at the very least, acting in a way that is closer to what we are obligated to do. To omit this fact in the comparison is to ignore the morality of the situation. And this seems wrong. An economist might reply that they are merely describing two different schemes of production and that their description need not get caught up in the morality of the situation. But we disagree. To ignore moral facts and to use the same standard of efficiency to describe these very different operations makes it seem as if both are permissible forms of production. But, if the ethicist is correct and that one producer is being unethical or less ethical, then this should, at the very least, be noted. Economics is a science, like conservation biology, that describes systems and situations that have moral elements to them. Preferably, the economist should not compare these different schemes of production using the same efficiency concept because it is not a fair comparison. To call the smallholder's operation inefficient is to ignore or at least eschew the constraints on their production that are produced by ethical duties—duties that the plantation is ignoring.

Furthermore, while it is possible to build ethical constraints into efficiency concepts, it doesn't seem meaningful to compare the two above operations with the same concept because they are producing a different kind of product. The fulfillment of ethical constraints creates a different product. This means that there is essentially a special market because the goods being produced by the different operations are heterogeneous.

We will now explore the idea that ethical production not only places a constraint that needs to be represented by the efficiency concept used to describe the production but also adds value to the good produced—in the sense that there are ethical consumers who value ethically produced goods.

3.4.2 Ethical Consumption and Ethical Production

Where would one begin to analyze markets for goods that are deemed heterogeneous because of the explicit consideration of ethical constraints on production? We start with the model of consumer theory of Lancaster (1966). Lancaster defines the consumer maximization problem as choosing the optimal consumption set of product characteristics, rather than the optimal set of goods. Any good purchased for consumption contains some set of identifiable characteristics or attributes. In food, there are intrinsic attributes including nutritional (calories, fat content, protein, salt, ...) and organoleptic (texture, color, smell, sweetness, ...). Lancaster posits that consumers combine the attributes in a number of purchased goods into complex consumption goods. Some attributes may be extrinsic, arising from advertising (Lancaster 1966, p. 150). These extrinsic characteristics may also attach to purchased goods due to origin or location (such as *terroir* in wine, and environmental attributes in a housing market), production methods (artisanal, organic, animal welfare-friendly), or perceived exclusivity.

The Lancasterian approach was elaborated by Rosen (1974) as the hedonic pricing model. This allowed differentiated products to be analyzed by comparing relative levels of several attributes bundled in purchased goods against the market prices of the purchased goods. Hedonic pricing has been used widely in evaluating housing markets, wherein the value of "environmental variables" associated with particular locations are imputed along with the values of the intrinsic structural attributes of particular properties. There have been some applications of hedonic pricing in agricultural commodities (e.g., Ratchford 1975; Lenz et al. 1994).

Implicit in the model of consumer behavior that is based on demand for attributes, including those that are intrinsic to the purchased good and those that are extrinsic, is that household choice behavior has complex tradeoffs. One can choose to buy commodity (undifferentiated) coffee and make a charitable donation to an NGO that supports economic and social development among smallholders. Or, one can purchase fair trade coffee that has an explicit, though extrinsic, attribute of returning higher incomes to smallholders growing the raw beans. Moreover, the consumer may make a choice among competing brands of fair trade coffee based upon the specific bundles of extrinsic characteristics associated with each brand. How much additional income is returned to growers? Do fair trade margins support market access for indigenous peoples? Is there an educational component? Are global agribusinesses in the marketing chain or not?

One can see that ethical production and marketing practices need not be limited to fair trade. It is evident in many developed countries that consumers are choosing products that are produced organically, locally, as free-range or other animal welfare-friendly schemes, and with other extrinsic attributes tied to production methods. Both Lancaster and Rosen considered the implications of the market that joined attribute-based consumption and attribute production. While the attainment of an explicit equilibrium is difficult to obtain computationally, the following quote from Rosen (1974) notes the implicit market-making.

> The spirit of these recent contributions is that consumers are also producers. Goods do not possess final consumption attributes but rather are purchased as inputs into self-production functions for ultimate characteristics. Consumers act as their own 'middle-men,' so to speak. In contrast, the model presented below interposes a market between buyers and sellers. Producers themselves tailor their goods to embody final characteristics desired by customers and receive returns for serving economic functions as intermediaries. These returns arise from economies of specialized production achieved by specialization and division of labor through market transactions not available outside organized markets with self-production (p. 36).

Thus, we move from a more primitive Lancasterian model, wherein all consumers bundle valued attributes in complex goods with high utility in consumption, to the observed markets, wherein producers construct their goods with different attribute bundles to generate higher selling prices because they make the exchange of extrinsic characteristics more efficient for consumers. The consumer spends less effort in household production and in search for their preferred attribute bundles.

We can see that we have "closed the market" between the producer who has additional constraints on the production function to accommodate ethical standards and the consumer who places positive value on ethical standards in her consumption choice set. In product characteristic space, the producer and consumer have co-located at the same point, to use Rosen's terminology. The implicitly higher costs associated with the ethical production constraints match with the implicit prices derived from the consumer's valuation of ethical attributes in the market goods available to her.

We can point to numerous examples where these active submarkets for ethical attributes exist. We have developed a number of markets for Fair Trade products, typically from tropical countries, including coffee, cocoa, sugar, and textiles. In most cases, the motivation for the development of a fair trade market is focused on a particular village or region and a single commodity where the social attributes of the exchange (e.g. higher incomes for the target producers) are presented directly to buyers. The development of Fair Trade submarkets is well documented in Raynolds et al. (2007)

We can find a number of other examples of ethical attributes marketed jointly with the food good, such as animal welfare and environmental sustainability. For the former, one can see the first pork marketing firm in North America that received certification by the American Humane Society: DuBreton of Québec. They now produce pork that meets certification standards from QAI Organic, USDA Organic, Humane Farm Animal Care, Global Animal Partnership, and the Safe Quality

Food Institute. Consumers get a choice in the market for three alternative bundles of ethical attributes from only antibiotic-free meat to humanely produced meat to humanely produced organic meat. This is clearly a manifestation of Rosen's specialized producers serving ethically-oriented consumers at a specific point in the market.

Does this development of ethically-centric submarkets meet the requirements of normative ethics? Clearly not. These duties are universal and cannot be satisfied by token operations in specialty markets. If there is a duty to produce meat like it is produced by DuBreton, then the fact that DeBreton is producing their meat this way does not negate or relieve the duty of other pork producers. Given that we have duties to animals, then necessarily any individual who engages in pork production—whether they believe it or not—will have duties to those animals. And to produce pork in disregard to those duties is wrong. Also, consumers would have a *prima facie* duty to only buy pork produced in that ethical way. Of course this means that we need to figure out what exactly our duty is. In this chapter we have only given evidence that such a duty does in fact exist. But we have remained silent on what the exact nature and extent of that duty is. We do not explore that knotty question. But we would like to note that determining the extent of our duty is necessary for creating efficiency concepts that build in ethical obligations as constraints. Thus economists and ethicists must communicate with each other.

While it is difficult to determine the extent of our ethical duties to workers, animals and the environment, it is clear that, currently, our duties are not all being sufficiently met. In the next section we explore how producers and consumers can become more ethical.

3.4.3 Institutionalizing Ethical Considerations in the Sector

The development of a market for ethical attributes described above requires no particular institutional instantiation, nor any prescribed regulatory intervention. It is often an organic process, though one can often find evidence of the institutionalization process described by Scott (1995). Scott describes the "three pillars" of institutions that provide structure and legitimacy to an institutional form (Table 3.1).

Ethical production can arise as an institution based upon any of the three pillars. It can be regulative or enacted policy or regulation: this is how it "must be" done. That is, the laws can reflect our ethical duties. It can be supported by a general moral concern for ethics—a normative foundation: this is how it "ought to be" done. That is, individuals can feel the pull of moral obligation and act accordingly. It can also be supported by a cognitive or mimetic process: this is how it "is" done. That is, once the ethical form of production becomes standard, fulfilling one's duty becomes automatic. Scott would argue that institutionalization often evolves temporally from regulative to cognitive, from a clear expedient of government intervention to the eventual attainment of a taken-for-grantedness. One might see this happening as regulation of one subsector or one production practice (e.g. labor law) that spreads by normative or mimetic processes to become industry-wide common practice.

Table 3.1 The three pillars of institutions

	Regulative	Normative	Cognitive
Basis of compliance	Expedience	Social obligation	Taken for granted
Mechanisms	Coercive	Normative	Mimetic
Logic	Instrumentality	Appropriateness	Orthodoxy
Indicators	Rules, laws, sanctions	Certification, accreditation	Prevalence, isomorphism
Basis of legitimacy	Legally sanctioned	Morally governed	Culturally supported, conceptually correct

Source: Scott (1995, p. 35)

Another temporal process would involve all three pillars developing at the same time, leading to a swifter adoption of ethical production carried by mutually reinforcing mechanisms.

Westgren (1999) examined a particular case of this legitimation process in the French poultry industry. A non-industry specific social movement against the industrialization of food production created the first poultry production systems based upon small scale on-farm units, stringent food safety, ecological and economic sustainability, and certified origin. The national government established some norms for production that set ethical production constraints that combined with the moral imperatives of the social movement. The mimetic process grew this system from two regional collectives to 23 in about 30 years. This would not have occurred without a concomitant development of a consumer segment that valued the bundle of ethical attributes (and the organoleptic attributes) at nearly a 100% price premium over industrial poultry production. Moreover, this systemic approach to ethical production has been adapted in markets for other animal products, fresh vegetables, and some processed products—certainly an example of broad mimetic adoption of ethical norms.

However, it is clear that the existence of a growing number of *Label Rouge* products in France, while indicative of a heightened awareness of various ethical production issues in large segments of the consuming public and of agriculturalists, does not fulfill the societal obligation toward ethical production. *Label Rouge* products are offered as explicit alternatives to industrial products whose production methods permit low wages in the processing facility and field operations that may be unsustainable. But the existence of these alternative products does not fulfill our obligations to universal norms of higher wages in the food system, to animal welfare, and to the environment.

3.5 Conclusion

In this chapter we have shown that ethics and efficiency are clearly not locked in antithesis. We show examples of the existence of efficient ethically-oriented production, where additional value is returned to smallholders and wage-earners and/or where animals are treated humanely and production is environmentally sustainable. Such operations are not traditionally characterized as efficiency-driven. However, we make it clear that such producers can be efficient, though they are constrained by their ethical production function to a cost structure that cannot achieve the same level of technical efficiency as an unconstrained competitor. Their efficiency is revealed when ethics are appropriately integrated into the analysis of their operations. We conclude that it is not just to compare their economic efficiency absent the explicit recognition of these constraints and that ethical constraints should be included into efficiency concepts and model equations used by economists.

We also conclude that the existence of ethically oriented firms as counterpoint to unconstrained, efficiency-driven production does not fulfill our obligations. We must see these duties to people, animals, and the environment as a universal obligation. To "do better for some" does not exhaust our duties to all.

Although our analysis sheds new light on the true efficiency of ethically oriented smallholders, it does not give *carte blanche* for inefficiency for inefficiency's sake. Smallholders using methods that are not ethically superior to the industrial behemoths do not get a free ride. Nostalgia is not morally relevant. All thing being equal, we do not have an obligation to maintain market access for agricultural producers of undifferentiated commodity product whose production technology and scale are inconsistent with prevailing norms of scale and efficiency in an increasingly industrialized, integrated, contract-governed agrifood sector.

We examined Scott's three pillars of the process of institutionalization to note the possible routes to better fulfillment of our obligations. While the existence of sub-markets for ethically produced foodstuffs are insufficient to fulfill our societal obligations, they are still useful in the process of institutionalizing more ethical production systems. They represent the (partial) recognition of a moral obligation, which can spread as a normative movement or as a cognitive (mimetic) process towards universality—or institutionalization. The institutionalization of ethical production norms will certainly be accelerated if those norms are supported by regulation. This outcome clearly requires much of ethicists, economists, and other stakeholders in the process.

We want to end by calling for more cooperation and dialogue between ethicists and economists. To invoke ethics in a discussion of agrifood sector production and market access or competition, one must speak to the nature and extent of our moral obligations to others (including non-human animals) and the environment in the sector. For instance, to simply say that wages should be higher or that smallholders should earn more from their farms is insufficient. To what extent are we morally obligated? Are there minima to which we are duty bound? Questions of this kind and questions about the extent and nature of our obligations are actively being worked on by ethicists. More work surely needs to be done but progress has been made and that progress should inform our efficiency concepts and the kind of constraints that are put into model equations. Working on these questions is not only important for economists but also for policy makers and the regulators who need to know the nature and extent of societal obligations for ethical production of food products. What does society owe smallholders and migrant laborers? What duties do we have toward the other species that provide our sustenance? What obligations have we with respect to the biotic and abiotic landscapes in which we practice modern agriculture? Policy makers can certainly leave these questions to the normative and cognitive pillars that Scott outlines and skirt the issues required for regulative intervention. And many would probably choose that course of inaction so as to avoid the necessity of addressing the complex issues we raised under the rubric, "what is ethics?". However, there is good evidence that these moral obligations exist in the arena of food production. And we, therefore, must sustain the conversation about the nature and extent of these duties, so that we can engage the policy process efficiently and ethically.

References

Charnes, A., W.W. Cooper, A.Y. Lewin, and L.M. Seiford. 1994. *Data envelopment analysis: Theory, methodology, and applications*. Boston: Kluwer Academic Publishers.

Farrell, M.J. 1957. The measurement of productive efficiency. *Journal of the Royal Statistical Society* (A, general) 120: 253–281.

Harsanyi, J. 1975. Can the maximin principle serve as a basis for morality? *The American Political Science Review* 69(2): 594–606.

Hobbes, T. 1651. *Leviathan or the matter, forme and power of a common wealth ecclesiasticall and civil*. London: Andrew Cooke.

Johnson, R. 2008. *Kant's moral philosophy. Stanford encyclopedia of philosophy*. Stanford: Stanford University Press.

Kant, I. 1971. *The doctrine of virtue. Part II of the metaphysics of morals*. Philadelphia: University of Pennsylvania Press.

Kant, I. 1998. *The groundwork for the metaphysics of morals*. Cambridge, MA: Cambridge University Press.

Korsgaard, C. 1996. *The sources of normativity*. Cambridge, MA: Cambridge University Press.

Lancaster, K.J. 1966. A new approach to consumer theory. *Journal of Political Economy* 74: 132–156.

Lenz, J.E., R.C. Mittelhammer, and H. Shi. 1994. Retail level hedonics and the valuation of milk components. *American Journal of Agricultural Economics* 76: 492–503.

Mill, J.-S. 1993. *On liberty and utilitarianism*. New York: Bantam Books.

Moore, G.E. 1903. *Principia ethica*. Cambridge, MA: Cambridge University Press.

Murillo-Zamorano, L.R. 2004. Economic efficiency and frontier techniques. *Journal of Economic Surveys* 18: 33–45.

Rachels, J., and S. Rachels. 2012. *The elements of moral philosophy*. New York: McGraw Hill.

Ratchford, B.T. 1975. The new economic theory of consumer behaviour: An interpretive essay. *The Journal of Consumer Research* 2: 65–75.

Raynolds, L.T., D.L. Murray, and J. Wilkinson. 2007. *Fair trade: The challenges of transforming globalization*. New York: Routledge.

Rawls, J. 1971. *A theory of justice*. Cambridge, MA: Harvard University Press.

Rawls, J. 1989. Themes in Kant's moral philosophy. In *Kant's transcendental deductions*, ed. E. Förster, 81–113. Stanford: Stanford University Press.

Rosen, S. 1974. Hedonic prices and implicit markets: Product differentiation in pure competition. *Journal of Political Economy* 82: 34–55.

Scott, W.R. 1995. *Institutions and organizations*. Thousand Oaks: Sage Publications.
Shafer-Landau, R. 2012. *The fundamentals of ethics*. New York: Oxford University Press.
Singer, P. 1975. *Animal liberation*. New York: Avon Books.
Westgren, R.E. 1999. Delivering food safety, food quality, and sustainable production practices: The Label Rouge poultry system in France. *American Journal of Agricultural Economics* 81(5): 1107–1111.

Chapter 4
The Fallacy of "Competition" in Agriculture

Michael E. Sykuta

Abstract Agriculture has long been viewed by economists as the best example of an industry characterized by perfect competition. However, the history of modern agriculture is marked with differences about just how competitive the industry is and whether competition is in fact a desirable thing. Present debates about competition in agriculture rally discontent with the competitive environment around the mantra of "free and fair competition." But this populist ideal presents problems of its own. First, what is the economic meaning of "free and fair" competition? Second, how does the argument about the need for free and fair competition meet with the facts of how the agricultural industry behaves? And finally, what are the ethical implications of arguments for government intervention in the agricultural economy?

4.1 Introduction

The concept of competition plays a critical role in economics. Competition underlies the very essence of the science of economics as the study of how scarce resources are allocated among *competing* wants. Without competition, at the most fundamental level, there is no effect of scarcity to result in positive prices for economic goods. Indeed, scarcity itself could be defined as the presence of competition to access or possess a good or service. In the context of the market, competition underlies the intuitive dynamics that lead to market equilibrium, as buyers and sellers of goods bid against one another. Competition, or more specifically the concept of "perfect competition," is the hallmark market attribute that results in social welfare-maximizing outcomes.

M.E. Sykuta, Ph.D. (✉)
Department of Agricultural & Applied Economics, University of Missouri,
135 Mumford Hall, Columbia, MO 65211, USA
e-mail: sykutam@missouri.edu

H.S. James Jr. (ed.), *The Ethics and Economics of Agrifood Competition*,
The International Library of Environmental, Agricultural and Food Ethics 20,
DOI 10.1007/978-94-007-6274-9_4, © Springer Science+Business Media Dordrecht 2013

And therein lies the problem. Competition is a term much used but little considered in most of the economics literature. Consequently, the term "competition" is used in a variety of contexts with little specificity as to its actual meaning or implication. Rather than focusing on the meaning and nature of competition itself, economists have instead separated static concepts of competitive structures from the actual process of competitive activity, focusing on the former with little regard for the latter. As a result, while pundits, politicians, and even academic economists romanticize the notion of competition and competitive markets, they blithely overlook the very nature of competition that makes markets work. They espouse competitive markets while denouncing the natural outcomes to which such markets sometimes lead. They embrace a fallacious notion of competition that may be inherently inconsistent with its own premises. This has been particularly true when considering US agriculture.

In the fall of 2009, the United States Attorney General and the Secretary of Agriculture announced that the Department of Justice (DOJ) and the Department of Agriculture (USDA) would embark on an historic alliance jointly to explore the state of competition in the US agriculture sector. In March 2010, at the first of a series of workshop hearings across the country, US Attorney General Eric Holder (2010) remarked:

> So we have to ask, is today's agriculture industry suffering from a lack of free and fair competition in the marketplace? That's the central question.
>
> And to answer this question, we must begin by examining what we know for sure. We know that a growing number of American farmers find it increasingly difficult to survive by doing what they have been doing for decades, and we've learned that some of them believe that the competitive environment may be, at least in part, to blame.

Holder's remarks reflect a common view of competition. Implicit in the question and the proposed answer are the idea that "free and fair" competition is good and the assumption that the inability of producers "to survive by doing what they have been doing for decades" implies a flawed economic environment. The problem with such a perspective is two-fold. First, "free and fair" competition is something about which economics has perhaps surprisingly little to say and is a term with more emotional than economic implication. Second, the assumption that some producers' inability to succeed is an indictment of the economic environment is, as we shall see, demonstrably inaccurate in any economic conception of competition.[1]

The purpose of this chapter is to illustrate the nature of the fallacy of competition in the context of US agriculture and agricultural policy debate. I argue that much of the debate about competition in agriculture is poorly grounded on either theoretical

[1]Part of the difficulty is Holder's imprecise use of the term "agriculture industry." Much of the DOJ/USDA workshops focused on issues of concentration at the farm inputs (e.g., seed) and commodity processing (e.g., grain handlers and meat packers) levels of the industry, not the production level. However, Holder made clear the assertion that the pressures facing (some) family farms were a result of reduced competition at the non-farm levels of the industry. Consequently, I focus on the producer level to illustrate why the changes observed there refute allegations of decreased competitiveness, whether arising on- or off-farm.

or empirical grounds, the result being a flawed focus on static market structures and on policies that restrict competitive behavior in the name of preserving this flawed conception of competition. I conclude with both a caution and a plea: that economists forebear from misuse and rampant imprecision in their discussions of competition, and that more intentional and holistic approaches to the nature and implications of competition be explored in future research.

4.2 The True Central Question of Competition: What Is It?

In order to answer the question of whether "today's agriculture industry is suffering from a lack of free and fair competition," one must first define what is meant by free and fair competition. If one cannot define "free and fair competition," one cannot presume to discern its presence or absence in a market economy. So the true central question that must be addressed is, "what does the concept of 'free and fair competition' mean, especially in the context of the agriculture industry?"

4.2.1 The Nature of Competition

A survey of economic textbooks, from first principles to advanced economic theory, reveals that the term *competition* is itself scarce, or at least scarcely defined in a meaningful way. To the extent the term is used, the implicit definition is something akin to that offered by Alfred Marshall (1920, p. 4) in his *Principles of Economics*: "The strict meaning of competition seems to be the racing of one person against another, with special reference to bidding for the sale or purchase of anything."

Marshall makes special reference to the activity of bidding for the sale or purchase of something. However, economic competition extends beyond bidding in the marketplace per se to include engaging in research, exploration, discovery, experimentation, and innovation either to secure additional scarce resources or to improve the agent's ability to engage in market bidding. Thus, we might extend Marshall's definition to read: competition seems to be the racing of one person (or firm) against another, with special reference to the acquisition, consumption, or exploitation of economic goods.[2]

In this context, competition is clearly an act or set of behaviors; a dynamic of interactions between competing parties. It reflects, even explains, Schumpeter's notion of "creative destruction," as economic agents race against one another for new ideas and new opportunities that displace less efficient and less effective

[2]Here I use the term exploitation in its most basic economic sense of extracting value from an economic good either by transformation or trade, without specific reference to its value of marginal product.

ideas, business practices and resource allocations. In *Capitalism, Socialism and Democracy*, Schumpeter writes (1950, pp. 84–85):

> Economists are at long last emerging from the stage in which price competition was all they saw. . . . In capitalist reality . . . it is not that kind of competition which counts but the competition from the new commodity, the new technology, the new source of supply, the new type of organization . . . competition which . . . strikes . . . existing firms . . . at their foundations and their very lives. This kind of competition is . . . much more effective than the other . . . and [is] . . . the powerful lever that in the long run expands output.

Thus competition, as an economic concept, implies a dynamic process in which economic agents race against one another in the pursuit of their own self-interest by exploiting human, physical and financial resources. Competition requires that individuals produce efficiently in order to effectively compete against their peers. The competition of "bidding for the sale or purchase" of goods and services is only one margin of competition, albeit critically important in establishing the value of goods and in creating the incentives that drive other margins of competition. The *process* of competition creates the incentive for economic efficiency in production and consumption that results in the maximization of social welfare.

4.2.2 'Free and Fair' Competition

If competition is the process by which individuals (and firms) race against one another in the pursuit of their own self-interests, what then are the characteristics of that racing implied by the label of "free and fair"? On this point, economists have perhaps a less concrete contribution. In fact, although the phrase is popularly used, it is not as common in the economics literature as one might first guess.[3] Rather, much of the phrase's use appears to be in legal and public policy research, without necessarily much consideration for or definition of a detailed understanding of the phrase's economic underpinnings.[4]

It is also important to recognize the difference between the two characteristics; namely, free and fair. Free is itself an economic term, normally suggesting the absence of cost or constraint. Free competition connotes a competitive process lacking arbitrary barriers to individuals' pursuits of their self-interests. It is an objective term in the sense that the presence or absence of such barriers may be objectively identified and their consequences for the competitive process analyzed. Fair, on the other hand, is necessarily a subjective term that falls outside the scope

[3] A search of the phrase "free and fair competition" in ECONLIT, one of the primary bibliographic databases in the profession, yielded only two publications from 1992 to present. Allowing a more flexible Boolean search of "free and fair" and "competition" yielded only seven.

[4] A search of the phrase in Google Scholar, which covers a much wider array of books, journals and disciplines than ECONLIT, yielded almost 1,300 results since 1993, the earliest year delimiter available.

of positive economic analysis. Moreover, the term "fair" presents problems of contradiction when used in the context of competition, a problem addressed later in this chapter.

4.2.2.1 Free Competition

If free competition is competition unfettered by arbitrary or artificial barriers in the ability of individuals to engage in the race, then one must consider the actions involved in running that race, as it were, and the types of barriers that might interfere with that activity. In defining the concept of competition, Marshall (1920) suggests that a starting point for considering the concept of free competition may lie in understanding the behavior of individuals that leads to the competition itself. He writes:

> This kind of racing ... is only a secondary, and one might almost say, an accidental consequence of the fundamental characteristics of modern industrial life. There is no one term that will express these characteristics adequately. They are ... a certain independence and habit of choosing one's own course for oneself, a self-reliance; a deliberation and yet a promptness of choice and judgment, and a habit of forecasting the future and of shaping one's course with reference to distant aims.

Thus one may start with the principle that the unrestrained exercise of individual liberty lies at the foundation of free competition. However, free and effective competition also requires institutions that support and protect property rights and their exchange in order for economic competition to occur, or at least to occur most effectively (North 1990).

Hayek (1944) provides a more concrete picture of what free competition may look like in the market economy. In explaining how the principle of competition most effectively organizes society and economic activity, he writes (p. 37):

> It is necessary ... that parties in the market should be free to sell and buy at any price at which they can find a partner to the transaction and that anybody should be free to produce, sell, and buy anything that may be produced or sold at all. And it is essential that the entry into the different trades should be open to all on equal terms and that the law should not tolerate any attempts by individuals or groups to restrict this entry by open or concealed force. Any attempt to control prices or quantities of particular commodities deprives competition of its power of bringing about an effective co-ordination of individual efforts, because price changes then cease to register all the relevant changes in circumstances and no longer provide a reliable guide for the individual's actions.

Free to sell and buy at any price. Free to produce, sell, and buy anything that may be produced or sold. Entry should be open to all on equal terms. Prices and quantities should not be controlled. Price should be allowed to reflect the economic circumstances so as to provide a reliable guide for individual's actions. These are the elements of free competition. And it is important to note that Hayek's reference to attempts to control prices or quantities in this context refers specifically to government intervention, not necessarily to the actions of individuals or groups in the market.

4.2.2.2 Fair Competition

Fair competition, as distinguished from free competition, appears to be more a legal concept than an economic one. The term fair has a distinctly moral or normative implication. We may say that it is unfair of someone to restrict market entry by force, but the economic justification for that judgment is based not on the disutility or disparate effects such actions have on the specific parties, but on its implication for free competition in the market and its resulting social inefficiencies. In this instance, unfairness is marked by the lack of freedom. However, the phrase "fair competition" generally carries a more utilitarian tenor and suggests a broader range of activities than may fit neatly within the more narrow economic perspective.

Within legal scholarship, the concept of unfair competition traces to the Industrial Revolution and a commensurate increase in dishonest practices as industry and commerce rapidly grew beyond the scope of traditional institutions for economic exchange. Heilbroner (1975) explains that the trend to big business in the 1800s and early 1900s, "extended and intensified" the degree of competitiveness of the market structure (p. 110). "The outcome was the emergence of 'cutthroat competition' among massive producers, replacing the more restricted, local competition of the small-business, small-market world" (p. 111). Some of these "cutthroat" practices gave rise to concerns of "unfair competition."

Writing about the development of the legal concept of unfair competition at that time, Haines (1919) describes the term "unfair competition" as being "even more indefinite" than "certain vague and indefinite phrases... such as 'unreasonable conduct' in the law of negligence, 'undue influence' in the law of wills, 'unreasonable restraint of trade' in the effort to check the growth of monopoly, and 'unfair discrimination' in the regulation of affairs of public carriers." Haines provides an instructive history of the concept of unfair competition in both the English and American legal systems, explaining how the first such concerns arose in response to trademarks and improper use of intellectual property. In describing the attempts of State governments to reduce unfair competition through statutes and anti-trust laws, Haines writes:

> Chief among this class of enactments are the prohibition of monopolies and pooling; agreements or conspiracies in restraint of trade; restraint of competition as distinct from restraint of trade such as price control, increasing prices, fixing a standard price or local price discriminations, limitation of output, division of territory or restraint on resales. While monopolies and agreements in restraint of trade involve the principle of unfair competition, *it is with the last of the three classes of acts that we are now chiefly concerned.* It is this type of law which is designed to provide that there may be "reason-able competition," and that aims to enact into law the doctrine of "free and fair competition," as an inherent right of the people (p. 11; emphasis added).

Price control, increasing prices, fixing a standard price or local price discriminations, limitation of output, division of territory or restraint on resale. The list follows closely the activities prohibited under the Clayton Act (1914) and its follow-on, the Robinson-Patman Act (1934), which continue to be primary restrictions on unfair competition today (Damanpour 2005).[5] The Packers and Stockyards Act of 1921 was passed to extend more specifically these protections against unfair competition to the livestock industry.[6]

It is also important to note that the above list of activities is primarily related to the behavior, or actions, of individuals and firms. The focus is on the process of competition. In this doctrine of "free and fair competition," what matters is how parties go about running the race. In that sense, the concept as thus defined is relevant to economics and economists. It affects the ability of individuals to engage in free competition and for markets to reflect society's true value of the things to be bought and sold, thereby providing "a reliable guide for individual's actions."

However, "fair competition" is also sometimes used not to describe the nature of the process, but the outcomes of the process. At this point, we move beyond economics and more deeply into the realm of ethics. This is not to say these two realms are mutually exclusive. How individuals interpret ethically the process of competition and the outcomes of competitive markets does inform their choices of how to engage in competitive behavior. However, the science of economics has little to offer in the evaluation of alternate distributions of outcomes aside from their tendency toward or away from economic efficiency and competitive behaviors. In short, economics is concerned more with maximizing social welfare than the allocation of that welfare among market participants.

On the other hand, the ethics view of "free and fair competition" tends often to focus on the distribution of wealth and on individuals' abilities to realize their desired outcomes. Indeed, the ethics literature often asserts that "fairness" and "distributional equity" are synonymous (Donaldson 2001). Unfortunately, the very premise that free and fair competition should result in either equitable outcomes or universal satisfaction is intrinsically inconsistent with the very concept of competition.[7]

The implication of competition being a race among parties is that not all parties can win. Not all parties will achieve the same outcomes. Not all parties will find themselves equally satisfied with the outcomes they achieve. Moreover, because competition is by its nature dynamic, it is unreasonable to suggest that any producer

---

[5]It is also interesting to follow how the interpretation and enforcement of these laws and the concept of unfair competition has evolved over the last century, including a liberalization around certain of these behaviors, such as predatory pricing, exclusive dealing territories, tying, and resale price maintenance. A history of US antitrust law and the economics of antitrust law is well beyond the scope of this essay.

[6]Sykuta (2010) addresses the use of the Packers & Stockyards Act to supplement antitrust enforcement in the livestock industry and argues that a failure to distinguish between competitive forces and anticompetitive effects makes effective enforcement of the Act difficult.

[7]Alesina and Angeletos (2005) study peoples' attitudes toward fairness and redistribution and find that fairness is not necessarily based on equity, but perceptions of whether those outcomes were achieved by valid means or by luck. This sense of fairness is more consistent with an economic understanding of free and fair competition.

should be able to continue to survive merely by doing what she has been doing for decades. As Schumpeter (1950, p. 82) explained, "Capitalism . . . is by nature a form or method of economic change and not only never is but never can be stationary." Thus the answer to Holder's second question is simply, "Yes, the inability of farmers to survive by doing the same thing they have done for decades is a result of the competitive environment." But that is the nature of a competitive environment. Rather than blaming the competitive environment for tending to its natural outcomes, the concept of competition would instead suggest blame is on the part of farmers who have continued to do what they have done for decades.

4.3 The Problem of Perfect Competition

One reason for confusion around the concept of competition and its application to policy is how economists most often characterize competition. Despite the dynamic nature of the competitive process, economists have instead focused on static models of industry structure that in many cases fail to capture the implications of the underlying competitive processes. If the term "competition" is listed at all in the contents of an economics text, it will often appear with at least the adjective "perfect" associated with it.

Perfect competition, or sometimes pure competition, is economists' hallmark of the ideal economic system. This notion of pure competition dates back to Adam Smith's *Wealth of Nations* (Smith 1776).[8] In its modern form, perfect competition is defined by a set of five structural characteristics:

1. *Many buyers and sellers*, meaning enough such that no one party can meaningfully affect the market price by increasing or decreasing the quantity they wish to sell or buy.
2. *Homogeneous goods*, meaning all units of a particular type of good are identical in any meaningful way, or that they are perfect substitutes.
3. *Perfect information*, meaning that all buyers and sellers have full information about the product, its price, and potential trading parties.
4. *Zero transaction costs*, meaning that there are no "frictions" in the market that would prevent buyers and sellers from meeting, negotiating, and settling the terms of mutually-beneficial transactions.
5. *Free entry (and exit)*, meaning new buyers and sellers are able to enter into or exit the market without penalty or some other impediment.

The first four of these characteristics ensure what economists call price-taking behavior, or that prices are exogenously determined for individual buyers and sellers by the aggregate interaction of all buyers and sellers. Because products are

[8] Rima (1986, p. 86) notes that "Smith's awareness of the role of competition in the pricing process becomes clear in his seventh chapter (of *The Wealth of Nations*). . . . Indeed, the only prerequisite of pure competition which he did not note is product homogeneity" (clarification added).

homogeneous, there is no reason why a buyer would ever pay more for one seller's items than for another's. Because there are many buyers and sellers, parties have ample alternatives with whom to trade. Because all parties have perfect information, no party can be fooled to believe a product is worth more or less than its market price or that other parties are willing to pay more or less than the offer price. Because transaction costs are zero, there is no reason why a buyer or seller would "settle" for a different price rather than continue to search for alternate trading parties or to make the cost of trading with one party greater than the cost of trading with another.

The natural result of this price-taking behavior is that consumers pay no more or less than their true valuation of the product (at the margin), meaning the prevailing price reflects society's value of the good. Similarly, because sellers can sell as many units of the good as they wish at the same market price, they produce at a level of output where the marginal cost of producing one more unit equals the market price. Since society's value of the product equals the marginal cost of producing the product, the socially-optimal level of output will be produced and exchanged.

Given this conclusion, it is perhaps not surprising that economists have embraced this fictional construct as the baseline against which market competition is measured. However, the result is that discussions of competition inevitably turn on the numbers of buyers and sellers in the market and the size of these buyers and sellers relative to one another. The concept of perfect competition creates a fallacious understanding of competition as merely the presence of many (presumably small) buyers and sellers, without regard to the actual behavior of the market participants. Given such an understanding, the appearance or presence of "large" players immediately raises suspicions and allegations of noncompetitive behavior, never mind how those large players came to be nor how they actually behave.

This brings us to the fifth of the five characteristics of perfect competition: free entry and exit. While the first four are sufficient to guarantee price-taking behavior in the short run, free entry and exit is the characteristic that drives competitive markets toward efficient outcomes in the long run. When entry is unrestricted, new buyers and sellers may enter the industry to take advantage of potential economic rents. These rents may result from a relative scarcity of supply of the product being sold, changes in relative prices of inputs and outputs, cost advantages attributable to size and scale, or cost advantages attributable to new technologies or organizational innovations. Particularly in the latter two cases, as new entrants adopt more efficient levels or means of production, prices for outputs go down, reducing the profitability of all firms in the industry. Incumbent producers must in turn adopt these new business practices or risk being underpriced by their more efficient peers. In the extreme, producers who refuse or are unable to adopt the more efficient practices will find themselves losing money and eventually exiting the industry.

Free entry and exit is the assumption that allows, indeed requires, the dynamic process of competition to play out. However, this raises a quandary for proponents of an ethics view of "free and fair competition" and for strict adherents to the perfectly competitive ideal as the hallmark of competition: What to make of competition that systematically eliminates some producers in favor of others, particularly when the tendency is toward fewer, larger producers over time?

Economists have really only dealt with this quandary in the extreme case in which competition would tend to result in only one surviving firm, a natural monopoly. In that case, neoclassical economists might argue for any of a variety of regulatory schema intended to limit the ability of the monopoly to exploit its monopoly status by restricting output below (and commensurately raising prices above) the social optimum. However, what happens in between the extremes of atomistic firms competitively replacing one another and increasing concentration to the point of monopoly remains undeveloped, dismissed as just a matter of degree.

And yet, a matter of degree is the basis of debate in the agriculture industry. The last century has witnessed a decline in the number of participants at just about every level of the agriculture industry. The number of farms is now less than one-third its peak in 1920, dropping from 64,500,000 to 1,912,000 in 1997.[9] As the number of farms has declined, average farm size has increased proportionally, growing from 148 acres in 1920 to 487 acres in 1997. The distribution of the value of agricultural production shifted such that a shrinking percentage of farms produce the vast majority of agricultural output (O'Donoghue et al. 2011). And it is this trend that raises concerns about the state of "free and fair competition" in agriculture, as the number of (typically smaller, family) farms decreases and as operators of such farms point to increasing non-farm concentration both up- and down-stream as the cause of their demise.

4.4 Competition in Agriculture

The agriculture industry has long been considered perhaps the best example of (near) perfect competition (Benedict 1954; Stiglitz 1974; Adams and Brock 1995). Indeed, one might even argue that agriculture served as the prototype competitive market in the development of modern economic theory (Rima 1986). Despite this general view, concerns about the state of competition in agriculture are nothing new.

4.4.1 The Demise of Competition in Agriculture?

In 1953, the American Economic Association (AEA) annual meeting featured a session titled "Is American Agriculture Still Essentially Competitive and Laissez Faire?" Between 1920 and 1950, the number of farms reported in the US Census of Agriculture dropped from 6,453,000 to 5,379,000. However, the focus of that

[9] Statistical methods were changed beginning with the 1997 Census of Agriculture, making direct comparisons with more recent years difficult. The 2007 Census shows a slight decrease in farms at 2,205,000 compared to 1997s adjusted number of 2,216,000, although average farm size decreased from 431 in 1997 to 418 in 2007.

session was not on the increasing concentration in or the declining number of farms in the US. Nor was it increasing concentration in the non-farm agriculture industry. Instead, the question was whether "the restrictionist character of some of the farm programs" that had emerged beginning in the 1930s had made agriculture less competitive (Benedict 1954).

M.R. Benedict (1954), one of the panel presenters, argues that the farm sector specifically sought government programs that would reduce the forces of competition in agriculture. What started in the early 1920s with a short-lived, private-sector movement suggested by Aaron Sapiro to create large-scale, national cooperative marketing associations to control quantities and prices, resulted eventually in the creation of the Farm Board in 1929, which effectively achieved a similar purpose. Benedict (1954, pp. 97–98) writes:

> Competition had come to be looked upon as 'destructive' and antisocial. ... [i]t seems fair to state that, ideologically, agriculture has moved rather far from its traditional position as the principal defender of the competitive system. Has it, in fact, been able to break away from it or are the forces of competition so powerful that they have continued to dominate the situation despite these major changes in policy? This as I see it is the problem to which we are seeking answers here.

There are two important points to recognize from this historical narrative. The first point is that decision makers, farmers and economists explicitly recognized the necessary link between competition and competitive outcomes. D. Gale Johnson, the other presenter in the 1953 AEA session on competition in agriculture, states:

> The assumption that competition is preferable to other means of organizing an area of economic activity is primarily a preference for the consequences that are supposed to follow from competition, not merely a preference for competition per se. But the consequences that are supposed to flow from competition do not necessarily occur, if we define competition in terms of the inability of any one firm to influence the price at which it buys or sells (1954, p. 107).

The nature of the farming enterprise, being removed from the final consumption of agricultural products, led individual farmers to maintain production regardless of changes in demand, barring extreme weather conditions or extreme prices that either discouraged or encouraged production. This means that changes in demand resulted in major price changes for farm products, and prices varied greatly from year to year. Moreover, this price variability was in contrast to less volatile prices for industrialized goods whose production was actively managed and controlled in industries that had witnessed increasing concentration resulting from greater economies of scale due to technological and institutional changes.

The second important point to recognize is that the role of government farm programs was specifically viewed as being anticompetitive, or as dampening the forces of competition and creating a "more favorable" distribution of wealth. Benedict (1954) asserts that when privately-organized attempts to collectivize and control prices through "anticompetitive" means failed in the early 1920s, farmers turned to the government to "monopolize" agriculture by regulatory control. The creation of the Farm Board in 1929, which set out to create federally-sponsored, national cooperative marketing associations, followed two previous legislative attempts promoted by farming interests, known as the McNary-Haugen plan. As the effects of the depression set in, new government programs were introduced that further centralized control of agricultural production and prices, including acreage controls, marketing quotas, import restraints, price support through government procurement of surpluses, and social programs such as the National School Lunch Program and the Food Stamp Plan, designed to make use of surplus commodities.[10]

Although the details have changed, many of these programs continue in some form even today. To the extent price support programs have been eliminated, income payment programs continue to reduce the effects of competition in agriculture. The difference between now and then is not the intended effect, but that the farm community and its supporters now represent those policies as being "pro-competitive" because they protect a large number of producers from the effects of competition. Thus, we now have an agriculture industry preserving the fallacy of competition by using anticompetitive policies to maintain a condition of having many sellers of agricultural goods, or more accurately, even more sellers of agriculture goods than would be the case otherwise.

4.4.2 The Shortcoming of Government Intervention

Despite the objectives of early farm programs to reduce the effects of competitive forces in the market, Benedict's assessment at the time suggests that, while government programs did have some marginal effects on farm operations, they did not effect long-term changes in the nature of the agriculture industry. He writes:

> Most of the government programs have not changed significantly the basic structure of agriculture nor have they brought about any large amount of self-sustaining change in the competitiveness of agriculture. If the legal authorizations for acreage controls, marketing quotas, and marketing agreements were to be repealed, agriculture would promptly revert to essentially the same type of highly competitive organization as it had before these controls were established. ... (Competition) still is the major organizational influence in the agriculture segment of the economy and is likely to remain so, except as government intervenes to hold it in check. Question may be raised also as to whether, even with government intervention, it is actually restrained *or merely diverted into other forms* (1954, pp. 99–100; emphasis added).

Although government programs arguably had an effect on the distributional outcome of agricultural markets, the fundamental forces of competition were not dispelled during these first few decades. Indeed, by assuming price risk for farmers,

[10]The National School Lunch Program originated informally during the depression to help dissipate the surplus of farm products and was formalized by Congress in 1946 after a review of the World War II military draft revealed a high correlation between physical deficiencies and childhood nutrition among rejected draftees (Taenzler 1970).

the government subsidized competition among farmers on non-price margins. Rather than competing based on commodity price, farmers competed for greater income and greater wealth through increased land holdings and bidding up land prices, adoption of new technologies, and greater productivity of inputs. Comparing input–output ratios in agriculture of the early 1950s with that of the late 1920s, Johnson (1954, p. 108) states, "these data do not give an indication of a stagnant, unchanging industry nor one in which governmental interference was used to place an effective upper limit upon output or to prevent changes in the inputs used." Benedict (1954, p. 104) concludes, "It would seem to me that the evidence of continuing and vigorous competition is incontrovertible."

4.4.3 Competition in Agriculture Today

As noted above, the number of farms today is less than one-third the number at its peak in 1920 and roughly 35% of the total in 1950. Despite that shrinking number of farms and the increasing concentration of agricultural production in a small percentage of total farms, agriculture is still an industry whose behavior is best understood in the framework of perfect competition (Adams and Brock 1995). In 2006, 2% of all US farms (those with annual sales of $1 million or more) accounted for 48% of the sales of US agricultural products. However, that 2% consisted of more than 35,000 farms. Researchers at the USDA's Economic Research Service (Hoppe et al. 2008) concluded "there are still too many million dollar farms . . . for any single farm to dominate agriculture or the production of specific commodities." Moreover, by 2007 the number of million dollar farms increased to over 55,500 (O'Donogue et al. 2011) and the US Census of Agriculture reported the number of farms with more than $500,000 in annual sales exceeded 116,000 farms.

These figures illustrate the recent truth of a longer trend in modern agriculture: Competitive forces, government programs notwithstanding, have been leading to an industry structure that is more concentrated in a relatively small percentage of farms, but the absolute size of the industry and number of participants remains indisputably competitive. In addition, the trend suggests the industry is getting more competitive (measured by numbers of farms) in the most meaning and productive ranges of farm size. Thus there seems to be no basis for claims that the agricultural production is growing less competitive over time.

4.4.4 So Whence Concerns About Competition in Agriculture Today?

Concerns about competition in agriculture today are less about competition than about the inability of large percentages of farms to effectively compete given changes in the competitive environment both up- and down-stream. As reflected

Table 4.1 Economic performance of family farms in 2004 and 2007

	Full-time family farms by sales size				
	Low	Medium	Large	Very large	All farms
Number of farms					
2004	395,781	133,299	86,087	71,708	2,107,925
2007	434,599	111,389	93,601	110,152	2,196,791
Operating profit margin					
2004	−36.1	−2.4	10.8	18.3	3.0
2007	−48.6	5.9	16.3	25.7	11.0
% with net income > 0					
2004	68.7	76.9	82.2	83.8	69.6
2007	60.6	81.0	82.9	83.8	63.0

Source: Hoppe et al. (2007) and Hoppe and Baker (2010) for 2004 and 2007, respectively. Figures only for occupational family farms, excluding small family farms with primarily off-farm income and non-family farms. Low sales farms have sales less than $100,000. Medium farms have sales from $100,000 to $250,000. Large have sales from $250,000 to $500,000. Very large have sales of $500,000 or more

in Holder's comments, a large number of farms are finding it more difficult to survive in today's competitive environment. That concern may best be captured by the profitability of farming operations.

Table 4.1 shows the average operating profit margins of occupational family farms by farm size for 2004 and 2007.[11] On average, small family farms, those having gross sales of less than $100,000, have large, negative operating profits in both years, while large farms tend to be more profitable. It is important to note that these averages mask a good deal of variance within each group. Table 4.1 also shows the percentage of farms in each class earning positive net income. A majority of low-sales farms earned positive net incomes. However, many low-sales farms do not record a salary for the operator of the farming operation. The USDA's operating profit margin imputes a charge of unpaid operators' labor and management, thus providing a better measure of the true economic returns to the farming operation.[12]

[11]Table 4.1 excludes roughly 1.4 million small family farms that rely primarily on off-farm income or are operated by retirees and roughly 50,000 non-family farms, which include cooperatives and corporations and tend to vary in size. Small family farms perform similarly to small-sales occupation farms in terms of operating margins. Non-family farms perform similarly to very large family farms. I focus on occupational family farms because they are most reliant on their agricultural production (among family farms) and concerns about the competitiveness of agriculture tend to focus on the viability of family farms.

[12]Neither net income nor operating profit margin account for the opportunity cost of assets in production. Given the role and importance of land, this is likely a significant omission for estimating economic profitability. However, some land is mortgaged and the cost of loan payments, which would approximate the cost of the land capital, is included in net income. Thus it is difficult to draw any strong conclusions in the aggregate.

Two points bear mention in regard to these figures. The first is that net income and operating profit margin both include government payments received by the farm operation. Thus, more than 30% of small farms in 2004 and almost 40% in 2007 earned negative net income even *after* government program payments. While it is true that the majority of commodity and working land payments go to large-scale farms, small farms receive a more than proportional share. Hobbe and Baker (2010) report that small-scale farms (which include the medium-sales farms in Table 4.1) received 24% of federal commodity payments while producing only 16.4% of the agricultural production in 2007.

The second is that both 2004 and 2007 were exceptionally good years in agriculture (Usset 2011). Thus, even in boom years of agriculture, the average small farm produced negative operating margins and fully one-third of farms failed to earn positive net income. While one-third of small farms seems like a relatively small percentage, bear in mind the total number of farms. Based on the figures in Table 4.1, fully 125,000 and 170,000 small, occupation farms failed to break even in 2004 and 2007, respectively. Add another 31,000 and 21,000 for negative net income medium-sales farms in the 2 years, and we have almost as many small and medium-sales farms losing money as there are large and very large farms in total!

4.4.5 What Does This Tell Us About Competition in Agriculture?

Does the persistent, negative profit of a minority of small farms suggest problems with the competitive environment? Simply put, no. At least not in the way that is asserted by critics or suggested by the comments of Secretary Holder. There are two arguments for dismissing the suggestion that either the level or nature of competition is to blame.

The first argument is that the pattern we observe over time in agricultural production is most consistent with a vigorous competition among producers. Despite the decline in farm numbers up until the 1990s, there is continual growth of output, productivity, and average farm sizes (in acres). The rapid adoption of biotechnologies such as genetically-modified field crops in the late 1990s and 2000s suggests vibrant competition among producers seeking cost and/or productivity advantages. Improvements in animal genetics and adoption of new production practices, particularly in hogs over the past two decades, reflect a high degree of competition among producers. And the fact that the number of large, more economically profitable farms has been consistently increasing over this period suggests that competition not only is well at work, but also is creating a self-sustaining competitive structure at scales of production appropriate to the technologies now available for agricultural production.

The second argument is that increased concentration in the non-farm sectors of agriculture is not responsible for the plight of small farmers and therefore the decline of family farms is not evidence of problems with the competitive environment. It is true that input markets have witnessed increasing concentration, especially for specialty-trait, biotechnology crops. It is true that concentration in meat and food processing has increased dramatically over the past few decades. It is also true that consolidation in the grain and oilseed industries has in some cases left farmers with fewer options for marketing their crops. The 2010 DOJ/USDA workshops investigating the state of competition in agriculture were clearly focused on these trends and their effects on farm profitability. However, blaming increased concentration upstream ignores the evidence of competition at the production level.

Exercise of monopoly (or monopsony) power leaves economic footprints beyond the simple profitability of a minority of counterparties. Monopsony is the case of a single (or limited number of) buyer(s) in a market who is able to keep prices for the product low by restricting the amount of product the monopsonist purchases. Farmers complaining about increased concentration downstream tend to allege the low prices they receive are a result of monopsony practices that artificially depress the price of farm products. However, the fact that more than 200,000 family farms generated large, positive operating margins in 2007 suggests that competitive, price-taking farms are perfectly capable of being profitable despite the increased concentration up- and down-stream. The fact that some farms are struggling to survive reflects more on the operations of those farms than it does on the changing structure of the non-farm agriculture sector. In short, blaming concentration in the non-farm sectors for the economic inviability of some farms is like unto standing in the rain without seeking shelter and blaming the rain for getting one wet.

If the competitive environment is responsible for the financial difficulty in which many farms find themselves, it is more likely due to what Secretary Holder described as farmers "continuing to do what they have done for decades." The nature of agriculture has changed and competition requires changes from those who wish to be successful. That not all producers can make those changes successfully is not an indictment of the competitiveness of the industry, but rather a reflection of it.

Consider, for instance, the practice of using contracts. O'Donoghue et al. (2011) show that the use of contracts (whether marketing or production) has stabilized over the last decade with roughly 40% of the value of agricultural production under contract and roughly 10% of farms using contacts. However, as McDonald and Korb (2008) show, small-scale farms are much less likely to use contracts for their output. Between 2001 and 2008, fewer than 7% of small-scale and medium-scale farms used contracts while over 50% of very large farms used contracts. These very large firms contracted just over 35% of the value of their production. The percentage of large-scale firms, those with gross sales between $250,000 and $500,000, using contracts increased from 40 to 53%, contracting just 25% of the value of their production.

Results of the USDA's 2008 Agricultural Resource Management Survey show further disparities between the behaviors of small and large-scale farms. Small-scale farm operators were less likely to

- shop beyond the nearest town for key inputs
- shop for the best price from suppliers

- negotiate price discounts
- lock in prices for inputs
- use market-based risk-management tools

While it is conceivable that small farms may not have the financial resources to make significant investments in capital and equipment that larger farms make, that in itself is not a symptom of a failing competitive market. Moreover, most of the activities in the preceding list do not necessarily require any particular scale or access to capital.

It seems clear from an examination of the evidence that competition is alive and well in the agriculture industry. Indeed, it would not be a stretch to call it a vibrant competition. The industry is exhibiting exactly the kinds of behaviors and dynamics that characterize economists' conception of perfect competition, or at least as much as possible given existing farm programs. While there are undoubtedly some farms that are unable to survive in this environment, even that is a signal that competition is alive and well. By and large, the farms that are struggling are farms that have failed to adapt with the industry, either in scale, technology, or effective business practices. These are precisely the kinds of firms a theory of competition would predict as unable to compete and thus likely to withdraw from the industry. To suggest that such changes are evidence of a failing competitive environment reflects a poor understanding of the nature and effects of competition.

4.4.6 Ethics and the Fallacy of Competition

The debate about competition in agriculture raises questions of an ethical nature, but not necessarily—or solely—the ones raised by critics of the current environment. Agricultural producers who find themselves struggling and those persons who sympathize with the plight of the small family farmer are prone to raising questions about the fairness (i.e., equitableness) of the distribution of welfare in the current system. That is a legitimate concern to express from a welfare and ethics perspective. However, proponents of a more equitable distribution of wealth among farmers need to understand—or admit—that the problem is not a lack of competition or competitiveness in the industry, but a lack of competitiveness on the part of those farming operations that fail to hold their own in the market. Populist concerns about the competitive nature of the market should embrace the more intellectually honest arguments of their forebearers in the 1920s and 1930s who explicitly sought to reduce the level of competition so as to make life easier for the less economically fit.

But that argument raises other ethical questions. For instance, what is the ethical basis for government to intervene in the market to reduce the financial pressures facing a minority of agricultural producers? Why are the interests of a minority of farmers, who are economically unable to compete, of greater value than the economic interest of the remaining farmers who make more effective use of their resources to compete in the market? Or of greater value than the welfare interests of consumers of agricultural goods? Or of greater value than the welfare interests of investors and employees in non-farm sectors of agriculture that may be negatively affected by government protections on behalf of small family farms or of investors in competing firms? On a grander level, what ethical framework endorses agricultural support policies that benefit domestic producers while depressing the livelihoods and well-being of agricultural producers in developing countries? Finally, what is the ethical basis for using government intervention to reduce "free competition" in order to promote some special group's self-interested sense of "fair competition"? This question extends well beyond agriculture, but the present case provides ample opportunity and evidence for reflection.

In his discussion of the concept of competition, Marshall (1920) recognizes that the term competition is sometimes viewed as a pejorative, especially by those for whom competition presents the reality of losing the race. His conclusion seems a fitting end for this chapter:

> We may conclude then that the term 'competition' is not well suited to describe the special characteristics of industrial life in the modern age. We need a term that does not imply any moral qualities, whether good or evil, but which indicates the undisputed fact that modern business and industry are characterized by more self-reliant habits, more forethought, more deliberate and free choice. There is not any one term adequate for this purse: but *Freedom of Industry and Enterprise*, or more shortly, *Economic Freedom*, points in the right direction (p. 8).

References

Adams, W., and J. Brock. 1995. *The structure of American industry*, 9th ed. Englewood Cliffs: Prentice Hall.

Alesina, A., and G.-M. Angeletos. 2005. Fairness and distribution. *American Economic Review* 95(4): 960–980.

Benedict, M.R. 1954. Attempts to restrict competition in agriculture: The government programs. *American Economic Review* 49(2): 93–106.

Damanpour, F. 2005. A comparative analysis of competition and Anti-Trust Law for the major industrialized nations. *International Business & Economics Research Journal* 4(6): 17–28.

Donaldson, T. 2001. The ethical wealth of nations. *Journal of Business Ethics* 31(1): 25–36.

Haines, C.G. 1919. Efforts to define unfair competition. *The Yale Law Journal* 29(10): 1–28.

Hayek, F.A. 1944. *The road to serfdom*. Chicago: University of Chicago Press.

Heilbroner, R. 1975. *The making of economic society*, 9th ed. Englewood Cliffs: Prentice Hall.

Holder, E. 2010. *Public workshops exploring competition issues in agriculture: A dialogue on competition issues facing farmers in today's agricultural marketplace* (transcript). Washington, DC: United States Department of Justice. http://www.justice.gov/atr/public/workshops/ag2010/index.html. Accessed 17 June 2011.

Hoppe, R.A., and D.E. Banker. 2010. Structure and finances of U.S. farms: Family farm Report, 2010 edition. *Economic Information Bulletin Number 66*. Washington, DC: Economic Research Service, United States Department of Agriculture.

Hoppe, R.A., P. Korb, E.J. O'Donoghue, and D.E. Banker. 2007. Structure and finances of U.S. farms: Family farm report, 2007 edition. *Economic Information Bulletin Number 24*. Washington, DC: Economic Research Service, United States Department of Agriculture.

Hoppe, R.A., P. Korb, and D.E. Banker. 2008. Million-dollar farms in the new century. *Economic Information Bulletin Number 42*. Washington, DC: Economic Research Service, United States Department of Agriculture.

Johnson, D.G. 1954. Competition in agriculture: Fact or fiction. *American Economic Review* 49(2): 107–115.

Marshall, A. 1920. *Principles of economics*, 8th ed. Philadelphia: Porcupine Press.

McDonald, J., and P. Korb. 2008. Agricultural contracting update: Contracts in 2008. *Economic Information Bulletin Number 72*. Washington, DC: Economic Research Service, United States Department of Agriculture.

North, D. 1990. *Institutions, institutional change, and economic performance*. Cambridge: Cambridge University Press.

O'Donogue, E., R. Hoppe, D. Banker, R. Ebel, K. Fuglie, P. Korb, M. Livingston, C. Nickerson, and C. Sandretto. 2011. The changing organization of U.S. farming. *Economic Information Bulletin Number 88*. Washington, DC: Economic Research Service, United States Department of Agriculture.

Rima, I.H. 1986. *Development of economic analysis*, 4th ed. Homewood: Richard D. Irwin.

Schumpeter, J. 1950. *Capitalism, socialism, and democracy*, 3rd ed. New York: Harper & Brothers, orig. pub. 1942.

Smith, A. 1776/1981. *An inquiry into the nature and causes of the wealth of nations*. Indianapolis: Liberty Classics.

Stiglitz, G. 1974. Incentives and risk sharing in sharecropping. *Review of Economic Studies* 41(2): 219–255.

Sykuta, M. 2010. Concentration, contracting and competition: Problems in using the Packers & Stockyards Act to supplement antitrust. *The CPI Antitrust Journal* 4(2).

Taenzler, S.A. 1970. The national school lunch program. *University of Pennsylvania Law Review* 119(2): 372–388.

Usset, E. 2011. One big bull. *Corn & Soybean Digest*. http://cornandsoybeandigest.com/marketing/one-big-bull. Accessed 3 Feb 2012.

Chapter 5
Efficiency, Power and Freedom

C. Robert Taylor

"Everything has changed but our ways of thinking, and if these do not change we drift toward unparalleled catastrophe."

–Albert Einstein

Abstract Efficiency is the dominant economic concept underlying most academic and governmental studies of competition in the agrifood system, yet key issues deal with equity, fairness, economic discrimination, independence, justice, economic freedom and economic liberty. This chapter seeks to widen the economic view of the agrifood system to include ethics along with efficiency, and to include the interface between law and economics as manifested in antitrust and competition law. Antitrust law began with broad socioeconomic goals emphasizing "free and fair competition." The original emphasis on fairness has essentially disappeared. Now aggregate economic efficiency dominates interpretation of this legislation. Without corrective legislation and a truly independent judiciary, recent legal interpretations will continue to shape the agrifood system, allowing it to become more integrated and concentrated. The need to rediscover the purposes for antitrust laws and their enforcement has never been more acute than now.

5.1 Introduction

Efficiency is the dominant economic concept underlying most academic and governmental studies of competition in agricultural markets. It is also the dominant explanation made by corporate executives and their hired economists when

C.R. Taylor, Ph.D. (✉)
Department of Agricultural Economics and Rural Sociology, Auburn University, Auburn, AL 36849, USA
e-mail: taylocr@auburn.edu

H.S. James Jr. (ed.), *The Ethics and Economics of Agrifood Competition*,
The International Library of Environmental, Agricultural and Food Ethics 20,
DOI 10.1007/978-94-007-6274-9_5,

confronted by displaced farmers and ranchers and others in the agricultural chain. Efficiency has long been the central framework for assessing competitive issues in agricultural markets and, to some, has become an ideology.

Many of the hotly debated agrifood competition issues are not about efficiency, in my opinion. At least efficiency should not be the only concern or even the dominant concern.

Key socioeconomic issues deal with equity, fairness, economic discrimination, independence, justice, economic freedom, economic liberty, and serfdom. Have these socioeconomic effects no value to individuals or society except to the limited extent that they may be factored into efficiency calculations? Can human life, happiness, and general well-being of society reduce to an efficiency calculus, a single number in a box? I think not.[1]

Blind pursuit of efficiency as a policy goal may, from an aggregate perspective, even lead to inefficiency. In the presence of economies of size in either production cost or market power, industry tends to become highly concentrated. Concentrated economic power often leads to concentrated, disproportionate political power. Disproportionate political power may be, and has been, used to influence legislation or subtly influence court interpretation of existing law in favor of the powerful. Oligopoly and oligopsony power can thus be strengthened and further entrenched, leading to monopoly inefficiencies and a widening chasm between income and wealth of the powerful and the rest of society.

We are well along this evolutionary path, I think, with the global economy in general as well as with industrialization of the agrifood system. The political, economic, social, and legal power struggle is reshaping the food economy. Analyzing this struggle with efficiency blinders on is a public policy travesty.

This chapter is an attempt to widen the economic view of the agrifood system to include ethics along with efficiency, and to include the interface between law and economics as manifested in antitrust and competition law. The chapter begins with an overview of broad issues, and then turns to a brief review of the limits of traditional economic aggregate efficiency calculus. This is followed by discussion of antitrust and competition law.

5.2 Overview

It is widely recognized that ethics and equity are value-laden concepts. Unfortunately, many contemporary economists advocate efficiency, or at least let efficiency considerations dominate their analyses, as though it were an objective concept. Past generations of economists have recognized that there is no such thing as value free

[1] Admittedly, the economic surplus concept can, and has been, expanded to include non-market effects. However, the typical application of economic surplus to agrifood competition issues has only considered primary market effects.

welfare economics. In fact, Frank Knight (1947, p. 19) commented, "No discussion of policy is possible apart from a moral judgment."

While economics tends to focus on efficiency, law tends to focus on justice, fairness, and equity. Discussions of ethics and economics of the agrifood system therefore necessitate consideration of the Rule of Law in general and antitrust law in particular. The Populist notion of antitrust law emphasized broad social objectives and was intended to insure "free and fair" competition, including preventing businesses from developing excessive economic and political power. The need for considering antitrust law in the context of agrifood systems is especially acute because farmers, especially sellers of perishable commodities, are particularly vulnerable to disproportionate economic and political power of large buyers.

The 1921 Packers & Stockyards Act (PSA) went further than Sherman and Clayton Antitrust law to protect vulnerable livestock producers from unfair business practices. Key words in the PSA are "unfair, unjustly discriminatory, undue or unreasonable preference, deceptive practice, and price manipulation." The Act prohibits practices with the "purpose (with intent) or effect (without intent)." The word efficiency is nowhere to be found in the PSA or, for that matter, in the Sherman or Clayton Acts. Not once. Yet, century old laws have been flipped over to where antitrust enforcement—in the rare cases where it actually occurs—is based on a narrow definition of economic efficiency at best.

From a broad economic system perspective, a fallacy of composition may exist with application of the efficiency framework to numerous small policy changes. The aggregate effect may be to alter the economic system to favor an economic system in which efficiency no longer matters.

Giant transnational agrifood corporations are increasingly using political clout that comes with economic power to influence legislation and to influence courts to interpret laws in their favor. Frederic Bastiat, a French political economist in the early 1800s, referred to effects of a similar power imbalance in French Socialism as "the law perverted" and the law converted into an instrument of plunder, which he labeled "legal plunder." Bastiat (1850, pp. 14–15) stated,

> As long as it is admitted that the law may be diverted from its true purpose—that it may violate property instead of protecting it—then everyone will want to participate in making the law, either to protect himself against plunder or to use it for plunder. Political questions will always be prejudicial, dominant, and all-absorbing. There will be fighting at the door of the Legislative Palace, and the struggle within will be no less furious. To know this, it is hardly necessary to examine what transpires in the French and English legislatures; merely to understand the issue is to know the answer. Is there any need to offer proof that this odious perversion of the law is a perpetual source of hatred and discord; that it tends to destroy society itself? If such proof is needed, look at the United States [in 1850]. There is no country in the world where the law is kept more within its proper domain: the protection of every person's liberty and property. As a consequence of this, there appears to be no country in the world where the social order rests on a firmer foundation.

Many recent developments in the political economy of the United States suggest that "firmer foundation" to which Bastiat referred is being undermined by legal plunder, the "fatal tendency of mankind" to "wish to live and prosper at the expense of others." Bastiat emphasized "perverted law causes conflict." Recent public protests in the US known as "Occupy Wall Street" confirm his assessment, as does the back alley fight between the few remaining independent farmers and ranchers, and the meat packers and their trade associations over proposed GIPSA (Grain Inspection, Packers & Stockyards Administration) Rules.

The fatal tendency of the powerful few has been to gain control over legislation and the courts (France et al. 2004). This undermines the notion of American Democracy in general and the agrifood system in particular. American Democracy and the firm foundation of capitalism to benefit the many are being turned into Wall Street capitalism, to benefit the few at the expense of many. The agrifood manifestation of Wall Street capitalism is commonly referred to as "industrial farming."

Farmers and ranchers are caught in an increasingly tightening vise (vice?) of monopoly power by input suppliers and monopsony power of raw commodity buyers. Statistics show a widening gap in income and wealth in the United States that has paralleled growth of size and power of domestic and transnational corporations. Corporate profits as a percent of domestic value added continue to climb, and the percent of income captured by the top few percent of our population has returned to levels experienced during the robber baron period.

Frank Knight (1947, p. 430) noted the tendency of the free exchange system toward increasing inequality,

> The major ethical problem of economic organization arises out of the grossly unequal distribution of economic capacity, and consequently of the product, among individuals, and the fact that distribution is determined for the most part by forces beyond the control of the disadvantaged individuals and classes, while the working of the free exchange system naturally tends toward increasing inequality. The simple and obvious remedy for inequality, insofar as it is unjust and is practically remediable, is not planning by a central authority, but progressive taxation, particularly of inheritances, with use of the proceeds to provide services for the poorer people.

Single minded pursuit of economic efficiency and the "free market" ideology has much to do with evolution of American's "firmer foundation" to which Bastiat referred in 1850 to the quagmire of what is now know as Wall Street capitalism, plutocracy, oligarchy, corporatocracy, and by other pejorative labels.

5.3 Aggregate Economic Efficiency

A review of assumptions and considerations underlying the efficiency argument—as embodied in aggregate economic surplus—is warranted.

First, efficiency assumes the existence of the coldly calculating rational consumer or producer, equating everything at the margin. However, it is not at all clear that many individuals or businesses are coldly calculating marginalists or, for that matter, rational.[2] Furthermore, the theory of second best says that if a single marginal

[2]Boulding's (1970, p. 67) view is, "The weakness of the traditional marginal analysis which postulated that businessmen would maximize their profits was that the data on which decisions

condition cannot be satisfied in an economy, then the "second best" solution may be to violate other, perhaps all, marginal conditions.

Second, efficiency assumes that individual utility functions are independent at a given point in time as well as across generations. Love, hate, jealousy, altruism, fairness, family values and other interpersonal and intergenerational effects are assumed away.

Third, efficiency assumes that the marginal utility of income is the same for all individuals, rich or poor. Does anybody really believe that assumption? Ironically, an economic surplus framework allowing for the marginal utility of income to be less for the rich than for the poor might reject a policy that increased economic efficiency in the traditional sense but that widened the gap between rich and poor. But the economic surplus framework, as applied in food competition and antitrust economics makes no such allowance.

Fourth, efficiency assumes a neutral effect of advertising. As typically implemented in agrifood competition studies, there is no distinction made between informational advertising and persuasive advertising. Social welfare consequences of persuasive advertising are far from clear, as it may be an instrument of social control (see, for instance, Bagwell 2001)

Fifth, evaluations of efficiency typically invoke the Pareto Criterion, which states that condition A is preferred to condition B if at least one person gains and no one loses, and the widely accepted Kaldor-Hicks compensation principle that an action (or business practice) is desirable if the gainers could compensate the losers. Decades ago, Boulding (1969, p. 5) emphasized that "Many, if not most, economists accept the Paretian optimum (and thus the Kaldor-Hicks principle) as almost self-evident. Nevertheless, it rests on an extremely shaky foundation of ethical propositions."[3] Typically the Kaldor-Hicks principle is applied to situations where the compensation never occurs. Theoretically, income taxes and other public policy could be used for equity adjustments, but rarely does this occur in practice. Consequently, because compensation does not occur, there can be a widening gap between the rich and poor, as we now observe throughout the world and even in America.

Sixth, it is important to recognize that actual markets are embedded within a social/institutional structure, including rules, laws and customs that affect market transactions. Empirical estimates of supply and demand and thus empirical estimates of economic efficiency are conditional on the underlying institutional setting. What is efficient in one institutional setting may not be efficient or even socially desirable in another setting.[4] Since empirical analysis is generally restricted to the institutional setting that generated the historical observations, applied economists

---

were supposed to be made often did not exist. If a firm does not know what effect a given decision will have on its profits, obviously it cannot maximize profits. We can never climb to the top of a mountain if we do not know whether we are going up or down."

[3]Additional discussions of the limitations of welfare economics are in Boulding's American Economic Association Presidential Address (1969) and subsequent book (1970).

[4]For additional discussion of the institutional bias inherent in efficiency analyses, see Bromley (1989), Lang (1980), Schmidt and Shaffer (1964), and Shaffer (1987).

are severely hampered in evaluating the aggregate consequences of "new" institutional settings because their only empirically operational metric is relative to the "old" institutional setting. We must be ever cognizant of the potential institutional bias inherent in economic surplus and efficiency analysis, as that bias may be acutely important in assessing "new" laws, rules and regulations affecting markets.

Finally, in imperfectly competitive markets, demand and supply estimated with historical price and quantity (and other) data may not provide the appropriate functions for efficiency analysis. Take, for example, the extreme case of pure monopoly. Observed price and quantity data points are on the product demand curve, but generally not on the monopolist's marginal cost curve (which is typically assumed to be the supply curve in a competitive market). Technically, there is no supply curve for a monopolist because product price is endogenous to the firm's decisions (Beattie et al. 2009). Empirical estimates may result in an estimated supply "relation," as Bresnahan calls it (1989), but this supply relation is not the marginal cost curve appropriate for traditional economic efficiency analysis. In general, demand and supply estimated with data points generated in the presence of imperfect competition—oligopsony as well as oligopoly—may not be the appropriate functions for efficiency analyses.[5] Theoretically, it may be possible to extract the appropriate curves for efficiency analyses from estimated supply and demand "relations," but that is in theory not practice. Hence, efficiency studies of farm program and agrifood policy that have competitive implications, such as proposed policies to prohibit captive supply agreements, are conceptually incorrect to the extent that they are based on supply and demand relations estimated with data points generated in markets where power was exerted unless, of course, the appropriate (marginal) functions are extracted for the efficiency analysis.

The elaborately constructed efficiency model is mathematically and graphically elegant, but nevertheless a house of cards built on dubious, if not preposterous, assumptions. Certainly, it is a useful concept to help understand aggregate economic and social issues, but how it could become dogma to so many academic economists is puzzling, to say the least. Paul Krugman (2009) asserts that the current generation of economists mistook beauty (of the utility maximizing consumer and associated efficiency calculus), clad in impressive looking mathematics, for truth. Boulding (1970, p. 115) observed that "mathematics in any of its applied fields is a wonderful servant but a very bad master; it is so good a servant that there is a tendency for it to become an unjust steward and usurp the master's place." I agree.

There is hope, however, for the economics profession. Konow (2003, p. 1188), in an extensive review of economic literature dealing with justice, notes the following:

---

[5]This problem is compounded if price discrimination has occurred and the analyst has only average prices available, as the average price will not be on the appropriate marginal function. Estimation bias can be eliminated if data are also available on the distribution of (discriminatory) prices at each point in time. Such distributional data are rarely available, thus the empirical analyst may not know if there is theoretical bias in an empirical analysis based on average price data.

> The view that 'By now we have substantial evidence suggesting that fairness motives affect the behavior of many people' is expressed in mainstream economics. This contrasts with the traditional belief of many economists that justice is chimerical or amorphous. A more sympathetic stance placed it outside the domain of economics, better left to philosophers, political scientists, or sociologists. There has been a steady trend, however, on increasing interest in and acceptance of justice in the economics profession, even partially displacing efficiency. This is not to say, of course, that economists are or should be abandoning their traditional interest in efficiency. Instead, stimulated by empirical evidence and, perhaps, the perception of increasing economic inequality, they are expanding their studies to encompass a wider set of distributive concerns.

With regard to the ongoing debate about agricultural competition issues, I never cease to be surprised by the number of practitioners who seem to think that their use of economic efficiency and economic surplus is somehow objective, while less elaborate and less quantitative models are subjective. As the great economic historian Mark Blaug (1996, p. 577) emphasized, "there is no such thing as 'value-free welfare economics' and, indeed, the phrase itself is a contradiction in terms. To say that something is an improvement in 'welfare' is to say that it is desirable and evaluator statements of this kind necessarily involve ethical considerations, that is, value judgments." Frank Knight (1947, p. 19) had a similar view,

> No discussion of policy is possible apart from a moral judgment. The argument of the body of this paper has shown that an appeal to maximum freedom as a 'standard' involves a fallacy. The result is dogmatic acceptance of an existing distribution of power (and income), which is an ethical proposition, a value judgment in disguise, and an ethically indefensible one.

Recognizing that economic efficiency is cloaked in value judgments and implausible assumptions, it is troubling that the concept has come to dominate antitrust case law and public policy in general, and to dominate for decades the analyses of agrifood competition issues by both academic and government economists.

5.3.1 The Free Market

The free market ideology grew out of the economic efficiency model. Few would question that this ideology has had a dominant effect on the politics of business policy in the United States and much of the planet for three decades. Under this ideology, the only acceptable regulation is no regulation. In the absence of traditional economies of size and in the absence of "power" economies of size, this ideology may have merit.

Social and economic problems arise, however, when there are substantial economies of size. Without regulation and public constraints on size, a few firms will come to dominate the economic system. A market or system dominated by one or a few firms is no longer free or unregulated because it is subject to the influence of the dominant firms. In an unregulated market with economies of size, the biggest and baddest gorilla gets most of the bananas; a market dominated by a big gorilla is by no means a "free" market or an "unregulated" market. The big gorilla rules such a market, so there are "rules and regulations" influencing economic transactions.

Frank Knight (1947, p. 443) noted that economic freedom would not necessarily occur without laws because "freedom does not mean unregulated impulse, or 'license,' but action directed by rational ideals and conforming to rational laws. The ideals and laws are to be discovered in individual and social life and recognized and imposed upon themselves by individuals and groups." Appropriate rules and enforcement of those rules are necessary for preservation of competitive markets, at least when substantial economies of size exist. But the laws and enforcement of laws must come from collective action and not from powerful special interests such as transnational corporations who want to rule and control the market.

5.4 Morals of Monopoly and Competition

Philosopher Homer Blosser Reed published an article in 1916 titled, "The Morals of Monopoly and Competition." Reed's thoughts and arguments have an uncanny applicability to ethics and economics of the contemporary agrifood system as well as to the global economy and thus bear repeating. Reed's first sentence is, "The changing character of morals is nowhere more conspicuous than in those of monopoly and competition" (p. 258). Reed continues,

> Underlying the changing character of morals is the conception that new conditions require new rules. It usually happens that when the conditions suddenly change old rules are applied unaltered, and are allowed to work serious havoc before their inertia is overcome and an effort made to formulate rules fitting the new situation. This state of affairs applies in particular to the morals of competition and monopoly. Within the last half century there has been an unrivaled development of industry from a simple agricultural stage to the extreme form of the factory system, or from industry as carried on by individuals each according to his preference to a condition of industry carried on by the combined efforts of many men bringing about large combinations and monopolies. But there has been no corresponding change in business methods or morals. On the contrary, competitive morals have been applied without alteration to conditions of monopoly and combination. This misapplication resulting from the unequal evolution between business morals and business conditions appears to be the fundamental cause of our present monopolies and other industrial problems engaging the serious efforts of our legislatures and courts.
>
> But if we introduce into this competitive system of approximately equal individual traders a large combination of individual traders having an enormous capital, then the competitive morals as practiced between the combination and the individual trader have an altogether different effect because of the inequality of capital. In a siege of price-cutting, in getting information of the competitor's business from their employees and from those of the railroads, in securing favorable advertising in the form of disinterested news and editorials, in delaying litigation by appeals, and in many other instances the combination can get advantages which are wholly denied to the small trader because of his small capital. The small trader may be a better manager than anyone in the combination; he may produce cheaper, treat his customers more considerately, give prompter service, and offer a superior quality of goods; but no matter what his merits are, he cannot possibly overcome the superior capital of the combination which as a consequence secure a monopoly. It then has power to oppress the public with unreasonable prices through which it may recoup its losses from the war of competition (pp. 258, 262–263).

Reed continues with public concerns,

> When such a result occurs, we begin to hear of 'unfair competition,' 'cut-throat and predatory competition,' 'tainted money,' 'anti-trust legislation,' 'the extortion of monopolies,' 'restraint of trade,' 'reasonable and unreasonable restraint of trade,' and similar phrases which indicate that the problem has arisen in the public consciousness and that the moral feelings have been aroused. The old adage, 'Competition is the life of trade,' begins to have an unsavory sound and these so-called laws of competition which have existed since time out of mind begin to be questions. The combination is dubbed an 'Octopus.' But as a matter of fact the combination has done nothing more than carry out the 'good, old fashioned laws of competition,' the very same methods practiced daily by those who raise the bitter cry against it. The only difference is that the combination profits, and the littler trader goes to the wall (p. 263).

We hear the same words and concerns expressed over the current state of the agrifood system.

Economists generally emphasize only unit costs in efficiency analyses. Capital, labor and management are simply viewed as inputs to production. Reed, however, raises a moral issue about capital, or size *per se*.

> The question arises, however, whether a combination can rightfully adopt the same methods practiced by small traders in competition and whether its large capital does not create a new situation in which the old morals of competition fail to function, and whether the combination should not adopt a new set of morals commensurate with its new situation. Here there is clearly a moral problem, and to show the form which it has taken we can do no better than to refer to some court decisions on the matter. It is probably that the conservatives will think the old system of competition good enough while those enlightened on new conditions will recommend a change. We shall find that they are averse to making distinctions between kinds of competition, and believe competition as such a part of the unchangeable order of nature (p. 263).

In our present situation, it is apparent that courts are unwilling to make distinctions between types of competition. Beginning with *London v Fieldale* in 2005, appellate courts have not only ignored the plain wording in the PSA—sections 202 (a-b) say nothing about competition—but have opined that plaintiffs must show a packer's business practice "harmed competition" without ever defining "competition." Court opinions muddle enforcement of the PSA because it is unclear whether they are referring to competition as a process, or the common antitrust interpretation of consumer harm.

Reed summarizes the historical roots of the competitive system.

> [W]e have found that the competitive system grew out of ancient conditions of monopoly and was approved by the judges of the transition period because it better satisfied the interests of the public. It did this because it allowed free range to individual incentive and capacity; and success depended, among other things, on good management, prompt service, considerate treatment of customers, ability to produce and sell goods of a quality and price demanded by the customers, and on capital, which, however, was only one element. With reference to the traders the system was a success because they were approximately equal in capital; and one could play 'rules of the game' as effectively as another. Under such conditions competition was the life of trade, that is, on the whole it was worth more to the public than it cost. When, however, a combination is introduced into these conditions then success depends principally upon the single element of capital against which the

> other elements of success in the small trader are of no avail. *Competition, as between the combination and the individual trader, instead of being the life of trade, becomes the restraint to trade, the outcome of which is inimical to the interest of the public* (pp. 277–278; emphasis added).

A century ago, many of the writings and discussion about antitrust and competition focused on "the public interest," as did Reed's observation. It now seems like the public mindset is more focused on "what's in it for me" than the public interest doctrine. To the extent that this is true, reinvigorating antitrust laws to again have a fairness element may require profound change in mindset and morals. Reed continues:

> When, under these conditions, a judge tells us that what is right for an individual is also right for a combination, he is basing rights upon the single element of capital. He fails to see that this element in the combination destroys all the other values of the old competitive system. He assumes that a difference in magnitude does not produce a difference in kind, and he is led into this assumption because in law both the individual trader and the combination possess the common name of 'person.' When, however, the individual person and the corporate person are analyzed and the elements of success in each are made distinct, then such propositions fall to the ground. In general the judge who commits such fallacies fails to analyze the situation in which the morals in question function. He is satisfied to refer to cases which have nothing more in common than simply some problem of competition, and then argues that, if in the case at hand nothing was committed which was forbidden in the past, the act complained of is just and lawful. This sort of procedure is quite correct when cases referred to and the act in question present identical situations. It is then a matter of prudence to apply to a present situation what has proved successful in the past in an identical situation, and only when such a motive is present in the consciousness of a judge is this reference to past cases profitable. But to say that what is lawful for individuals is lawful for combinations is wholly to ignore their respective situations and to deal only with rules in the abstract. … *The difference in magnitude between a private individual and a corporation is important here.* When a corporation becomes so large that its capital, business organization, and number of employees equals that of the government itself, and when it supplies an article of necessity (food) to every community throughout the state's territory, it holds within its grip the fortunes of individuals quite as much as the state itself and is equally affected with a public interest (pp. 278–279, 280–281; emphasis added).

The "difference in magnitude" between a private individual and a corporation obviously has not been recognized in US Supreme Court decisions granting corporate personhood and, in 2010, giving corporations free rein to make unlimited political contributions in *Citizens United v. Federal Election Commission*. These and other Supreme Court opinions carry over to antitrust law and to the PSA.

5.5 Antitrust and Competition Policy

Current socioeconomic issues are not unlike they were in an earlier time in America's history, the late 1800s and early 1900s, as is evident from Reed's writing. The Populist notion of antitrust took hold during this "robber baron" period, resulting in the Sherman Antitrust Act in 1890, the Clayton Act in 1914,

Court ordered divestiture of the meat packer cartel in 1920, the PSA in 1921, and the Capper-Volstead (agricultural cooperative) Act of 1922 that made agricultural cooperatives a limited exception to antitrust so farmers and ranchers could cooperate to countervail market power.

Since antitrust laws were legislated, however, economists have "had their way" with interpretation of antitrust laws. Aggregate economic efficiency has come to dominate interpretation of antitrust laws. Federal Judge and Chicago economist Richard Posner's view of an economic approach to antitrust law based essentially on consumer's surplus has prevailed. He asserts that "the only goal of antitrust law should be to promote efficiency in the economic sense. Efficiency is the ultimate goal of antitrust, but competition a mediate goal that will often be close enough to the ultimate goal to allow the courts to look no further" (2001, p. 2). The need to rediscover the purposes for antitrust laws and their enforcement has never been more acute than now.

In the first substantive decision interpreting the Sherman Antitrust Act, Justice Peckham wrote, "[I]t is not for the real prosperity of any country that such changes should occur which result in transferring an independent business man . . . into a mere servant or agent of a corporation ... having no voice in shaping the business policy ... and bound to obey orders issued by others" (quoted in Carstensen 2000). Haines (1919), in a law article titled "Efforts to Define Competition," also comments on the broad intent of antitrust law,

> It is this type of (antitrust) law which is designed to provide that there may be 'reasonable competition,' and that aims to enact into law the doctrine of 'free *and fair* competition,' as an inherent right of the people. This country, the court said on one occasion, has always been committed to the principle of fair competition and the Sherman act has been interpreted as a means to bring about this desired condition (p. 11; emphasis added).

Haines also maintained that under the "free and fair competition" interpretation of antitrust law, "The grounds for giving relief in cases of unfair competition are held to be: to promote honesty and fair dealing, to protect the purchasing public, (and) to protect the rights and property of individuals" (p. 9). Noting the evolution of antitrust law, Haines states:

> The law of unfair competition is beginning to be conceived as the body of rules designed to regulate the conduct of those striving for goodwill and trade advantages for themselves. And with slow and halting steps the courts have been approaching the formulation of a principle now definitely recognized by the Supreme Court of the United States, namely 'that no one shall be permitted to appropriate to himself the fruits of another's labor.' This view if carried out and extended, as seems likely, will, it is readily understood, basically alter the former conception of unfair competition (p. 22).

Recent Wall Street and other financial scandals, tax policy for the rich, *Citizens United Opinion,* governments spending beyond their means, the revolving door in Washington, the squeezing of farmers and ranchers by input suppliers and commodity buyers, courts opining of the need to show harm to competition under the PSA, and numerous other contemporary economic developments suggest that courts have largely abandoned the principle "that no one shall be permitted to appropriate to himself the fruits of another's labor."

Justice William O. Douglas believed that bigness threatened our capitalistic and free enterprise system and thus that antitrust law should be used to check corporate power. In an article on the antitrust legacy of Justice Douglas, Rogers (2007, p. 19) states,

> Douglas ... thought it was just a bad idea, as a matter of policy, to permit such wealth and financial power in the hands of so few. In his view, the decisions of those few could tip the national scales towards prosperity or depression. Further, Douglas cautioned that unabated bigness threatened our capitalistic and free enterprise system because it threatened competition, individual initiative and freedom of opportunity. He believed it would transform 'a nation of shopkeepers' into 'a nation of clerks' which would stifle individual initiative and independence. Even beyond that, Douglas believed that large corporations fostered dishonesty and 'resulted in ruthless sacrifices of human values.' They are so impersonal and remote from their investors, Douglas argued, that management feels free to serve themselves rather than the enterprise they work for. 'There can be no question that the laxity in business morals has a direct relationship to the size of business.'

Rogers (2007, p. 20) continues by noting that "Douglas, characterize(ed) as 'financial termites' those opportunists who prey on other people's money and destroy the legitimate function of finance and investment. Among the several factors that provided hospitable conditions for the termites were the curse of bigness and the centralization of financial power." While Justice Douglas' views were expressed during the robber baron era of the late 1800s and early 1900s, his concerns with bigness are equally applicable to our present economic situation.

Broad social goals for antitrust law carried over to the 1940s. Thurman Arnold, who was in charge of the Antitrust Division of the Department of Justice from 1938 to 1943, also believed in a variety of non-economic justifications for antitrust as part of the attack on concentrated economic power in a democracy that was both inefficient and had destroyed local business and drained away local capital. In the celebrated work, *The Folklore of Capitalism*, Arnold (1955, pp. 207–208) wrote, "The most significant evil at which the antitrust laws are aimed is the evil of absentee ownership and industrial concentration that makes for such depressions. We were slow to learn after 1929 that great corporate organizations cannot continue to take money out of local communities without somebody putting it back."

The 2007 Census shows that absentee ownership of America's farmland averaged about 40% and much higher for cropland (USDA 2009, p. 268). Small but rapidly growing amounts of hedge funds and speculative funds by people far removed from the land are now coming into agriculture as well (OECD 2010, p. 2). In a letter to the journalist Alfred Friendly, Arnold wrote that,

> The purpose of the antitrust laws is to ensure freedom of business opportunity. They are not designed to protect small business from larger and efficient competitors. They are not designed to prevent the growth of nationwide business enterprises so long as that growth is a product of industrial efficiency. Even if, through greater efficiency in operation and distribution, a corporation achieved a monopoly, that in itself would not violate the Sherman Act. But this has never yet happened. Monopolies have been built up by using financial strength to buy out competitors or force them out of business. It is this sort of growth and only this sort that the antitrust laws are designed to penalize ... This process repeated in industry after industry during the period between the first World War and the depression

> created a system of absentee ownership of local industries which made industrial colonies out of the West and South, prevented the accumulation of local capital and siphoned the consumers' dollars to a few industrial centers like New York and Chicago (quoted in Waller, 2004, p. 611).

Massive consolidation and integration of the global food (and non-food) economy in the last few decades has once again created a system of absentee ownership that has siphoned dollars out of local and rural economies and off to international financial centers. Vertical integration in the poultry industry has make growers exactly what Justices Peckham and Douglas argued against.

Judge Posner has been most influential in redirecting antitrust law from a broad view reflected in Justice Peckham's opinion to a narrow efficiency view, as noted previously. Posner (2001, p. 35) opines,

> Populists would like the interpretation of the antitrust laws to be guided neither by the common-law background nor by economics, but instead by the prominent vein of populist thought that runs through the legislative history of all the major federal antitrust statutes. But the motive and meaning of legislation are different things. No doubt most of the legislators whose votes were essential to the enactment of these statutes cared more about the distribution of income and wealth and the welfare of small businesses and particular consumer groups than they did about allocative efficiency, especially since the economics profession itself had no enthusiasm for antitrust policy. But these legislators did not succeed in writing into the statutes standards that would have enabled judges to order these goals and translate them into coherent, administrable legal doctrine without doing serious and undesirable damage to the economy. For guidance the courts perforce turned elsewhere. After a century and more of judicial enforcement of the antitrust statutes, there is consensus that guidance must be sought in economics. There is no generally accepted principle of statutory interpretation that shows that the courts were wrong to go this route.

A corollary of Judge Posner's view of legislative intent that applies for the past few decades is that most of the legislators (and judges) have *not* "cared about the distribution of income and wealth and the welfare of small businesses and particular consumer groups" (p. 35). Consequently mergers and acquisitions that have increased market power and changed the distribution of income and wealth have been essentially rubber stamped by the Department of Justice and the Federal Trade Commission, the two agencies charged with enforcing antitrust law in the United States.

Judge Posner's opinion that historically "legislators did not succeed in writing into the statutes standards that would have enabled judges to order these goals and translate them into coherent, administrable legal doctrine ..." is worthy of reexamination in light of recent efforts to promulgate Rules under the Packers & Stockyards Act, as called for by legislators in the 2008 Farm Bill. One issue is that since 2005, many federal judges have ignored what is known in legal circles as the *Chevron* deference. The Supreme Court opined in *Chevron U.S.A. Inc. v. Natural Resources Defense Council, Inc.*, (467 U.S. 837, 1984) that the lower courts should give deference to the interpretation of law by the agency assigned responsibility for enforcing that law. The USDA is responsible for enforcing the PSA. Yet, courts have recently turned a blind eye not just to the plain language of the law, but also to

USDA's long-standing interpretation that Sections 202 (a-b) do not require showing "harm to competition."[6]

The second issue is that recently proposed GIPSA Rules were an effort to translate the PSA words such as "unfair, unjustly discriminatory, undue or unreasonable preference, and deceptive practice" into administrable legal doctrine. Yet the legislative and judicial clout of giant transnational agribusiness corporations and their trade associations essentially killed the proposed rules. To many of the dominant firms, the only acceptable rules and regulations are no rules and regulations.

Haines (1919) attributed growth of the branch of law dealing with unfair and dishonest practices to the

> use of unfair and dishonest practices parallels the growth of commerce, and the keen rivalry of modern commercial methods has brought a great increase in fraudulent methods of competition. Many attempts have been made to condemn unfair commercial practices and to foster honest trading. The first statutes and judicial decisions appear to have served as a obstacle to the grosser forms of monopoly and of unfair trading, and with the growth of commerce and of industry accompanying the Industrial Revolution came a *demand for free and unrestricted competition* which swept away practically all of the statutes and almost removed the restraint formerly exercised by the courts (p. 1; emphasis added).

The "demand for free and unrestricted competition" in domestic and global commerce over the last three decades has once again "swept away the restraint formerly exercised by the courts." Haines observes that since the aim of antitrust is to prevent unfair business practices, a more exact definition of unfair competition is imperative.[7] According to Posner, workable legal definitions did not emerge, allowing the narrow concept of efficiency to prevail in the courts. One wonders if antitrust case law would be fundamentally different had economists devoted as much collective effort in the last 100 years to operationalizing the concept of unfair as they did to operationalizing the concept of efficiency. Haines (1919, p. 23) also noted that, "those who suffer from unfair practices are often the small but efficient business establishments which find it impossible to carry their cases to the courts."

The colloquial counterpart to Haines statement is the adage that "the color of justice is green." Large firms often literally overwhelm plaintiff attorneys (and the courts) with paperwork from more expensive lawyers. In such instances, the scales of justice are tilted in favor of large, powerful businesses and individuals.

---

[6]USDA has filed numerous *Amicus Curiae* briefs in PSA litigation consistently stating their interpretation that a plaintiff need not show harm to competition under sections 202 (a-b) of the PSA. The Department of Justice has also filed similar *Amicus Curiae* briefs in PSA litigation.

[7]Haines (1919, pp. 1–2) continues: "For a long time it was assumed that the best interests of society were subserved by the regulation of prices and the control of business through the operation of the economic laws of supply and demand." These days, representatives of giant agribusiness continue to claim that markets are competitive (without defining competition) and that prices are "determined by the laws of supply and demand." Virtue (1920, p. 653) noted that this was a claim by the meat packers leading up to the 1921 PSA. Since one can say that "price is determined by supply and demand" even in a monopoly, it is ironic that a meaningless economic phrase continues to get traction in public debated about the industrialized agrifood system.

Consequently, there can be a problematic power imbalance not just in markets and politics, but also in litigation and protection of smaller firms and individuals without the financial wherewithal to match corporate legal spending.

5.5.1 Collusion in Fixing the Rules of the Marketplace

With size comes the economic wherewithal to influence legislation through political contributions and intense, even deceptive, lobbying. Adam Smith (1776, pp. 219–220) warned about allowing economic power to be used to influence legislation,

> The interest of the dealers, however, in any particular branch of trade or manufacture, is always in some respects different from, and even opposite to, that of the public. To widen the market and to narrow the competition is always the interest of the dealers. To widen the market may frequently be agreeable enough to the interest of the public; but to narrow the competition must always be against it, and can serve only to enable the dealers, by raising their profits above what they naturally would be, to levy, for their own benefit, an absurd tax upon the rest of their fellow citizens. The proposal of any new law or regulation of commerce which comes from this order, ought always to be listened to with great precaution, and ought never to be adopted, till after having been long and carefully examined, not only with the most scrupulous, but with the most suspicious attention. It comes from an order of men, whose interest is never exactly the same with that of the public, who have generally an interest to deceive and even to oppress the public, and who accordingly have, upon many occasions, both deceived and oppressed it.

While antitrust law applies to collusion in the marketplace, the Supreme Court has opined that it does *not* generally apply to efforts to influence legislation and courts interpretation of law. Under Supreme Court opinions collectively known as the *Noerr-Pennington doctrine*, private entities are immune from liability under the antitrust laws for attempts to influence the passage or enforcement of laws, even if the laws they advocate would have anticompetitive effects. Furthermore, private entities are immune from antitrust even when they employ deceptive and unethical tactics to influence legislation.[8] Corporations and individuals are treated equally under Noerr-Pennington (AAI n.d.). Although trade associations are typically watched closely by their antitrust attorneys as a potential vehicle for collusion in the marketplace, trade associations have no antitrust limits on trying to influence legislation or the courts to favor interests of their members.

Although there is a "sham" exception to *Noerr-Pennington*, it appears to be limited only to petitioning activities that are nothing more than a *direct* attempt to interfere with the business activities of a competitor (FTC 2006). Minda (1990, pp. 907–908) summarizes concerns with *Noerr-Pennington*:

---

[8]The *Noerr-Pennington doctrine* is derived from the following two US Supreme Court decisions: *Eastern Railroad Presidents Conference v. Noerr Motor Freight, Inc.*, 365 U.S. 127, 135 (1961), and *United Mine Workers v. Pennington*, 381 U.S. 657, 670 (1965).

> Because business competes for the favor of government as much as for the trade of customers, government has become an alternative marketplace for corporate America. It is thus not surprising to find corporations, trade associations, and their political action committees working, unilaterally or in concert, to manipulate state and local government for purely private economic advantage. Nor is it surprising to learn that corporate interests have reaped the benefits of legislation and administrative regulations that subsidize private interests adverse to the public interest, causing distortions and inefficiencies in the normal operation of market competition. Truly surprising, and deeply troubling, is the fact that the courts have been largely unable to develop a workable legal framework under the Sherman Antitrust Act to regulate predatory conduct of business in the governmental sphere even though such conduct presents potentially serious danger to market competition.

Plain language of the PSA prohibits "deceptive" business practices. But since the Supreme Court extended *Noerr-Pennington* protection outside antitrust law, it appears that the courts would not treat intentional deception about PSA issues as a violation. Meat packers, poultry integrators, their trade organizations, and agricultural organizations they control thus hid behind *Noerr-Pennington* in successfully defeating recently proposed GIPSA Rules under the PSA. Giant corporations and their trade associations can thus collude, or practice conscious parallelism, to block legislation intended to preserve competitive markets. The athletic equivalent is allowing one team to make rules of the game and to control referees and penalties, the consequence of which is a lopsided, uncompetitive game.

Although Judge Posner has long advocated efficiency as the goal of antitrust, he does express concern with firms collaborating to influence legislation. Posner (2001), pp. 78–79) states that "where firms cooperate in lobbying Congress and the regulatory agencies, or industries in which most firms are vertically integrated and therefore are each other's customers or suppliers as well as competitors, the executives of the competing firms get to know and maybe trust each other and have opportunities to discuss pricing without arousing suspicions. The personal relations thus forged and opportunities for communication thus created reduce the cost of collusion." Thus there may be indirect adverse market consequences of firms cooperating or colluding to fix the rules of the game.

Powerful special interests not only try to influence legislation in their favor, they seek appointment of judges who are politically and ideologically aligned, particularly to appellate courts. Writing in a *Business Week* magazine cover story titled "The Battle Over the Courts: How politics, ideology, and special interests are compromising the US justice system," France et al. (2004) state the following:

> When you get right down to it, all of the (judicial) trappings are designed to build faith in the core ideals of the American judiciary: that judges are fair, objective, principled, and nonpartisan. That's the theory. ... So here's where things stand: Conservatives blame liberals for the current debauched state of judicial politics, and liberals fault conservatives. The truth is that both sides are culpable—and seem to be racing to see who can capture lower ground. So long as the two sides remain locked in partisan warfare and the country's overall civic culture continues to degenerate into ever more antagonism, there seems little reason to hope that politics will soon loosen its tightening grip on the judiciary.

Has the dream of an independent judiciary envisioned by the Founding Fathers of the United States been hijacked? Ideology and politics have, in my opinion, had more to do with recent PSA litigation that objective interpretation of law. Collusion or conscious parallelism to influence legislation and the courts in favor of corporate interests, along with intentional deception permitted under *Noerr-Pennington*, may be as bad long-term if not worse than collusion in current market activities. Furthermore, the long-term effect of collusion to fix the rules of the game may, and to some extent has, been to replace a competitive market place with one based on central planning. The cumulative effect of *Noerr-Pennington, Citizens United,* and a narrow, piece meal efficiency view of antitrust law may be to concentrate power and wealth, which is problematic for a democratic economic and political system.

5.5.2 Knightian Welfare Economics

Frank Knight (1923, p. 605), who many view as the father of the "Chicago School" of Economics, wrote in a paper titled *"The Ethics of Competition"* the following:

> As long as we had the frontier and there was not only 'room at the top' but an open road upward, the problem (distribution of economic power, opportunity and prestige) was not serious. But in a more settled state of society, the tendency is to make the game very interesting indeed to a small number of 'captains of industry' and 'Napoleons of finance,' but to secure this result by making monotonous drudgery of the lives of the masses who do the work.

Knight is widely known for his classical 1921 book "Risk, Uncertainty and Profit," in which he made an important distinction between risk and uncertainty. This book and subsequent writings are much more significant than this distinction alone, however, because they reflect an evolving social and economic theory embracing not just risk and uncertainty, but imperfect competition and welfare economics.[9]

The economic milieu in which Knight's ideas were formed was one in which a few firms dominated some markets, particularly oil and meat-packing. Out of this environment came our existing Antitrust Laws and, in the same year that his book was published, the Packers and Stockyards (P&S) Act. These antitrust laws led to divestiture in some highly concentrated markets. As we enter the twenty-first century, however, we have witnessed an unprecedented wave of mergers, acquisitions and joint ventures leading to horizontal concentration, to vertical integration, and to a web of interlocked firms that may have more economic and political power than dominant firms during Knight's era.

Knight cautioned against the single-minded pursuit of economic efficiency. In his view, the general welfare of society depended jointly on three policy goals: (a) economic efficiency, (b) an acceptable balance of economic power, and

[9]For a summary interpretation of Knight's view of the role of uncertainty in a competitive economy, and his view of a welfare pyramid involving efficiency, power and freedom, see Taylor (2003).

(c) economic freedom. In his view, the proper role of the government was to balance these three factors. He claimed that pursuit of economic efficiency alone would be at the expense of economic freedom and the balance of economic power.

5.5.3 *Economic Freedom for Farmers and Ranchers*

Breimyer (1965, p. 287; emphasis added) emphasized the economic freedom dimension of industrialization:

> ... the significance of vertical integration as an institution of agriculture is judged best from the standpoint of market structure. In particular does that approach to a study of integration shift the focus from its meaning in isolated cases—which may be insignificant—to what would result if it were to become pervasive. In this light, *vertical integration appears the greatest threat to individual freedom* in agriculture in those instances in which two conditions prevail: (1) There is a direct, inescapable linkage through successive stages in production and marketing. In other words, where the marketing sequence makes it hard for any farmer or firm to shift resources easily. And (2), a firm integrating vertically also is large and powerful at one or more of the stages. When both these conditions are met, vertical integration can be a massive force. *Under those conditions, integration is not primarily a means to efficiency but an instrument of power.*

Growing chickens was a family business but now it happens only by "invitation." One who wants to produce chickens must have a contract with an integrator. Deliveries of sickly or underweight chicks, late deliveries, bad feed deliveries, and bad advice from the integrator's field representative, or simple pricing power can all ruin the producer's business. It is well known in the chicken industry that producers dare not speak out against integrators (Taylor and Domina 2010).

After contracting to be a grower, the integrator has near total economic control over profitability in the grow-out operation. The grower's capital, labor, management and risk bearing are all captive to the integrator. In economics the relationship between the grower and integrator is an extreme power imbalance; in law this is a contract of adhesion; in colloquial terms this is serfdom—with a mortgage. Individual freedom is sacrificed.

Leading up to the jointly sponsored Department of Justice and USDA/GIPSA public hearings on competition issues in the poultry industry in 2010, many contract growers were strongly "discouraged" by their integrator's representatives for attending or testifying. Strength of discouragement by integrators ranged from a suggestion that the grower not attend to outright threats. Disutility associated with being threatened has yet to be factored in as a cost in efficiency analyses.

A half century ago, Breimyer (1965, p. 287) warned about inequities inherent in a vertically integrated, horizontally concentrated industry like poultry. He said, "And, as a farmer in Illinois protested, 'of the elements integrated, the stronger or dominant element in the integration will be the recipient of all, or at least the lion's share, of the benefits." This is precisely what has happened to poultry growers in the intervening years; their integrator has siphoned off profits and transferred environmental and economic risk to the growers (Taylor and Domina 2010).

5.5.4 Serfdom

The heart of the debate over the structure of agricultural markets, while infrequently articulated by producers, is about economic freedom, economic liberty, and economic systems, in my opinion. As Breimyer (1995, p. 199; emphasis added) said, "The salient feature of industrialization of agriculture and the food system is that it replaces the time honored system of markets. *It substitutes centralized management for open exchange markets as the principal, though not exclusive, coordinating instrument.* In the Boulding sense of putting first things first, that is the heart of what the argument is about."

Concerns are not only about the economic freedom and social status of farmers and ranchers, but also about how central economic planning by giant transnational companies affect consumers, governments and people in general. Reed (1916, p. 268) commented on industrialization by noting that "within the last 50 years (prior to 1919) there has been a rapid change in the industrial order; a change from individual, competitive, and small-scale production to co-operative, monopolistic, and large-scale production; a movement from an undirected, unorganized, and separate control of the many to the directed, organized, and unified control of the few."

In the 1940s Friedrich Hayek warned of the danger of economic tyranny and serfdom that results from government control of economic decision making through central planning. Certainly central economic planning inherent in fascist and socialist systems can lead to serfdom. But there are many other roads to serfdom. Central economic planning inherent in a vertical integrated and horizontally concentrated industry may also lead to serfdom. That road is paved with efficiency. We have traveled far down that road.

The vertically integrated poultry industry is often held up as a model to be emulated in other agricultural and food sectors. Those who promote this economic structure seemingly overlook the fact that poultry producers are nothing more than servants. A half century ago, Breimyer (1965, p. 292) warned, "... (poultry) growers have been enrolled in contracts that sharply reduce the entrepreneurial role of farmers and make exploitation possible." His warning went unheeded. The vertically integrated poultry industry is nothing more than a modern day plantation system or industrial feudalism where growers bring not only labor but also capital, captive labor and capital.

Many hog producers and captive cattle feeders are well down this road. Some of the larger captive cattle feeders have a contractual relationship with a single packer, such as Cargill's contract with Friona Industries, which has a combined one-time capacity approaching a million head. These captive feeders may not know it yet, but their status is little different from a poultry grower. They are locked in to their relationships with packers and may have no escape route other than exiting the business.

The American Dream of starting one's own business is fading as agribusiness becomes more integrated with entry into the vertical chain at the invitation of the integrated firm and not necessarily as result of competitive forces. Thus, there are important economic freedom dimensions to the industrial model of an agrifood system.

5.5.5 *Economic Freedom for Consumers*

Economic freedom for consumers is also a component of the ethics and economics of agrifood competition. Few would argue that informational advertising is problematic. But persuasive advertising may be an instrument of social control. Historically, many growing agribusiness firms claimed that their success was due to offering what the consumer wanted. Now, however, there are increasing efforts to persuade consumers that the products of industrial farming and associated production technology, is what they really want.

With the industrial model now losing market share to "local foods," the recently formed US Farmers and Ranchers Alliance appears to be a well-funded corporate effort to convince consumers that all is well with the industrial model of the agrifood system. In one of his last articles in a long career, Breimyer (1995, p. 197) said, "I reject the often-heard line that current structural changes in agriculture and the food system are consumer driven. I turn that line bottom side up. The system is driving consumers, or trying to, about as much as consumers drive it." Whether the food consumer is the driver or the passenger merits careful consideration in analyses of the ethics and economics of our present industrialized agrifood system.

5.5.6 *Innovation and Democracy*

Dynamics of innovation are also an important consideration in discussion of ethics and economics of the agrifood system. In a truly competitive market, we expect innovation to occur by some market participants at all levels, from raw material suppliers, to farmers and ranchers, to processors, and to retailers. Certainly in the poultry model, the entrepreneurial role and thus innovative role of famers has been largely eliminated. Breimyer (1965, pp. 287–288) quoted George Mehren's 1963 testimony to the House Ag Committee as follows: "(Integration) carried to a distant and perhaps never-to-be-realized but still logical extreme, present trends could well mean that competitive independence may one day be restricted basically to the retailing segment—and such competitive independence may be greatly different from that which prevails today." Breimyer (1995, p. 198) also stated, "What is the essence of industrialization? I call it the designing and imposing of systematic order; that is to say, management, on all economic processes. Intricate, sophisticated, precisely controlled management."

In the industrial model, the captains of industry want to control all aspects of the economic process, including innovation and the consumer. We are well along the path to which Mehren and Breimyer cautioned against. Along with loss of competitive independence may come loss of ability to capture any potential benefits of innovation. Innovation of products and development of new markets is occurring by small farms and businesses, but these have been niche markets. However, as evolution of the organic food industry illustrates, products and markets developed by small businesses may be appropriated by corporate agribusiness, displacing the innovators. For local food entrepreneurs to survive, there must be appropriate predator control—antitrust—to prevent the hostile takeover of products and markets developed by entrepreneurs whose business grew larger than niche status.

Boudreaux (2002, p. 1) summarizes the current state of antitrust law and economics by stating that "Conflicting goals—such as protecting small producers from the competition of larger, more-efficient firms, or keeping industries unconcentrated as a means of nurturing democratic values—are no longer taken seriously as appropriate aims of antitrust." Cumulative effects of merger and acquisition approval may concentrate economic power. Concentrated economic power often translates into disproportionate political power favoring dominant corporations. This can have equity, justice, and even efficiency implications. If a powerful few gain hold of the agricultural and food economy, monopoly and oligopoly inefficiencies will eventually occur.

5.6 Concluding Remarks: Back to the Agrifood System

Knight proposed a system that I think is a better framework for discussing and analyzing contemporary agrifood competition issues. His framework gets us past efficiency as the sole metric. Unlike efficiency, which can often be quantified, the concepts of power balance and economic freedom are difficult to quantify, but no less important. The key issues are fairness, preferential treatment of the "chosen ones," economic freedom and economic liberty.

Delong (2011, p. 2) raises issues that apply not only to academic macroeconomists but also to agricultural economists who seem to be wearing efficiency blinders.

> Perhaps academic economics departments will lose mindshare and influence to others—from business schools and public policy programs to political science, psychology, and sociology departments. As university chancellors and students demand relevance and utility, perhaps these colleagues will take over teaching how the economy works and leave academic economists in a rump discipline that merely teaches the theory of logical choice. Or perhaps economics will remain a discipline that forgets most of what it once knew and allows itself to be continually distracted, confused, and in denial. If that were to happen, we would all be worse off.

Heilbroner and Milberg (1955, p. 8) expressed a similar view: "Our ... most contentious point of all is that we further believe that unless the social setting of economic behavior is openly recognized, economics will be unable to play a useful role as explicator of the human prospect. Once the dismal science, it will become irrelevant scholasticism. That is what is at stake."

In one of his last articles of a career spanning six decades, Breimyer (1995, p. 201) emphasized the stresses coming from industrialization of agriculture: "Put in fewest words, it is that the discontent and distrust that is so obvious in our nation today can be viewed as a revulsion against the disciplines that industrialization imposes, both directly and via the instrument of government."

And, I might add, of the discipline that the captains of industry imposed on us through their disproportionate influence on governments and even the land-grant system and academics. Will academic economists broaden their view, or continue to worship a narrow concept of economic efficiency? We should heed Breimyer's (1995) challenge: "If individual freedom is a timeless principle, if economic and social institutions are but transitory inventions, and if the human mind is capable of designing its institutions to fit its standards of freedom, therein lie opportunity and challenge for those who will frame a policy for agriculture for years of the future."

In America we have the confluence of compelling political and economic forces as manifested in: (1) the US Supreme Court recently allowing unlimited political contributions by corporations, (2) the *Noerr-Pennington* Doctrine that makes private entities legally immune for attempts to influence passage or enforcement of laws, even to the point of permitting outright lies and deception of legislators by corporations and trade associations, and (3) re-interpretation of antitrust laws from broad social objectives to narrow economic efficiency objectives that do not necessarily nurture democratic values. These forces threaten the very soul of American democracy and the American Dream.

Without corrective legislation and a truly independent judiciary, these legal interpretations will continue to shape the agrifood system, allowing it to become more integrated and concentrated, not just in the United States, but on the planet Earth. Those who control inputs to food production—seed, technology, fertilizers, water & energy—control food. Those who control food control people. Those few who now seem to have a firm foothold on control of food do not apparently have ethical and moral values that support democracy.

Efficiency cannot be the main issue. Rather, key issues in the food system and society generally ought to consider economic and political power, economic and physical sustainability of the food system, economic freedom, fairness, equity and justice.

References

American Antitrust Institute (AAI). No date. Noerr-Pennington Doctrine. http://www.antitrustinstitute.org/content/noerr-pennington-doctrine. Accessed 18 Jan 2012.

Arnold, T. 1955. The economic purpose of antitrust laws. *Mississippi Law Journal* 26: 207–208.

Bagwell, K. 2001. The economics of advertising, introduction. In *The economics of advertising*, ed. K. Bagwell, 1–20. Cheltenham: Edward Elgar.

Bastiat, F. 1850. *The law*, trans. by Seymour Cain, 1995, Irvington-on-Hudson: The Foundation for Economic Education.

Beattie, B.R., C.R. Taylor, and M.J. Watts. 2009. *The economics of production*. Malabar: Kreiger Publishing Company.

Blaug, M. 1996. *Economic theory in retrospect*, 5th ed. New York: Cambridge University Press.

Boudreaux, D.J. 2002. The second edition of Judge Posner's Antitrust Law: A tempered appreciation. *The Antitrust Source,* Chicago, IL: American Bar Association, March.
Boulding, K.E. 1969. Economics as a moral science. *American Economic Review* 59: 1–12.
Boulding, K.E. 1970. *Economics as a science*. New York: McGraw Hill.
Breimyer, H.F. 1965. *Individual freedom and the economic organization of agriculture*. Chicago: University of Illinois Press.
Breimyer, H.F. 1995. Understanding the changing structure of American agriculture. In *Increasing understanding of public problems and policies*, ed. S.A. Halbrook and C.E. Merry. Oak Brook: Farm Foundation.
Bresnahan, T.F. 1989. Empirical studies of industries with market power, Chapter 17. In *Handbook of industrial organization*, ed. R. Schmalensee and R. Willig. North Holland: Elsevier.
Bromley, D. 1989. Institutional change and economic efficiency. *Journal of Economic Issues* 23(3): 735–759.
Carstensen, P.C. 2000. *Beyond antitrust: The case for change*. Paper presented at the USDA Agricultural Outlook Forum, February 24
DeLong, J.B. 2011. Economics in crisis. *The Economists' Voice* 8(2): 2.
Federal Trade Commission (FTC). 2006. *Enforcement perspectives on the Noerr-Pennington* Doctrine, FTC Staff Report.
France, M., L. Woellert, and B. Grow. 2004. The battle over the courts: How politics, ideology, and special interests are compromising the U.S. justice system. *Business Week*, September 27.
Haines, C.G. 1919. Efforts to define unfair competition. *Yale Law Journal* 29(Nov): 1–22.
Heilbroner, R., and W. Milberg. 1955. *The crisis of vision in modern economic thought*. New York: Cambridge University Press.
Knight, F.H. 1921. *Risk, uncertainty and profit*. Boston: Hart, Schaffner & Marx; Houghton Mifflin Co.
Knight, F.H. 1923. The ethics of competition. *Quarterly Journal of Economics* 37(4): 579–624.
Knight, F.H. 1947. *Freedom & reform: Essays in economics and social philosophy*. New York/London: Harper & Bros.
Konow, J. 2003. Which is the fairest one of all? A positive analysis of justice theories. *Journal of Economic Literature* 41(Dec): 1188–1239.
Krugman, P. 2009. How did economists get it so wrong? *The New York Times*, September 6.
Lang, M.G. 1980. Economic efficiency and policy comparisons. *American Journal of Agricultural Economics* 62(4): 772–777.
Minda, G. 1990. Interest groups, political freedom, and antitrust: A modern reassessment of the Noerr-Pennington Doctrine. *Hastings Law Journal* 41(April): 937–942.
Organization for Economic Co-operation and Development (OECD). 2010. *Private financial sector investment in farmland and agricultural infrastructure*, Working Party on Agricultural Policies and Markets, Trade and Agricultural Directorate, Committee for Agriculture, JT03287310.
Posner, R.A. 2001. *Antitrust law*, 2nd ed. Chicago: University of Chicago Press.
Reed, H.B. 1916. The morals of monopoly and competition. *International Journal of Ethics* 26(2): 258–281.
Rogers, C. P. 2007. The antitrust legacy of justice William O. Douglas and the curse of the curse of bigness. Selected works of C. Paul Rogers III. http://works.bepress.com/c_paul_rogers/1/. Accessed 23 Jan 2012.
Schmidt, A.A., and J.D. Shaffer. 1964. Marketing in social perspective. In *Agricultural market analysis*, ed. V.L. Sorensen. East Lansing: Michigan State University.
Shaffer, J.D. 1987. Does the concept of economic efficiency meet the standards for truth in labeling when used as a norm in policy analysis? In *Economic efficiency in agricultural and food marketing*, ed. R.L. Kilmer and W.J. Armbruster, 91–97. Ames: Iowa State University.
Smith, A. 1776/1991. *Wealth of nations*. Amherst: Prometheus Books.

Taylor, C.R. 2003. The role of risk versus the role of uncertainty in economic systems. *Agricultural Systems* 75: 251–264.

Taylor, C.R., and D.A. Domina. 2010. *Restoring economic health to contract poultry production*, Report prepared for the Joint U.S. Department of Justice, U.S. Department of Agriculture Workshops on Agriculture and Antitrust Enforcement Issues in Our 21st Century Economy, May 13, Normal, AL.

United States Department of Agriculture (USDA). 2009. *2007 census of agriculture*, United States Summary and State Data, 1, AC-07-A-51.

Virtue, G.O. 1920. The meat-packing investigation. *Quarterly Journal of Economics* 34(4): 626–685.

Waller, S.W. 2004. The antitrust legacy of Thurman Arnold. *St. John's Law Review* 78(3): 569–613.

Chapter 6
Networks, Power and Dependency in the Agrifood Industry

Harvey S. James Jr., Mary K. Hendrickson, and Philip H. Howard

Abstract We review research on power, dependency and the concentration of agrifood industries and report updated concentration figures for selected agrifood sectors. We then utilize network exchange theory to identify principles of dependency and network relations and describe network relationships within the broiler, beef and commodity crop sectors. We argue that this study demonstrates that network analysis can inform on the nature, source and extent of differential dependencies and asymmetric power relationships within the agrifood sector.

6.1 Introduction

The agrifood industry has experienced significant structural changes during the second half of the twentieth century. While much has been written about these changes from a variety of perspectives, what we are most interested in is whether these changes have negatively affected the competitive advantages of farmers vis-à-vis industry firms. As an illustration, consider the fact that in 1990 the top four firms in the pork packing industry controlled 40% of the market, whereas by 2010 the four firm concentration ratio had increased to 67% (GIPSA 2011; Wise and Trist 2010). If the number of pork packers buying hogs declines, then there will be fewer

H.S. James Jr., Ph.D. (✉)
Department of Agricultural & Applied Economics, University of Missouri,
146 Mumford Hall, MO 65211 Columbia, USA
e-mail: hjames@missouri.edu

M.K. Hendrickson, Ph.D.
Department of Rural Sociology, University of Missouri, 200B Gentry Hall,
MO 65211 Columbia, USA

P.H. Howard, Ph.D.
Department of Community Sustainability, Michigan State University,
316 Natural Resources Bldg, MI 48824 East Lansing, USA

H.S. James Jr. (ed.), *The Ethics and Economics of Agrifood Competition*,
The International Library of Environmental, Agricultural and Food Ethics 20,
DOI 10.1007/978-94-007-6274-9_6,

firms competing for hogs from hog producers. Basic economics suggests that this would result in an increase in the market power of pork packers collectively relative to hog producers. This is a concern because of a greater likelihood that pork packers will engage in competitive practices that are harmful to hog producers.

Legal, social and economic analyses have raised questions about power relationships within the agrifood industry by examining how the existence and exercise of market power actually works and to whose advantage it is used (e.g., Carstensen 2008; Foer 2010; Zheng and Vulkina 2009), how power can structure global relations of production and consumption and political institutions (McMichael 2000, 2009; Friedmann and McMichael 1989; Heffernan 1984; Friedland 1984, 1994) or discipline labor and other groups within the food system (UFCW 2010). This chapter addresses the question of how the structure of the agrifood industry relates to the relative power of agribusiness firms and farmers. In doing so we stress that while the question of relative power applies to all segments of the agrifood industry, our concern is primarily directed at the perspective and position of farmers and producers. Specifically, we focus on the extent to which structural characteristics of the agrifood industry affect power issues arising from a farmer's position in and connection to networks of exchange relationships that exist in different agricultural commodities. The reason for our focus on farmers is simple: the question of whether there is adequate competition in the agrifood industry is generally not raised by or on behalf of agribusiness firms. Rather, the question of adequate competition and its economic, social and political benefits is raised on behalf of farmers.[1]

Other than analyses of market power (e.g., monopoly, monopsony) and antitrust issues, and with perhaps a few other exceptions (e.g., Kuhn 1964), economists have offered relatively little commentary on the subject of "power" (Oleinik 2011). Moreover, legal interpretations in antitrust law have shifted primarily to a prioritization of consumer welfare – mostly defined in terms of price – which leaves little room for exploring questions of harm to producers and others within the supply chain (Carstensen 2008; Foer 2010). For instance, Shelanski (2010, pp. 184–185) of the Federal Trade Commission testified that

> Monopsony, the power of buyers, can become a concern when buying power becomes concentrated in too few hands, although reduced payments to upstream suppliers may not harm and instead can benefit final consumers when benefit is measured in terms of their food bills. So some of the buying power that agricultural providers make in front along the supply chain may be beyond the scope of traditional antitrust enforcement.

A study of power within the agrifood industry is complicated by the fact that there are many definitions and conceptualizations of power, some of which are contradictory, and there are competing perspectives of how and why power

[1]Five different workshops on competition within the agrifood system were held in 2010 in the US, in locations that allowed access and participation by farmers and producers. Transcripts of the hearings can be found at USDA-DOJ (2010).

arises and is used. Weber (1978) defines power in terms of the ability to impose one's will on others, in spite of their resistance. Some scholars view power as a relational process (Foucault 1980; Lukes 1974) and as embedded in social networks (Granovetter 1985). Political power theorists consider specific behavior and decision-making processes (Dahl 1961), arguing that while power may be manifested in the non-decision (i.e. structuring formal agendas) and through the structure of relationships, power is ultimately manifested in domination or control, where the basic maxim is '*Control the resource or control the people*' (see Lukes 1974; Giddens 1984). Critical theorists have long studied power and resistance, particularly in development theory through the lens of the intertwined power of capital (accumulation) and state (legitimation), with the latter also being a forum for resistance by those without access to capital (McMichael 2000; O'Connor 1973).

Because there are contradictory views of power, we approach the problem indirectly by drawing on Emerson (1962) and other sociologists who define power in terms of dependency. Dependency is the state of relying on the actions of others in order to achieve some objective. According to Emerson (1962, p. 32), "the dependence of one party provides the basis for the power of the other." Sociological and similar literatures on dependency are helpful because they link the structural relationships of actors, such as those defined by network relations, to relative dependency. Dependency is also more tractable as an analytical device than is power because dependency is "a less evasive concept than power, one more easily operationalized" (Marsden 1987, p. 147). Therefore, in this chapter we identify principles of dependency and network relations and describe network relationships within the broiler, beef and commodity crop sectors in order to identify and articulate the nature, source and extent of dependencies and power relationships of farmers vis-à-vis agribusiness firms.

6.2 Previous Research on Agrifood Industry Structure

Structural analysis of the food system has long been of interest to social scientists, particularly the social, economic and ecological impacts of power and agency in the global agrifood system. They have often placed farmers – or at least a focus on production – front and center in their analyses. In a series entitled "Who Will Control Agriculture?" published in 1973, agricultural economists influential in policy arenas warned that the changing organization of agriculture did not enhance the efficiency or productivity of the system, but could instead exact social and psychological costs on farmers and society, including limiting the economic freedom of individuals (Breimyer et al. 1973). Using four case studies, one of which examined the broiler industry, Breimyer (1965) argued for agriculture policies that would keep a competitive system of agriculture in place.

Writing since the 1970s, rural sociologists and political scientists interested in agrifood developments analyzed how power was expressed through intertwined economic and political processes, generally viewing capital (or actors with more capital) as having the upper hand with distinct negative impacts on farmers, workers, consumers and the environment (e.g. Heffernan 1972; Friedland et al. 1981; Friedmann and McMichael 1989; Burch and Lawrence 2009; Bonanno and Constance 2008). In the 1990s, scholars critiquing what they considered a rigid structuralist view of power in the food system focused on how actors shaped the local manifestations of restructuring in agriculture and food (Goodman and DuPuis 2002; Miele and Murdoch 2002). For these scholars, producers and consumers exerted agency by resisting changes in the food system and spearheading the development of alternative agrifood networks (for a discussion of these alternative networks, see Allen 2004). In the latter view, power circulated through nodes with no one actor dominating completely. Bridging these camps, Wilkinson (2006) built on the work of Granovetter (1985) to develop the notion of global production networks that exerted a certain amount of influence in shaping the global agrifood system but acknowledged that individual actors could change these networks through a variety of options.

Another important strand of work has focused on more narrowly defined competition issues that seek to explore structure and conduct from economic and legal perspectives. The interest is competitive markets *per se* because of the important benefits they are assumed to provide for society in terms of price, choice, or democratic action and other social goods (Lynn 2009). Because of these benefits, government has an interest in ensuring a competitive environment. To this end, economists and other social science scholars, including government regulators, have regularly examined and reported the state of agrifood industry concentration either through measures such as the concentration ratio of the top four firms in an industry (CR4) or the Herfandal-Hirschman Index (HHI) which estimates the amount of competition between firms based on the size of firms in an industry. Table 6.1 reports the CR4 for a dozen agricultural commodities and sectors.

We think it is valuable to give farmers, in addition to scholars, policymakers and other stakeholders in the food system, a snapshot picture of the marketplace as presented in Table 6.1 for two different reasons. First, in most cases we report both market share data figured in the simple CR4, as well as the dominant firms in each sector. This picture allows farmers to understand the wide reach of corporate actors. Second, we believe it is important for farmers to have information on their position in the marketplace. Many already have this knowledge as lived experience but might not possess the information across a variety of sectors.

While it is true that competition has been traditionally measured and litigated through the analysis of structure (mostly using an HHI index) and conduct (i.e., specific acts of uncompetitive behavior), more recent analysis has critiqued market share as imperfect and an often misused analysis of structure (Domina and Taylor 2009). Instead, these scholars have focused on differences between buyer and seller

Table 6.1 Concentration ratios and dominant firms for selected agrifood sectors

Industry sector and representative firms	CR 4	Date and source notes
Beef slaughter (Steer & Heifer) Cargill Tyson JBS National beef	82%	2009 figures quoted in GIPSA (2011). Firm names taken from *2011 Feedstuffs Reference Issue*, September 15, 2010. Note that rankings are based on capacity while CR4 is based on actual slaughter
Beef production (Feedlots) JBS fiver rivers cattle feeding (838,000) Cactus feeders (relationship with Tyson) 520,000 Cargill cattle feeders LLC (350,000) Friona industries (275,000)	Top 4 have one-time capacity for 1,983,000 head	Head numbers cited as one-time capacity from *Feedstuffs* (2010)
Pork slaughter: Smithfield foods Tyson foods Swift (JBS) Excel corp. (Cargill)	63%	2009 figures with 2008 at 65%, quoted in GIPSA (2011). Firm names listed based on capacity reported in *Feedstuffs* (2010)
Pork production: Smithfield foods (876,804) Triumph foods (371,000) Seaboard (213,600) Iowa select farms (157,500)	Top 4 have 1,618,904 sows in production	*Successful Farming* (2010). *Feedstuffs* (2010) includes higher sow numbers for Smithfield at 922,251, Triumph at 371,500, and lower ones for Iowa Select at 152,500
Broiler slaughter: Tyson Pilgrim's pride (owned by JBS) Perdue Sanderson	53%	2009 figures, with 2008 at 57% are quoted in GIPSA (2011). Firm names reported in Thornton (2010)
Turkey slaughter Butterball (Smithfield/Goldsboro) Jennie-O (Hormel) Cargill Farbest foods	58%	2009 figures with 2008 at 51%, quoted in GIPSA (2011). Firm names reported in Thornton (2010, p. 18). Note that Butterball is a joint venture of Goldsboro Milling and Smithfield Foods
Animal feed Land O'Lakes Purina LLC Cargill animal nutrition ADM alliance nutrition J.D. Heiskell & Co.	44%	CR 4 from 2007 Economic Census, US Census Bureau (2011), percent of value added. Firm names are rankings from Feedstuffs (2010) based on annual manufacturing capacity
Flour milling Horizon milling (Cargill/CHS) ADM ConAgra	52%	2007 Economic Census, US Census Bureau (2011), percent of value added. Firm names are based on author calculations

(continued)

Table 6.1 (continued)

Industry sector and representative firms	CR 4	Date and source notes
Wet corn milling ADM Corn products international Cargill	87%	2007 Economic Census, US Census Bureau (2011), percent of value added. Firm names are based on author calculations
Soybean processing ADM Bunge Cargill Ag processing	85%	2007 Economic Census, US Census Bureau (2011), percent of value added. Firm names are based on author calculations
Rice milling ADM Riceland foods Farmers rice milling Producers rice mill	55%	2007 Economic Census, US Census Bureau (2011), percent of value added. Firm names are based on author calculations; among the largest rice processors, not necessarily listed in order of size
Grocery Walmart Kroger Safeway Supervalu	42–51%	*NY Times*, January 2011, reported Wal-Mart at 33%, and Kroger, Safeway and Supervalu at 4–9% each (see Clifford 2011). *Grist*, December 2011, reported Wal-Mart at 25% (see Mitchell 2011) The top 20 grocery stores today account for roughly 65% of US grocery store sales, an increase from 39% in 1992 (Shelansky 2010). Rankings from Moran and Chanil (2010)

power, particularly as it relates to farmers.[2] Wise and Trist (2010) conclude there is significant evidence of buyer power in the hog market and join with Domina and Taylor in calling for empirical analysis that is "farm-centered" and reliant upon "detailed economic data." As Domina and Taylor (2009, p. 14) assert

> Governmental agencies charged with antitrust enforcement must recognize complex and unique characteristics of each individual market chain, or system. The ways in which market power is manifested in the poultry industry are considerably different than in the beef industry, for example. Therefore, a single metric or—have model will travel approach to competition analysis is woefully inadequate.

[2]Domina and Taylor (2009) and Carstensen (2008) are concerned that buyer power and seller power have different measures and impacts. Analysis of market share is hard to calculate because of the difficulty in establishing the parameters of the market – in particular the geographical nature of markets; the inelasticity of particular market sectors like most in the agrifood industry, and the fact that competitive circumstances are very different in different sectors of the food system (e.g. the poultry industry has completely different parameters than the beef industry).

These commentators distinguish between buyer power and seller power because they argue that power is exercised differently in each situation and both buyer and seller power can compromise the competitive nature of the market. Antitrust law has focused for the most part on seller power, in the sense that in a monopoly situation, sellers can command a price above the level considered competitive which harms consumer welfare in the form of higher prices. Buyer power has often been considered the mirror image of seller power, which many scholars vehemently reject (Chen 2008; Grundlach and Foer 2008; Foer 2010; Carstensen 2008; Domina and Taylor 2009). Foer (2010) testified at a workshop on competition in agriculture organized by United States Departments of Agriculture and Justice that seller power takes effect in very highly concentrated markets (which he estimates at 60–70% market share) while buyer power can be exhibited in relatively unconcentrated markets (for example around 20%). Thus, the traditional focus on HHI is not an adequate metric in measuring buyer power. Chen (2008) dissects the definition of buyer power, relying on concepts of *monopsony* and *countervailing power* (bargaining power).[3] For Chen, monopsony power that is exercised in the presence of perfect competition among sellers is deadweight loss and bad for consumers.[4] When there is some sort of countervailing power present, then consumer welfare can sometimes be enhanced.

Carstensen (2008) argues that the source of buyer power, the capacity and incentive of the buyer to exploit their market power, and the incentives to discriminate among sellers all must be considered when examining buyer power. For instance, high switching costs on the part of a supplier (which reflect the time and effort necessary for a supplier to find another buyer) or the quantity and proportion that a buyer takes from a supplier (c.f. the notion of *captive draw* introduced when the Department of Justice filed to stop the merger of grain giants Cargill and Continental)[5] can enhance buyer power. Other examples of enhanced buyer power occur when the monopsonist operates in both monopsonistic and competitive markets, which affects the prices paid to suppliers in different areas. Buyer power can also occur in an all-or-nothing arrangement that exists when suppliers use economies of scale to supply that buyer at a particular price, but will experience significant diseconomies if the buyer abandons that supplier. Foer (2010) also

---

[3]Chen's (2008, p. 247) definition: "*Buyer power* is the ability of a buyer to reduce price profitably below a supplier's normal selling price, or more generally the ability to obtain terms of supply more favorably than a suppliers' normal terms. The normal selling price, in turn, is defined as supplier's profit-maximizing price in the absence of buyer power. In the case where there is perfect competition among suppliers, the normal selling price of a supplier is the competitive price, and the buyer power is *monopsony power.* On the other hand, in a case where competition among suppliers is imperfect, the normal selling price is above the competitive price, and the buyer power is *countervailing power.*"

[4]Lynn (2006, 2009) argues that Wal-Mart uses its monopsonistic power to force concessions from suppliers rather than collecting higher prices from consumers.

[5]US v. Cargill and Continental. United States District Court for the District of Columbia. Civil No. 1: 99CV01875. Section VI, Paragraphs 20–26.

cautions about the "waterbed" effect where one buyer forces a discriminatory low price on a supplier which gains that buyer a competitive advantage, while at the same time the supplier tries to recoup some profit in selling to other buyers, thereby putting them at a disadvantage in the market place vis-à-vis buyer number one. Foer (2010, p. 223) calls this a "double whammy" that leads to the first buyer becoming an "ever-increasing behemoth."

This discussion shows that different forms of power can exist in agricultural networks, that these different forms of power have different impacts, and that legal and economic theories need to "catch up" to the realities of how agricultural and food markets are operating. What is missing is a better conceptual model that helps to explain the existence and exercise of power within the agrifood system. In what follows we use the concept of relative dependencies created through networks to identify principles that can help us understand what is going on in various networks of relationships in the agrifood system. Our exploration and explanation of farmer positions within the networks will help scholars recognize the complexity of dependencies among actors connected in agrifood networks, and even the possibility that dependencies may not change when industry concentration changes (or can change when industry concentration does not).

6.3 Networks, Dependency and Power

We draw on network exchange theory in order to understand better dependency and power within the agrifood arena. Network exchange theory is based on the work of Emerson (1962), Cook and Emerson (1978), Cook et al. (1983), Markovsky et al. (1988) and others. Like economic models, in network exchange theory (NET) the focus of analysis is the exchange (e.g., transactions), and actors are assumed to be rational and to maximize benefits (see Cook et al. 1983, f.n. 12). Unlike economic models, however, behavior of actors is not assumed to be a function of incentives derived directly from profit (or utility) maximization calculations. Rather, the behavior of actors is assumed to be derived from power imbalances that arise from differences in the dependencies of potential exchange partners. Thus, the concept of dependency is central to the NET perspective on power.

An actor is dependent on another when he or she must rely on the actions of others. Dependency is affected positively by the value of the assistance or participation a person requires of another in order to achieve his or her objective and negatively by the number and quality of resources available because of that assistance.[6] Emerson (1962) equates power with dependency, so that the more

[6]Emerson (1962, p. 32) provides this specific definition: "The dependence of actor A upon actor B is (1) directly proportional to A's motivational investment in goals mediated by B, and (2) inversely proportional to the availability of those goals to A outside of the A-B relation."

dependent an actor is on a second actor, the more power the second actor has over the first. The power-dependence relation is expressed as follows:

$$P_{ab} = D_{ba},$$

which reads as "the power of A over B is equal to, and based upon, the dependence of B upon A" (Emerson 1962, p. 33). When parties within an exchange relation are equally dependent on each other, then power is balanced and neither party will possess a power advantage. However, if the dependencies are unequal so that one party is more dependent on the other, that is, if there are "differential dependencies" (Cook 1987, p. 216) so that $D_{ab} > D_{ba}$ (the dependency of A on B is greater than the dependency of B on A), then there will be a power imbalance in favor of the least dependent of the two parties (see also Molm 1987).

This perspective provides important insights about power, which will be discussed next, but it also embodies a significant weakness reflected in the difficulty of identifying imbalances in an exchange relationship or network. What would a perfectly balanced exchange relationship and network look like? Are there objective indicators showing that exchange partners are, or are not, equally dependent on each other? These are difficult questions to answer. However, we argue that NET can advance our understanding of power because it offers a means of establishing clear principles and objective, identifiable indicators. This chapter provides a step in this advancement.

A key insight of network exchange theories is that the structural characteristics of the network affect the differential dependencies and hence relative power of actors within the network. This chapter focuses on two aspects: position within a network and type of network connection. First, position within the network is important because differential dependency is by definition defined relative to others. For example, other things being equal, the more central an actor is within the network, the more alternative opportunities that actor is expected to have relative to others within the network, such as actors located along the periphery (see Hanneman and Riddle 2005, chapter 10). While centrality within a network is an important indicator of network power, centrality and number of alternatives are not perfect indicators of differential dependencies, because there is no consensus as to their definition and measurement (Freeman 1979).

Second, the effect of relative network position is attenuated by the types of connections linking actors within the network and the overall configuration of the network (Cook et al. 1983). There are two general types of connections linking actors with the network that affect relative dependency: *negative* connections and *positive* connections. In negatively connected networks, a decision to exchange with one actor implies that exchanges with other actors do not occur. In positively connected networks, an exchange with one actor facilitates or requires a complementary exchange with other positively connected actors. Moreover, like electronic circuits that can be connected either in parallel or series, positive connections can exist in parallel or series. A positive connection is parallel when, for instance, the purchase of an input requires the purchase of a second input. A positive connection is in series along a value chain, where a purchase of an input by a processor results in a later sale of a product to another buyer (indeed, all connections along a value chain are by definition positive).

Positive and negative connections in networks have different implications. According to Yamagishi et al. (1988, p. 849), in networks characterized by negative connections, "the availability of resources from alternative exchange relations determines the distribution of power." Importantly, this is the basis for the standard economic perspective in which (market) power is determined largely by the number of competitors or alternatives a market participant faces. In positively connected networks, "the local scarcity of resources determine the distribution of power" (Yamagishi et al. 1988, pp. 849–850), meaning that the agent possessing the (relatively) more scarce resource has more power than others within the network because scarcity affects the dependence of others. Importantly, positive connections both affect local scarcity and transmit the effects of local scarcity along the network. Positive connections create local scarcity when they act as barriers to resource transmission through the network. For instance, an intermediary or "middleman" can facilitate an exchange between two actors, but it also acts as a barrier if the only way for two actors to interact is through the intermediary. Moreover, while positive connections are not the only source of local scarcity – geography, contract, technology and other factors can influence local scarcity and thus create dependencies – these effects are transmitted along positively connected networks (in series) and are amplified by the effect of intermediary "barriers."

Within a network it is the combination of positive and negative network connections that matters, not just the number of negative connections, in determining the relative dependency of actors. Thus, Cook et al. (1983, pp. 288–289) state that "An important point to be made is that treating number of alternatives as a perfect indicator of resource availability can result in erroneous predictions when applied to connected sets of exchange relations and suffers from the same deficiency as a simple degree-based measure of centrality." As shown next, the presence, position, and number of positive connections can amplify or attenuate the effect of a change in the number of alternative (negative) exchange relations.

For example, suppose assemblers of a product purchase inputs from one of a dozen different input suppliers. Suppose further that these suppliers produce similar goods of comparable quality and that they are also similarly priced. In this situation, let's say that there is a relative balance of power within the network consisting of assemblers and suppliers. In other words, initially neither assemblers nor suppliers have a power advantage (or dependency disadvantage) over the other. Now, suppose there is a change in technology or some other exogenous change so that the purchase by the assemblers of the input from the suppliers requires a complementary or parallel purchase of a second input from a second group of sellers. Examples might include hybrid seeds that are planted closer together that require different planting and harvesting equipment or improved poultry or swine breeds that require the

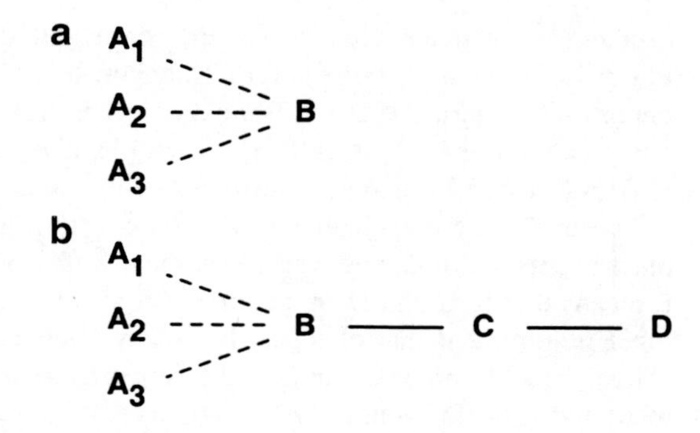

Fig. 6.1 Simple network structures (**a**) shows negative connections between Ai and B (**b**) shows the addition of positive connections linking C and D to B

purchase of antibiotics due to increased susceptibility to disease (e.g., Rich 2008).[7] It should be clear from this change that the relative dependency of the assemblers *cannot* remain static. Because of the addition of a parallel exchange within the network – characterized by the requirement that a purchase from one supplier requires the purchase of a second input from another supplier – assemblers are made relatively more dependent upon suppliers collectively. The reason is simple. When the assemblers purchase one input, the exogenous change means that they cannot complete assembly of the product without the addition of the second input, making the assemblers dependent on that input's supplier. Whereas originally a dependency did not exist, the change creates a relative dependency for the assemblers as depicted by the existence of an additional positive network condition.

Furthermore, if the complementary input is supplied (only) by the supplier of the original input, then the increased dependency of the buyer is mirrored by increased power of the input supplier. For example, Howard (2009, p. 1277) provides this example:

> In 2003 Syngenta began to extend the strategy of bundling transgenic seeds and proprietary chemicals to its non-transgenic seeds. UK farmers that purchased a new hybrid barley seed were required to also buy a package of plant growth regulators and fungicides. This heightened concerns first raised by transgenic seed agreements, that seed/chemical companies would use their oligopoly power to increasingly dictate production decisions to farmers through contracts.

Consider a further illustration of the effect of positive connections on networks, based on the simple network relations given in Fig. 6.1. The networks depicted here contain agents, labeled A through D, and paths connecting them. The dashed lines representing connections between A_i and B are *negative*, meaning that if B exchanges with one relation it does not exchange with the others. In contrast, the solid lines representing B-C and C-D connections are *positive*, meaning that

---

[7] A critique of the green revolution is that hybrids required higher levels of inputs such as fertilizer and irrigation water, thus the suggestion by Vandana Shiva that they not be called "higher yielding varieties" but "high responsive varieties" (Shiva 1991).

exchanges are not exclusive but are contingent upon each other. As shown in Fig. 6.1a, B has three options for exchanges, while each A_i has only one exchange opportunity. Therefore, B's power exceeds that of A_i because B is less dependent on a particular A_i than A_i is on B. For example, if A_1 does not offer terms acceptable to B, B can seek exchange opportunities with either A_2 or A_3.

In Fig. 6.1b, the exchange network connecting A_i and B is expanded to include other agents within the network. Specifically, the addition of C and D in series with B means that B, C and D are positively connected. Like the addition of the parallel input requirement that changes the relative dependency of assemblers described above, the addition of C and D to the network *cannot* leave the relative dependency of A_i and B unchanged. In order to understand the change in dependency resulting from the addition of a series of positive connections, one must assess which agent possesses the (relatively) more scarce resource. In the case of Fig. 6.1b, as explained by Yamagishi et al. (1988), B has more power than A_i not only because the negative connection between A_i and B offers more opportunities for B to exchange with A_i than for A_i to exchange with B, but also because the introduction of the positive connections with C and D within the network places B between A_i and C. The result is that resources or advantages offered to the network by C and D are now relatively scarcer to A_i than to B because A_i has to go through B to obtain them, thus further increasing B's power over A_i. Similarly, because D has to go through C in order to obtain whatever advantage the participation of A_i and B provide to the network, C has more power than D; that is, resources or advantages offered by A_i and B are relatively scarcer to D than they are to C. In the B-C relation, note that because B has multiple alternatives for exchange opportunities with respect to A_i, B's ability to become locally satiated in the A_i-B relation – that is, to be able to obtain resources from A_i – is greater than the ability of C to become locally satiated in the C-D relation. Therefore, relative to B, C controls the more scarce resource or advantage, thus giving C more power than B. Accordingly, it is predicted that C's power over B will in turn affect A_i, thus diminishing B's power over A_i. These results have been supported in experimental studies (see Yamagishi et al. 1988, for a complete discussion).

The lesson here is that relative dependency, and hence relative power, within a network can be determined through a careful and comprehensive examination of not only the number of exchange options that a particular actor has within a network but also the nature of that exchange relation relative to other connections the actor has within the network and the relative scarcity of resources exchanged within the network. That is, specific dependencies can only be determined through analyses of specific network structures and actors. That said, the NET framework does provide some basic hypotheses for understanding the dependency and power in the agrifood industry. From the perspective of an agent within the network, we offer the following:

Hypothesis 1: *A reduction in the number of negative exchange connections in a network increases the relative dependency of the agent, other things being equal.*

Hypothesis 2: *The addition of a positive exchange connection in parallel with other connections in a network will generally increase the relative dependency of the agent, other things being equal.*

Hypothesis 3: *The addition of a positive exchange connection in series with other connections in a network may increase or decrease the relative dependency of the agent, other things being equal, depending on whether the agent is locally more or less satiated from exchanges with others in the network.*

Hypothesis 4: *A combination of changes in negative and positive exchange connections within a network can either compound the relative dependency of the agent or have countervailing effects, depending on how the connections affect the relative scarcity of resources.*

As an illustration, compare the *relative* dependency of farmers engaged in three types of crop farming: genetically-modified (GM), conventional, and organic. For GM farming, producers purchase seeds that contain a gene that makes the plant tolerant to herbicides like glyphosate. For conventional farming, producers purchase non-GM seeds and control weeds and pests with a number of different chemical inputs. For organic farming, producers use conventional seeds but do not use chemical inputs to control for weeds and pests. If the GM farmer and conventional farmer purchase the same types of inputs (e.g., seeds, chemical herbicides, labor and machinery), then the *relative* dependency of the conventional farmer is less than it is for the GM farmer, other things being equal. Even though both conventional and GM farmers have the same number of parallel positive connection (four in this example: seeds, chemicals, labor and machinery), the fact that the herbicide tolerant seed requires a specific type of chemical herbicide means that the number of negative exchange connections between GM farmer and seed company and between GM farmer and farm chemical companies is smaller than the number for the conventional farmer. In contrast, because the organic producer does not rely on any farm chemical input (e.g., he or she has positive connections with only seeds, labor and machinery), the organic producer is relatively less dependent than the conventional and GM farmers, other things being equal.

Of course, the *absolute* level of dependency of the GM farmer, conventional farmer and organic farmer will depend on substantially more considerations than just seeds and chemical inputs. Dependency can arise at any point of exchange. All exchange points need to be considered before a final assessment of dependency can be made for a particular agent. For example, the dependency advantage that an organic farmer has over conventional crop producers because he does not face a positive exchange connection with chemical herbicide producers may be eroded if there is scarcity in the farm labor market and the organic farmer has a greater reliance on farm labor for weed control than the conventional farmer. Similarly, if the number of outlets to which an organic producer can sell his output is smaller than the number of places a GM producer can sell his output, then one must balance the dependency advantage the organic farmer has upstream relative to the GM farmer with the dependency disadvantage the organic farmer has downstream.

In summary, NET can provide an important perspective on dependency and power in the agrifood industry, particularly from the perspective of farmers. Specifically, NET analysis suggests the following insights. First, the differences between buyer and seller power explained above become very important to the farmer and impact whether relationships between farmers and other actors are characterized by positive or negative connections. Second, by looking at simple measures of concentration, like CR4 or HHI, one emphasizes the disappearance of negative connections available for farmers, but overlooks the implications of positive connections in the network. Third, it is important to explore the implications of positive and negative connections collectively between farmers and other actors in the agrifood system in order to understand how dependencies are created and how they impact power relationships in the network. For instance, changes in agricultural technologies might result not only in the disappearance of a negative connection, but also force farmers into a positive connection that then defines other relationships that are available to or required by them. Finally, the study of relative dependency is best made by examining changes in the network structure over time, for instance, by noting not only the change in the number of negative exchange connections but also the existence and nature of positive exchange connections within the network.

6.4 Differential Dependencies in Stylized Agrifood Networks

Farmers are in a unique position within the network connecting all players in the agrifood system. At the center of the network, farmers take agricultural inputs, such as seeds and genetics, labor, machinery, fertilizer and weed control products, and convert these inputs into agricultural commodities. As actors along the periphery of the agrifood network, agricultural input suppliers are dependent upon farmers collectively as buyers of their products and as gatekeepers to exchange connections further along the agrifood value chain. Similarly, food processors and retailers are dependent upon farmers for their primary product inputs, namely agricultural commodities. The positional advantage of farmers within the agrifood system, however, is attenuated by the nature of the negative and positive connections that bind them within the network of all actors and participants in the agrifood system. Although scholars have documented extensively the changes in the number of participants resulting from consolidation and other structural changes that have been occurring in the agrifood system over the previous decades, we draw on insights from network exchange theory to highlight how these changes have affected the relative dependency of farmers and producers in the specific cases of broilers, beef and corn and soybean growers. Admittedly our characterization of these networks is somewhat stylized. The relative dependencies of farmers and actors in specific agrifood networks will depend on their unique circumstances. However, these analyses illustrate the insights an NET perspective provides on power and dependency in the agrifood industry.

6.4.1 Broilers

The relationships that exist in the broiler industry are well-documented. In this volume Constance et al. summarize the evolution of the contract broiler system. A classic study comes from Heffernan (1972, 1984), who examined how farmers and communities benefitted from investment in poultry production in Union Parish, Louisiana. Over the course of 30 years – field research was conducted in 1969, 1982 and 1999 – the structural position of the producer changed greatly. In the early days, when four locally-owned integrators competed for growers, farmers and the community enjoyed economic and social benefits. These benefits declined as competition for growers decreased (two integrators operating in the county in the late 1970s dwindled to one by 1982). By 1999, poultry growers believed they had few options, that they would continue in debt, and that they would not recommend poultry production to their children (Hendrickson, et al. 2008). As options decreased, farmers felt less powerful and more dependent on the integrators.

Today a typical arrangement for broiler production looks like Fig. 6.2. In this particular instance, a grower (farmer) enters into a contract relationship with an integrator (poultry firm) to provide chicks, reasonable veterinary care, feed, scheduling of flocks, chicken catching, transportation and processing. In exchange, the grower contracts to provide labor and growout houses for the chicks. Growers typically obtain financing from banks or other lending institutions in order to construct, maintain, and upgrade growout houses.

Within this network, the connections between the grower and poultry firm and bank are positive. The contract with the integrator requires a growout house, which in turn requires financing from a lender. Importantly, a number of factors significantly enhance the dependency of growers on the integrator and lender. For instance, no other integrator will enter the geographic area (represented in Fig. 6.2 by the dashed circle encompassing the farmer and grower) of their competitors.[8] According to Taylor and Domina (2010), most broiler processors locate processing plants so that they have growers within 50–60 miles of the plant, suggesting that geographically a single integrator may have 100% of the local market. This assertion is supported by poultry growers who testified at the USDA-DOJ workshop on antitrust in the poultry industry (USDA-DOJ 2010) that once they entered a contract with a company, that was their only option, even if other integrators operated within their county.[9] Virtually all inputs used by

[8]McDonald and Korb (2006) showed that 30% of broiler growers reported no other operation near them.

[9]The Department of Justice has argued that such a "captive draw" area in grain should trigger antitrust concerns. In their suit opposing the acquisition of Continental Grain by Cargill, the Department of Justice argued that there were significant geographic areas where the two firms competed for grain products that would be reduced to a *captive draw* area if the acquisition was approved. See US v Cargill and Continental. US District Court for District of Columbia. Civil No. 1: 99CV01875.

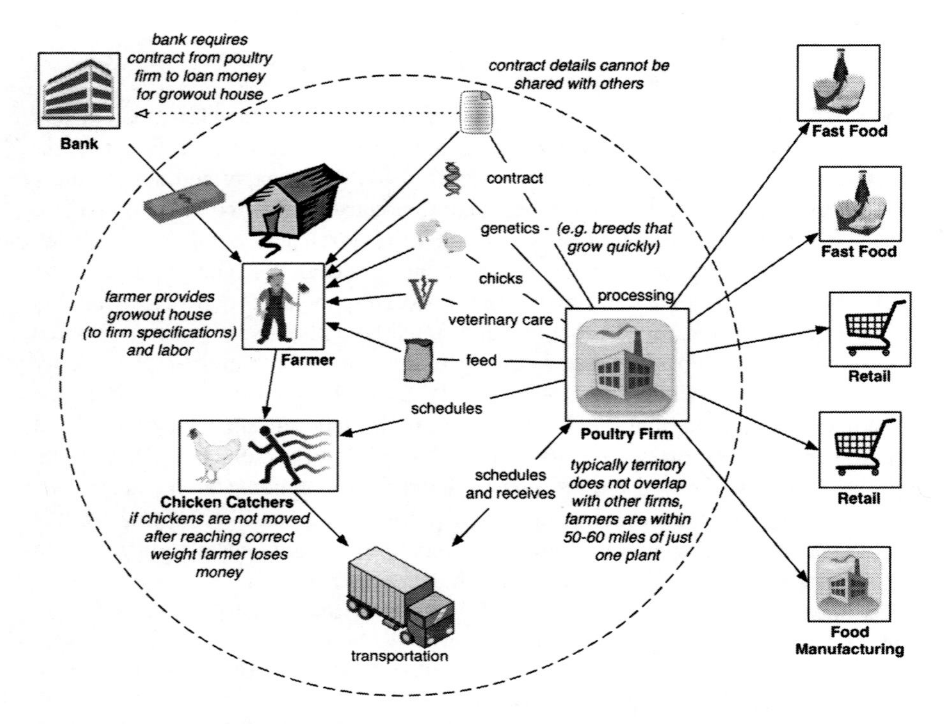

Fig. 6.2 Typical relations among broiler growers, integrators and other agents in broiler growing networks

growers in raising chicks come from the single integrator, thus compounding the dependency of the grower on the poultry firm because these multiple inputs are positive connections; farmers cannot grow chicks unless all inputs are provided. Moreover, because of the perishability of the product – the flock needs to move out as soon as possible after it reaches market weight or the grower begins losing money – and because the grower must rely on the poultry firm to catch and transport the chicks, the grower's dependency on the poultry firm is magnified. As is widely documented, the grower cannot select different genetics, feed, vet care, or when chicks arrive or depart from his/her facility (Taylor and Domina 2010; Constance et al. 2013), yet the grower's profitability is dependent upon these factors. The grower needs a cash-flow contract to arrange financing from a bank, but typically these contracts do not cover the entire investment period of the facility. Contracts can be 12 months or less in length (see MacDonald and Korb 2006) in contrast to 10 years or longer for terms of bank lending. In addition, the integrator can require upgrades and facility changes when negotiating a new contract, thus perpetuating the dependency between the grower and the lending institution. All of these factors suggest that there is a significant dependency disadvantage of growers relative to integrators.

An important question is why the grower wants to enter into this dependent relationship? Two possible answers to this question illustrate the extent of the differential dependencies growers face relative to poultry firms. First, the grower is most likely socially integrated into the community with family life and social ties embedding him/her into the community. We cannot account for these kind of relationships and the network connections they engender in the simple schema presented here. However, the concept of embeddedness, which is a common concern of network theorists, might be very important in this case. For example, Heffernan (1984) showed that the rural lifestyle – hunting, fishing, social activities, etc. – could be an important part of embedding the grower into the community and subjecting him or her to the limited economic activities available. Second, Taylor and Domina (2010) argue that the terms of the contract often change over time; the integrator offers better contracts at the beginning of contract poultry production, which enticed many growers into borrowing money to construct facilities, thus creating positive connections with integrators, who then change contracts mid-stream with the effect of increasing grower dependencies.

What is perhaps most interesting about the broiler case is that relative dependencies we document in these networks were apparent by the late 1950s, with the network structure changing relatively little since (see Constance et al. 2013; Breimyer 1965). However, between the 1960s and the early 1980s broiler contracts actually helped farmers in low-income farming areas improve the quality of their life as documented in North Georgia by Weinberg (2003) and in Union Parish, Louisiana, by Heffernan (1984).[10] Growers were able to get out of debt and build nice homes. Even though Breimyer (1965) reported limited dissatisfaction from growers in the early 1960s, there is now almost universal concern about broiler contracts, even from successful poultry growers (e.g. testimony at the May 2010 USDA-DOJ antitrust hearing in Alabama). Even though we agree with critiques of CR4 and HHI measures of concentration, it is important to note that the CR4 ratio stayed constant at 18% from 1964 to 1976 (Rogers 2002) and then started to increase to today's 53%. This may indicate that emerging grower dissatisfaction could result from the elimination of choice of integrators (e.g. the four integrators present in Union Parish, Louisiana in 1969 versus one today) even though the overall structure of the each network has stayed the same.

[10]Weinberg (2003) gives the example of a North Georgia family who were able to upgrade from a four room house with no indoor toilet to a seven room house with two baths after 20 years in the poultry business (1961–1982). "We all owe that to Gold Kist," [the farmer] said. "Chickens have been mighty good to this family." However, Heffernan (January 2012, personal conversation) says that farmers in Louisiana in his 1982 restudy were starting to show signs of distress but almost every survey participant would say 'go talk to so and so, you'll see what's happening' rather than openly reporting issues. Thus, he was unable to document this discontent for his study.

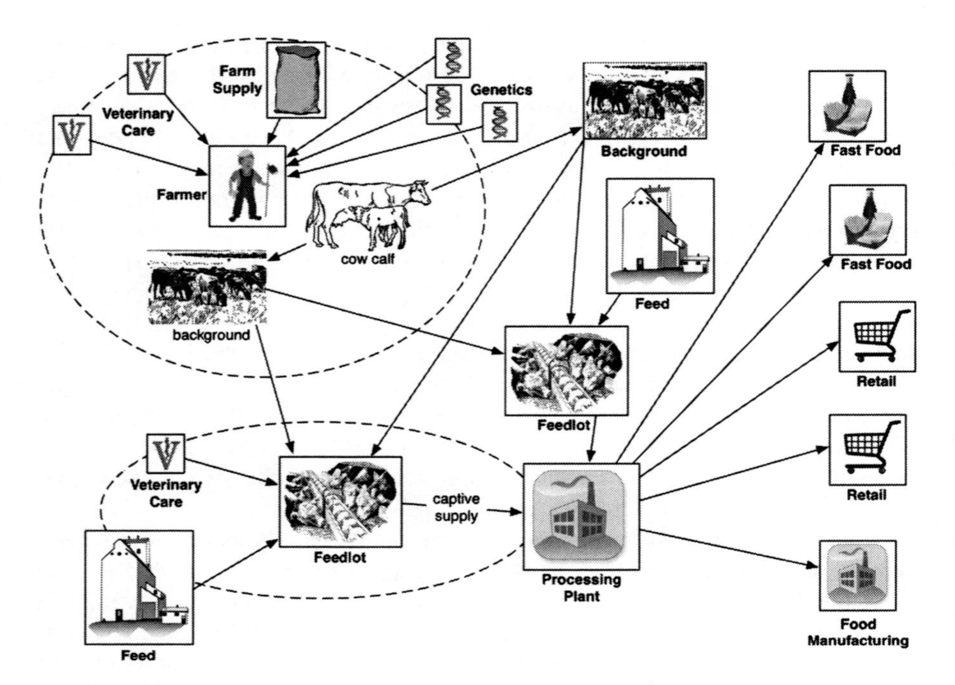

Fig. 6.3 Typical relations among cattle growers, feedlots and other agents in beef cattle networks

6.4.2 *Beef*

While the relative dependency of poultry growers is well-known and well-documented (Becker 2007; USDA-DOJ 2010), the networks in which beef producers operate show a different and more complicated mix of negative and positive network connections (see Fig. 6.3). In beef production, there are a large number of cow-calf operations in the US (758,000 farms had beef cows in 2007 according to the Census of Agriculture), which are dispersed across large geographical areas (MacDonald and McBride 2009; McBride 1997). Thus, a typical beef producer faces less consolidated markets for inputs than either the poultry growers of Fig. 6.2 or the grain operators discussed below, because the producer can choose how to maintain the health of his animals as well as what genetics to use and what to feed. In other words, even though beef producers require a number of positively connected inputs like chicken growers, there are multiple options along each network path, thus attenuating the potential for adverse differential dependency. Ownership of beef genetics, for instance, is much less concentrated than dairy, pigs or poultry genetics (Gura 2007). A cow-calf operator can choose to sell his calves as weanlings to a backgrounder operation or feed them longer before sending them on to a feedlot, which may or may not be located within the same geographic confine as the producer or backgrounder.

However, some feedlots are in a positively connected relationship with a specific beef processor either through outright ownership or a contracting supply relationship, while the independent feedlots negatively connected to processors face a significant amount of buyer power at the processing level where the CR4 is equal to 81%. While processors like Tyson, JBS and Cargill possess relatively significant buying power from the beef producer or independent feedlot's perspective, their selling power is perhaps less significant as one of their buyers, Wal-Mart, is America's largest grocer with an estimated quarter or possibly a third of the grocery market.[11] This disadvantage for them is increased by the fact that because there are a large number of cow-calf and feedlot operations from which they can source beef cattle, they can become quickly satiated with product – that is, it is relatively easy for them to obtain production inputs – and as noted in the discussion of Fig. 6.1, network actors locally satiated are at a dependency disadvantage relative to their trading partners.

The integrator relationship that exists in poultry and is expressed through production contracts is different, and to some extent less pronounced in the beef sector. For instance, in 2006/2007, roughly one-third of the production value in cattle was under contract versus nearly 90% for poultry and eggs (O'Donoghue et al. 2011), although this is changing. There is a great deal of concern in the beef industry about the use of "committed procurement methods" on the part of processing plants or packers, generally expressed through marketing agreements. These methods bypass openly negotiated markets, which tend to have negative connections and thus options for alternative trading alternatives. The use of these methods rose in the latter half of the last decade, and in at least one area, the Texas-Oklahoma regional market, "the proportion of the trade accounted for by the negotiated market ... declined 13 percentage points from mid-2008 to mid-2009" (GIPSA 2011, p. iv). That said, producer dependencies could increase if the use of production contracts in beef increases and if such packers begin specifying specific genetics, veterinary care and feed formulas, as is the case in broiler production.

Other changes also occurred in the structure of the beef industry between the late 1960s and today. The number of farms feeding out cattle declined by 40% between 1978 and 1992 (McBride 1997), with feeder cattle becoming concentrated in the Central and Southern Plains States by the early 1990s. According to McDonald and McBride (2009), today 262 feedlots could feed out 16,000 or more head at any one time, and such feedlots account for 60% of the fed-cattle marketings. Moreover, the beef industry essentially functions as a North American industry with Canadian producers involved in similar networks as US farmers (Adcock et al. 2006).[12]

[11]Today, the top 20 grocery stores have a combined 65% of the grocery market (Shelansky 2010), with estimates for Wal-Mart's share running from 23 (UFCW 2010) to 33% (Clifford 2011). Regardless, Mitchell (2011) and UFCW (2010, p. 5) note that Wal-Mart grew from 6% of grocery sales in 1998 to having larger grocery sales today than the "combined sales of its three closest competitors ...."

[12]It is also important to note that beef processing plants largely left unionized areas of the Midwest in the 1980s and 1990s after the introduction of boxed beef production created the opportunity for

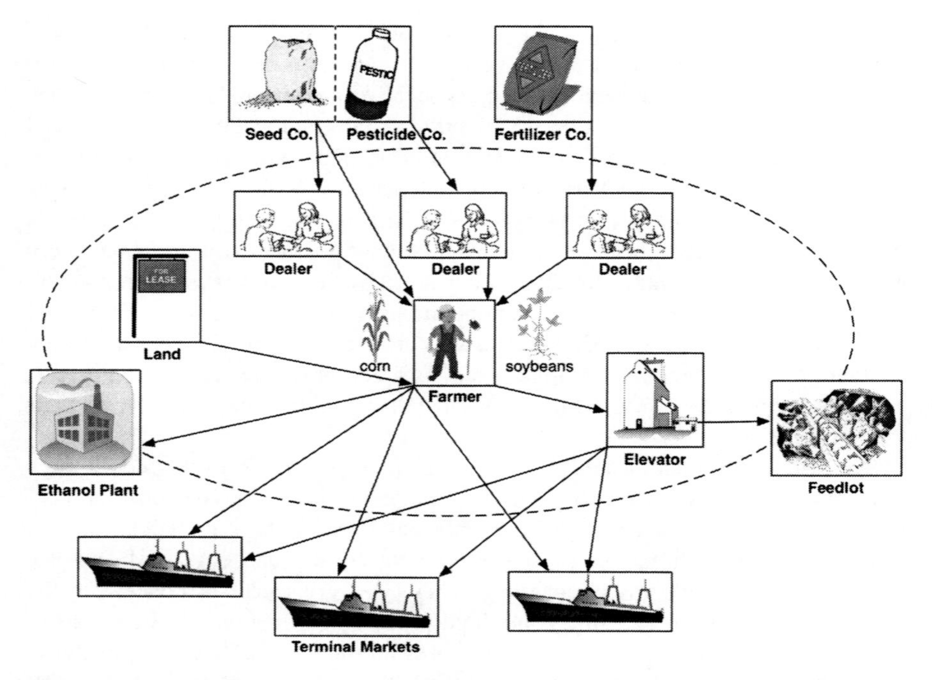

Fig. 6.4 Typical relations among farmers and other agents in corn and soybean commodity crop growing networks

6.4.3 Corn and Soybeans

The last situation we will discuss is based on a typical corn or soybean row-crop producer network from the Midwest or South of the US. As depicted in Fig. 6.4, the network relationships of corn and soybean growers are relatively less complex when compared with broiler and beef producers. Positionally, corn and soybean growers are more central within the network than broiler and beef producers, thus giving them the power advantage of centrality. However, like broiler and beef producers, the number of corn and soybean farmers relative to the number of input suppliers and buyer is large, thus increasing their degree of relative dependency.

The corn and soybean farmer requires a number of inputs, such as seeds, fertilizer, and other inputs, representing positive connections. In the case of seeds,

beef packers to build larger plants with faster processing speeds (and deskilled, less costly labor) in the Great Plains (Gouveia 1994; Stull et al. 1995). Thus, a system of relatively dispersed slaughter plants and farmer feeders changed to a more geographically concentrated industry accompanied by changes in the CR4 where 36% of steers and heifers were slaughtered by the top firms in 1980 compared to 81% in 2009 (GIPSA 2011).

for instance, the farmer has a number of options. The farmer can often source these among locally based seed dealers who are often neighbors or buy directly from seed companies. However, the dependency of positively connected relationships at this level is affected by the nature of the farm production methods chosen, as argued above in the previous section. It is most significant, other things being equal, when the decision to buy an herbicide-tolerant seed necessitates the accompanying purchase of herbicides owned by the same owner of the seed genetics (e.g. Round-up Ready soybeans or corn requires use of Round-up herbicide in order for farmers to benefit from the purchase of the GM seed). Moreover, there is greater seller power at the seed genetics level, with estimates that two firms, DuPont and Monsanto, controlled 70% of the US corn seed market and 59% of the soybean seed market in 2009 (Pollack 2010), and that the top four firms account for 53% of proprietary seed sales at the global level (ETC Group 2008).[13]

In addition, soybean and corn production is heavily reliant on fertilizer, especially in the form of nitrogen, phosphorus and potassium. Potash and phosphorous production has long been organized in cartels (Blas 2010; Etter 2008), where three cartels are thought to account for 70% of the global trade in these two fertilizers (Blas 2010).

When farmers wants to sell their corn or soybeans, they face concentrated buying power, although they have options, such as selling to local grain elevators or ethanol plants (although in the latter case farmers are often required to be members of cooperatives). Moreover, most grain elevators are dependent on moving grain to terminal elevators located on major waterways or ports that are often controlled by large grain traders like ADM, Bunge or Cargill. Buyer power is also represented by the fact that the top four soybeans processors control 85% of the market, while the top four wet corn millers account for 87% of the market. Ethanol, which in 2011 outpaced feed in terms of corn utilization, is also a consolidating market (Glenna and Cahoy 2009).

6.5 Ethics of Dependency

Ethical issues involve questions about what is right or wrong, good or bad, or acceptable and unacceptable, particularly with regard to how humans ought to act (see, for instance, Singer 1994). Ethical issues always arise when there is a conflict of interests and/or values. As differential dependencies emerge between network actors, their respective interests will increasingly conflict, thus creating ethical tensions. These tensions in turn raise a number of important ethical questions,

[13]For further discussion of the competitive nature of these markets see Moss (2010, 2011); Shi et al. (2008) and Hubbard (2009). For an animated representation of changes in the seed industry from the mid-1990s to present see Howard (2009).

including: Do differential dependencies create unfair advantages and disadvantages to actors in a network? Do the duties and obligations of actors in a network change when conditions create differential dependencies in their favor? Should network actors in these circumstances take into consideration how their use of the power, which differential dependencies give them, affects other actors in the network? What is the nature of the harm that actors experience when others in the network take advantage of differential dependencies in their favor? What does it mean to "take advantage of differential dependencies"?

A comprehensive discussion of these and other questions is beyond the scope of this chapter. Scholars have commented extensively on many of these themes, such as power, dependency, harm and fairness.[14] However, unlike parent–child, teacher-student, employer-employee, king-subject and similar relationships in which differential dependency is inherent to and thus expected in the relationship, and in which norms have developed governing these relationships, differential dependencies are not, or ought not to be, automatically expected or presumed in agrifood networks. When they arise they deserve a careful ethical consideration of their nature and implications, particularly with respect to the norms that govern and ought to govern interactions between actors within the networks. Our assessment of the broiler, beef and corn and soybean production networks presented above is that ethical concerns arising from differential dependency are strongest in the case of broiler production but guarded in beef and commodity crop production. Nonetheless, more work is needed to address ethical issues arising from network relationships in the specific case of the agrifood system, especially from the perspective of farmers and producers.

One potential direction is a consideration of how differential dependencies affect the ethical behavior of actors within the network. Ethical behavior, like economic behavior, is affected by the constraints that people face. Dependencies impose constraints on behavior. Hendrickson and James (2005) argue that constraints can increase the likelihood that agents will engage, or at least be tempted to engage, in behavior they consider unethical. When differential dependencies arise because of the characteristics of network relationships, there might be an increase in incentives for adversely affected actors to engage in or rationalize unethical conduct. For example, if farmers increasingly believe that they are at a disadvantage because of the dependencies they face in agrifood networks, then we might observe an upward trend in unethical behavior of farmers, which has support in research presented by James and Hendrickson (2008).

[14]It is not possible to provide a comprehensive list of contributors. However, we are reminded of Davis and Blomstrom's (1971, p. 95) Iron Law of Responsibility, which states that "in the long run, those who do not use power in a manner which society considers responsible will tend to lose it."

6.6 Conclusions

Our analysis demonstrates that farmers involved in different commodity networks face different issues – and thus different relative dependencies created by the distribution of positive and negative connections in the network. Within agrifood networks, buyer and seller dependencies are different, as argued forcefully by Carstensen (2008), Grundlach and Foer (2008) and Domina and Taylor (2009), especially because the entities who rank near the top in CR4 can experience significant dependency advantages on the buying end (e.g. beef packers with a CR4 of 82%) but when selling, the power resulting from differential dependencies is dissipated by the fact that other entities may possess significant buying power relative to them (e.g. Wal-Mart with somewhere between a quarter and one-third of the grocery market). More importantly, farmers experience buyer power and seller power differently in the three networks we examined, depending on how they are connected and the nature of the connections. For instance, row-crop producers tend to face seller power on the input side, and buyer power on the grain markets side, while for cow-calf producers the issue tends to be the buying power exerted on the feedlots with which they must deal.

We have also shown that dependencies can be created differently in the networks that we have examined. For instance, in the broiler arena the dependency disadvantage of parallel positive connections representing grower inputs are compounded by the fact that they usually are linked to a single input supplier that is also the only output buyer. This differential dependency is in turn compounded by the confines of geography and social embeddedness. Most likely, it is because poultry integrators do not operate in the same geography, and that farmers are searching for options that allow them to stay in place for family and lifestyle reasons, that they accept contractual obligations that create and expand relative dependency. Thus, we believe it is important to identify principles such as geographic constraints, embeddedness and the nature of contractual relations in particular commodities to understand more fully the farmers' relative position of dependency and power within an extended network structure.

What does this analysis mean for furthering our understanding of the competitive nature of the marketplace, the distribution of power within networks, and the relative power of the farmer in these networks? First, network exchange theories (NETs) can help bridge the gap between the focus on the structure of the marketplace (i.e. number of firms) and the conduct within that marketplace (i.e. exercise of market power, or the exertion of agency in the face of power) by highlighting the linkages that exist and what the impacts of those linkages are. By looking simply at the concentration ratio (whether CR4 or HHI) one emphasizes the disappearance of negative connections within the networks in specific commodities, but such an emphasis overlooks the effects of other connections within the network.

Second, NET can make a significant contribution to studies of agrifood concentration and the distribution of power within the agrifood system because it brings us straight back to a basic social reality – humans are social creatures who are dependent upon one another because we exist in networks of relationships. This reality is neither good nor bad, but NET theory and its focus on relative dependencies help us to explicate these basic relationships in new ways.

Third, if farmers are at a dependency disadvantage because of the structure of the negative and positive connections linking them to other parts of the agrifood network, is there anything that they can do to improve their situation? One of the reasons farmers and producers are at a dependency disadvantage is because there are so many of them, at least relative to other actors in the network. Both sellers to them, and buyers of their products, often face a significant number of negative network connections, thus providing substitutes if one farmer, for instance, chooses not to accept the terms offered by either seller or buyer. Could farmer organizations collectively bargain successfully on behalf of farmers? (It should be noted that past efforts like those of the National Farmers Organization have had mixed successes.) Academics like Levins (2002) have argued for the need to create countervailing power in certain networks that could ameliorate dependencies created through positive connections in the network.

While we do not have answers for these questions, we believe that exploring network exchange theory can help social scientists, legal experts and policymakers better understand the nature of the relationships that exist within the agrifood industry. Such an understanding can help society in fashioning remedies that improve the position of the farmer in these networks, if that is indeed a societal goal.

References

Adcock, F.J., D. Hudson, P. Rosson, H.M. Harris, and C.W. Herndon. 2006. The global competitiveness of the North American livestock industry. *Choices* 21(3): 171–176.

Allen, P. 2004. *Together at the table: Sustainability and sustenance in the American agrifood system*. University Park: The Pennsylvania State University Press.

Becker, G. 2007. *Livestock marketing and competition issues*. Washington, DC: Congressional Research Service Report for Congress, Order Code RL33325.

Blas, J. 2010. End looms for fertiliser cartels. *Financial Times*, August 19.

Bonanno, A., and D.H. Constance. 2008. *Stories of globalization: Transnational corporations, resistance, and the state*. University Park: The Pennsylvania State University Press.

Breimyer, H.F. 1965. *Individual freedom and the economic organization of agriculture*. Urbana: University of Illinois Press.

Breimyer, H.F., H.D. Guither, and W.B. Sundquist. 1973. *Who will control U.S. agriculture? A series of six leaflets*. University of Illinois College of Agriculture Special Publications, vol. 28. Urbana: University of Illinois Cooperative Extension Service.

Burch, D., and G. Lawrence. 2009. Towards a third food regime: Behind the transformation. *Agriculture and Human Values* 26(4): 267–279.

Carstensen, P.C. 2008. Buyer power, competition policy, and antitrust: The competitive effects of discrimination among suppliers. *Antitrust Bulletin* 53(20): 271–331.

Chen, Z. 2008. Defining buyer power. *Antitrust Bulletin* 53(2): 241–249.

Clifford, S. 2011. Groceries fill aisles at stores like CVS. *New York Times*, January 17, B1.

Constance, D.H., F. Martinez, G. Aboites, and A. Bonanno. 2013. The problems with poultry production and processing. In *The ethics and economics of agrifood competition*, ed. Harvey S. James Jr.. Dordrecht: Springer, 155–175.

Cook, K.S. 1987. Emerson's contributions to social exchange theory. In *Social exchange theory*, ed. K.S. Cook, 209–222. Newbury Park: Sage Publications.

Cook, K.S., and R.M. Emerson. 1978. Power, equity and commitment in exchange networks. *American Sociological Review* 43(5): 721–739.

Cook, K.S., R.M. Emerson, M.R. Gillmore, and T. Yamagishi. 1983. The distribution of power in exchange networks: Theory and experimental results. *The American Journal of Sociology* 89(2): 275–305.

Dahl, R.A. 1961. *Who governs? Democracy and power in an American city*. New Haven: Yale University Press.

Davis, K., and R.L. Blomstrom. 1971. *Business, society, and environment: Social power and social response*, 2nd ed. New York: McGraw-Hill.

Domina, D., and C.R. Taylor. 2009. *The debilitating effects of concentration in markets affecting agriculture*. Lincoln: Organization for Competitive Markets. http://farmfutures.com/mdfm/Faress1/author/2/OCM%20competition%20report.pdf. Accessed 11 July 2011.

Emerson, R.M. 1962. Power-dependence relations. *American Sociological Review* 27(1): 31–41.

ETC Group. 2008. Who owns nature? Corporate power and the final frontier in the commodification of life. http://www.etcgroup.org/sites/www.etcgroup.org/files/publication/707/01/etc_won_report_final_color.pdf. Accessed 29 Dec 2011.

Etter, L. 2008. Lofty prices for fertilizer put farmers in a squeeze. *Wall Street Journal*, May 27, A1.

Feedstuffs. 2010. Feed marketing and distribution. *Feedstuffs Reference Issue*, September 15, 3–14.

Foer, A. 2010. Agriculture and antitrust enforcement issues in our 21st century economy. In *Proceedings of the December 8, 2010, workshop*, 219–252. Washington, DC: US Department of Agriculture and Department of Justice. http://www.justice.gov/atr/public/workshops/ag2010/dc-agworkshop-transcript.pdf. Accessed 11 July 2011.

Foucault, M. 1980. *Power/Knowledge: Selected interviews and other writings 1972–1977*. Trans. Colin Gordon. Brighton: Harvester Press.

Freeman, L.C. 1979. Centrality in social networks: Conceptual clarification. *Social Networks* 1: 215–239.

Friedland, W.H. 1984. Commodity systems analysis: An approach to the sociology of agriculture. *Research in Rural Sociology and Development* 1: 221–235.

Friedland, W.H. 1994. The global fresh fruit and vegetable system: an industrial organization analysis. In *The global restructuring of agro-food systems*, ed. Philip McMichael, 173–189. Ithaca: Cornell University Press.

Friedland, W., A. Barton, and R. Thomas. 1981. *Manufacturing green gold: Capital, labor, and technology in the lettuce industry*. New York: Cambridge University Press.

Friedmann, H., and P. McMichael. 1989. Agriculture and the state system. *Sociologia Ruralis* 29(2): 93–117.

Giddens, A. 1984. *The constitution of society: An outline of the theory of structuration*. Cambridge: Polity Press.

Glenna, L., and D.R. Cahoy. 2009. Agribusiness concentration, intellectual property, and the prospects for rural economic benefits from the emerging biofuel economy. *Southern Rural Sociology* 24(2): 111–129.

Goodman, D., and E.M. DuPuis. 2002. Knowing food and growing food: Beyond the production-consumption debate in the sociology of agriculture. *Sociologia Ruralis* 42(1): 5–22.

Gouveia, L. 1994. Global strategies and local linkages; The case of the U.S. meatpacking industry. In *From Columbus to ConAgra: The globalization of agriculture and food,* eds. A. Bonanno, L. Busch, W.H. Friedland, L. Gouveia, and E. Mingione, 125–148. Lawrence: University of Press of Kansas.

Grain Inspection Packers and Stockyards Administration (GIPSA). 2011. *2010 Annual report of the packers & stockyards program*. Washington, DC: USDA Grain Inspection Packers and Stockyards Administration.

Granovetter, M. 1985. Economic action and social structure: The problem of embeddedness. *The American Journal of Sociology* 91(3): 481–510.

Grundlach, G., and A. Foer. 2008. Buyer power in antitrust: An overview of the American Antitrust Institute's invitational symposium on buyer power. *The Antitrust Bulletin* 53(2): 233–240.

Gura, S. 2007. *Livestock genetics companies: Concentration and proprietary strategies of an emerging power in the global food economy.* Ober-Ramstadt: League for Pastoral Peoples and Endogenous Livestock Development. http://www.psas-web.net/documents/Info/livestock_gen_gura.pdf. Accessed 29 Dec 2011.

Hanneman, R.A., and M. Riddle. 2005. *Introduction to social network methods*. Riverside: University of California.

Heffernan, W.D. 1972. Sociological dimensions of poultry production in the United States. *Sociologia Ruralis* 12(3/4): 481–499.

Heffernan, W.D. 1984. Constraints in the U.S. poultry industry. *Research in Rural Sociology and Development*, vol. 1, 237–260. Greenwich: JAI Press Inc.

Hendrickson, M.K., and H.S. James Jr. 2005. The ethics of constrained choice: How the industrialization of agriculture impacts farming and farmer behavior. *Journal of Agricultural and Environmental Ethics* 18(3): 269–291.

Hendrickson, M.K., W.W.D. Heffernan, D. Lind, and E. Barham. 2008. Contractual integration in agriculture: Is there a bright side for agriculture of the middle? In *Food and the mid-level farm*, ed. T.A. Lyson, G.W. Stevenson, and R. Welsh, 79–100. Cambridge, MA: The MIT Press.

Howard, P.H. 2009. Visualizing consolidation in the global seed industry: 1996–2008. *Sustainability* 1(4): 1266–1287.

Hubbard, K. 2009. *Out of hand: Farmers face the consequences of a consolidated seed industry.* Washington, DC: National Family Farm Coalition.

James Jr., H.S., and M.K. Hendrickson. 2008. Perceived economic pressures and farmer ethics. *Agricultural Economics* 38(3): 349–361.

Kuhn, A. 1964. Bargaining power in transactions: A basic model of interpersonal relationships. *American Journal of Economics and Sociology* 23(1): 49.

Levins, R. 2002. Collective bargaining for farmers. *Choices* 4th Quarter, 15–18.

Lukes, S. 1974. *Power: A radical view*. London: Macmillan.

Lynn, B. 2006. Breaking the chain: The antitrust case against Wal-Mart. *Harper's Magazine* 313(1874): 29–36.

Lynn, B. 2009. *Cornered: The monopoly capitalism and the politics of destruction*. Hoboken: Wiley.

MacDonald, J., and P. Korb. 2006. *Agricultural contracting update: Contracts in 2003*. Economic Research Service Electronic Information Bulletin EIB-9. Washington, DC: US Department of Agriculture, Economic Research Service.

MacDonald, J., and W. McBride. 2009. *The transformation of U.S. livestock agriculture: Scale, efficiency, and risks*. Economic Research Service Electronic Information Bulletin EIB-43. Washington, DC: US Department of Agriculture, Economic Research Service.

Markovsky, B., D. Willer, and T. Patton. 1988. Power relations in exchange networks. *American Sociological Review* 53(2): 220–236.

Marsden, P.V. 1987. Elements of interactor dependence. In *Social exchange theory*, ed. K.S. Cook, 130–148. Newbury Park: Sage Publications.

McBride, W.D. 1997. *Change in U.S. livestock production, 1969–92*. Economic Research Service Agricultural Economic Report No. AER754. Washington, DC: US Department of Agriculture, Economic Research Service.

McMichael, P. 2000. The power of food. *Agriculture and Human Values* 17: 21–33.

McMichael, P. 2009. A food regime analysis of the 'world food crisis. *Agriculture and Human Values* 26: 281–295.

Miele, M., and J. Murdoch. 2002. The aestheticisation of food: Taste, time and typicality. *Sociologia Ruralis* 42(4): 312–328.

Mitchell, S. 2011. Eaters beware: Wal-Mart is taking over our food system. *Grist*, 30 December. http://www.grist.org/food/2011-12-30-eaters-beware-walmart-is-taking-over-our-food-system. Accessed 13 Jan 2012.

Molm, L.D. 1987. Linking power structure and power use. In *Social exchange theory*, ed. K.S. Cook, 101–129. Newbury Park: Sage Publications.

Moran, M., and D. Chanil. 2010. Super 50: Steadfast leaders. *Progressive Grocer*, May. http://www.progressivegrocer.com/inprint/article/id664/super-50-steadfast-leaders/. Accessed 13 Jan 2012.

Moss, D. 2010. Transgenic seed: The high technology test of antitrust? *CPI Antitrust Journal* 2: 1–7.

Moss, D. 2011. Competition and transgenic seed systems. *Antitrust Bulletin* 56(1): 81–103.

O'Connor, J. 1973. *The fiscal crisis of the state*. New York: St. Martin's Press.

O'Donoghue, E.J., R.A. Hoppe, D.E. Banker, R. Ebel, K. Fuglie, P. Korb, M. Livingston, C. Nickerson, and C. Sandretto. 2011. *The changing organization of U.S. farming*. Economic Research Service Electronic Information Bulletin EIB-88. Washington, DC: US Department of Agriculture, Economic Research Service.

Oleinik, A. 2011. Market as a weapon: Domination by virtue of a constellation of interests. *Forum for Social Economics* 40(2): 157–177.

Pollack, A. 2010. After growth, fortunes turn for Monsanto. New York Times, October 4. http://www.nytimes.com/2010/10/05/business/05monsanto.html?_r=0. Accessed 1 May 2012.

Rich, R. 2008. Fecal free. Biology and authority in industrialized Midwestern pork production. *Agriculture and Human Values* 25(1): 79–93.

Rogers, R.T. 2002. Broilers: Differentiating a commodity. In *Industry studies*, 3rd edn, ed. L.L. Duetsch, 59–95. New York: M.E. Sharpe, Inc.

Shelansky, H. 2010. Agriculture and antitrust enforcement issues in our 21st century economy. In *Proceedings of the December 8, 2010, workshop*, 182–252. Washington, DC: US Department of Agriculture and Department of Justice.

Shi, G., J-P. Chavas, and K. Stiegert. 2008. An analysis of bundle pricing: The case of the corn seed market, Working Paper Series FSWP2008-01. Madison: University of Wisconsin-Madison, Food System Research Group.

Shiva, V. 1991. The green revolution in the Punjab. *The Ecologist* 21(2): 57–60.

Singer, P. 1994. Introduction. In *Ethics*, ed. P. Singer, 3–13. Oxford: Oxford University Press.

Stull, D., M. Broadway, and D. Griffith (eds.). 1995. *Any way you cut it: Meat processing and small town America*. Lawrence: University of Press of Kansas.

Successful Farming. 2010. U.S. Pork powerhouses 2010, November. http://www.agriculture.com/uploads/assets/promo/external/siteimages/powerhouses2010.pdf. Accessed 13 Jan 2012.

Taylor, C.R., and D. Domina. 2010. Restoring economic health to contract poultry production. Report prepared for the Joint U.S. Department of Justice and U.S. Department of Agriculture/GIPSA Public Workshop on Competition Issues in the Poultry Industry, Normal, 21 May 2010.

Thornton, G. 2010. Shake-up at the top, growth in the ranks. *Watt Poultry USA*, February, 14–22.

UFCW. 2010. *Ending Walmart's rural stranglehold*. Washington, DC: UFCW.

US Census Bureau. 2011. Economic census. Sector 31: Manufacturing: subject series: Concentration ratios: Share of value added accounted for by the 4, 8, 20, and 50 Largest Companies for Industries: 2007. Washington, DC: US Census Bureau.

US Department of Agriculture/Department of Justice (USDA-DOJ). 2010. *Agriculture and antitrust enforcement issues in our 21st century economy*. Washington, DC: US Department of Agriculture & US Department of Justice. http://www.justice.gov/atr/public/workshops/ag2010/index.html. Accessed 1 Dec 2011.

Weber, Max. 1978. *Economy and society*. Berkeley: University of California Press.

Weinberg, C. 2003. Big Dixie chicken goes global: Exports and the rise of the North Georgia poultry industry. *Business and Economic History On-line* 1: 1–32.

Wilkinson, J. 2006. Network theories and political economy: From attrition to convergence? *Research in Rural Sociology and Development* 12: 11–38.

Wise, T.A., and S.E. Trist. 2010. Buyer power in U.S. hog markets: A critical review of the literature. Global Development and Environment Institute Working Paper No. 10-04, Tufts University, Medford.

Yamagishi, T., M.R. Gillmore, and K.S. Cook. 1988. Network connections and the distribution of power in exchange networks. *The American Journal of Sociology* 93(4): 833–851.

Zheng, X., and T. Vulkina. 2009. Do alternative marketing arrangements increase pork packers' market power? *American Journal of Agricultural Economics* 91(1): 250–263.

Chapter 7
Reaping and Sowing for a Sustainable Future: The Import of Roman Catholic Social Teaching for Agrifood Competition

Patrick Flanagan

Abstract Roman Catholic social teaching is a comprehensive normative social theory from which principles and directives for agriculture and, in turn, agrifood competition can be drawn. This chapter offers an overview of the rich cache of Roman Catholic social teaching specific to agriculture and argues that such a moral theology tradition can supply new insights for the neglected area of agrifood competition. Particular texts from the Church's social teaching – rooted in Judeo-Christian scripture and 2,000 years of tradition – are presented as motivations to pay attention to possibly overlooked concerns and identifying viable action steps not considered by others in this tenuous area. Finally, a conceptual framework for thinking about agriculture and agrifood competition, based on the Church's social teaching, is presented for consideration.

7.1 Introduction

In 2009, the world's most powerful leaders assembled for the annual G8 summit in the earthquake ridden Italian city of L'Aquila. In their discussion of pressing economic issues, they admitted the horrible gravity of global hunger, which they concluded was a grave consequence of the world's fiscal reality. Their subsequent conversation sought to understand more acutely the etiology of such an overwhelming and dehumanizing reality. They laid blame for the global hunger situation on "insufficient investment in farming over the past few decades" exacerbated more acutely by the economic crisis. Additionally, the leaders of the world's strongest economies noted that "food security is closely connected with economic growth

P. Flanagan, Ph.D. (✉)
Department of Theology & Religious Studies, St. John's University, 8000 Utopia Parkway, NY 11439 Jamaica, USA
e-mail: flanagap@stjohns.edu

H.S. James Jr. (ed.), *The Ethics and Economics of Agrifood Competition*, The International Library of Environmental, Agricultural and Food Ethics 20,
DOI 10.1007/978-94-007-6274-9_7,

and social progress as well as with political stability." In response, the G8 leaders announced the "L'Aquila Food Security Initiative" to counter "the tendency of decreasing official development aid and national financing to agriculture." These costly "initiatives for food security and aid" marked a poignant shift from sporadic emergency food aid to sustainable long-term investments in farming, particularly in the developing world. This new evenhanded approach acknowledged "the combined effect of longstanding underinvestment in agriculture and food security, price trends and the economic crisis [that] have led to increased hunger" (Hooper 2009).

In one of his weekly broadcasts right on the heels of the G8 summit, Pope Benedict XVI made similar observations and acknowledged that "there are inequalities in the world that can no longer be tolerated which demand a coordinated strategy, in addition to necessary immediate interventions, in the search for lasting global solutions" (Benedict 2009a). Benedict XVI remarked that the Roman Catholic Church, hereafter cited as "the Church," "has no technical solutions to propose but, as an expert in humanity, offers to all the teaching of Sacred Scripture on the truth about mankind [sic], and proclaims the gospel of love and justice." In his remarks, Benedict XVI's expressed the hope that the range of concerns the G8 accounted for in their plans would be expansive enough not to exclude any pressing global situation. At the same time, to ensure this, Benedict proposed the wisdom and insight that the Church had to offer sought to supplement the G8's leadership agenda.

Benedict XVI's actions are not isolated from his predecessors. He joins a long line of popes who have examined critical societal issues through the lens of the rich cache of Church's social teaching. This chapter focuses on the Church's social teaching specific to agriculture. The Church's theological tradition can supply new insights into agriculture and, in turn, for the neglected area of agrifood competition. To accomplish this, the chapter will first offer an overview of this rich canon of instruction in social justice the Church values. While some might quickly dismiss the Church's social teaching as too parochial or personal, this chapter will demonstrate its import for the broader global community even though, admittedly, it stems from a specific theological context. The chapter will then identify and explain specific selections from the Church's social teaching that are relevant to agriculture and the issue of agrifood competition. These particular choices from the Church social teaching provide motivation for paying attention to possibly overlooked concerns and for identifying viable action steps not considered by others in this tenuous area. Finally, this chapter will present a conceptual framework for thinking about agriculture and agrifood competition, based on the Church's social teaching.

7.2 Roman Catholic Social Teaching

Roman Catholic Social Teaching, hereafter cited as "RCST," is a comprehensive, systematic, and normative social theory from which principles and directives for a more just social, economic, and political global community can be drawn. RCST's foundation is built upon a living tradition or, as John Paul II taught in his 1999 apostolic exhortation *Ecclesia in America (para. 55)*, "rests upon the threefold cornerstones of human dignity, solidarity, and subsidiarity" (John Paul II 1999). RCST is firmly rooted in Judeo-Christian scriptures. RCST is founded upon the central understanding, gleaned from Judeo-Christian scripture, that the human person is an "imago Dei." Made in the image of God, as the book of Genesis records, the human person is not an isolated entity, but created in and for community. God has given humanity dominion over all creation charging humanity with the obligation to be faithful stewards of their resources. Correlatively, situated within the context of a community, the human person has a social responsibility towards others, particularly those who suffer poverty and are victims of injustice. Correlatively, the 1997 *Catechism of the Catholic Church* teaches that RCST is an integral part of the Church (Catechism of the Catholic Church 1997). The Church's social mission is not an adjunct one or extracurricular, but part and parcel of what the Church believes it is.

RCST concerns itself more with ethics than morality. It offers guiding principles and proposes a moral framework for life in common. Legitimate differences may ensue then as to how these principles shape reality. Some might see only similarity between the two academic venues, but for the purposes of understanding RCST more precisely, a distinction is helpful. Consider the other like combination of the "Internet" and the "World Wide Web." Upon closer examination, the difference becomes clear. The Internet is that which undergirds the World Wide Web; the Web relies on the Internet's protocols for its operations. In a comparative vein, morality is built upon ethics. What appears on a Web page or in reality, the moral life, is informed, supported, and validated by the Internet or ethics. Realistically, there is an ongoing dynamic conversation that occurs between these two and as time proceeds morality can, in fact, transform one's ethics.

The canon of RCST consists of letters and documents promulgated by the teaching authorities of the Church with some, like those written by a pope or disseminated from a worldwide council, having more weight. The following papal letters are those generally included in the library of RCST: *Rerum Novarum* (1891); *Quadragesimo Anno* (1931); *Mater et Magistra* (1961); *Pacem in Terris* (1963); *Populorum Progressio* (1967); *Octagesima Adveniens* (1971); *Laborem Exercens* (1981); *Solliciudo Rei Socialis* (1987); *Centesimus Annus* (1991); and *Caritas in Veritate* (2009). This catalog of social justice documents and their dating reveals two important aspects of the Church. First, in every age, the Church has sought to be true to its mission, which its bishops of the world made clear in their document *Justice in the World*: "Action on behalf of justice and participation in the transformation of the world fully appear to us as a constitutive dimension of the preaching of the gospel, or, in other words, of the Church's mission for the redemption of the human race and its liberation from every oppressive situation" (World Synod of Bishops 1971). Second, as it notes in its 1965 pastoral constitution on the church in the modern world, *Gaudium et spes*, the Church has sought consistently to examine closely the "signs of the times" through its lens of sacred scripture and tradition and offer a meaningful response to timely concerns (Vatican Council II 1965).

Modern RCST was initiated with Pope Leo XIII's publishing of *Rerum Novarum*, often referenced as the *magna carta* of letters, for it set in motion an organic tradition of scholarship that critiques the political socio-economic status quo and presses civil society, particularly its leadership, to work for the transformation of unjust structures. RCST did exist prior to Leo XIII, of course. The organic tradition of RCST was initiated in the Judeo-Christian scriptures and continued in the writings of theologians throughout the history of the Church. Since the dawn of modern era, documents and letters from popes, bishops, and groups of them generally have been the method RCST has been communicated. Michael Schuck (1991) provides the most comprehensive review of the papal texts of the pre-Leonine heritage, those immediate to the ones considered in this chapter.

Popes writing in the area of RCST after Leo XIII built upon Leo's initial critique particularly with respect to labor, capital, politics, and philosophical ideas. These successive popes often published their texts in anniversary years using Leo XIII's seminal papal letter as a benchmark. In doing so, they sought to update RCST in light of the particular challenges their era face whether they be advances in industrialization, movements in modernization, technological progress, global expansion, or similar.

The major themes of RCST reflect the Church's ethics. They tease out more of the aforementioned logic. They are: the life and dignity of the human person; call to family; community; participation; rights and responsibilities; an option for the poor and vulnerable; the dignity of work and the rights of workers; the virtue of solidarity; and, care for God's creation. This list is taken from Sharing Catholic social teaching: challenges and directions approved by the United States Conference of Catholic Bishops' (1998). There are others that try to attend to themes that need fuller expression. For instance, Thomas Massaro (2008) proposes a list of nine key themes: the dignity of the every person and human rights; solidarity, the common good, and participation; family life; subsidiarity and the proper role of government; rights and responsibilities; the dignity of work, the rights of workers, and support for labor unions; colonialism and economic development; peace and disarmament; and, option for the poor and vulnerable. William Byron's (1999) list consists of the principles of human dignity; respect for human life; association; participation; preferential protection for the poor and vulnerable; solidarity; stewardship; subsidiarity; human equality; and, the common good. Whatever themes are employed, they can serve as a critical evaluative lens to assess some pressing concerns like the agricultural system and, in turn, propose criteria for agricultural policy and advocacy.

7.3 Agrifood Competition in Roman Catholic Social Teaching

While the previous part offered an overview of what RCST is, the following section delves more deeply into specific letters from the canon of RCST as well as related complementary insights from other Church documents in order to illustrate the Church's teaching on agriculture and subsequent regard for agrifood competition.

7.3.1 Rerum Novarum (1891)

When Leo XIII wrote *Rerum Novarum* (*Of New Things* or *On Capitol and Labor*)[1] in 1891, he was addressing a vastly changed landscape than his papal predecessors. The revolutions in Europe were concluded, but their aftereffects were still confounding cultures and economies. African and Asian countries continued to be dominated by European imperialist leaders while America wielded powerful control in Latin America. Karl Marx and Friedrich Engels had issued *The Communist Manifesto* further pressing the import of an atheistic socialism.

More specific to this chapter, the Industrial Revolution was in full force. Workers began to organize into unions, and strikes increasingly were polarizing. Urbanization, commercialization, and industrialization had taken firm root. The agricultural way of life seemed to have lost its attraction as people moved from their villages and farms to the cities in pursuit of work. A capitalist economy was in full force. While *Rerum Novarum* focused its energy on the rights and duties of capital and labor and concomitant responsibilities of the State in a new economy, Leo XIII did acknowledge agricultural concerns.

In speaking about the dignity of humankind, Leo XIII notes that humanity has needs and that the "fruits of the earth" offer humankind "provision for the future" giving "fresh supplies" for needs that "forever recur." Humanity's pursuit of these fruits does not need to involve the State, "for Man precedes the State" and the "right of providing for the substance of his body." Where humanity seeks to cultivate the soil may be, in fact, one's own private property by virtue of ownership, "fixed by man's own industry and by the laws of individual races." This concern for private property initiated by Leo XIII's discussion in this letter will continue to occupy all subsequent RCST discussions. Even though there may be private ownership, the benefits reaped from the private land redound to all:

> Those who do not possess the soil contribute their labor; hence, it may truly be said that all human subsistence is derived either from labor on one's own land, or from some toil, some calling, which is paid for either in the produce of the land itself, or in that which is exchanged for what the land brings forth (para. 8).

Leo XIII emphasizes that private property is "accordance with the law of nature" and no one should violate that right. The fruits of the soil yield a plentiful harvest for preserving and extending human life. Clearly, this line of thought was contrary to the increasingly popular tenets of socialism that preferred common property over that which is "equitably divided."

Private ownership renders three "excellent results." The first, as noted above, is that there is a clear division of property. Admittedly, Leo XIII recognized, this

---

[1]Papal social encyclicals take their name from the first two Latin words of the document. The Latin translation is the RCC's official one. This as well as other translations can be found on the Vatican website (http://www.vatican.va). The title is often accompanied by a literal translation and a more popular one that captures the meaning of the document. All three will be identified in this chapter for each papal encyclical discussed.

may result in an even wider chasm between the wealthy and powerful and "needy and powerless multitude." However, the acquisition of private property may prompt the latter class to work harder to procure their own. Second, Leo XIII indicates, with private property there will be a greater harvest. Owners are ever more intent in their care and concern for that which is theirs personally. "Men always work harder and more readily when they work on that which belongs to them; nay, they learn to love the very soil that yields in response to the labor of their hands, not only food to eat, but an abundance of good things for themselves and those that are dear to them." The final positive outcome would be an increased commitment to one's own native land. There would not, the pope observes, this ambition to emigrate to some place "better" if that which is sustainable is found in one's own country. All these "excellent results" should enjoy the State's support and not be subjected to "exhaustive taxation" which clearly could yield, in fact, very detrimental results.

7.3.2 *Quadragesimo Anno (1931)*

Pius XI's 1931 *Quadragesimo Anno*, also known as *The Fortieth Year* or *Reconstruction of the Social Order*, like Leo XIII's and subsequent RCST texts, was a response to the then contemporary milieu.[2] Forty years had passed since Leo XIII initiated modern RCST and the intervening years had been more than troubling. Politically, revolutions in Europe, South America, and Asia toppled established governments. The names of Lenin and Hitler became hopes for the masses only eventually to evolve into unrelenting despots. World War I, "the Great War," ensued during this interregnum followed by the "Great Depression" which toppled long-standing financial industries. This depression or "the Crash" led to increased destitution, staggering rates of unemployment, and surging demands for labor justice. The world went from the materialism, captured well by the image of the "roaring 1920s," to depression in just a decade.

Like Leo XIII, Pius XI continued to tackle the "social question" of labor and capital that would occupy all of modern RCST. In Pius XI's text there is passing reference to farmers forming beneficent and charitable associations and organizations that under the guise of the Church and its priests to mutually assist and support one another. The associations, or unions, that Leo XIII encouraged, had proved to be most helpful in leading workers, "among farmers and others of the

---

[2]In the chronology of popes, Benedict XV (1914–1922) followed Leo XIII and Pius XII (1939–1958) followed Pius XI. Benedict XV's papacy was in the midst of the World War I and its subsequent share of difficulties. He did not promulgate any letters, although his sermons and addresses did address the promise and practice of peace. None, however, were admitted formally into the canon of RCST. While assuredly attentive to RCST, Pius XII's letter concerns centered on challenges of a quickly evolving society not the least included sexual, authority, and family concerns. Additionally, Pius XII in his writings contended with advancements in the scientific community,

middle class," to spiritual and economic flourishing. These associations particularly assisted "non-owning workers" that could advance themselves "through industry and thrift advance to the state of possessing some little property" of their own.

These associations seek to assist the "non-owning" class in their efforts to be "paid a wage sufficient to support him and his family." The pope has in mind a decent enough "just salary" so that women and children do not have to be relied upon as they are "in the families of farmers" which he considers "grossly wrong." For Pius XI, his appreciation of work is a highly charged masculine environment. Wives and mothers' responsibilities, Pius XI contends, lie with the home, in particular, the family. Children have their youth to enjoy and grow. The pontiff terms it "an intolerable abuse" that should "be abolished at all cost" if a wife and mother has to work to supplement the husband and father's income. "Social justice" demands adjustment in places where such exists.

Pius XI suggests further that there should not be any wide disparity between wages and salaries. When it comes to wages and salaries, Pius XI argues that they should be in "right proportion" to the prices of goods sold. Particular to this chapter, Pius XI teaches that agriculture and manufacturing are two main concerns that must be "properly maintained." When this balance is achieved "the various occupations will combine and coalesce into, as it was, a single body and like members of the body mutually aid and complete one another." If this is realized, a just "social economy" would offer all economic players an opportunity to flourish. Much work needs to be done, particularly in the field of agriculture "wherein the greater portion of mankind honorably procures its livelihood ... is being crushed with hardships and with difficulties."

7.3.3 Excursus: César Chávez

César Chávez (1927–1993) serves as an example of someone who built his life's work upon RCST. After suffering miserable losses from the Great Depression, his family and he migrated from his birthplace of Yuma, Arizona to San Jose, California for work as migrant workers. While a short stint in the Navy offered his family and him some financial solace, it was only temporary, forcing them back to migrant farming now to support his own family of eight children. Donald McDonnell, an Irish-American Catholic priest, befriended Chávez and introduced him to the wisdom of the Catholic Church's social encyclicals, at least those available in the late 1950s, namely those of Leo XIII and Pius XI discussed in the previous sections. Chávez was so taken by the challenging and insightful texts that he organized the Farm Workers Association in 1962 to protect migrant workers from unjust treatment by grape growers in central California. This organization served as a rich resource for farmworkers' economic need including wage negotiation, housing conditions, and working environment issues.

Buoyed by his foundational Catholic beliefs in the God-given dignity of every person and the sacredness of pilgrimage, Chávez organized a strike against replacement workers, more commonly referred to as "scabs," used to quickly replace any agricultural workers that refused to work because of what the workers considered unjust conditions. First, Chávez encouraged a national boycott of purchasing grapes. Second, Chávez organized his "Plan for Delano," a journey from the center of grape region to the Sacramento, the state capitol, to publicize farmworkers' rights struggle. In seeking support for his efforts from his Catholic Church, he was initially met with hesitancy, which eventually developed into activity participation in negotiation efforts and the establishment of the Bishops' Ad Hoc Committee on Farm Labor in 1969. Although Chávez' work had its fits and stops, particularly with the United States Catholic bishops' initially reserved support and the Teamsters Union's attempt to usurp control over the union, Chávez' efforts to ensure economic justice for Farmworkers succeeded. In fact, the Catholic bishops' initial hesitancy to active participation in negotiation efforts.

7.3.4 Mater et Magistra (1961)

In a very precarious and volatile era in human history, Pope John XXIII publishes *Mater et Magistra*, literally *Mother and Teacher*, and more commonly titled *Christianity and Social Progress*, in 1961. A second world war had been fought destroying lives, leveling nations, extinguishing cultures, and depleting treasuries. Hitler has risen and fallen. So had the atomic bomb. John XXIII faced a global community that was increasingly jettisoning long-held moral traditions and challenging established authority. There were signs of hope though. The United Nations (UN) had been established and, in one of its first acts, issued a declaration on human rights. Individual nations declared their independence from their foreign colonizers. Space exploration had begun.

In the midst of profound disparity, John XXIII examined "new aspects of the social question" in *Mater et Magistra*. In this letter, John XXIII offers the most comprehensive treatment of farming to date. He acknowledged its rich interconnectedness with so much of life:

> It brings into its service many branches of engineering, chemistry and biology, and is itself a cause of the continued practical development of these sciences in view of the repercussions of scientific and technical progress on the business of farming. It is a work which demands a capacity for orientation and adaptation, patient waiting, a sense of responsibility, and a spirit of perseverance and enterprise (para 145).

Further, farming for the Christian is tied up with one's vocation:

> In the work on the farm the human personality finds every incentive for self-expression, self-development and spiritual growth. It is a work, therefore, which should be thought of as a vocation, a God-given mission, an answer to God's call to actuate His providential, saving plan in history. It should be thought of, finally, as a noble task, undertaken with a view to raising oneself and others to a higher degree of civilization (para 149).

Despite the loftiness of farming, the pope contended that there is a "depressed state of agriculture." His remarks that follow about this reality were couched in a concern that the just "social economy" Pius XI had encouraged had not taken root. Justice and equity were lacking in the dynamic system of economic relationships – amongst workers, managers, owners, political parties, countries, and industry itself.

The exodus from the farms to the cities throughout the world that began with the Industrial Revolution has continued, the pope observed, leading to an acutely low number of people involved with agriculture. The cities, he continues, offer greater prospects of financial growth, entertainment, and freedom that the "confining surroundings" of the farm "offer little." While there may be many underlying reasons, one main one is that farming "has become a depressed occupation. It is inadequate both in productive efficiency and in the standard of living in provides."

The pontiff recognizes that this reality poses a fundamental problem across the globe:

> What can be done to reduce the disproportion in productive efficiency between agriculture on the one hand, and industry and services on the other; and to ensure that agricultural living standards approximate as closely as possible those enjoyed by city dwellers who draw their resources either from industry or from the services in which they are engaged? What can be done to persuade agricultural workers that, far from being inferior to other people, they have every opportunity of developing their personality through their work, and can look forward to the future with confidence? (para. 125)

While faced with this panoply of questions that teases out the depressed state of agriculture, John XXIII does offer some clear solutions. These remedies are providing essential public and more modernized services to agricultural "country" areas, striving for a balanced development of the economy that incorporates agricultural concerns, and the development of a suitable economic policy that allows for a more just and equitable tax structure, expansion of credit banks for necessary capital at more accommodating rates of interest, social security for workers comparable to other economic sectors and social insurance for agricultural produce, price protection, and the creation of ancillary industries that will promote the role of the farm and its produce.

Economic development for the future can retrieve from the past some important lessons in order to attain a proper economic balance between all the constituencies involved with farming. Developing nations must not be tempted, however, to exploit more depressed agricultural economies by offering what John XXIII calls "disinterested aid." Such assistance always comes with a price, whether it is political or economic. Motivations like this yield "a new form of colonialism" and do little to assist "less developed nations achieve their own economic and social growth." Further, some countries and cultures may reject these opportunities for development. The pope counsels that in such instances a nation's individuality must be respected. A resistant nation must not be forced into a "mold."

John XXIII understood the structure of the farm unit as multifaceted. There is not a singular model for the arrangement of a farm. They can be as different from one to the next. However, the pontiff proposes a Christian appreciation of the farm as a family owned enterprise whereby all involved are working toward a common goal guided by principles of justice. "Every effort must be made in the prevailing circumstances to give effective encouragement to farming enterprises of this nature." While family farming is the ideal the Church proposes, John XXIII also admits that the family needs to be supported in its efforts through education and professionals provided from the State. The family should undertake its own efforts to bond with other family farm owners and organize in such a way to have a public impact. They should also form a flourishing system of cooperative undertakings, and organize themselves in solidarity through professional venues to take an effective part in public life, both on the administrative and the political level, to promote their agricultural industry.

The pope extolled the work of the Food and Agriculture Organization (FAO) of the UN, which has sought to promote solidarity amongst nations particularly those who have a rich agricultural economy. The FAO is also commended for its attentiveness towards marginalized countries, in their work to update their farming methods, and, in the end reduce global hunger. While highlighting the tremendous efforts of the FAO, he also summons wealthy nations to take responsibility for the process of development. "The solidarity which binds all men together as members of a common family makes it impossible for wealthy nations to look with indifference upon the hunger, misery and poverty of other nations whose citizens are unable to enjoy even elementary human rights." All are "equally responsible for the undernourished people." "Everything must be done to minimize the ill effects of overproduction, and to spread the burden equitably over the entire population." The pontiff also employs the theological framework of "the Mystical Body of Christ" to amplify this obligation towards those who are suffering. As members of this divine union, Christians and all those sympathetic to the Church's message have a responsibility to each other to effect a decent standard of living.

Cooperation must not only come from the political community, but also from the science, technology and financial industries. Many of these agencies have provided notable efforts towards emergency relief in the midst of their agricultural depravity and famine conditions. What is needed, the pope believed, was the continued training and associated capital these industries have provided, particularly in those areas of the world where the need was most urgent. These international and regional industries can continue to assist the farming industry with more modernized methods in farming and economic development. At the same time, the values that the scientific, technological, and financial industries espouse, must respect their place in what the Church calls "the true hierarchy of values" which are drawn from the themes of RCST, including respect for the dignity of the human person, freedom of the conscience, care of the marginalized, valuation of the common good, economic and environmental justice, and participation. The values that industries promote are "essentially instrumental in character, not supreme values in themselves" as those culled from the themes of RCST.

The Church, the pope contends, has a special regard for all people. Its history supports this as it has "brought [people] many social and economical advantages." Its goal is unity not uniformity. Catholic citizens, particularly those in developed nations, have a keen responsibility in "to increase the effectiveness of the social and economic work that is being done for the poorer nations."

Closely aligned with the concern for the "depressed state of agriculture" are the question of population increase and the supply of food. John XXIII asks the pressing poignant question: "How can economic development and the supply of food keep pace with the continual rise in population?" There was not then "any immediate or imminent world problem arising from the disproportion between the increase of population and the supply of food." John XXIII considers "arguments to this effect" having little base, "unreliable and controversial data that can only be of very uncertain validity." The resources given to humankind, through God, the pope notes are "well-nigh inexhaustible." To focus on the challenge of population and seek to resolve it could disrupt the "established moral order ... and ... attack human life at its very source." In doing such, "an utterly materialistic conception" of life could emerge. Science, the Church upholds, always should be at the service of humanity.

The pope offers another solution. Combined with the scientific technological intelligence of humanity "to discover ways and means of exploiting these resources for personal advantage and livelihood," science can open up "limitless horizons." People must work in solidarity in mutual trust espousing "true human values" that concern human dignity and "the immense worth of each individual life." At the same time, solidarity must yield to a cooperation where there is a lively intercourse of intellect, finances, scientific skill, and technological know-how.

In all of this, the Church called for the acknowledgement of the moral order, as they understood it. A moral order for the Church is one that is "transcendent, absolute, universal, and equally binding upon all." Without such an appreciation for a divinely inspired order, an understanding, no less agreement, can be achieved on issues of justice.

7.3.5 Pacem in Terris (1963)

Pacem in Terris (*Peace on Earth*, or more commonly titled *On Establishing Universal Peace in Truth, Justice, Charity, and Liberty*) was written in 1963, a time of heightened concern for peace that has become a fragile commodity in the midst of the Vietnam conflict, the Cuban missile crisis, and the emerging Cold War. In this letter, John XXIII does not offer the in-depth analysis of agriculture as he did in his previous text. There are two places in this letter that the pope alludes to the subject when speaking on the topic germane to this chapter. The first area is the question of rights. Following his concern for the decreasing amount of food available, particularly for developing nations, he names food a human right. The right to food is connected intimately with "bodily integrity and the means necessary for the proper development of life." Food then must be a central concern for humanity, especially the State.

In another section of *Pacem in Terris*, John XXIII describes what the Church understands as the proper balance between population, land, and capital. The pope records the imbalance that exists between "arable land and the number of inhabitants" as well as "the richness of resources and the instruments of agriculture available." Following the suggestion of his previous letter, he encourages solidarity to share material resources, skills, and intellect. Finally, John XXIII proposes that work be brought to workers allowing them to stay in place so as to preserve social cohesion.

7.3.6 *Populorum Progressio (1967)*

Following the Church's second worldwide Vatican council, Paul VI addresses the rapid developments in the world in his 1967 letter *Populorum Progressio* (*The Progress of Peoples* or *On the Development of Peoples*). These developments occurred in the advancement of nuclear technology and consequent ownership of this potentially enhancing or threatening power. War continues to mark the international scene both in Eastern Europe and the Arab peninsula. Large demonstrations, many dotted by large assemblies of youths, occurred in Europe and the United States protesting these wars and demanding more accountability from authorities.

In this letter, Paul VI acknowledges the latter. He notes that humanity is ambitious to reach "complete development" in its attempt to "remove every obstacle which offends man's dignity" through "continually striving to exercise greater personal responsibility." While many people were striving to reach their fulfillment, Paul VI observes, there was such a vast portion of the global community that "live amid conditions that frustrate these legitimate desires." The gap was widening increasingly between the wealthy and the poor; the pace of development in each is frightening staggeringly. Evidence of this was seen in the imbalance of food market: "While some nations produce a food surplus, other nations are in desperate need of food or are unsure of their export market."

All of these harsh economic realities, Paul concluded, have led to social unrest, particularly for the farmer. The "acute restlessness" that industrialized countries have experienced now has spread to the countries where agriculture is an economic basis of support. "The farmer is painfully aware of his 'wretched lot.'" This is apparent not only in the material goods that the wealthier class enjoys, but also in the political power they are able to wield.

Given this reality it is no wonder fewer people will choose to continue in an agricultural economy. It is a battle between the mainstays of the tradition and the novelties of the new. Traditions might be abandoned easily by the younger generation, but the older generation finds in them fulfillment for them and their families. Paul VI observes:

> The conflict between generations leads to a tragic dilemma: either to preserve traditional beliefs and structures and reject social progress; or to embrace foreign technology and foreign culture, and reject ancestral traditions with their wealth of humanism. The sad fact is that we often see the older moral, spiritual and religious values give way without finding any place in the new scheme of things (para. 10).

Concomitant with this reality, there can be other salvos that a younger generation might invest that only tend toward "public upheavals, civil insurrection, and the drift toward totalitarian ideologies."

Paul VI sought to resolve this situation by a number of proposed solutions including a discussion of the nobility of work. Humanity had been endowed by God with an incredible intelligence and diligence that allows him to continue the work of the Creator God. The worker leaves an imprint on the work done and participates in a common project. The farmer is one of those particular occupations, Paul VI notes, which accomplish this task.

Another area that will narrow the gap between rich and poor is the availability of a basic education to all, particularly those who are illiterate. "Lack of education is as serious as the lack of food; the illiterate is a starved spirit." When education occurs, not only do people learn some basic reading, writing, and arithmetic, but a confidence not known before ensues to perform better at a task and develop as a person. It is a State's responsibility in the cause of development of itself and its people.

A State may need assistance. Following the Christian virtue of charity as founded in the Church's sacred scriptures, Paul VI urges well-off nation-states to be more attentive and caring towards the developing ones. There are, he observes, "whole populations [that] are immersed in pitiable circumstances and lose heart." Paul VI commends the work of the FAO in their efforts in solidarity with the Church to assist developing nations particularly as they combat those areas stricken with famine.

Finally, for the purposes of this chapter, the pope notes the growing distortion between the "haves" and the "have-nots." There are those "highly industrialized nations" with an economic edge that permits them not only to manufacture their own goods but also to export them to other nations. On the other hand, "less developed nations" have only their "raw materials and agricultural crops." The costing problem can be quite acute for farming communities who wish to sell their products and produce given the constraints of competition:

> As a result of technical progress, the price of manufactured products is rising rapidly and they find a ready market. But the basic crops and raw materials produced by the less developed countries are subject to sudden and wide-ranging shifts in market price; they do not share in the growing market value of industrial products (para. 57).

Because of this reality, the burdens that developing nations can bear can be incredible. They do not enjoy the same opportunities for exporting as wealthier nations do. In turn, their economy remains depressed as well as opportunities for further development. The situation is not without hope as some "highly developed nations" have assisted these developing nations. They have done so, at times, "at the price of sacrifices," but more often motivated to improve competition in their own markets.

7.3.7 *Octagesima Adveniens (1971)*

Octagesima Adveniens, literally *On the Coming Eightieth* and commonly known as *A Call to Action*, is not a typical social letter. It is a 1971 apostolic letter to Maurice Roy, president of the Church's Council on the Laity and of the Pontifical Commission of Justice and Peace in anticipation of the World Synod of Bishops that would took place in the fall of 1971. In this text, Paul VI remarks about the contemporary situation:

> These problems of course are particular to each part of the world, but at the same time they are common to all mankind, which is questioning itself about its future and about the tendency and the meaning of the changes taking place. Flagrant inequalities exist in the economic, cultural and political development of the nations: while some regions are heavily industrialized, others are still at the agricultural stage; while some countries enjoy prosperity, others are struggling against starvation; while some peoples have a high standard of culture, others are still engaged in eliminating illiteracy. From all sides there rises a yearning for more justice and a desire for a better guaranteed peace in mutual respect among individuals and peoples (para. 2).

These observations offer a preparatory agenda examining "new needs of a changing world." Additionally, it is also a letter, like previous ones, that marks the eightieth anniversary year of *Rerum Novarum.*

The part of *Octagesima Adveniens* that concerns this chapter has to do with Paul VI's remarks on what Paul VI identifies as a new social problem, namely that of urbanization. "Agrarian civilization is weakening," Paul VI writes. At the same time, he questions whether this reality has been conceded or can aid be given to rectify the "inferior" life and, at times, "miserable economic situation" of those whose lives are devoted to agriculture. The "unceasing flight" from the farm to the city seems to be irreversible, he suggests, but wonders if citizens really know what they are involving themselves with and truly understand what they are abandoning. The promises of the city can be misleading and unforgiving. Realistically the "megalopolis" with its burgeoning populations can yield a proletarianism not known to those who enjoyed the personal and intimate life of the farm. Notwithstanding, there are exceptions, for instance a "medium-sized town," but more and more people are opting for the larger more urban centers.

The environment is another one of his social problems discussed in this letter. Humanity, Paul VI records, is beginning to consider more and more the effect of their historical actions in the environment. Humanity has been the destructive force that now faces destruction itself by its careless and inattentive actions towards the environment. Such a frightening prospect calls for greater solidarity to work towards a healthier future. Perhaps, his placement of his concern for the environment in the list of new social problems that includes urbanization is not without merit. While Paul VI does not say it forthrightly, there seems to be an implication that with the abandonment of agrarian society, there has been a loss of the sense of preciousness of nature and the environment.

7.3.8 *Laborem Exercens* (1981)

Two years into his pontificate in 1981, on the occasion of the ninetieth anniversary John Paul II published his third letter entitled *Laborem Exercens* (*The Exercise of Labor* or *On Human Work*). The topic of human work was central to John Paul II's priestly life. Prior to his election as pope, Karol Wojtyla, as he was known prior to his papal election, was heavily involved with the formation of the solidarity union which sought to restore dignity to the working class.[3]

The document emphasizes that at the center of Leo XIII's "social question" is work. Work involves the human person in the creative work of God as outlined in Genesis, the first book of the Judeo-Christian scriptures. It also generates an income to make life together, particularly as a family, more meaningful. While there may be a temptation to treat capital over labor, John Paul II stridently rails against such a self-serving opportunity. Employers have a responsibility to provide just wages, benefits, and safe working conditions. The right to unionize as well as that to hold private property is highly supported, but both are subordinated to the common good. When considering the various economic systems, John Paul II does not find solace in either the collectivist extreme of Marxism or that of the excesses and, at times, manipulative nature of capitalism. Early on in his text, John Paul II speaks about the dignity of agricultural work. Like all work, it has what the pope calls an "objective and subjective dimension." The objective is the agricultural work itself and the subjective being the one who reaps what is sown. Agricultural work is not particular to any one country but exists throughout the world. This work is "of *fundamental importance*." How this work is arranged may vary from location to location depending on the interests and skill of the people, but also upon the "recognition of the just rights of agricultural workers and, finally, on the level of awareness regarding the social ethics of work."

Social ethics of work and for the workplace are necessitated in that there are some "objectively unjust situations" that need correction. Such "objectively unjust situations" John Paul II and the Catholic Church would hold are or, at least, should be obvious. They are not alone in their belief. Certain philosophers also would contend that we can have objective knowledge of the goodness or badness of situations, conditions, or things, including the unjustness of situations. Specific to the field of agriculture and realistically in all areas of morality, the Catholic Church believes a person can have objective normative knowledge about the farmer, farm, and agricultural system. That is, value knowledge about the goodness and badness of situations, conditions, and things is *a priori*. For instance, the Catholic Church would hold that a farm worker or, legitimately, any worker should never be treated as

[3]During the Second World War, John Paul II (Karol Józef Wojtyła at the time) gained firsthand experience as a worker while working in a chemical factory during the war. For more information on Pope John Paul II's life, see Holy See Press Office (2005).

a means to an end. The human person is always a subject and never an object. Labor must not be compromised for the sake of capital. Unfortunately, recognition of "obviously unjust situations" like long working hours, hazardous labor conditions, lack of access to food and relief stations during work, unfair labor management practices, subjection to toxic environments, are just a few examples as to what could be catalogued under this heading.

Even without any of the exploitative activity that can sometimes go along with agricultural work, farming itself is not easy. It can be physically draining. Compounded by the social stigma that some in society can assign farm work, it can be further degrading evening making "people feel that they are social outcasts." This only motivates them to abandon their work in the fields and seek more urban pastures which, as noted in *Populorum Progressio*, can be offer only illusory promises.

John Paul II suggests education in farming and training in the associated methods and equipment as a venue for liberation for agricultural workers. If one does not have a proper education, one's options are limited even within the confines of the agricultural system itself. With an education, farm hands do not have to be consigned to slave-like conditions. They may even generate enough income to purchase their own parcel of land for cultivation.

A healthy just socio-economic economy protects its workers. Those in the agricultural industry, John Paul II observes, do not enjoy that same kind of security. The benefits of health and welfare enjoyed by so much of the developed world can be so foreign to agricultural workers. Even the concept of an 8-hour working day with legitimate breaks, John Paul II notes, can be so alien.

A healthy economy, John Paul II observes, must account for agricultural work. It cannot be jettisoned as a burden on the economy or left to the regard of the powerful. Legal titles to land must be honored and not overlooked as they often are. Farm workers must not be left out of the conversation about agricultural work. They should enjoy the same opportunity for input as those responsible for scientific and technological development enjoy.

7.3.9 Solliciudo Rei Socialis (1987)

To commemorate the twentieth anniversary of Paul VI's *Populorum progresio*, John Paul II promulgates *Sollicitudo Rei Socialis* (*On Social Concern* in both literal and common parlance) in 1987. While John Paul II focuses on the increased optimism and global innovations made since Paul VI's letter, he also more squarely desires to address some areas of concern that have developed. Much that should have been accomplished in the two decades that have passed has not. The chasm between the rich and the poor has become wider. John Paul II, in this letter, speaks about such division when refers to the incredible distance between the northern and southern hemispheres. There is such an incredible amount of underdevelopment that the "third world" has given way to an even harsher "fourth world."

What has precluded so many of the underdeveloped nations from progress have been economic structures that extend colonialist control, enslave in debt, fail to cooperate and act in solidarity, and exchange and trade goods and monies solely with other advanced States. Socio-economic development seems to be stymied at all points for struggling nations. Yet, development is what humanity is all about which makes the blockage all the more frustrating. The Judeo-Christian bible texts remind humanity that they are charged "to have dominion" over the earth, "to cultivate the garden." Not having that option for humanity frustrates the designs of God for the Christian as articulated in Judeo-Christian scriptures.

Development is a process, but begins with an inner corporate drive:

> Each of them must act in accordance with its own responsibilities, not expecting everything from the more favored countries, and acting in collaboration with others in the same situation. Each must discover and use to the best advantage its own area of freedom. Each must make itself capable of initiatives responding to its own needs as a society. Each must likewise realize its true needs, as well as the rights and duties which oblige it to respond to them (para. 44).

While there may be a temptation for a developing country to be like another to which it has been privy, perhaps one in particular, the pope says the most ideal development is when it moves in concert on its own accord. Solidarity with others, however, should accompany the process.

The task of development is a challenging but noble task. What will continue to be important for developing nations is basic education. Literacy serves as an incredible catalyst to development. As development does transpire, there will be those countries that need to find more sources of food production "for sustenance and daily life." Starvation and famine, for too long, have accompanied underdevelopment. It would be ideal if a nation developed so much that they not only have enough food to feed their population, but also are able to export their products.

In the end, the pope renews a call for solidarity amongst nations of the world. The prospect of the positive hopeful development he elaborates on will never be realized without such. Wealthier, more powerful, and more advanced nations should seek to assist the less developed ones. Additionally, nations, particularly in the same geographical area, should seek to foster interdependence and thus relinquish the debt in which some more powerful nations hold them.

7.3.10 Centesimus Annus (1991)

The centennial anniversary of *Rerum Novarum* in 1991 was marked by John Paul II's letter *Centesimus Annus* (*The Hundredth Year* in both literal and common parlance). John Paul II catalogues the many promising "new things" that have transpired recently including the fall of communism in the Eastern bloc, and freedom for nations and individuals held hostage. There is also, unfortunately, continuing escalating wars in the mid-East.

The letter is an opportunity for the pope to level criticisms at the operative economic systems of socialism and capitalism. The former, the pope alleges, purports an atheistic appreciation of humankind failing to admit any transcendence held by the Church. The latter in its unrestricted strain is just as volatile. Yet, capitalism has more promise. As the pope notes "free market is the most efficient instrument for utilizing resources and effectively responding to needs," but points out that the market and enterprise "need to be oriented toward the common good."

"New things" have made the pope rethink private property and the universal common good. As the pope relates, much as he did in *Laborem Exercens*, work has an objective and subjective dimension. Humanity does the objective work, but in turn the work takes on personal dimension through a worker's investment, the subjective dimension. "The right to private initiative and ownership" are outgrowths of one's work. At the same time, when considering work in the ultimate sense, all work is related. Humankinds' work is connected as each worker engages in labor "not only for his own sake but also *for others* and *with others.*" Thus, the worker in performing the labor initiates a string of solidarity. Those who are owners of the "means of production," here with respect to agriculture, the pope says, is "just and legitimate if its serves useful work." Owners must not use their equipment for exploitation and demeaning motives. It severs solidarity and has no justification. According to John Paul II, such an activity represents an abuse in the sight of God and man.

7.3.11 Caritas in Veritate (2009)

Building upon the richness of *Populorum Progressio* and certainly in the line of tradition with *Rerum Novarum*, Benedict XVI published *Caritas in Veritate*, meaning *Charity in Truth* literally or more fully *On Integral Human Development in Charity and Truth*, in 2009. The global milieu in which Benedict writes has experienced a massive economic challenge, not as debilitating at the crash of 1929, but quite staggering.[4] Persistent terrorist actions have contributed negatively to the crippling economies. Death and destruction have also come at the hands of tyrannical despots like in Rwanda, Yugoslavia, Iraq, the Sudan, and Bosnia. There are signs of hope though. The long Cold War has ended; there is greater international solidarity, particularly with the creation of the European Union, peace in Northern Ireland, and South Africa. World leaders have agreed to *UN Millennium Development Goals* that they hope to meet by 2015. The World Wide Web, disseminated to the public in the early 1990s, had connected the global village, in a way never known to humanity before, through its incredible network. As for the

[4]Shortly before becoming Pope Benedict XVI, Joseph Ratzinger warned that "we are living in a period of great dangers and great opportunities both for man and for the world, a period that also imposes a great responsibility on us all." (2006, p. 25).

Church, it is a bit of a challenging time. The second edition of *The Catechism of the Catholic Church* in 1997 is released as well as *Compendium of the Social Doctrine of the Church* in 2006. At the same time, an incredible amount of serial pedophilia amongst a wide range of priests has resulted in an exodus of many members as well as a decreased appreciation for the moral authority of the Church.

Benedict XVI laments the horrible reality that there still exists so much poverty and much of it is intimately connected with food shortages. Despite the ethical injunction found in Judeo-Christian scriptures and rooted in solidarity to "feed the hungry," hunger has become a justice issue of global proportion. Food and water are natural rights. Rights held should not be trumped by "entitlements" or eclipse concomitant personal and corporate responsibility. "Hunger is not so much dependent on lack of material things as on shortage of social resources, the most important of which are institutional."

Benedict XVI proposes that "a network of economic institutions capable of guaranteeing regular access to sufficient food and water for nutritional needs, and also capable of addressing the primary needs and necessities ensuing from genuine food crises" whatever their etiology. These crises must be transformed by systematic change that promotes true economic growth. This would involve investment in "rural infrastructures, irrigation systems, transport, organization of markets, and in the development and dissemination of agricultural technology that can make the best use of the human, natural and socio-economic resources that are more readily available at the local level." Any decisions regarding such outlay must include the underdeveloped communities themselves – the virtue of subsidiarity. These peoples could perhaps offer a traditional appreciation of agriculture previously unknown to developed States.

Echoing his predecessor, Benedict XVI makes the connection between the environment and care of self. The pope directs humankind to reflect on its attraction to consumerism and even hedonism which seem to so dominate post-modern culture. They, in his opinion, are empty goals; they militate against solidarity and "civic friendship." These values have led to conflicts, sometimes even wars; selfishness, at times the amassment of valuable resources; and, an inattentiveness, even blindness, towards those who are suffering from famine or underdevelopment. In their place, he prompts humanity to engage in "the quest for truth, beauty, goodness and communion with others for the sake of common growth are the factors which determine consumer choices, savings and investments." Agreements rooted in peace and solidarity will provide care for a wider group of people as well as the environment itself.

Finally, Benedict XVI comments on international aid in the same strain of thought as some of his predecessors. Assistance to underdeveloped nations must not be guided by a paternalistic agenda, but by the principles of subsidiarity and solidarity. Throughout history, generous nations have assisted poorer regions, but, in some instances, their financial assistance has not been without additional conditions, "secondary objectives." Benedict XVI rails against such manipulative behavior for it sets up a debtor economy that can choke a nation for generations. He suggests that the negotiation and acceptance of any aid must involve a wide range of constituencies in a given country not without a hitch. "Indeed, the most valuable resources in countries receiving development aid are human resources: herein lies the real capital that needs to accumulate in order to guarantee a truly autonomous future for the poorest countries." The monies given should assist developing countries in the increase of their product market, especially making them more in demand and more competitive. A "just and equitable international trade," must involve the importation of products, particularly agricultural ones, from underdeveloped countries to shore up growing economies.

7.4 A Conceptual Framework

In late June 2011, the United Nations (UN) declared a famine in two large regions of the African nation of Somalia. Twenty years earlier, the UN had passed the same judgment on Somalia. Somalia's neighboring nations of Ethiopia and Sudan had experienced famine earlier, the former in 1984 and again in 2000, and the latter in 2008. Outside these countries of the African horn, the Democratic People's Republic of Korea had its own famine in 1996. While the recurrent droughts have not yielded land fertile for planting, these nations' plights have been further complicated by oppressive governments who stymie efforts by the international community to bring aid to an increasingly starving populace.

Access to food is a serious moral issue. In the world today, there are 925 million people who lack proper nutrition. In the United States, out of a population of almost 300 million people, less than 1% of the population actually farm for a living. Thirty-seven percent of land in the world is agricultural land.

The Church does not seek to offer specific solutions to the issues involving the agrifood industry. Rather, the Church seeks to serve as a global conscience, ensuring that world leaders know and understand their responsibilities to the world community. Benedict XVI amplified this in his 2005 *Deus Caritas Est*: "Church is duty-bound to offer, through the purification of reason and through ethical formation, her own specific contribution towards understanding the requirements of justice and achieving them politically" (Benedict XVI 2005, para 28a). On a more local level, the United States Conference of Catholic Bishops (2003), in its statement on food and agriculture, established criteria for agricultural policy and advocacy. It was an effort to define parameters to overcome hunger and poverty. These included "providing a safe, affordable, and sustainable food supply, ensuring and decent life for farmers and farmworkers, sustaining and strengthening rural communities, and expanding participation."

Using the key themes of RCST explained at the beginning of this chapter, the bishops desired to use them as lens to assess contemporary agricultural concerns and subsequent benchmarks for evaluation. The primary theme of RCST concerns human life and dignity and renders a "right to enough food to sustain a life with dignity." This right is supported by the reality that the human person is social and part of a community bound by commitments of justice, their second theme.

In accordance with RCST, decisions affecting the livelihood of farmers and related agricultural concerns should involve members of the farming community and not merely be left to corporations. This is the virtue of solidarity in practice where individuals appreciate themselves as inexorably linked to one another in a common project. Concomitantly, it is also the principle of subsidiarity applied whereby decisions that can be made on the lowest platform should be made on such a level. Such tasks seek the dignity of farmers, supports their rights and duties of workers and owners, and esteems creation. To this end, the bishops in their 2003 document *For I was hungry and you gave me food (Mt 25:35)*: *Catholic reflections on food, farmers, and farmworkers* asked governments and corporations to evaluate critically agricultural policies using the following questions:

> Do these policies help to overcome hunger and poverty?
> Do they provide a safe, affordable, and sustainable food supply?
> Do they ensure a just and decent life for farmers and farmworkers?
> Do they sustain and strengthen rural communities?
> Do they protect God's creation?
> Do those affected by agricultural policies have a real opportunity to participate in their development?

Ideally, if an agribusiness firm could answer the above questions affirmatively, there would not even be a debate about the "ethics" of agrifood competition. But, there is such a debate, especially in unbridled and unregulated economies, mainly because of concerns regarding the exploitation of agricultural resources for the sake of both corporate and political profit and greed. These themes and critical benchmarks from the Church's rich cache of RCST are thus an important and often unattended voice. They seek to support and sustain a more just agrifood competition. The Church challenges agribusiness firms to exercise their due diligence in being morally responsible by paying attention to the ethical guidelines the Church has outlined. If they do so, all could have the opportunity to flourish.

Such concerns are evident in recent Summer letters to the Appropriations Committees on Agriculture in the Senate and in the House of Representatives from the United States bishops' committee on domestic justice and human development and the committee on international justice and peace anticipating discussion of the Federal Budget. The bishops' letters annually address critical concerns about the future of agriculture from the perspective of RCST. In 2011, the bishops' committee wrote to "express deep concerns that the House proposal calls for significant cuts to both domestic and international food aid, conservation, and rural development programs ... [which] would greatly affect programs that serve hungry, poor and vulnerable people in our nation and around the world" (Blaire and Hubbard 2011). Subsequently, in 2012, the bishops' committee asked the Senate "to draw a 'circle of protection' around resources" for the poor. They went onto say that "the moral measure of the agricultural appropriations process is how it serves 'the least of these'" (Blaire and Pates 2012). These letters are only the latest in a series from the United States bishops that seek to shape more just agricultural policies.

7.4.1 Deeper Investigation of Conceptual Framework

Undergirding this appreciation for agriculture and agrifood competition, as evidenced in the history of RCST, has been a high regard for agricultural work and workers. The Church consistently has esteemed its invaluable nature. Agricultural efforts allow humanity to fulfill some of its primary needs, including acquiring food and monetary provisions, participating in a social economy, and realizing one's human dignity and worth. As noted above, work itself has an objective and subjective dimension. The worker makes or does something and, consequently, the work does something to the laborer. It is a process of self-actualization.

The Church teaches the value of private property, but not without limitation of the demands of the common good, of course. Owning private property, such as land for agricultural development, however, does establish a clear delineation of one's goods. Private property can prompt a farmer to exercise greater care in the land that is owned. Ownership of the land can also engender pride and provide a venue for increased production and greater competition. A byproduct of ownership can be a greater respect and care for creation.

Clearly, there are challenges to realizing the ideal reality whereby people who want to engage in farming and fair competition can do so. Farming takes time and attentiveness. It involves incredible responsibility and steadfast perseverance. Despite farmers' best efforts, there can be many militating factors tempting farmers to jettison their work. Farming is a multifaceted activity, the Church acknowledges, and involves not only the hard sciences, but also the attentive and generous support of States and corporations that will assist them in their efforts. Farming can be painstaking enough given the constellation of economic challenges such as trade embargos, taxation, price structures, and banking loan policies. This noble profession should not be held hostage or dominated by industries or political parties seeking narrow self interests, but rather be equipped with the appropriate tools, have access to education and training, and engage in more cooperative farming. The establishing of unions or associations that not only assist the farming community in just competition and wages, but also generate relationships among members of the farming community, is a viable option the Church suggests.

In each generation, as the papal letters indicate, agriculture has been a challenge. Some pockets of society have just abandoned it, leaving farming in that wretched state and depressed condition of which the popes spoke. This does not have to be. The leaders at the G8 summit have recognized this and made the connections between farming, food, and economic growth (G8 Experts Group on Global Food Security 2009). The field of agriculture offers incredible promise and hope for so much of the world's population, particularly the more depressed cultures. Global economic leadership, including the FAO, have the opportunity to change the present system by paying attention to some of the critical insights RCST offers, particularly solidarity, subsidiarity, and the preferential option for the poor. Lack of regard for this burgeoning concern for building up agricultural societies and agrifood competition can lead to a continued unfortunate hemorrhaging of the global economy.

7.5 Conclusion

Unfortunately, having explained and extolled the value of RCST for the agricultural community, it is a tragic reality that RCST is so little known. The bishops of the United States acknowledged this fact in their 1998 document *Sharing Catholic Social Teaching: Challenges and Directions* in which they reflect on RCST and how much import in and impact on politics, economic life, and society. It was a sad reality, they noted, that so few people, particularly Roman Catholics, knew of RCST. In an effort to circulate word of this invaluable resource, they encouraged dissemination of RCST into different educational, pastoral, and liturgical venues.

How unfortunate it would be for the Church's rich treasure of social doctrine to remain what many theologians have termed the Church's "best kept secret." RCST offers Christians, as Augustine of Hippo (354–430) taught in *The City of God*, an orientation as to how to live in the City of God while living *and influencing* the City of Man. Understanding, appropriating, and appreciating RCST can also has a universal appeal to non-Christians and how to arrange a more just common good. While its language might be theological, philosophical reasoning provides access and perhaps even affirmation of RCST. Admittedly, RCST does have its detractors who contend that it is too Western in orientation, borders on a Marxist communism, male dominated, and not enough energy and reflection given to burgeoning environmental concerns. However, the RCC's teaching is deeply rooted in biblical teaching and theological principles that stretch more than 2000 years. In addition, and particularly with respect to the criticism about RCST being too Marxist, what RCST offers is specific benchmarks and boundaries by which institutional economic structures might be redirected to account for human needs. It does not champion a pure socialism any more than it espouses an unbridled capitalist economy.

This chapter has offered an exposure to RCST with regard to agriculture and an overture to agrifood competition. Its goal has been to disclose the secrets of wisdom that are found in RCST vis-à-vis agriculture, farming, food, and economic competition. Agriculture itself has always been at the forefront of the Christian message. Throughout the Judeo-Christian scriptures, there are rich references to agriculture. In Christian scriptures alone, Jesus uses the farmer, the land, and the seed and other earthy images in parables to teach lessons of steady work, attentiveness, and responsibility. The challenge of disseminating the rich and timeless evaluation of RCST, rooted in these same biblical texts, may be quite daunting and beg transformation, but it is apparent, to borrow a metaphor, the Church together with the global community can no longer "bury its head in the sand."

References

Benedict XVI. 2005. Deus Caritas Est. http://www.vatican.va/holy_father/benedict_xvi/encyclicals/documents/hf_ben-xvi_enc_20051225_deus-caritas-est_en.html. Accessed 28 Sept 2012.

Benedict XVI. 2009a. Angelus. http://www.vatican.va/holy_father/benedict_xvi/angelus/2009/documents/hf_ben-xvi_ang_20090712_en.html. Accessed 28 Sept 2012.

Benedict XVI. 2009b. Caritas in Veritate. http://www.vatican.va/holy_father/benedict_xvi/encyclicals/documents/hf_ben-xvi_enc_20090629_caritas-in-veritate_en.html. Accessed 28 Sept 2012.

Blaire, Stephen, and Howard Hubbard. 2011. Letter to senate on agriculture appropriations.http://www.usccb.org/about/domestic-social-development/upload/letter-senate-agriculture-appropriations-2011-09-06.pdf. Accessed 28 Sept 2012.

Blaire, Stephen, and Richard Pates. 2012. Joint letter to senate appropriations subcommittee on agriculture, FY 2013. http://www.usccb.org/issues-and-action/human-life-and-dignity/agriculture-nutrition-rural-issues/upload/Joint-Letter-to-Senate-2012-04-16.pdf. Accessed 28 Sept 2012.

Byron, William. 1999. Ten building blocks of catholic social teaching. *Catholic Education: A Journal of Inquiry and Practice* 3(1): 7–14.

Catechism of the Catholic Church. 1997. http://www.vatican.va/archive/ENG0015/_INDEX.HTM. Accessed 28 Sept 2012.

G8 Experts Group on Global Food Security. 2009. G8 efforts towards global food security. http://www.g8italia2009.it/static/G8_Allegato/G8_Report_Global_Food_Security%2c2.pdf. Accessed 28 Sept 2012.

Holy See Press Office. 2005. His holiness John Paul II short biography. http://www.vatican.va/news_services/press/documentazione/documents/santopadre_biografie/giovanni_paolo_ii_biografia_breve_en.html. Accessed 28 Sept 2012.

Hooper, John. 2009. Silvio Berlusconi wants G8 to be in earthquake-stricken city of L'Aquila. http://www.guardian.co.uk/world/2009/apr/24/silvio-berlusconi-g8-laquila. Accessed 28 Sept 2012.

John XXIII. 1961. Mater et Magistra. http://www.vatican.va/holy_father/john_xxiii/encyclicals/documents/hf_j-xxiii_enc_15051961_mater_en.html. Accessed 28 Sept 2012.

John XXIII. 1963. Pacem in Terris. http://www.vatican.va/holy_father/john_xxiii/encyclicals/documents/hf_j-xxiii_enc_11041963_pacem_en.html. Accessed 28 Sept 2012.

John Paul II. 1981. Laborem Exercens. http://www.vatican.va/holy_father/john_paul_ii/encyclicals/documents/hf_jp-ii_enc_14091981_laborem-exercens_en.html. Accessed 28 Sept 2012.

John Paul II. 1987. Sollicitudo Rei Socialis. http://www.vatican.va/holy_father/john_paul_ii/encyclicals/documents/hf_jp-ii_enc_30121987_sollicitudo-rei-socialis_en.html. Accessed 28 Sept 2012.

John Paul II. 1991. Centesimus Annus. http://www.vatican.va/holy_father/john_paul_ii/encyclicals/documents/hf_jp-ii_enc_01051991_centesimus-annus_en.html. Accessed 28 Sept 2012.

John Paul II. 1999. Ecclesia in America. http://www.vatican.va/holy_father/john_paul_ii/apost_exhortations/documents/hf_jp-ii_exh_22011999_ecclesia-in-america_en.html. Accessed 28 Sept 2012.

Leo XIII. 1891. Rerum Novarum. http://www.vatican.va/holy_father/leo_xiii/encyclicals/documents/hf_l-xiii_enc_15051891_rerum-novarum_en.html. Accessed 28 Sept 2012.

Massaro, Thomas. 2008. *Living justice: Catholic social teaching in action*. Lanham: Rowman and Littlefield Publishers, Inc.

Paul VI. 1967. Populorum Progressio. http://www.vatican.va/holy_father/paul_vi/encyclicals/documents/hf_p-vi_enc_26031967_populorum_en.html. Accessed 28 Sept 2012.

Paul VI. 1971. Octagesima Adveniens. http://www.vatican.va/holy_father/paul_vi/apost_letters/documents/hf_p-vi_apl_19710514_octogesima-adveniens_en.html. Accessed 28 Sept 2012.

Pius XI. 1931. Quadragesimo Anno. http://www.vatican.va/holy_father//pius_xi/encyclicals/documents/hf_p-xi_enc_19310515_quadragesimo-anno_en.html. Accessed 28 Sept 2012.

Ratzinger, Joseph. 2006. *Christianity and the crisis of cultures*. San Francisco: Ignatius Press.

Schuck, Michael. 1991. *That they be one: The social teaching of the papal letters 1740–1989*. Washington, DC: Georgetown University Press.

United States Conference of Catholic Bishops. 1998. Sharing catholic social teaching: Challenges and directions. http://www.usccb.org/beliefs-and-teachings/what-we-believe/catholic-social-teaching/sharing-catholic-social-teaching-challenges-and-directions.cfm. Accessed 28 Sept 2012.

United States Conference of Catholic Bishops. 2003. For I was hungry and you gave me food (Mt 25:35): Catholic reflections on food, farmers, and farmworkers. http://nccbuscc.org/bishops/agricultural.shtml. Accessed 28 Sept 2012.

Vatican Council II. 1965. Gaudium et Spes, Pastoral Constitution on the Church in the Modern World. http://www.vatican.va/archive/hist_councils/ii_vatican_council/documents/vat-ii_cons_19651207_gaudium-et-spes_en.html. Accessed 28 Sept 2012.

World Synod of Bishops. 1971. Justice in the world. http://www.osjspm.org/files/officeforsocialjustice/files/Justice%20in%20the%20World.pdf. Accessed 28 Sept 2012.

Part II
Assessing Agrifood Competition

Chapter 8
The Problems with Poultry Production and Processing

Douglas H. Constance, Francisco Martinez-Gomez, Gilberto Aboites-Manrique, and Alessandro Bonanno

Abstract This chapter employs a commodity systems analysis combined with a sociology of agrifood studies conceptual framework to investigate ethical issues in the poultry industry. The poultry industry was the first livestock sector to industrialize. While it emerged in the Northeast in the 1930s, by the 1950s the locus of activity had shifted to the South, where the vertically-integrated commodity model based on contract production and non-union labor became the norm for the industry that persists today. By the 1980s mergers and acquisitions had increased horizontal integration, often leading to regional monopsonies. This organizational innovation, vertically-integrated poultry firms anchoring agro-industrial districts, is diffusing into other commodity sectors and globally. It has been argued that the poultry industry system developed in the US South is the model of agricultural globalization based on flexible accumulation forms of commodity-chain organization. Although the modern poultry industry efficiently produces low-priced chicken for consumers, this Southern Model has been criticized as a system of asymmetrical power relationships that marginalize contract producers, processing plant workers, and rural communities. This chapter focuses on the ethical dimensions of the Southern Model for contract growers and processing plant workers. We conclude that the Southern Model of poultry production developed in the US South under specific historical circumstance is the original model of flexible accumulation that is now the basis of agrifood globalization. The problems with poultry raise critical questions regarding the ethical implications of the diffusion of this innovation globally and into other commodities.

D.H. Constance (✉) • A. Bonanno
Department of Sociology, Sam Houston State University, CHSS Room 270, Huntsville, TX 77341, USA
e-mail: soc_dhc@shsu.edu

F. Martinez-Gomez • G. Aboites-Manrique
Centro de Investigaciones Socioeconomicas, Autonomous University of Coahuila, Saltillo, CP 25080, Mexico

H.S. James Jr. (ed.), *The Ethics and Economics of Agrifood Competition*,
The International Library of Environmental, Agricultural and Food Ethics 20,
DOI 10.1007/978-94-007-6274-9_8,

8.1 Introduction

The modern poultry industry developed in the US South in the 1950s under a specific set of socio-economic circumstances characterized by a history of plantation agriculture and vertical and horizontal integration. This Southern Model of poultry production based on flexible forms of accumulation will likely be the model of agrifood globalization as it spreads into other commodities (Boyd and Watts 1997; Constance 2008a; Heffernan 2000; Little and Watts 1994; Marion 1986; Thu and Durrenberger 1998; Vocke 1991).[1]

The rationalization of the poultry commodity system reduced costs and increased profits for the integrators, as well as lowered prices to consumers resulting in increased market share compared to other meat sectors. Although quite successful as an economic model, the poultry industry has been criticized for numerous ethical failures. Agrifood scholars have reported asymmetrical power relationships in the industry between the integrators and growers in production (Boyd and Watts 1997; Breimyer 1965; Burch 2005; Constance 2008a; Davis 1980; Heffernan 1984; Hendrickson et al. 2008; Stull and Broadway 2004; Taylor and Domina 2010) and exploitative labor patterns in processing (Boyd and Watts 1997; Griffith 1995; Human Rights Watch 2005; Striffler 2005; Stull and Broadway 2004; Stull et al. 1995). Others have noted the negative community quality of life impacts of the industry (Burmeister 2001; Constance 2001; Constance et al. 2003; Constance and Tuinstra 2005; Molnar et al. 2001), as well as animal welfare issues related to the industrial production methods (Harrison 1964; Mason and Singer 1990).

This chapter employs a commodity systems analysis (Friedland 1984) combined with a sociology of agrifood studies framework to investigate ethical issues in the poultry industry.[2] It begins with a review of the history of the poultry industry focusing on its peculiar development in the US South. The history sets up two primary areas of investigation: processing and production. The section on poultry processing investigates briefly some ethical concerns regarding the informal labor relations and the rapid Latinization of the workforce. The section on poultry production contracts investigates more thoroughly the ethical implications of a sharecropping system where the grower (farmer) raises broiler chickens owned by the company (integrator). The last section of the case documents the diffusion of the innovation globally. The chapter ends with a discussion of how the Southern

[1]Constance (2008a) discusses the historical context in the US South that generated the Southern Model of poultry production. Flexible accumulation refers to the organization of supply chains that include flexibility for the company, such as informal labor relations (non-union), production contracts, and multiple input sources.

[2]Commodity systems analysis (Friedland 1984) is a research methodology used to investigate the power relations of a commodity supply chain within its socio-historical context that includes state policies, corporate structure, labor relations, and scientific environment. A sociology of agrifood framework analyzes the changing structure of the agrifood system from production through consumption with special attention to power differentials and social stratification among actors that participate in the various commodity systems that make up the agrifood system.

Model of poultry production serves as an early model of flexible forms of capitalist accumulation that is now the preferred organizational model of the globalization of the agrifood system.

8.2 A History of the Poultry Industry

Broilers were initially the male offspring, called cockerels, of layer hens that were eaten in Spring and part of a household-based subsistence strategy on most family farms (Gordy 1974; Sachs 1983). The broiler industry emerged in the DelMarVa region in the 1930s as egg producers increased their cockerel production to sell in Northeast markets and regional processing facilities switched from the declining fishing industry to poultry.[3] By 1935 the DelMarVa area accounted for about two-thirds of US broiler production. Today, broilers are a distinct genetic line of meat chickens that includes both the male and female birds.

This early broiler production system was comprised of independent breeders, hatcheries, farmers, feed dealers and manufacturers, slaughterhouses, truckers, live and "New York dressed" retail markets, commission agents, and merchants. Broilers were raised by independent growers who paid cash for the chicks and feed, and then sold them on the open market (Gordon 1996). Technological developments in poultry husbandry supported by industry, government, and land grant universities rationalized the production process, which allowed large batches of broiler to be grown indoors (Bugos 1992; Strausberg 1995). During WWII the government commandeered DelMarVa's poultry production for the war. Broiler growing areas in the South emerged to fill the national demand (Gilsolfi 2007; Reimund et al. 1981; Tobin and Arthur 1964; Williams 1998).

From 1950 to 1960 the structure of the industry shifted from the independent system developed in the Northeast to one controlled by vertically-integrated firms at the center of agro-industrial districts in the South (Boyd and Watts 1997; Gilsolfi 2007; Heffernan 1984; Kim and Curry 1993). The southern postwar political economy provided social and institutional context for the contract-based model of integration that became the industry standard (Boyd and Watts 1997; Griffith 1995). Underemployed farm labor, a favorable climate, lower wages and less unionization, cotton-crop failures, and the stabilization of feed prices all contributed to the increasing advantage of the South (Breimyer 1965; Easterling et al. 1985; Reimund et al. 1981). In the South there was an ample availability of surplus labor to work in the processing plants (Daniels 1985), an abundance of marginal farmers on the periphery of the cotton belt who needed alternative livelihood strategies and saw contract broiler production as an attractive way to supplement their incomes, and a culture of merchants and feed dealers extending credit to small farmers, who saw broiler contracts as sharecropping and part of the agricultural

[3] DelMarVa refers to the region where the states of Delaware, Maryland, and Virginia share borders.

history of the region (Griffith 1995; Martin and Zerring 1997; Skully 1998). By the 1970s, the South accounted for 90% of national broiler production, but dropped to about 75% by 2002 as the model diffused to other regions (Lasley 1983; Reimund et al. 1981).

As the Southern Model diffused to other regions of the US, technological improvements made it possible to grow larger numbers of uniform broilers in less time. The number of farms growing more than 100,000 birds rose from zero in 1954, to about 30% in 1970s and to nearly 100% in the 1990s (Reimund et al. 1981; Welsh 1996), with about 90% on contract and 10% from company-owned facilities (Welsh 1997). During this same time the development of mechanized killing and processing lines followed models established by industrial factories (Reimund et al. 1981). Increased productivity and efficiency based on flexible vertical integration supported the industries' growth and market share increases against beef and pork.

8.3 From Vertical to Horizontal Integration

The process of vertical integration was accompanied by horizontal integration and industry consolidation. Vertical integration is a business strategy to reduce risk. As the independent firms continually found themselves in cost–price squeezes due to volatile commodity markets, some feed dealers and companies began to integrate into hatcheries, feed mills, and later processing plants. Integration and rationalization reduced transaction costs and increased efficiencies. By the end of the 1950s, the integrated firm had become the industry norm, with 90% of production by early 1960s (Tobin and Arthur 1964). During this time, several independent firms were forced out of the business as major corporations such as Pillsbury and Ralston Purina dominated the market (Strausberg 1995; Striffler 2005). Vertical integration moved broiler production from a farm sideline to a highly developed agribusiness (Lasley 1983).

Vertical-integration fueled growth, but it did not resolve the problem of commodity cycles and overproduction. Broiler firms adopted further-processing and value-added products to reduce the vulnerability to overproduction, but it remained a problem (Bjerklie 1995). When the major firms divested their poultry holdings in the late 1960s and early 1970s due to commodity cycles losses, regional integrators such as Tyson, Holly Farms, and Perdue stepped in to the fill the void, often buying up portions of the larger companies vertically-integrated systems (Marion and Arthur 1973).

The main strategies to generate profits were to increase volume through increasing market share (horizontal integration), increase productivity through technological innovations (mechanization and line speed), lower labor costs (immigrants/contractees), innovate with value-added products (nuggets), and dispose of surplus production (exports). The efforts to increase market share generated a rash of mergers and acquisitions in the 1980s and 1990s leading to industry consolidation. For example, after Tyson Foods bought Lane, Valmac, Hudson Foods, and Holly

Farms in the 1980s, it became the largest poultry processor in the world (Heffernan and Constance 1994). Heffernan (2000) notes that while in the early 1980s about 95% of broilers grown in the US were under contract with less than forty companies, by 1998 the largest four firms controlled about half of production.

Several other researchers have documented the increasingly oligopolistic market structure of the broiler industry over time (Breimyer 1965; Marion 1986; Marion and Arthur 1973; Rogers 1963; Tobin and Arthur 1964). As industry consolidation progressed, regional monopsonies emerged resulting in decreased venues for growers to sell their birds (Hendrickson et al. 2008; Heffernan 2000). Over this time farm bill policies subsidized grain production and resulting overproduction reduced feed prices, which acted as implicit subsidies for poultry integrators and allowed them to buy feedstocks at below the costs of production (Starmer et al. 2006).

By 2003 the largest four broiler firms accounted for 58% of production. In 2002 Tyson Foods, Inc. bought Iowa Beef Packers, (IBP), then the largest pork and beef company in the world, and became the world's largest meat company (Constance 2008a). The Tyson/IBP merger created a company with 30% of the beef market, 33% of the chicken market, and 18% of the pork market that accounted for about 30% of the 400,000 workers in the meat and poultry processing industry (Meat Industry 2001; MigrationInt 2003).

8.4 The Processing Plant and Informal Labor

During the 1950s and 1960s, the integrators connected surplus labor with assembly line technologies to increase productivity. The different aspects of slaughtering broilers were broken down into specific tasks that could be performed by unskilled and low wage labor. Automation and increased line speed further rationalized the processing plant. The labor force slowly changed from poor Whites to African Americans and females, but with substantial geographic variability. The industry employed women and older children who were needed at peak farm times but were available off-season for work in the processing plants and on the growout farms (Fite 1984; Griffith 1995; Schwartz 1995). Social structures, such as Evangelical Christianity, racism, white supremacy, and anti-union attitudes recreated the traditional authority of men over women, whites over blacks, and primary over supplementary wage earners (Griffith 1995).

In the 1980s, the labor supply shifted rapidly toward Hispanic, and some Asian, immigrants as many local workers left their processing jobs for better opportunities (Griffith 1995; Striffler 2005; Stuesse 2009). Latino workers made up a small proportion of the workforce in 1981 but had increased to about 25% by 1993 (Griffith 1995). By 2005 Latinos made up about three-fourths of processing plant workers, with most of the remainder from Southeast Asia and Micronesia (Striffler 2005). During the same period the real wages of poultry workers remained largely stagnant as line speeds increased, repetitive motion injuries increased, and the industry continued to block unionization (Human Rights Watch 2005; Striffler 2005).

The flow of immigrants reduced labor costs and served as a constant reminder to native workers that their jobs could be filled by workers who work harder and complain less. Plant managers frequently employed kinship and friendship networks within the Latino community to generate a continuous supply of new workers who rotated between agricultural field-work, broiler processing work, and return migration to Mexico (Griffith 1995; Striffler 2005; Stuesse 2009). High turnover rates, often greater than 100%, necessitated a constant supply of flexible labor (Boyd and Watts 1997). The integrators preferred immigrant workers, often illegal, who were willing to work under the dangerous and difficult situations and who the integrators could better exploit because of their undocumented status (Human Rights Watch 2005).

Another example from Tyson Foods, Inc. illustrates this pattern. In 1997, the Immigration and Naturalization Service began a two and a half year undercover investigation of Tyson Foods related to hiring undocumented workers (Tanger 2006). A grand jury indicted Tyson Foods, Inc. and six Tyson managers in 2001 on 36 counts of conspiracy to smuggle illegal aliens into the US, provide them fraudulent documents, and employ them illegally (USDOJ 2001). The jury acquitted Tyson and the remaining managers (one committed suicide and two pled guilty) of all charges in 2003. The managers who pled guilty reported that the lack of labor locally, mostly due to the low level of wages offered, combined with the intense pressure to fully staff the processing line forced them to seek other options to meet production quotas. These plant managers paid established Latino migrants to smuggle more workers from Mexico and Central America (Sack 2002). Despite the huge volume of undercover audio and video tapes and subpoenaed documents presented by the government prosecutors who argued the trial was about corporate greed, the Tyson defense was successful in convincing the jury that the illegal hiring activities were the actions of a few rogue plant managers and that Tyson Foods, Inc. officials above the level of plant manager were not aware of these activities (Day 2003a, b; Rosenbloom 2003).

8.5 Contract Broiler Production

The broiler industry has a special geography and farm structure. The biological aspects of broilers necessitate a specific spatial pattern to the vertical integration system (Boyd and Watts 1997; Heffernan 1984; Kim and Curry 1993). The transport of live broilers (to growout barns and back to slaughter plants) and the different types of feed rations required at different stages of the growth cycle, demanded that the growout operations be centrally located, generally within a 25 mile radius of the feed mill and processing facilities. These kinds of spatial requirements combined with physosanitary risks associated with monoculture confinement production and the preference for contracts (as opposed to tying up capital in company-owned grow out facilities) required a special kind of farm structure to make the vertically-integrated system work. That farm structure existed in the US South in the form of small, marginal farms in close proximity (Boyd and Watts 1997).

The most important factor in broiler industry industrialization was the organizational innovation of vertical integration (Reimund et al. 1981). Vertical integration rationalized the broiler industry as it brought all aspects of the production chain (e.g., breeding, hatching, growing, feed mills, transportation, and processing plants) under the control of the integrating firm. At the center of the vertically-integrated system was the contract grow-out arrangement that emerged in the South in the 1940s and 1950s. In the early 1940s the local feed dealers sold feed and baby chicks to local farmers, and then offered to buy back the full-grown broilers. This informal contract system worked well as long as the number of birds was relatively small. As consumer demand grew and the flocks became larger, to facilitate expansion the feed dealers offered the baby chicks and feed on credit to the growers, and retained "first call" on either buying back the full-grown broilers or the profits on the sale of the birds by the grower (Gordy 1974). By the 1950s, these informal contractual agreements were formalized into written contracts. The growers became more dependent on the feed dealers for inputs, credit, feed, and chicks. Under these formal contracts, the feed dealer retained ownership of the birds that the farmer grew using the dealer's feed and then returned to the dealer. This sharecropping arrangement based on formal contracts developed as a way for feed companies to expand their markets without the fixed cost of buying land or paying production workers. Broilers were a lucrative way to add value to feed, as well as provide supplemental income to the local farmers. Consumer demand for chicken rose steadily and the industry expanded to meet the demand.

As increased production led to commodity cycle price crises, feed dealers increased their use of formal contracts with growers to ensure a minimum return for the grower while retaining ownership of the birds. In broilers, the integrating firms did not buy land and build growout facilities, firms "vertically coordinated" and contracted with marginal land owners to supply the broilers for slaughter (Knoeber 1989). The formalized contracts allowed the feed dealers to better control the genetics, feed, and standardized management practices in the growout facilities (Martinez 1999; Southern Cooperative Series 1954). Without the flexibility afforded by contracts, it is doubtful the "new entrants, primarily feed manufacturers and dealers, would have considered broiler production very attractive" (Reimund et al. 1981, p. 8).

While the relationship between feed dealers and growers began as an informal system whereby the farmer bought the feed and baby chicks and then sold them back to the feed company, as the industry grew, the dealers encouraged the farmers to grow bigger flocks of birds. To facilitate this expansion, the dealers first offered the feed and chicks on credit with a retainer clause, then moved to a formal contract system that specified the division of labor, capital, and inputs. This shift from informal to formal contracts "marked the evolution from a simple credit arrangement to a tightly interlinked credit, input, and labour contract" (Boyd and Watts 1997, p. 200). Through the contract, the integrator secured a reliable product stream to supply the processing plant but avoided the land and labor cost of company-owned production facilities.

Under the modern contract system, the integrator pays the grower to raise its broiler chickens in a share cropping arrangement. The integrating firm provides the farmer (grower) with day-old chicks, feed, medication, and technical support. The grower provides the built-to-specifications growout buildings, labor, utilities, and is responsible for disposal of the dead chickens and manure. In most cases, the farmer mortgages his/her land to build the growout buildings; most often multiple buildings that cost $250,000 each or more. In this system, the farmer receives a guaranteed payment based on the feed conversion ratio (how much weight the birds gained on a certain amount of feed), and a bonus or discount based on how the farmer's particular flock compared to other similar flocks – a controversial ranking system called "the tournament" (Knoeber 1989; Tsoulouhas and Vukina 2001).[4] At the end of the grow-out term, the integrator retrieves the mature broilers and brings another batch to the grower.

The contract and tournament system allows poultry integrators to adapt quickly and cheaply to changing market conditions and productivity levels without the burden of fixed costs of company-owned land and buildings (Knoeber 1989). The company does not have to renew the growers' contract which is offered on a "take it or leave it" basis and is usually batch to batch with no guarantee beyond the current batch. The grower's debt often persists as the integrators require technological upgrades (FLAG 2001; Greene 2011; Hendrickson et al. 2008; Striffler 2005; Vukina and Leegomonchai 2006b). The tournament system combined with the debt associated with contract production creates a penalty system that self-selects for high quality growers willing to adopt the newest technologies (Knoeber 1989). Asset specificity due to single expensive purpose buildings and the fear of hold up and/or contract termination encourage low-performing growers to increase their efforts without an increase in compensation. Grower provision of investments provides an efficient way for integrators to finance expansion, as well as weed out low-performing growers. From an integrator perspective, grower provision of capital is the fee for entering the possible long-term relationship with the integrators (Tsoulouhas and Vukina 2001).

While the contract offered a guaranteed income and took much of the risk out of raising chickens, the grower was in substantial debt and dependent on the integrator for birds. The grower also assumes all responsibility and risks regarding manure disposal (Hamilton 2002; Molnar et al. 2001), leading to both community conflicts with neighbors (Constance 2001; Constance et al. 2003; Constance and Tuinstra 2005), as well as regulatory conflicts with state and federal environmental agencies (Burmeister 2001). The contract system allows the integrating firm to control the methods of production but avoid the fixed costs of building and land investment, as well as the responsibility and liability related to environmental protection and community disruption (Constance 2008a; Hendrickson et al. 2008). The integrator

---

[4]The payment system is two-tiered. First, a guaranteed payment is calculated based on the feed conversion ratio specified in the contract (how many pounds of feed it takes to produce one pound of poultry). Then, the first payment is adjusted (bonus/discount) based on comparison to other growers' flocks.

can "to take advantage of the chief assets of the family farm – cheap, 'docile', and flexible labour – without the burdens of equity or the costs of wage labour" (Boyd and Watts 1997, p. 211).

8.6 Integrator Power and the Contract Grower

Mooney (1983) sees the contract system as an example of how capitalist relations penetrate agriculture by detouring around obstacles such as the control of production practices without formal ownership. He agrees with Davis (1980) that the contract producer is a propertied laborer that compromises autonomy for security; who becomes a "semi-autonomous employee" that still holds title to their land but has lost decision-making control. The high costs and single purpose characteristics of the poultry barns (asset specificity) made poultry growers more insecure and vulnerable than other forms of contract production such as fruits and vegetables (Heffernan 1984). Similarly, because of the limited alternative uses of the growout barns, the integrators can use the threat of termination of contracts to force the growers to adopt new technological improvements (Greene 2011; Lewin-Solomons 2000; Wilson 1986). Roy (1972) concluded that contract farmers are in a position similar to a sharecropper. Vogeler (1981) put contract growers in a transitional status between family farmer and agricultural worker. Breimyer (1965) referred to broiler growers as serfs on the land. Some growers commented that they were the only slaves left in the country (Wellford 1972). Constance (2008a) refers to the situation as debt slavery.

Contracts help coordinate production but also act as a policing mechanism that provides positive and negative incentives to induce certain behaviors from growers who operate in an asymmetrical relationship with integrators (Taylor and Domina 2010; Wolf et al. 2001). Growers are disadvantaged in their disputes with integrators and "stories of abuse and intimidation are commonplace" (Stull and Broadway 2004, p. 50). Hendrickson et al. (2008) document the erosion of grower sovereignty and well-being as horizontal integration advances and monopsony markets emerge. As horizontal integration leads to poultry industry consolidation, growers have fewer integrators in their area to contract with. Other researchers have also discussed the asymmetrical market power that integrators hold over contract producers (Clouse 1995; Gilsolfi 2007; Hamilton 2002; Striffler 2005; Taylor and Domina 2010) and warned about the adoption of the poultry model in other agrifood sectors (Little and Watts 1994; Morrison 1998; Thu and Durrenberger 1998). Vertical integration combined with horizontal integration creates the possibility of monopsony opportunism.[5]

[5] It is important to note that growers report that in the early phases of industry expansion that the contract system was acceptable and often worked well. As consolidation advanced and growers were left with only one integrator in their region, instances of monopsony opportunism increased.

Production contracts helped fuel the remarkable growth of the poultry industry, but during the same time the integrator-grower relationship has deteriorated. The media started covering the increasing tensions between growers and integrators, turning poultry contracts into a social problem (FLAG 2001; Taylor and Domina 2010; Vukina 2001). The National Contract Poultry Growers Association formed in 1991 to advocate for growers' rights. Industry commentators soon identified grower discontent in general, and with the tournament system of payment in particular, as the most volatile issue in the industry (Bjerklie 1996; Hamilton 1995). In 1995, three broiler growers from Alabama, Maryland, and Kentucky committed suicide due to despair over their contract situation (Countryman 1996). Several southern states including North Carolina, Mississippi, Alabama, and Louisiana tried unsuccessfully to pass legislation to regulate the contracts and protect the rights of growers to organize (Tsoulouhas and Vukina 2001; Vukina and Leegomonchai 2006b). After the Mississippi Contract Growers Association failed to get a bill passed to increase growers' rights, the President of the Association commented that his, and the previous President's, organizing activities had resulted in the termination of their contracts (Cullen 1996).

The National Commission on Small Farms recommended that the USDA evaluate the need for federal legislation to regulate poultry contracts. In 1999, the National Contract Poultry Growers Association sued ConAgra in Alabama for under-weighing birds (Morrison 2001). The same year Representative Marcy Kaptur of Ohio introduced the Poultry Farm Protection Act in the House and in 2000 Senator Harkin of Iowa introduced the Agricultural Producer Protection Act in the Senate; both bills died in committee. The Iowa Attorney General proposed legislation called the Producer Protection Act to protect contract growers. The model was endorsed by attorney generals in 16 states but received little structural support during the political process as many mainstream agricultural organizations opposed the protections (Vukina and Leegomonchai 2006b). These state and national level attempts to reform the contract system were generally unsuccessful due to stiff resistance from the poultry industry.

Through the mid- and late-1990s, the USDA funded research to address and document the growing controversy over agribusiness concentration in general, and poultry contracting in particular (USDA/GAO 1997). The USDA Fund for Rural America provided monies for research on integrator-grower relationships and GIPSA began rulemaking actions to address the growers' concerns, including: the tournament system of payment, lack of information about weight of feed and market broilers, quality of chicks, mandatory upgrades to growout barns, and unequal bargaining power (FLAG 2001; Hamilton 2002; Ilvento and Watson 1998). State extension services and rural NGOs developed guidesheets to help growers better understand the advantages and disadvantages of broiler contract production (Doye et al. n.d.; FLAG 2001).

Some of the USDA monies supported research carried out by agricultural economists and rural sociologists regarding these controversial aspects of poultry production, especially the tournament system and monopsony opportunism that facilitates hold up due to asset specificity. Tournaments are a ranking system integrators use to measure the efficiency of their growers. The growers get paid a base price, but then receive a bonus or penalty determined by how they compare with their neighbor growers during the same time period. Growers maintain that the tournament system can be biased by preferential distribution of the production inputs of chick and feed quality and market bird weight, all factors that are under exclusive control of the integrator.

Tsoulouhas and Vukina (2001) found that although the tournament system of payment is theoretically the optimum for both growers and integrators,[6] many growers are opposed to tournaments and prefer a fixed payment system. They compared the efficiencies of the tournament versus fixed performance schemes and found that grower welfare increases and integrator welfare decreases in fixed payment systems. They concluded that a switch from the tournament to fixed payment systems would require government intervention as the firms would never initiate such a move themselves. Wu and Roe (2006) found that grower opposition to the tournament payment system and support for fixed performance contracts was related to their perception of fairness in the contract. Accordingly, even in the absence of integrator opportunism growers may view tournaments as unfair, therefore integrators should consider a "fairness premium" in their dealings with growers. Tsoulouhas and Vukina (2001) also noted that other controversial aspects of the contract process such as hold up due to asset specificity needs more research, especially in geographic regions characterized by monopsony.

Rogers and Sexton (1994) found that markets for raw agricultural products, including broilers, are likely to be structural oligopsonies or monopsonies. Integrator market power may contribute to opportunism, especially in circumstances with geographic restrictions. Given the fact that government actions to address this issue have been blocked by the industry at the state and federal levels, they suggest growers organize into bargaining associations or marketing cooperatives. They comment though that this strategy has been unsuccessful to date as integrators have been successful in using a "divide and conquer" strategy.

Vukina and Leegomonchai (2006b) compared the utility of the public interest theory of regulation with interest group theory to explain why virtually all legislative attempts at the state and federal level to regulate broiler contracts had failed. According to public interest theory, government intervention in markets is a response to public pressure to address perceived market failure by enacting policies (laws, taxes, and/or subsidies) that restrict certain types of behavior. Interest group theory maintains that government regulations are the outcome of supply and demand dynamics that determine the value of regulation to various groups. More powerful groups are able to enact (or resist) regulation by using the coercive power of the state to protect their interests. They conclude that public interest theory with its focus on market failure is at best ambiguous in explaining the lack of government

[6] While the tournament is assumed to be economically optimal for both parties, the fact that growers prefer another method of payment indicates that the assumptions of the model are lacking some dimension important to growers.

regulation regarding poultry contracts. The fact that growers find themselves in asymmetrical monopsony relationships with integrators should result in government regulations to address the market failure, but such regulations have not occurred. Instead, interest group theory with its focus on asymmetrical competition between groups to influence government policy (or the lack thereof) better explains why legal and legislative attempts to regulate the poultry industry have been unsuccessful. Poultry integrators are powerful corporate actors in national, but especially state and local politics. Growers are at a distinct organizing disadvantage, especially since some growers are not critical of their integrators. Although integrator opportunism and holdup due to asset specificity may serve as a justification for government intervention, the lack of grower unity and power in the face of integrator market and political power severely constrain the success of regulatory initiatives. The result is a status quo situation whereby the integrators use their political influence to curtail state regulation and thereby perpetuate their monopsony power over the growers.

Vukina and Leegomonchai (2006a) investigated the evidence on oligopsony power, asset specificity and hold up in the broiler industry. Because most poultry contracts are short-term flock to flock contracts with no guarantee of other flocks, but grower investments are long-term covering specific-use buildings with little value outside the relationship with poultry integrators, integrators may exercise market power and opportunism through hold up to capture quasi-rents from the grower. Hold up is especially problematic at the time of contract renewal, as integrators may require growers to invest in expensive upgrades to the poultry barns, thereby increasing the level of asset specificity. Fear of contract termination in the face of huge debt may force growers to acquiesce to integrator demands for upgrades, effectively increasing grower costs while integrator payments remain the same (Lewin-Solomons 2000). Since contracts are renewed several times a year, there are numerous opportunities for integrators to exercise hold up, resulting in diminished grower negotiating power. Vukina and Leegomonchai (2006a) found that grower's perceptions and management decisions in response to possible hold up depends on the market structure. In situations of monopsony, growers were less willing to invest in upgrades and thereby increase asset specificity. Similarly, in situations of monopsony increases in asset specificity decreases grower compensation rates. They conclude that based on their research there is enough evidence of hold up in the broiler industry to warrant further research, especially in situations of monopsony.

8.7 Grain Inspection, Packers and Stockyards Administration

Title IX of the 2008 Farm Bill included specifics instructions to the USDA Grain Inspection, Packers and Stockyards Administration (GIPSA) to clarify regulations and enforcement regarding competition and unfair practices (Greene 2011). The USDA/USDOJ convened the Agricultural Competition Joint Task Force which organized a series of public workshops to explore competition around the US. These workshops were held in 2010, with the poultry workshop held in Birmingham, Alabama in March. The transcript of the workshop (USDOJ/USDA 2010) reveals that growers are most concerned about the regional monopsonies in poultry, the lack of transparency concerning the weight of the feed and grown broilers, the tournament ranking system for establishing payments, favoritism in placement of chicks and feed quality, renewal of contracts from long to short term, and contract termination if equipment upgrades were not carried out. Many growers reported that they felt threatened with termination of their contracts if they did not sign the new contract and/or upgrade their facilities. Some growers saw this as a form of extortion where the choice became lose the farm or sign the contract; some felt they would be "blacklisted" and retaliated against if they complained.

Growers reported that they were asset rich but cash poor. Mandatory upgrades kept them in debt bondage and dependent on the integrator for chicks to pay the bills with no way out. Growers noted that they faced two kinds of economic concentration. First, economic concentration in the poultry industry had steadily reduced the number of poultry firms in a region. Many growers had only one company in their region, a regional monopsony. Even in areas with multiple firms, the companies rarely "crossed lines" to sign with other growers. Second, and more importantly, the regional monopsonies put the growers at a substantial disadvantage regarding contract negotiations, as described above. Growers want USDA/DOJ to protect them from market power of the integrators. The Campaign for Contract Agriculture Reform organized to support efforts to protect growers from integrator market power (RAFI-UDA 2010).

In June 2010, GIPSA released the Proposed Rule for public comment (USDA/GIPSA 2010). The Rule included relevant sections regarding poultry to increase transparency, to eliminate favoritism, to eliminate the tournament system, and to regulate upgrades and contracts (Greene 2011). During the public comment period over 60,000 comments were received and the period was extended as advocates and critics of the Rule expressed their concerns and support. In April, 142 agricultural organizations send letter of support to House and Senate for GIPSA Proposed Rule (NSAC 2011). In May several agricultural industries and 147 congressmen called for the Obama Administration to withdraw and rewrite the Proposed Rule; USDA declined the suggestion (SEFP 2011). Through 2011 GIPSA was still analyzing the comments.

8.8 The Global Diffusion of the Innovation

In the 1950s and 1960s, large feed firms like Continental Grain, Ralston Purina, and Cargill started broiler operations in developing countries (Morgan 1979). These dominant grain companies were followed by Tyson, Pilgrim, and other US and foreign integrators in the 1980s. By the early 1990s transnational agribusinesses had created a global poultry agrifood complex that linked the most favorable areas of production to profitable consumer markets (Constance and Heffernan 1991). Burch (2005) has documented similar patterns of vertical and horizontal integration and global expansion by the Thai firm Charoen Pokphand (CP) in Southeast Asia and China.

By 2003, Tyson had joint-venture poultry operations in Argentina, Brazil, China, Denmark, Indonesia, Japan, Korea, Malaysia, Panama, Philippines, Spain, United Kingdom, and Venezuela (Tyson Foods, Inc. 2005a, b). After entering the Mexican market through a joint venture in 1987, by 2003 Tyson de Mexico was the largest producer of value-added chicken for both retail and foodservice in Mexico and was expanding into other areas of Latin America and Asia (Constance et al. 2010; Morais 2004). Following the model it developed in Mexico, in 2008 Tyson expanded its presence in China and acquired established vertically–integrated operations in India and Brazil. The three Brazilian broiler companies were bought to supply domestic demand and exports to Asia and Europe (Tyson Foods, Inc. 2009).

In addition to Tyson, Pilgrim's Pride, Inc. has also been very active in Mexico. In 2007, Pilgrim's Pride, Inc. was the largest broiler producer in the US and the world with its acquisition of Goldkist. Pilgrim's entered the Mexican market in 1995 with the purchase of five vertically-integrated broiler companies from Purina and was soon the second largest broiler company in Mexico and the largest in Puerto Rico (Pilgrim's Pride 2005, 2007). In 2008, Pilgrim was bought by JBS of Brazil, the largest multi-protein corporation in the world (JBS 2009). In 2010, Tyson de Mexico, JBS/Pilgrim's Pride, and Bachocho (Mexican corporation) controlled 67% of the market (Constance et al. 2010). The vertical integration system developed in the US South around agro-industrial districts is now the model for the low cost production systems that are the "social basis of competitiveness in a now global industry" (Boyd and Watts 1997, p. 207).

8.9 Discussion and Conclusions

The overview of the history of the poultry industry illustrates the peculiar development of the Southern Model of agro-industrial poultry production in the US and its diffusion globally. The description of these events reveals ethical concerns related to both the processing and production dimensions of broiler production. The growing reliance on Latinos, often undocumented, as the processing plant workforce introduces a new dimension of exploitation and labor suppression. Although historically the poultry processing workforce was non-union and often minority, the immigrant status of the Latinos provided integrators lower costs and increased flexibility. Integrators preferred immigrants who would work hard and not complain, especially the undocumented. Immigrants provided integrators more flexibility to expand and contract the processing labor supply as needed. The Tyson labor lawsuit illustrates the techniques the integrators use to source labor.

The ethical concerns regarding the production contract are more particular to the poultry commodity system. Recall that the flexibility of the vertically-coordinated contract system that allowed the integrator to source and control production without buying land or paying employees is the key variable in the success of industry. Several rural social scientists criticize the production contract arrangement as an erosion of farmer autonomy in an asymmetrical power relationship that is harmful to the growers, referring to the contract growers as serfs on the land, propertied laborers, or living in debt slavery. The production contract allowed for control of the labor process without the formal responsibilities of the company/worker relationship such as wages and benefits. Control without ownership and responsibility is a key aspect of flexible accumulation strategies (Harvey 2005).

Horizontal integration consolidated the industry resulting in regional monopsonies. Monopsony opportunism generates debt bondage through asset specificity and the gaming of the tournament system of payments. Growers and their supporting groups have organized to express their grievances and the state has responded with academic and bureaucratic inquiry. The integrators have used their political influence at the state and federal levels to block attempts to reform the system to be fairer to the growers. Regional monopsonies limit the flexibility of the grower to the advantage of the integrator. The tournament, combined with holdup during contract renewal, suppresses grower resistance to integrator power. Both dimensions provide the integrator with flexible accumulation options to expand or contract production based on market needs with the costs being born by the growers.

In the sociology of agrifood literature the Agrarian Question asks, "How does capitalism take hold of agriculture?"(Buttel and Newby 1980; Constance 2008b). Agriculture tends to be an unattractive investment for capital due to high risk, high fixed costs, and long production cycles. The poultry industry is a prime example of detours around these barriers to capitalist investment. Vertical coordination of contracts plus appropriation upstream and substitutionism downstream[7] rationalize the commodity chain into a very efficient industrial system, thereby making it attractive for corporate investment and entry (Goodman et al. 1987). It is the social basis of this model grounded in flexible labor processes in processing and production that makes poultry the preferred and copied organizational model.

Flexible organizational forms are a key component of the globalization of the agrifood system (Bonanno and Constance 2008). McMichael (2005) extends Harvey's work (1989, 2005) in presenting his Corporate Food Regime as the third regime in agrifood studies (see Friedmann and McMichael 1989). Harvey (2005) argues that globalization is an organized attack on the civil rights successes of the social-democratic movements. Globalization is based on the concepts of neoliberalism, flexible accumulation and the hyper-mobility of capital. Neoliberalism refers to a corporate strategy to minimize state regulation of industry and maximize organizational flexibility in constructing global commodity chains.

[7] Appropriation refers to the practice of replacing on farm inputs with off farm inputs and thereby appropriating some of that revenue at the level of corporate input suppliers. Substitutionism refers to the practice of further processing farm products beyond the farm gate and thereby capturing value at the corporate instead of farm level.

Global agribusinesses seek to employ flexible accumulation strategies such as the decentralization of production, the informalization of labor, and global sourcing to enhance capital accumulation and minimize government regulation. The hyper-mobility of capital refers to the ability of capital, both financial and productive, to move rapidly around the globe in search of profits. Agribusinesses also source their factors of production globally to avoid restrictive regulations and create global value chains based on flexible accumulation (Bonanno and Constance 2008). McMichael (2005) argues the Corporate Food Regime based on neoliberalism and flexible forms of capital accumulation is the model of agrifood production that the North is imposing on the South through the WTO. Neoliberalism transfers the governance function that regulates commodity chains from the public to the private sector as governments deregulate and privatize their economies to attract foreign direct investment. In the process, substantive forms of democracy are diminished in favor of market privilege.

We argue that the Southern Model of poultry production is the original model of flexible accumulation, developed in the US South under a historically conducive set of circumstances. Vertical integration in the poultry industry is a good example of privatized governance that reduced economic risk and attracted corporate investment. Horizontal integration at the global level is a good example of the hyper-mobility of capital whereby poultry agrifood TNCs diffuse the model into developing countries. The chapter reveals that the poultry industry's flexible accumulation strategy has harmed many contract growers and generated a legitimation crisis that produced social movement organization that is being mediated by the state, at the local and federal levels. To date, the integrators have been able to use their political power to block significant changes to the contracting system. The GIPSA investigation is evidence of the persistent and substantial ethical problems with poultry.

The Southern Model is a form of sharecropping that replaced slavery in the US South as the dominant form of agriculture production. For many contract poultry growers, debt bondage represents a modern form of slavery with no escape, what Araghi (2003, pp. 60–61) calls, "slavish conditions of employment... without visible slavery." As the industry matured, vertical and horizontal integration created regional monopsonies that facilitated integrator opportunism and hold up resulting in a system where it is not possible for new growers to rationally assess long-term prospects and for existing growers to equalize bargaining power. The growers' testimonies at the GIPSA hearing support the position that this is a self-perpetuating cycle of dependence that appears to be deepening. A critical evaluation of the situation can easily cast the integrators are the global planters spreading a system of debt slavery that is harmful to the growers, as well as the processing plant workers and rural communities where they locate (see Winders 2009).

This research documents the problems with poultry and points to ethical concerns with the diffusion of the model globally. This model grounded in neoliberal approaches that privilege the market over democracy is powered by Tyson, JBS, CP, and other agrifood TNCs. There are many opportunities for researchers concerned with the ethical implications of the restructuring of global agrifood system to join in comparative and collaborative research on the global poultry commodity chain and its diffusion into other commodities. If you want to see the future of the global agrifood system, study the poultry industry.

References

Araghi, F. 2003. Food regimes and the production of value: Some methodological issues. *Journal of Peasant Studies* 30(2): 60–61.

Bjerklie, S. 1995. On the horns of a dilemma: The US meat and poultry business. In *Any way you cut it: Meat processing and small town America*, ed. D. Stull, M.J. Broadway, and D. Griffith, 41–60. Lawrence: University Press of Kansas.

Bjerklie, S. 1996. Dark passage: Part 1. *Meat and Poultry*. August.

Bonanno, A., and D.H. Constance. 2008. *Stories of globalization: transnational corporation, resistance, and the state*. University Park: The Pennsylvania State University Press.

Boyd, W., and M. Watts. 1997. Agro-industrial just-in-time: The chicken industry and postwar capitalism. In *Globalizing food: Agrarian questions and global restructuring*, ed. D. Goodman and M.J. Watts, 192–225. London: Routledge.

Breimyer, H. 1965. *Individual freedom and the economic organization of agriculture*. Urbana: University of Illinois Press.

Bugos, G.E. 1992. Intellectual property protection in the American chicken-breeding Industry. *The Business History Review* 66(Spring): 127–168.

Burch, D. 2005. Production, consumption and trade in poultry: Corporate linkages and North–south supply chains. In *Cross-continental agrifood chains*, ed. N. Fold and B. Pritchard, 166–178. London: Routledge.

Burmeister, L. 2001. Lagoons, litter and the law: CAFO regulation as social risk politics. *Southern Rural Sociology* 18(2): 56–87.

Buttel, F.H., and H. Newby (eds.). 1980. *The rural sociology of advanced societies*. Montclair: Allenheld, Osmun, and Co.

Clouse, M. 1995. Farmer net income from broiler contracts. Pittsboro, NC: RAFI-USA.

Constance, D.H. 2001. Globalization, broiler production, and community controversy in East Texas. *Southern Rural Sociology* 18(2): 31–55.

Constance, D.H. 2008a. The southern model of broiler production and its global implications. *Culture and Agriculture* 30(1): 7–31.

Constance, D.H. 2008b. The emancipatory question: The next step in the sociology of agrifood systems? *Agriculture and Human Values* 25(2): 151–155.

Constance, D.H., and W.D. Heffernan. 1991. The global poultry agrifood complex. *International Journal of Sociology of Agriculture and Food* 1: 126–141.

Constance, D.H., and R. Tuinstra. 2005. Corporate chickens and community controversy in East Texas: Growers' and neighbors' views on the impacts of industrial broiler production. *Culture and Agriculture* 27(1): 45–60.

Constance, D.H., A. Bonanno, C. Cates, D. Argo, and M. Harris. 2003. Resisting integration in the global agro-food system: Corporate chickens and community controversy in Texas. In *Globalisation, localisation, and sustainable livelihoods*, ed. R. Almas and G. Lawrence, 103–118. Burlington: Ashgate Press.

Constance, D.H., F. Martinez, and G. Aboites. 2010. The globalization of the poultry industry: Tyson foods and Pilgrim's pride in Mexico. In *From community to consumption: New and classical statements in rural sociological research. Research in rural sociology and development*, vol. 16, ed. A. Bonanno, H. Bakker, R. Jussaume, Y. Kawamura, and M. Shucksmith, 59–76. Bingley: Emerald Group Publishing Ltd.

Countryman, C. 1996. Chicken fat goes to processors while growers go bankrupt. *The Progressive Populist* 2(2): 6.

Cullen, Jim. 1996. Poultry growers seek rights in Mississippi. *The Progressive Populist.* April. http://www.populist.com/4.96.Poultry.html. Accessed 15 Apr 2011.

Daniels, P. 1985. *Breaking the land: The transformation of cotton, tobacco, and rice culture since 1880.* Urbana: University of Illinois Press.

Davis, J.E. 1980. Capitalist agricultural development and the exploitation of the propertied laborer. In *The rural sociology of advanced societies*, ed. F.H. Buttel and H. Newby, 133–154. Montclair: Allenheld, Osmun, and Co.

Day, S. 2003a. Prosecutors in smuggling case against Tyson contend trial is about "corporate greed." *New York Times.* February 6, A26.

Day, S. 2003b. Jury clears Tyson Foods in use of illegal immigrants. *New York Times.* March 27, A1, 14.

Doye, D., B. Freking, and J. Payne. n.d. Broiler production: Considerations for potential growers. Oklahoma Cooperative Extension Service. F-202. http://pods.dasnr.okstate.edu/docushare/dsweb/Get/Document-3099/AGEC-202web.pdf. Accessed 1 Sept 2011.

Easterling, E.E., C.H. Braschler, and J.A. Kuehn. 1985. The South's comparative advantage in broiler production, processing, and distribution. Presented at the annual meeting of the Southern Agricultural Economics Association, Biloxi, February.

Fite, G. 1984. *Cotton fields no more: Agriculture in the U.S. South.* Lexington: University of Kentucky Press.

FLAG (Farmer's Legal Action Group). 2001. Assessing the impact of integrator practices on contract poultry growers. September. http://www.flaginc.org/topics/pubs/poultry/poultrypt1.pdf. Accessed 13 May 2011.

Friedland, W.H. 1984. Commodity systems analysis. In *Research in rural sociology*, vol. 1, ed. Harry Schwarzweller, 221–235. Greenwich: JAI Press.

Friedmann, H., and P. McMichael. 1989. Agriculture and the state system: The rise and fall of national agriculture. *Sociological Ruralis* 29(2): 93–117.

Gilsolfi, M. 2007. *From cotton farmers to poultry growers: The rise of industrial agriculture in upcountry Georgia, 1914–1960.* New York: Columbia University Press.

Goodman, D., B. Sorj, and J. Wilkinson. 1987. *From farming to biotechnology.* Oxford: Blackwell.

Gordon, J.S. 1996. The chicken story. *American Heritage* 47(5): 52–67.

Gordy, J.Frank. 1974. Broilers. In *American poultry history*, ed. John L. Skinner, 371–443. Madison: American Printing and Publishing, Inc.

Greene, J.L. 2011. USDA's proposed rule on livestock and poultry marketing practices. Congressional Research Service. 7-5700. R41673. http://nmaonline.org/pdf/USDAs_Proposed_Rule_on_Livestock_and_Poultry_Marketing_Practices.pdf. Accessed 12 July 2011.

Griffith, D. 1995. Hay trabajo: Poultry processing, rural industrialization, and the Latinization of low-wage labor. In *Any way you cut it: Meat processing and small town America*, ed. D. Stull, M.J. Broadway, and D. Griffith, 131–150. Lawrence: University Press of Kansas.

Hamilton, N.D. 1995. State regulation of production contracts. *University of Memphis Law Review* 25(3): 1051–1106.

Hamilton, N.D. 2002. Broiler contracting in the United States: A current contract analysis addressing legal issues and grower concerns. *Drake Journal of Agriculture Law* 7(1): 43–55.

Harrison, R. 1964. *Animal machines.* London: Vincent Stuart, Ltd.

Harvey, D. 1989. *The condition of post-modernity.* Oxford: Basil Blackwell.

Harvey, D. 2005. *A brief history of neo-liberalism.* Oxford: Oxford University Press.

Heffernan, W.D. 1984. Constraints in the poultry industry. In *Research in rural sociology and development*, vol. 1, ed. Harry Schwarzweller, 237–260. Greenwich: JAI Press.

Heffernan, W.D. 2000. Concentration of ownership in agriculture. In *Hungry for profit: The agribusiness threat to farmers, food, and the environment*, ed. F. Magdoff, J.B. Foster, and F.H. Buttel, 61–76. New York: Monthly Review Press.

Heffernan, W.D., and D.H. Constance. 1994. Transnational corporations and the globalization of the food System. In *From Columbus to ConAgra: The globalization of agriculture and food*, ed. A. Bonanno, L. Busch, W.H. Friedland, L. Gouveia, and E. Mingione, 29–51. Lawrence: University Press of Kansas.

Hendrickson, M., W.D. Heffernan, D. Lind, and E. Barham. 2008. Contractual integration in agriculture: Is there a bright side for agriculture of the middle? In *Food and the mid-level farm: Renewing an agriculture of the middle*, ed. T.A. Lyson, G.W. Stevenson, and R. Welsh, 79–100. Cambridge: The MIT Press.

Human Rights Watch. 2005. Blood, sweat and fear: Workers' rights in U.S. meat and poultry plants. January 24. http://www.hrw.org/en/reports/2005/01/24/blood-sweat-and-fear. Accessed 13 Nov 2008.

Ilvento, T., and A. Watson. 1998. *Poultry growers speak out: A survey of Delmarva poultry growers*. Newark: University of Delaware, College of Agriculture and Natural Resources.

JBS. 2009. JBS SA announces the acquisition of Pilgrim's Pride Corp. and the association with Bertin SA. September 16. http://www.slideshare.net/jbsri/acquisition-of-pilgrims-pride-and-association-with-bertin-sa. Accessed 23 Apr 2010.

Kim, C.K., and J.C. Curry. 1993. Fordism, flexible specialization, and agro-industrial restructuring: The case of the US broiler industry. *Sociologia Ruralis* 33(1): 61–80.

Knoeber, C.H. 1989. A real game of chicken: Contracts, tournaments, and the production of broilers. *Journal of Law, Economics, and Organizations* 5(2): 271–292.

Lasley, F.A. 1983. The U.S. poultry industry: Changing economics and structure. Agricultural Economics Report No. 502. Washington, DC: USDA, ERS. http://www.ers.usda.gov/publications/err3/err3.pdf. Accessed 1 Sept 2011.

Lewin-Solomons, S.B. 2000. Asset specificity and hold-up in franchising and grower contracts: A theoretical rationale for government regulation. Working paper. Cambridge, UK: University of Cambridge, Department of Applied Economics.

Little, P.D., and M.J. Watts (eds.). 1994. *Living under contract: Contract farming and agrarian transformation in sub-Saharan Africa*. Madison: University of Wisconsin Press.

Marion, Bruce W. 1986. *The organization and performance of the U.S. food system*. Lexington: Lexington Books, D.C. Heath and Co.

Marion, B.W. and H.B. Arthur. 1973. Dynamic factors in vertical commodity systems: A case study of the broiler system. Ohio Agricultural Research and Development Center, Research Bulletin 1065, Wooster.

Martin, L., and K. Zerring. 1997. Relationships between industrialized agriculture and environmental consequences: The case of vertical coordination in broilers and hogs. *Journal of Agricultural and Applied Economics* 29: 45–56.

Martinez, S.W. 1999. Vertical coordination in the pork and broiler industries: Implications for pork and chicken products. Economic Research Service, Report No. 7777. Washington, DC: USDA, ERS.

Mason, J., and P. Singer. 1990. *Animal factories: What agribusiness is doing to the family farm, the environment, and your health*. New York: Harmony Books.

McMichael, P. 2005. Global development and the corporate food regime. In *New directions in the sociology of global development: Research in rural sociology and development*, vol. II, ed. F.H. Buttel and P. McMichael, 265–299. New York: Elsevier, Ltd.

Meat Industry. 2001. Tyson wins battle: Buys IBP for $3.2B. January 7. http://www.spcnetwork.com/mii/2001/010126.htm. Accessed 15 Nov 2012.

MigrationInt. 2003. Sanctions: Tyson acquitted, airports. Laws: April, Number 2. http://www.migrationint.com.au/news/tahiti/apr_2003-02mn.asp. Accessed 24 May 2006.

Molnar, J.J., T. Hoban, and G. Brant. 2001. Passing the cluck, dodging pullets: Corporate power, environmental responsibility and the contract poultry grower. *Southern Rural Sociology* 18(2): 88–110.

Mooney, P.H. 1983. Toward a class analysis of Midwestern agriculture. *Rural Sociology* 48(4): 279–291.

Morais, R.C. 2004. Prodigal son. *Forbes Global* 7(17):1.

Morgan, D. 1979. *Merchants of grain*. New York: Viking.

Morrison, J.M. 1998. The poultry industry: A view of the swine industry's future. In *Pigs, profits, and rural communities*, ed. K.M. Thu and E.P. Durrenburger, 145–154. Albany: State University of New York Press.

Morrison, C. 2001. Contract poultry farming. *American Agricultural Movement Newsletter* 7(4):4. http://www.aaminc.org/newsletter/v7i4/v7i4p4.htm. Accessed 11 June 2011.

NSAC (National Sustainable Agriculture Coalition). 2011. Letters to congress in support of increased fairness for farmers and ranchers. April 28. http://sustainableagriculture.net/blog/gipsa-rule-support-letter/. Accessed 14 Sept 2011.

Pilgrim's Pride, Inc. 2005. Pilgrim's pride Mexico. http://www.pilgrimspride.com.mx. Accessed 30 Sept 2005.

Pilgrim's Pride, Inc. 2007. Pilgrim's pride completes acquisition of Goldkist. http://www.pilgrimspride.com/investors/GoldKist/jan09announcement.aspx. Accessed 13 July 2007.

Reimund, D.A., J.R. Martin, and C.V. Moore. 1981. Structural change in agriculture: The experience for broilers, fed cattle, and processing vegetables. Technical Bulletin No. 1648, ERS/USDA. http://naldc.nal.usda.gov/catalog/CAT81757950. Accessed 1 Sept 2011.

Rogers, G.B. 1963. Credit in the poultry industry. *Journal of Farm Economics* 45: 412–413, May.

Rogers, R.T., and R.J. Sexton. 1994. Assessing the importance of oligopsony in agricultural markets. *American Journal of Agricultural Economics* 76(5): 1143–1151.

Rosenbloom, J. 2003. Victims in the heartland: How immigration policy affects us all. *The American Prospect.* June 30. http://www.questia.com/library/1G1-104522644/victims-in-the-heartland-how-immigration-policy-affects. Accessed 2 Nov 2009.

Roy, E.P. 1972. *Contract farming and economic integration.* Danville: Interstate Printers and Publishers.

Rural Advancement Foundation International-USA (RAFI-UDA). 2010. Rules would level playing field for contract poultry farmers. http://www.rafiusa.org/docs/usdarulesreleaseshort.pdf. Accessed 15 June 2011.

Sachs, C. 1983. *The invisible farmers: Women in agricultural production.* Boulder: Westview Press.

Sack, K. 2002. Under the counter, grocer provided workers. *New York Times.* January 14. http://www.nytimes.com/2002/01/14/us/under-the-counter-grocer-provided-workers.html?pagewanted=all. Accessed 16 Jan 2012, A1, 13.

Schwartz, H. 1995. *Seasonal farmworkers in the United States.* New York: Columbia University Press.

Skully, D. 1998. Opposition to contract production: Self-selection, status and stranded assets. Presented at the annual meeting of the American Agricultural Economics Association, Salt Lake City, August.

Southeastern Farm Press (SEFP). 2011. Congressional letter corners USDA on proposed GIPSA rule. May 19. http://southeastfarmpress.com/government/congressional-letter-corners-usda-proposed-gipsa-rule. Accessed 15 July 2011.

Southern Cooperative Series. 1954. *Financing production and marketing of broilers in the South, Part 1: Dealer phase.* Auburn: Agricultural Experiment Stations of Southern States.

Starmer, E., A. Witteman, and T.A. Wise. 2006. Feeding the factory farm: Implicit subsidies to the broiler chicken industry. Working paper No. 06.03 June. Medford, MA: Global Development and Environment Institute, Tufts University.

Strausberg, S.F. 1995. *From hills and holler: The rise of the poultry industry in Arkansas.* Fayetteville: Arkansas Agricultural Experiment Station.

Striffler, S. 2005. *Chicken: The dangerous transformation of America's favorite food.* New Haven: Yale University Press.

Stuesse, A. 2009. Race, migration, and labor control: Neoliberal challenges to organizing Mississippi's poultry workers. In *Latino immigrants and the transformation of the U.S. South,* ed. M. Odem and E. Lacy, 91–111. Athens: University of Georgia Press.

Stull, D., and M.J. Broadway. 2004. *Slaughterhouse blues: The meat and poultry industry in North America.* Belmont: Wadsworth.

Stull, D., M.J. Broadway, and D. Griffith (eds.). 1995. *Any way you cut it: Meat processing and small town America.* Lawrence: University Press of Kansas.

Tanger, S.E. 2006. Enforcing corporate responsibility for violations of workplace immigration laws: The case of meatpacking. *Harvard Latino Law Review* 9: 59–89.

Taylor, C.R., and D.A. Domina. 2010. Restoring economic health to contract poultry production. Report prepared for the joint U.S. Department of Justice and U.S. Department of

Agriculture/GIPSA Public Workshop on Competition Issues in the Poultry Industry, Normal, May 21 http://www.dominalaw.com/ew_library_file/Restoring%20Economic%20Health%20to %20Contract%20Poultry%20Production.pdf. Accessed 22 June 2011.

Thu, K.J., and E.P. Durrenberger (eds.). 1998. *Pigs, profits, and rural communities*. Albany: State University of New York.

Tobin, B.F., and H.B. Arthur. 1964. *Dynamics of adjustment in the broiler industry*. Boston: Harvard University.

Tsoulouhas, T., and T. Vukina. 2001. Regulating broiler contracts: Tournament versus fixed performance standards. *American Journal of Agricultural Economics* 83(4): 1062–1073.

Tyson Foods, Inc. 2005a. About Tyson International. http://www.tysonfoodsinc.com/international. Accessed 13 May 2005.

Tyson Foods, Inc. 2005b. Tyson Foods, Inc. announces international initiatives. http://www.tysonfoodsinc.com/corporate/news/. Accessed 21 May 2005.

Tyson Foods, Inc. 2009. Fiscal 2009: Fact book. http://phx.corporate-ir.net/External.File?item=UGFyZW50SUQ9MjQ1NDd8Q2hpbGRJRD0tMXxUeXBlPTM=&t=1. Accessed 23 Apr 2010.

USDA/GAO. 1997. Concentration in agriculture. http://www.ams.usda.gov/concentration/home.htm. Accessed 17 June 2002.

USDA/GIPSA. 2010. Farm bill regulations: Proposed rule outline. http://archive.gipsa.usda.gov/psp/Farm_bill_rule_outline.pdf. Accessed 13 Apr 2011.

USDOJ (US Department of Justice). 2001. INS investigation of Tyson Foods, Inc. leads to 36 count indictment for conspiracy to smuggle illegal aliens for corporate profit. December 19. http://www.usdoj.gov/opa/pr/2001/December/01_crm_654.html. Accessed 6 May 2008.

USDOJ/USDA. 2010. *Public workshops exploring competition in agriculture: Poultry workshop*. Normal: Alabama A&M University, June 21. http://www.justice.gov/atr/public/workshops/ag2010/alagama-agworkshop-transcirpt.txt. Accessed 13 Apr 2011.

Vocke, G. 1991. Investments to transfer poultry production to developing countries. *American Journal of Agricultural Economics* 73(3): 951–954.

Vogeler, I. 1981. *The myth of the family farm: Agribusiness dominance in U.S. agriculture*. Boulder: Westview Press.

Vukina, T. 2001. Vertical integration and contracting in the US poultry industry. *Journal of Food Distribution Research* 81: 61–74.

Vukina, T., and P. Leegomonchai. 2006a. Olipogsony power, asset specificity, and hold up: Evidence from the broiler industry. *American Journal of Agricultural Economics* 88(3): 589–605.

Vukina, T., and P. Leegomonchai. 2006b. Political economy of regulation of broiler contracts. *American Journal of Agricultural Economics* 88(5): 1258–1265.

Wellford, H. 1972. *Sowing the wind*. New York: Grossman Publishers.

Welsh, R. 1996. The industrial reorganization of U.S. agriculture: An overview and background report. Policy Studies Report #6. Greenbelt: Henry A. Wallace Institute for Alternative Agriculture.

Welsh, R. 1997. Vertical coordination, producer response and the locus of control over agricultural production decisions. *Rural Sociology* 62(4): 491–507.

Williams, W.H. 1998. *Delmarva's chicken industry: 75 years of progress*. Georgetown: Delmarva Poultry Industry.

Wilson, J. 1986. The political economy of contract farming. *Review of Radical Political Economy* 18(4): 40–47.

Winders, B. 2009. *The politics of food supply: U.S. agricultural policy in the world economy*. New Haven: Yale University Press.

Wolf, S., B. Heuth, and E. Ligon. 2001. Policing mechanisms in agricultural contracts. *Rural Sociology* 66(3): 359–381.

Wu, S., and B. Roe. 2006. Tournaments, fairness, and risk. *American Journal of Agricultural Economics* 88(3): 561–573.

Chapter 9
Agricultural Contracting and Agrifood Competition

Ani L. Katchova

Abstract The industrialization of agriculture is associated with tighter supply chains where vertical coordination between farmers and processors is facilitated by the use of agricultural contracts. An overview is provided on the recent trends in the use and structure of agricultural contracts followed by an examination of how the competition among processors may affect agricultural contracts. Many reasons exist for using agricultural contracts, including improved risk management and reduced transaction cost. On the other hand, the growing use of agricultural contracts and processor concentration raises concerns that processors may exercise market power, for example by offering lower contract prices in absence of local competition. Previous studies using the new empirical industrial organization models show that processing industries are not perfectly competitive but the price distortions are very small. The focus here is on examining price competition from a farmer's instead of an industry's point of view. Recent studies using farm-level data that show that the absence of other contractors or spot markets in producers' areas does not lead to statistically significant price differences in agricultural contracts for most commodities. These findings provide evidence that most agricultural processors do not exercise market power by reducing prices when other local buyers are not available. Therefore, the recent trends of industrialization and increased vertical coordination in agriculture are likely occurring for reasons other than processors exercising market power.

A.L. Katchova, Ph.D. (✉)
Department of Agricultural Economics, University of Kentucky,
320 Barnhart Bldg, 40546 Lexington, KY, USA
e-mail: akatchova@uky.edu

H.S. James Jr. (ed.), *The Ethics and Economics of Agrifood Competition*,
The International Library of Environmental, Agricultural and Food Ethics 20,
DOI 10.1007/978-94-007-6274-9_9,

9.1 Introduction

The industrialization of US agriculture is typically associated with tighter supply chains that include greater concentration of production on a decreasing number of farms, more vertical coordination in the production and marketing system, and significant concentration downstream from the farm (Ahearn et al. 2005). These structural changes are partially motivated by consumer demands for specific attributes of agricultural products. More vertical coordination in the supply chain facilitates farmer-processor interactions and ensures that the desired quality and quantity of products will be provided to consumers as demanded. The increased coordination and concentration of the production and marketing systems are facilitated by the use of agricultural contracts between farmers and downstream processors.

The use of agricultural contracts, which is one of the major structural changes in the agricultural sector, has been generally increasing over time. For example, in 2008 producers used marketing and production contracts to market 39% of the value of US agricultural production, up from 36% in 1991 and 11% in 1969 (MacDonald and Korb 2011). According to USDA statistics, the concentration of the food manufacturing industry has also been increasing with the mean industry four-firm concentration ratio increasing from 35% in 1982 to 46% in 1997. An important policy question is whether the increased concentration in the processing industry and the increased use of agricultural contracts are a desirable result of cost efficiencies in production or the undesirable effect of market power from agribusiness processors (Ahearn et al. 2005).

Several questions are important to consider when examining industrialization, consolidation, and contracting trends, which affects competition in the agricultural sector. For example, farmers may have different reasons for using agricultural contracts or for marketing independently in the spot markets. Processors may have different reasons for locating in a specific geographic area, competing with other local buyers in that area, selecting an appropriate size of their operations, and structuring their contracts with local producers. Agricultural markets have unique characteristics due to the nature of agricultural production, marketing, and processing which often occur in a narrow geographic region. Consequently, the market structure and competition in a local market for agricultural commodities have important implications for processors' pricing behavior and interactions with farmers.

The main focus here is on examining price competition from a farmer's instead of an industry's point of view. Studies using farm-level data that show that the absence of other contractors or spot markets in producers' areas does not lead to statistically significant price differences in agricultural contracts for most commodities. These findings provide evidence that most agricultural processors do not exercise market power by reducing prices when other local buyers are not available. Therefore, the recent trends of industrialization and increased vertical coordination in agriculture are likely occurring for reasons other than processors exercising market power.

This chapter begins by describing the vertical coordination in the agricultural sector and the most commonly used types of agricultural contracts. It then discusses current trends in agricultural contracting, as well as reasons for and concerns about the use of agricultural contracting. It next defines and examines various types of market power that can be exercised by agricultural processors especially when agricultural contracts are used. Several studies on agricultural contracts are discussed, followed by studies examining the price competitiveness of agricultural contracts when farmers have limited marketing options. The final section concludes and provides policy recommendations.

9.2 Vertical Coordination in the Agricultural Sector

Agricultural production can be organized in several ways depending on how commodities are transferred from the farm to the next player in the supply chain: spot (cash) markets, vertical integration, and agricultural (marketing and production) contracts. When farmers deliver their products to the spot markets, they are paid the prevailing market price for their commodities when the ownership is transferred. When using spot markets, farmers make production, financial, and marketing decisions and retain full control and ownership of the commodities until an agreement is reached at or after harvest when the commodities are delivered. There may be premiums or discounts paid based on commodity attributes but such characteristics have to be observable and easily measurable.

Under vertical integration, the farm is jointly owned by a producer and the next player in the production process. Decisions are made internally as a part of the same control unit rather than by using contracts. Considering different types of vertical coordination, spot markets and vertical integration lie at the opposite ends in terms of grower independence to make decisions and bear production and marketing risk.

Finally, the production of commodities can be coordinated through marketing or production contracts. Marketing contracts represent an agreement between a farmer and a contractor that specifies a price or price mechanism, a delivery outlet, and a quantity to be delivered of a given commodity. Paulson et al. (2010) examine these characteristics for corn and soybean marketing contracts used by Midwest farmers. They find that 13% of the contracts specify a price formula, 21.4% of the contracts specify a premium or discount for commodity attributes, and 76.2% specify a quantity to be delivered. Marketing contracts are predominantly used to reduce price risk for farmers. The farmer owns the commodity during the production process and exercises control over managerial decisions. Marketing contracts are used predominantly in crop production.

Production contracts specify farmer and contractor responsibilities in terms of production inputs and practices and a fee payment for the farmer. The contract specifies the services that will be provided by the farmer, the contractor provision of inputs, and the payment mechanism for the farmer's services. The farmer's payment in production contracts is in the form of a fee or compensation for his/her services, instead of a payment for the commodity value, as is the case for marketing contracts. Under production contracts, farmers do not have ownership of the commodity and have limited decision making power throughout the production process. Production contracts are predominantly used in livestock production.

9.3 Current Trends in Agricultural Contracting

The primary data source for studying agricultural contracting in the US is the USDA's Agricultural Resource Management Survey (ARMS). It is conducted annually by the US Department of Agriculture and provides comprehensive statistics on marketing and production contract use by US farm businesses. ARMS is the USDA's primary source of information on financial conditions, marketing practices, and resource use by US farms and the economic well-being of US farm households. The ARMS questionnaire includes questions on marketing and production contracts, including the quantity contracted and the price or fee received for each commodity under contract. In select years, the ARMS questionnaire also includes information on contract design regarding price formulas, quantity and attribute specifications, type of contractor (a cooperative or an investor-owned firm), and availability of other marketing options in the farmers' area.

Farmers have been using agricultural contracts for the last few decades. While the proportion of farms using contracts has remained relatively stable between nine and 12% since 1969, the value of production under contract has increased from 11% in 1969 to 39% in 2008 (MacDonald and Korb 2011). This increasing trend has stabilized and even reversed in the last decade, with 36–41% of agricultural production being under contract. This is partially due to the recent commodity price trends in which the prices of five major field crops (corn, soybeans, wheat, cotton, and rice) have increased but these commodities are less likely to be produced under contract. According to the ARMS data, the percent of farms using contracts was 11.2% in 2001, 11% in 2005, and 10.4% in 2009, while the volume of production under contract was 38.4% in 2001, 40.7% in 2005, and 37.4% in 2009 (see Table 9.1). Therefore, contracting activities have remained relatively stable during the most recent decade.

The use of contracts varies depending on farm size; larger farms are more likely to use contracts and contract higher proportion of their production (Katchova and Miranda 2004). ARMS defines rural residence farms as family-operated farms with less than $250,000 in gross sales whose primary occupation is not farming; intermediate farms as family-operated farms with less than $250,000 in gross sales whose primary occupation is farming; and commercial farms as those with sales exceeding $250,000 and all non-family farms. Table 9.1 shows that rural residence farms are not very actively involved in agricultural contracting; only 3.4% of rural residence farms used contracts and they contracted 11.2% of their production in 2009. On the other hand, commercial farms are actively using contracts; 46.9% of

Table 9.1 Percent of production under contract by US farms

	All farms	Rural residence farms	Intermediate farms	Commercial farms
Percent of farms contracting				
2001	11.2	3.6	16.4	43.3
2005	11.0	4.1	15.8	45.6
2009	10.4	3.4	10.7	46.9
Percent of production under contract				
2001	38.4	13.5	24.3	45.0
2005	40.7	12.7	20.0	47.4
2009	37.4	11.	12.9	42.6

Source: USDA-ARMS data

Table 9.2 Percent of production under contract by commodity

Commodity	Percent	Commodity	Percent
Crops	25.8	Livestock	52.0
Corn	22.7	Cattle	25.5
Soybeans	23.5	Hogs	66.7
Wheat	15.2	Poultry and eggs	90.1
Sugar beets	73.7	Dairy	52.0
Rice	30.9		
Peanuts	66.5		
Tobacco	60.1		
Potatoes	53.8		
Cotton	36.3		
Fruit	33.9		
Vegetables	46.7		

Source: 2009 USDA-ARMS data. The numbers represent the percent of production under contract to total production for each commodity

commercial farms used contracts and they contracted 42.6% of their production in 2009. Therefore, larger farms are more involved with contracting both in terms of percent of farms contracting as well as the proportion of production contracted.

The use of contracts also varies depending on the commodities that farmers are producing and contracting. Contracts are less commonly used for crops (25.8% of the crop production was under contract in 2009) than for livestock (52% of the livestock production was under contract in 2009) (see Table 9.2). Among crops, the highest shares of production under contracts are for sugar beets, peanuts, tobacco, potatoes, and vegetables. The lowest shares of production under contract are for wheat, corn, soybeans, rice, fruit, and cotton. Among livestock, contracting is most prevalent in the poultry industry, where 90.1% of the production was under contract in 2009, followed by hogs, dairy, and cattle.

The recent trends indicate that while contracting has been relatively stable in the last decade, contract use varies depending on the size of farms and commodities that the farms produce, among other factors. These factors need to be taken into consideration when examining agricultural contracting and competition.

9.4 Reasons for Agricultural Contracting

Producers may prefer to use contracts instead of spot markets to market their commodities for a variety of reasons, including improved risk management and reduced transaction costs. Specifically, farmers may use contracts in order to reduce the price and income risk that they face. When farmers enter marketing or production contracts, these contracts usually specify a price or fee to be paid to producers. Therefore, contracts allow for risk shifting from a farmer to a processor that may be better able to hedge against price risk.

Contracts also provide farmers with incentives to improve their incentives to lower production costs and deliver commodities with specific attributes. This transaction-cost approach may facilitate the process of coordination with downstream entities by increasing the information flow and sharing of management responsibilities and production decision making. The production of certain agricultural commodities requires extensive capital investments in new technology and/or specific assets. Farmers may be reluctant to invest in land and other agricultural assets when they have limited marketing options. In this case, contracts can be used to assure farmers of secure markets, and therefore a steady income stream to pay off new investments.

Three characteristics of agricultural production facilitate the trend toward increasing contract adoption and use: asset-, site-, and time specificity (Williamson 1985). Asset specificity indicates that assets employed in agricultural production are highly specialized for agricultural use, and therefore have limited options for alternative uses. Site specificity refers to the fact that the transportation of some agricultural commodities is costly, and therefore requires that the commodities be marketed in the geographic region where production occurs. Time specificity indicates that many agricultural products are perishable and must therefore reach processors within a specified, relatively limited period of time. Because of asset-, site-, and time specificity, contracts are an attractive way for farmers to market their commodities.

Farmers and processors may also use contracts to secure specific commodity attributes. Some attributes (such as using specific production practices or growing a specific variety of a commodity) cannot be observed or are hard to measure in spot markets. Farmers may not be willing to produce commodities with specific attributes unless they can be assured of a certain market and a price premium. In the case of unobservable or hard-to-measure attributes, processors may be willing to offer farmers contracts to guarantee the quantity and specified qualities for the commodities they need.

Another reason for using agricultural contracts is that it may be more cost efficient for a processor to offer contracts and thereby secure stable supply from farmers in order to realize economies of scale (Allen and Lueck 1998). This is especially true for markets characterized by limited competition and/or thin markets, where contracting may be the only option to secure stable supply for processor's operations.

9.5 Concerns About Agricultural Contracting

Contracts have certain advantages for both producers and processors but they can also introduce new risks for producers. These risks include: (1) production-shortfall risks associated with the use of contracts, (2) hold-up risks because of asset-, site-, and time specificity and limited buyer competition, (3) thinning spot markets and decreasing price information transparency, and (4) market power that processors may potentially exercise (MacDonald et al. 2004).

Agricultural contracts typically specify price, quantity, quality, and a time frame for delivery of a commodity. While contracts can reduce price and income risks, they may also introduce other types of risks for farmers. For example, in case of production shortfall when the contract specifies a particular quantity to be delivered, farmers will have to obtain the additional quantity needed at the spot market at an uncertain price in order to fulfill their contract. Also, in case farmers are unable to meet the specific attributes in the contract, they may have to sell their products at a discount or not be able to deliver on the contract.

Contracts may help farmers make long-term investments by allowing farmers to obtain credit to finance such investments. However, it is often the case that contracts have much shorter terms than the time required to pay back these investments. At the time of contract renewal, farmers may incur hold-up risks where processors offer lower prices to them if farmers have limited alternative uses of agricultural assets and limited alternative marketing options for their commodities. Therefore, asset-, site-, and time specificity and limited regional competition facilitate the hold-up risks that farmers may face.

Another concern about agricultural contracting is that as more volume is produced under contract, too few transactions would take place in the spot markets for these markets to function. This trend further encourages more contracting because farmers need to find a reliable market for their production, especially when there are a limited number of buyers. The poultry industry is an example where most of the production is under contract and spot markets are no longer viable. While contracts have many advantages, spot markets play an important role in providing price information and transparency. Contract prices remain confidential or they are hard to observe, which makes it easier for processors to exercise market power.

9.6 Contracting, Market Power, and Local Competition

In economics, market power is defined as the ability of a firm to affect either the total quantity or the price of a good or service in the market. A monopsony is defined as having only one buyer, and an oligopsony is defined as having only a few buyers in the relevant market. When there are a limited number of processors in the market (increased concentration and consolidation), there is a concern that buyers make take advantage of the lack of competition and act anti-competitively, by offering lower prices to farmers or restricting the quantity of commodities purchased.

Processors may use several strategies to exercise market power: (1) contractors may deter entry by other local buyers, (2) they may limit price competition among existing buyers, (3) they may use captive supplies, (4) they may engage in discriminatory pricing, and (5) they may offer lower prices when farmers have limited other options to market their commodities to other contractors or spot markets in the farmers' area (MacDonald and Korb 2011; Katchova 2010a; Ward 2005). When processors have secured a large share of the local production under agricultural contracts, it may be costlier for new processors to enter the local market. The reason is that processors need to be large enough to realize economies of scale and operate their businesses profitably. When one processor has contracted a substantial portion of the local production, a potential entrant will have to pay substantially higher prices to secure an adequate supply for their processing facilities.

Contracts may also be structured to incorporate pricing mechanisms that limit competitive bidding for commodity prices. For example, the top-of-the-market pricing used in cattle contracts sets the base price at the highest spot market price paid for cattle during the established period. This pricing clause may limit aggressive price bidding by contractors in the spot markets as they procure additional local supply, because they have to offer this price on all existing contracts. If there are only a few contractors in the farmer's area, the contractors may collude to bid less aggressively and offer farmers lower prices.

Packers may also engage in captive supplies in order to procure livestock for their operations. Captive supplies are slaughter livestock that are committed to a specific buyer (meatpacker) through a contract or marketing agreement 14 or more days prior to slaughter. Packers may exercise market power by reducing competition on the spot markets and offering lower prices on the spot markets when they hold a captive supply of cattle.

Contractors may also offer different prices to farmers for commodities of the same quality and attributes. It may be hard to detect if price differences are due to differences in quality and attributes of the marketed commodity or due to the exercise of market power if prices are not completely transparent in the market. This is particularly true when there are confidentiality clauses that forbid farmers from disclosing details of their contracts to others. If contractors have monopsony power, they can offer lower prices to secure most of the local supply and then pay marginally higher prices only on the additional supply that they need.

Contracts can be designed in a way that allows buyers to exercise market power by offering lower prices to farmers. Because of the spatial nature of agricultural production, transportation costs, and commodity perishability, many farmers are restricted to selling their production within their geographic areas. Therefore, competition from other buyers located near the farm business, such as other contractors and spot markets in the farmer's area play an important role. Where farmers do not have such alternative marketing options, it is easier for contractors to exercise monopsony market power.

9.7 Studies on Agricultural Contracts

Agricultural contracting is typically studied using the principal-agent economic framework, where the contractor is the principal and the farmer is an agent. In the principal-agent framework, the principal contracts with the agent to pursue the principal's interest. However, because of incomplete and asymmetric information, the agent may not fully act in the principal's interest (moral hazard), making the principal's return risky. The principal-agent model is frequently used to explain the reasons farmers choose to use agricultural contracts, because of the risk shifting from a farmer to a contractor.

The two most common reasons for using contracts are improved risk management and reduced production and transaction costs. The empirical research is mixed on which reason is more important but there is evidence of farmers using both reasons to justify using contracts (Allen and Lueck 1995; Key 2004). On the other hand, the increased use of agricultural contracts raises concerns that processors may exploit market power. For example, contracting in the livestock industry is especially controversial where a few meatpackers handle most of the livestock purchases while quantities sold on the spot markets continue to decrease. In response to these concerns, Congress has passed laws in an effort to regulate livestock contracts and require mandatory price reporting for the processing industry.

The literature examining agricultural contracts is relatively limited mostly due to the fact that data on commodity contracts are scarce. Furthermore, because contract types and characteristics vary widely across commodities, it is difficult to generalize results from individual commodities to the entire agricultural sector. In addition to collecting data on the contracts themselves, it is useful to collect relevant data on contracting parties, contract outcomes, and the economic environment, since relatively little is known about how observed producer and contractor characteristics influence the design of marketing contracts (Hueth et al. 2007).

Paulson et al. (2010) use contract theory to investigate the existence of a link between the principal (contractor) and agent (farmer) characteristics and the resulting contract between the parties, after accounting for the endogenous matching between agents, contractors, and activities. In the case of corn and soybeans, they find evidence of producer characteristics (such as the use of crop insurance, farm size, leverage, and whether the farm is a hobby farm) having an impact on the decision to enter contract agreements. However, they find almost no evidence of observed producer or contractor characteristics influencing contract attributes such as pricing, quality, and quantity provisions of their contracts. Katchova and Miranda (2004) find similar results where producer characteristics such as farmer's age and education affect their likelihood of adopting marketing contracts but not do influence the quantity contracted, number of contracts, or type of contracts that farmers use. Their findings indicate that factors other than the proxies used for farmer risk preferences may play a more dominant role in determining the specific structure of agricultural marketing contracts. Another explanation is that monopsony market power of the contractor might also limit the menu of contract options available to producers as well as the producers' bargaining power with respect to contract terms.

Some empirical studies have examined farmers' decisions to adopt marketing and production contracts and the types of contracts they adopt. Some farmers use marketing contracts to respond to price risk, while others use marketing contracts for price enhancement (Harwood et al. 1999). Marketing contracts can reduce income risk and improve access to credit, particularly when used jointly with crop insurance. However, despite the benefits associated with marketing contracts, surveys have found that farmers use fewer marketing contracts than implied by theoretical optimal hedge models (Goodwin and Schroeder 1994; Musser et al. 1996; Sartwelle et al. 2000). Contracting is also found to be positively associated with the scale of production for farm businesses (Key 2004).

Other studies have compared contract and independent producers to identify distinguishing characteristics and reasons for contracting. These studies discuss the effects of risk, transaction costs, and autonomy when selecting marketing arrangements (Davis and Gillespie 2007). Key (2005) further shows that farmers' decisions to contract or produce independently depend on the distribution of income and the attributes associated with both contract and independent production arrangements.

Studies have also examined market prices in livestock spot markets in the presence of captive supplies and contracts with pricing clauses. The principal-agent model is used within a market equilibrium model of contract and cash markets to analyze the impact of contracting on spot market prices, finding that the formula-price contracts can theoretically increase or decrease cash market prices (Wang and Jaenicke 2006). Empirically, top-of-the market pricing has been shown to have anticompetitive consequences when the same buyers who purchase contract cattle with top-of-the-market clause also compete to procure cattle in the spot market (Xia and Sexton 2004). Zhang and Sexton (2000) further show that the spot price is inversely related to the incidence of contract use in the market, but this effect is not significant in markets where the spatial dimension is less important.

Numerous studies have examined market power in the processing industries, typically using the new empirical industrial organization (NEIO) structural models with aggregate industry-level data. The conceptual models include non-cooperative games, Nash's equilibrium, and various forms of dynamic games. Many interactions in agriculture can be represented as a game when production, pricing, and consumption are set in the first stage and players receive payoffs in the second stage. A key consequence of the industrialization of agriculture is that market power can be present at multiple stages of the market chain including processors and retailers. Most of these studies find that while processors exercise market power, the resulting price distortions are small in magnitude (Sexton 2000).

Several studies examine agricultural contracting and price competitiveness from a farmers' perspective using farm-level data rather than from a processing industry's perspective supported by industry data. Katchova (2010a) has proposed a new approach to examine price distortions due to processor concentration, where competition from local buyers such as other contractors and spot markets play an important role. In addition, Katchova (2010b) has examined how the bargaining power of farmers affects contract price competitiveness depending on the organizational type of the contractor (cooperative or investor-owned firm). The price competitiveness of agricultural contracts is examined in greater detail in the next section.

9.8 Price Competitiveness of Agricultural Contracts

The recent trend of increasing processor concentration and the widespread use of contracts has resulted in reduced competition in many local markets. These conditions create an opportunity for processors to act anti-competitively and offer lower prices to farmers. However, it is an empirical question of whether or not processors take advantage of the situation when farmers have limited marketing options and offer them lower prices.

Katchova (2010a) examines the price competitiveness of marketing and production contracts depending on the availability of alternative marketing options (other local contractors or spot markets). Specifically, the study tests if prices on comparable agricultural contracts are significantly lower for farmers lacking alternative marketing channels. Unlike other studies that compare spot market with contract prices, this study compared only contract prices based on whether or not farmers have alternative options.

Contract data for six commodities (corn, soybeans, wheat, cotton, milk, and broilers) were obtained from the Agricultural Resource Management Survey for 2003–2005. The availability of alternative marketing options differs based on the commodities farmers produce. Most farmers producing crops have other local contractors as well as local spot markets. About two-thirds of the marketing contracts for corn, soybeans, wheat, and cotton were located in areas with other contractors, and even higher proportion of these contracts (about 83–95%) had local spot markets. About 77% of milk marketing contracts had other local contractors, but only 23% had local spot markets. About half of the contracts for broilers were located in areas with other contractors, while only 3% of them had local spot markets.

Katchova (2010a) compares the prices for contracts that have other local buyers in the area (such as other contractors or open markets) with contracts that do not have other marketing options in the area. The propensity score matching methods were used to estimate price differences in order to compare contracts with similar characteristics. The findings show that only a few commodities had statistical differences in commodity prices above 3–5%. Corn growers receive 3.5% statistically significant higher prices if other local contractors are present and corn growers receive 3.9% statistically significant higher prices if there are local spot markets. The rest of the commodities have estimated price differences that are smaller than the 3–5% level needed to detect statistical significance. Overall, results from the Katchova (2010a) study show lack of statistically significant price distortions exceeding 4–5% in agricultural contracts between producers and processors. These findings are consistent with the explanation that the upward trend in contract use is likely not due to the exercise of price setting market power by processors but may be due to other factors such as increased efficiency associated with the vertical coordination in the production and marketing of agricultural commodities.

In addition, Katchova (2010b) examines commodity price differences for agricultural contracts depending on the organizational form of the contractors. In particular, marketing and production contract prices are compared for farmers marketing their commodities with cooperatives versus investor-owned firms (IOF). The study addresses the question of whether farmers who are members of cooperatives receive market prices for their commodities as expected according to cooperative principles. The propensity score matching method is used to estimate price differences in agricultural contracts to ensure comparison of similar contracts.

The analysis was conducted for six commodities (corn, soybeans, wheat, cotton, milk, and broilers) using data from the USDA's Agricultural Resource Management Survey for 2003–2005. Contracting with cooperatives differs based on the commodities farmers produce. Farmer contracting with cooperatives is most prevalent for milk contracts, with about 79% of the milk contracts being with cooperatives. A quarter to a half of the contracts for corn, soybeans, wheat, and cotton are with cooperatives. Only 6% of the broiler contracts are with cooperatives. The results in Katchova (2010b) show that the organizational form of the contractor generally does not lead to significant differences in contract prices for most commodities. The fact that prices received on contracts do not seem to be different based on the type of contractor provides indirect evidence of a cooperative benefit since the members do not have price penalties in contracting with cooperatives but retain the upside potential of a patronage payment.

The structure and performance of agricultural contracts are influenced by the competition among processors to offer farmers either more appealing terms or contract prices (Sykuta and Cook 2001). In comparison to most other industries, agriculture remains more heterogeneous in the organizational forms of contractors even though the contractors provide similar contracting services.

Using a different approach to study competition uniquely from a farmer's point of view, the findings by Katchova (2010a and 2010b) are also consistent with the limited evidence for market power in the processing industry found in other studies using the NEIO structural models. The two studies examined price competitiveness of agricultural contracts depending on the availability of alternative marketing options and the type of contractor finding and found limited evidence of contract price differences.

9.9 Concluding Remarks

The increased contracting use and processor concentration represent key trends in the industrialization of agriculture. Contract use has generally increased over time but its intensity still varies greatly among commodities. Contracts now dominate the exchange of several commodities such as tobacco, peanuts, sugar beets, broilers, and hogs. Other commodities such as corn, wheat, and soybeans continue to be sold predominantly on the spot markets. Because contracting is an alternative way to market agricultural production, producers may be more likely to switch to contracts when the markets are already thin; this further accelerates the trend of increased contracting. Contracts are more likely to be used in geographic areas which have a limited number of buyers, which raises concerns that processors may be exercising market power. Despite the prevalence of contracts in the agricultural sector, there is limited evidence that processors are exercising market power in terms of offering lower prices to farmers who may not have other marketing options in their areas. Farmers may also switch to contracting for other reasons such as guaranteeing a secure market outlet, obtaining credit, and making capital investments in agricultural specific assets.

The shift from spot markets to contracting also raises concerns about whether spot markets will be a viable option in the future or the majority of agricultural production will be produced under contract. When more output is marketed with contracts, the lower traded volume on the spot markets may induce a tipping point where the thinness and uncertainty of spot markets can force independent producers to accept contracts (MacDonald et al. 2004). Additional evidence by Katchova (2010a) shows that the absence of spot markets does not lead to lower commodity prices offered by the processing industry. This means that new regulations regarding the increasing concentration of processors may not be needed at this time, but government intervention may still be desirable to ensure that there is no loss in price information because of contracting. For example, the Livestock Mandatory Reporting Act of 1999 requires large packers and importers to report to USDA the details of all transactions involving purchases of livestock. Such regulations ensure transparency of commodity prices when the sector undergoes structural changes toward more contracting. Price transparency is of crucial importance for farmers since the consolidation in the processing industry may lead to a decreasing bargaining power for producers when negotiating prices and contract terms. Evidence shows that farmers marketing with investor-owned firms do not receive lower prices than those marketing with cooperatives (Katchova 2010b), indicating again that processors may not be exercising market power.

There may also be beneficial effects for moving toward increased contracting and reducing spot market transactions. From a government policy perspective, the shift away from spot markets toward contracting facilitates the traceability of food and food ingredients in the agricultural supply chain. The increased vertical coordination in the production and marketing of agricultural commodities is typically associated with ensuring food safety and delivering quality assurances to consumers, especially when commodity attributes are not easily observable.

The agricultural economics literature has examined market power using the NEIO structural models and aggregate industry-level data and has concluded that the processing industry is exercising market power but it is small in magnitude (for an overview, see Sexton 2000). Additional studies using farm-level data have examined imperfect competition among local processors uniquely from a farmers' perspective by taking into consideration the spatial nature of agricultural production and marketing (Katchova 2010a). These new findings are also consistent with the limited evidence for market power in the processing industry found in other studies. While the absence of local competition from other buyers currently does not lead to lower prices, the bargaining power of farmers will likely continue to weaken as more production shifts to contracting with larger processors. Therefore, policy makers need to monitor these structural changes in agricultural contracting as more government intervention may be needed in the future to prevent anti-competitive behavior by processors in absence of local competition.

References

Ahearn, M.C., P. Korb, and D. Banker. 2005. The industrialization and contracting of agriculture. *Journal of Agricultural and Applied Economics* 37: 347–364.

Allen, D.W., and D. Lueck. 1995. Risk preferences and the economics of contracts. *American Economic Review: Papers and Proceedings* 85: 447–451.

Allen, D.W., and D. Lueck. 1998. The nature of the farm. *Journal of Law and Economics* 66: 343–386.

Davis, C.G., and J.M. Gillespie. 2007. Factors affecting the selection of business arrangements by U.S. hog farmers. *Review of Agricultural Economics* 29: 331–348.

Goodwin, B.K., and T.C. Schroeder. 1994. Human capital, producer education programs, and the adoption of forward-pricing methods. *American Journal of Agricultural Economics* 76: 936–947.

Harwood, J., R. Heifner, K. Coble, J. Perry, and A. Somwaru. 1999. Managing risk in farming: Concepts, research, and analysis. Agricultural economic report 774. Washington, DC: Economic Research Service, U.S. Department of Agriculture.

Hueth, B., E. Ligon, and C. Dimitri. 2007. Agricultural contracts: Data and research needs. *American Journal of Agricultural Economics* 89: 1276–1281.

Katchova, A.L. 2010a. Agricultural contracts and alternative marketing options: A matching analysis. *Journal of Agricultural and Applied Economics* 42: 1–6.

Katchova, A.L. 2010b. Agricultural cooperatives and contract price competitiveness. *Journal of Cooperatives* 24: 2–12.

Katchova, A.L., and M.J. Miranda. 2004. Two-step econometric estimation of farm characteristics affecting marketing contract decisions. *American Journal of Agricultural Economics* 86: 88–102.

Key, N. 2004. Agricultural contracting and the scale of production. *Agricultural and Resource Economics Review* 33: 255–271.

Key, N. 2005. How much do farmers value their independence? *Agricultural Economics* 22: 117–126.

MacDonald, J., and P. Korb. 2011. Agricultural contracting update: Contracts in 2008. Economic information bulletin no. 72. Washington, DC: Economic Research Service, U.S. Department of Agriculture.

MacDonald, J., J. Perry, M. Ahearn, D. Banker, W. Chambers, C. Dimitri, N. Key, K. Nelson, and L. Southard. 2004. Contracts, markets, and prices: Organizing the production and use of agricultural commodities. Agricultural economic report number 837. Washington, DC: Economic Research Service, U.S. Department of Agriculture.

Musser, W.N., G.F. Patrick, and D.T. Eckman. 1996. Risk and grain marketing behavior of large-scale farmers. *Review of Agricultural Economics* 18: 65–77.

Paulson, N.D., A.L. Katchova, and S.H. Lence. 2010. An empirical analysis of the determinants of marketing contract structures for corn and soybeans. *Journal of Agricultural and Food Industrial Organization* 8(4): 1–23.

Sartwelle, J., D. O'Brien, W. Tierney Jr., and T. Eggers. 2000. The effect of personal and farm characteristics upon grain marketing practices. *Journal of Agricultural and Applied Economics* 32: 95–111.

Sexton, R.J. 2000. Industrialization and consolidation in the U.S. Food Sector: Implication for competition and welfare. *American Journal of Agricultural Economics* 82: 1087–1104.

Sykuta, M.E., and M.L. Cook. 2001. A new institutional economics approach to contracts and cooperatives. *American Journal of Agricultural Economics* 83: 1273–1279.

Wang, W., and E.C. Jaenicke. 2006. Simulating the impacts of contract supplies in a spot market-contract market equilibrium. *American Journal of Agricultural Economics* 88: 1062–1077.

Ward, C. 2005. Beef Packers' captive supplies: An upward trend? A pricing edge? *Choices* 20: 167–171.

Williamson, O. 1985. *The economic institutions of capitalism*. New York: The Free Press.

Xia, T., and R.J. Sexton. 2004. The competitive implications of top-of-the-market and related contract-pricing clauses. *American Journal of Agricultural Economics* 86: 124–138.

Zhang, M., and R.J. Sexton. 2000. Captive supplies and the cash market price: A spatial markets approach. *Journal of Agricultural and Resource Economics* 25: 88–108.

Chapter 10
Trading on Pork and Beans: Agribusiness and the Construction of the Brazil-China-Soy-Pork Commodity Complex

Emelie K. Peine

Abstract As "food crises" appear to increase in both frequency and severity around the world, renewed attention is focused on the political economy of the global food system. Specifically, the emerging production and consumption powerhouses of Latin America and China are drawing attention to the reconfiguration of trade flows and the role of powerful multinational agribusinesses in that process. This chapter examines the emergence of the Brazil-China-soy-pork commodity complex as a lens on global agro-food restructuring. As China has shifted pork production to an intensified, industrial model, its demand for imported soy to feed hogs has skyrocketed. Brazil has largely stepped in to meet that demand, which has led to the integration of the Chinese pork sector and the Brazilian soy sector in a highly interdependent commodity complex. The emergence of this commodity complex signals a shift away from the traditional production and consumption centers of soy (the US and EU/Japan, respectively) towards new South-South trade flows. What has remained the same—at least to this point—is the control exercised over that commodity complex by the four primary transnational soybean brokers and processers: Archer Daniels Midland, Bunge, Cargill, and Louis-Dreyfus. The level of control wielded by these four companies is not without challenges from farmers, governments, and NGOs in both China and Brazil. However, because of the structure of the industry and the extent of their reach down the supply chain, these firms maintain significant influence over the governance of this global commodity complex. This chapter addresses the structuring of the global soy market through the interaction of policy and the private sector in Brazil and China, and concludes with a discussion of the consequences of this new commodity system for food, farmers, and the environment.

E.K. Peine, Ph.D. (✉)
Department of International Political Economy, University of Puget Sound,
1500 N. Warner #1057, 98416 Tacoma, WA, USA
e-mail: epeine@pugetsound.edu

H.S. James Jr. (ed.), *The Ethics and Economics of Agrifood Competition*,
The International Library of Environmental, Agricultural and Food Ethics 20,
DOI 10.1007/978-94-007-6274-9_10,

10.1 Introduction

The increasing frequency and severity of spikes in global food prices over the past decade have raised grave concerns over the ability of the world's farmers to feed a growing, and increasingly affluent, global population. Although there are many reasons for this price volatility, including climate change (Eriksen et al. 2011) and the diversion of food crops for biofuels (McMichael 2009a), many point to the "meatification" (Weis 2007) of Asian diets as one of the primary factors putting pressure on grain reserves, as more grains and oilseeds are fed to livestock instead of people (Bello 2009; McMichael 2009b). Demand from China in particular has increased exponentially in recent years, creating a dramatic listing of the global agricultural economy away from traditional importers in the global north (EU and Japan). For an even longer period of time, since the mid-1980s, Latin America has been quietly creeping up on the United States and agricultural powerhouses of the global north, threatening their position as undisputed export leaders (Barbier 2003). Therefore, we see two concurrent trends in the global economy: increasing demand pressures on the global food supply that contribute to price volatility, and shifting agricultural trade flows from north-north to south-south.

This chapter focuses specifically on the integration of the Brazilian soybean and Chinese pork industries as an illustration of the negotiation of these new political-economic relationships by transnational agribusiness. As the world's largest (respective) consumer and exporter of soy, China and Brazil exemplify the brave new world of global agricultural markets, and the actions of transnational corporations (TNC)s in those markets reveal some emerging contours of a new food regime.[1] In the post-Washington Consensus era, political-economic power structures are not as clear-cut, and the negotiations between China, Brazil, and transnational agribusinesses in consolidating a global protein complex often reveal internal contradictions.

This chapter shows that the new political-economic landscape of the global soy industry presents potential challenges to the decades-long dominance of the sector by four TNCs: ADM, Bunge, Cargill, and Louis-Dreyfus Commodities, known simply as Dreyfus (hereafter referred to as "ABCD").[2] The Chinese and Brazilian governments, Chinese and Brazilian farmers, and domestic processers in both countries have every reason to circumvent the control that these companies have over the sector. However, I argue that because of the *depth* and *breadth* of their involvement in the supply chain, it is unlikely that a clear alternative will emerge in the near future. The primary reasons are (1) the crucial importance of these companies in financing Brazilian soy production; (2) monopoly of processing

---

[1] For a more detailed analysis of this geographic and political-economic shift, see Wilkinson (2009).

[2] In national markets other important players command substantial market share, like Groupo Maggi in Mato Grosso, Brazil and many state-owned agribusiness in China. However, these companies have generally not expanded their business transnationally, and so therefore do not compete in the *global* commodity chain in the same way.

technology; (3) control of transportation; and 4) the conflict of Chinese and Brazilian interests in the soy sector. The conflict is multifaceted, but includes China's desire for self-sufficiency in food. As will be discussed below, this policy has driven Chinese investors to purchase farmland abroad so as to circumvent the market for strategically important food products. In Brazil, the government has pushed back by prohibiting foreign ownership of farmland.[3]

Although the international soy trade—importers, exporters, producers, consumers, etc.—is framed as consisting of competing *national* interests, the fact remains that the global market is largely facilitated by this small handful of transnational corporations. These companies exploit the relative competitiveness of US and Brazilian producers and strategically invest in Chinese crushing in order to create the most profitable supply chain possible. Those strategic decisions are, in turn, structured by the various policies and market conditions that pertain in different places. In the end, there is not a unidirectional exercise of power by corporations over states (or farmers) or vice versa. Rather, the constant negotiation between transnational capital, government, producers and consumers reveals a contested landscape where the oligopolistic power of ABCD may, indeed, face serious threats.

Whether there is adequate competition in the global soybean industry is a difficult question, and the answer would be different depending on whom you ask. For both producers and consumers (industrial and individual alike), the answer is probably no, but the reasons behind that answer are very different. For Brazilian soybean farmers, ABCD exercise oligopolistic control over *every stage* of the process, from inputs and credit to drying, storage, processing, and shipping. Therefore, the anti-competitive atmosphere is an economic disadvantage. Because of the nature of the contracts that growers sign with these TNCs (to be discussed in more detail below), farmers feel that they are prohibited from taking advantage of the booming international soybean market, a market that they perceive as decidedly not "free." The competitiveness of the individual farmer, therefore, is undermined by the oligopoly.

In China, the implications of the oligopoly are both economic and strategic. For Chinese processors, feed companies, and pork consumers, soybeans imported from Brazil are much cheaper than soybeans grown domestically, and so the entry of transnational soy traders is good for their bottom line. However, the overwhelming reliance on imports for such a crucially important part of one of the most significant food value chains in China is anathema to the Chinese political emphasis on food self-sufficiency. As foreign interests have consolidated control even farther down the Chinese supply chain, buying and building significant crushing capacity on the Chinese mainland, the loss of sovereignty over the supply chain becomes even more concerning to the Chinese state. Therefore, from this perspective, the problem with the lack of competition is perhaps less economic and more strategic.

---

[3]Ironically, US farmers have been moving to Brazil to grow corn and soybeans for decades, purchasing land without provoking any reaction from the state.

For Chinese soybean farmers, however, the flood of cheap soybeans is of course a more directly economic problem. Even domestic crushers with a directive from the state to source soy as domestically as possible cannot compete with foreign crushers who do not have to follow the same guidelines. All of these relationships will be discussed in detail below, but the point is that the question of adequate competition in the global soybean industry has different implications for different constituents, but because the commodity system is truly globally integrated, the relationships between farmers, processers, domestic and transnational capital, states, and consumers must be understood relationally. The fate of the transnational oligopoly, therefore, must be understood as a function of the *relations* between very different political economic contexts of China and Brazil.

10.2 The Making of a South-South Commodity Complex

Much has been made of the increasing political and economic ties between China and Latin America, and many have lauded the emergence of a "south-south" alliance that challenges the long-held assumptions of the Washington Consensus (Ramo 2004; Jilberto and Hogenboom 2010; Kennedy 2010; Gallagher and Porzecanski 2010).[4] This alliance has shown its political relevance in the disruption of and continued stalemate in WTO negotiations, and its economic relevance in the increasing importance of the Brazil, Russia, India and China (BRICs) countries as trading partners, both for one another and for the global north. Since 1994, trade in the BRICs countries has increased almost sevenfold (UNCTAD 2009).

Trade, however, is not only a political phenomenon. Though we often speak of *countries* trading with one another, it is actually *companies* that do the actual work of moving goods across national borders. The primary economic actors in global trade—transnational corporations—must therefore negotiate rapidly changing political landscapes as supply chains are stretched across increasingly vast geographic spaces. Over the last three decades, the four leading soybean trading firms have successfully integrated a global soybean supply chain that has dominated markets in every major soybean producing and consuming country in the world. However, that landscape has changed significantly, as shown in Fig. 10.1, as the traditional producing and consuming powerhouses have been supplanted by rising powers in the global South. Until the mid-1990s, the United States was the undisputed global leader in soybean production, and most of the large transnational grain traders come out of the US as well. With the discovery of soil amendments that made the vast stretches of *cerrado* savannah in the Central-West

[4]The term "Washington Consensus" refers to the set of policies prescribed by the International Monetary Fund and the World Bank to encourage development and help countries of the global South "grow" themselves out of debt in the 1980s. These policies followed the principles of neoliberalism (privatization, small government, trade liberalization, producing for export, etc.) and were institutionalized in the structural adjustment programs that indebted countries were forced to accept as conditions of IMF loans.

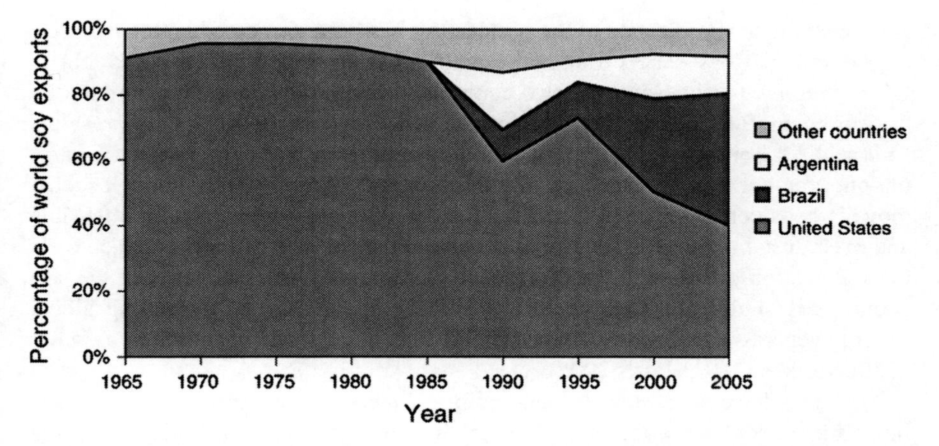

Fig. 10.1 Percentage of world soy exports by country (Source: USDA FAS (2011))

region of Brazil appropriate for soy cultivation, Brazil quickly came to rival the US for the designation of top soy producer and exporter. Argentina comes in a close third.

Likewise, since the 1950s, Europe and Japan were by far the largest importers of soybeans. In fact, Japanese investment helped to spark the soy revolution in the *cerrado* after US supplies were disrupted, threatening Japanese food security (Warnken 1999). In 1996, China switched from being a net exporter to a net importer of soybeans. In the years that followed, the market profile rapidly shifted, and by 2005 China was importing half of the world's soybeans.

The primary driving factor behind this shift is pork. China both produces and consumes half of the world's pork, and in the last 20 years, an increasing number of China's pigs have been raised in confinement, which means a growing demand for commercial pig feed (Schneider 2011). Soy is the primary source of protein in pig feed, and so China's insatiable appetite for pork is directly linked to perpetually tight soybean supply margins, despite production growth rates that average almost 5% per year (Masuda and Goldsmith 2009).

These new trade relationships are of more than just economic significance. Touted as a new "south-south alliance," leaders from China and South America frame increasing trade as a political strategy to circumvent the structures and ideologies of the Washington Consensus. In advance of a visit to China to cement trade deals in everything from oil and gas to airplanes to soybeans, former Brazilian president Luís Inácio Lula da Silva said, "The great economic lesson of the twenty first century did not come from the failure of some emerging country, but from the post-graduates of the world economy who know everything when a crisis hits Bolivia, Brazil and Russia, but know nothing when the crisis is in their own backyard" (Arce 2009). Two years later, Chinese president Hu Jintao said in a press release issued by the Foreign Ministry, "the China-Brazil strategic partnership has become a successful example of South-South cooperation and has an increasing global impact and strategic significance" (Xiaokun et al. 2011).

The strategic significance of the partnership has been expressed both concretely and symbolically, as leaders from both countries use the opportunity to cast doubt on US hegemony. For instance, the two countries proposed denominating commodity trade in yuan, the Chinese currency, instead of US dollars. In 2009, then-president Lula said, "It's absurd if two important trading nations such as ours continue to carry out our commerce in the currency of a third nation" (Arce 2009). Although such a move is considered—even by Brazilian finance officials—economically infeasible and even destabilizing for the global economy, the rhetoric of independence from the US is strong. Although the divergence of economic interests between the two countries is significant, their rhetorical alliance against the long-standing global superpower has significantly shaped WTO and other trade negotiations (Halper 2010; Narlikar 2010; Harris 2005).

Soybeans have become a strategic point of interest between the two countries. International soybean prices are listed on the Chicago Board of Trade, and while prices are influenced by weather conditions and harvest forecasts in all major producing countries, trades and contracts are essentially brokered through this exchange. Officials from Brazil and China have proposed opening a new commodity exchange based in the global South, or shifting the bulk of futures trading to the Dailan Exchange in northeast China (Merco Press 2006). Again, though these gestures are mostly symbolic, they illustrate the strategic importance of increasing economic integration between the two countries.

As Brazil and China solidify their respective roles as soy producing and consuming powerhouses, the strategic goals of the partnership may be as important as the economic ones. Because of that, the political contexts in which the commodity markets function may prove to be less permissive of the oligopolistic control exercised by transnational corporations, especially when the exercise of that oligopoly acts against domestic interests. In fact, both Brazilian soybean farmers and the Chinese state (via Chinese soy processors and other industrial consumers) are looking for ways around the ABCD bottleneck that currently exists in the global soy trade. Soy promises to be a battleground for these interests because of its crucial role in the global protein complex.

10.3 Let Them Eat Pork: The Rise of the Brazil-China-Soy-Pork Commodity Complex

The "meatification" (Weis 2007) of Asian diets has been singled out as one of the primary reasons for the global food demand squeeze that has triggered two significant food price "crises" in less than a decade (Bello 2009; Conceicao and Mendoza 2009; McMichael 2009c). Many argue that, since meat production—especially in the industrial livestock model—is much more calorie-intensive than cereal production, the more profitable livestock industry will successfully compete with the grain industry for farmland, and there will be fewer food crops planted (as opposed to feed or fuel crops), hence driving up the price of food. While others

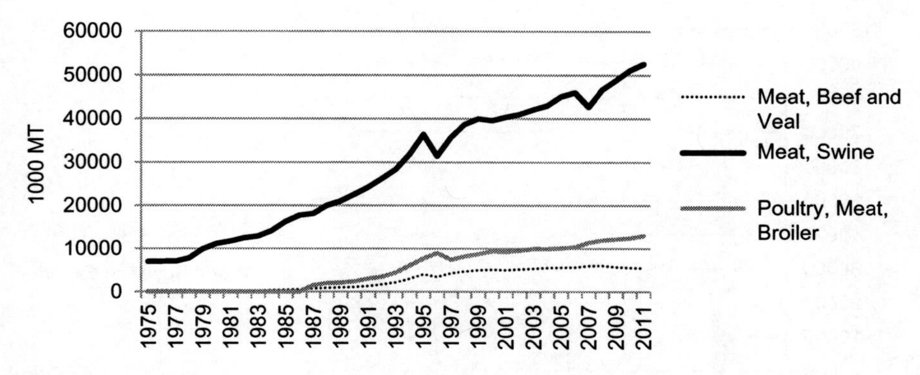

Fig. 10.2 Meat consumption in China (Source: USDA FAS (2011))

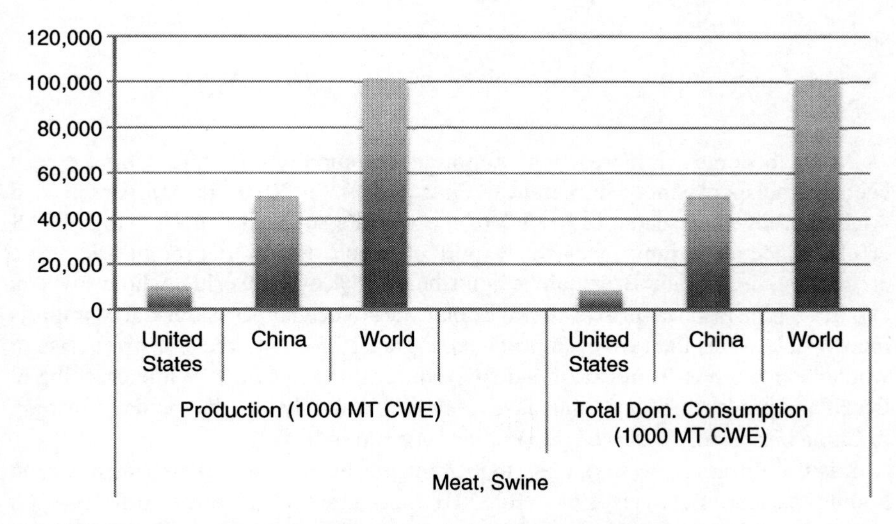

Fig. 10.3 Swine meat production and consumption (Source: USDA FAS (2011))

argue that this is less important than financial speculation in commodity markets as a precipitating factor in recent crises, the fact remains that the world's appetite for meat is on the rise. That increase in demand is especially intense in China. As seen in Fig. 10.2, far more pork is consumed in China than any other meat. In fact, as shown in Fig. 10.3, China is the largest producer and consumer of pork in the world, dwarfing totals in the United States. The rise in pork production has fueled demand for soy-based industrial feed products so that China's soybean economy—including both the livestock feed as well as edible cooking oil sectors—has been booming since the mid 1990s. In 1995, China was a net exporter of soybeans. Today, China imports over 50% of the world's exported beans (see Fig. 10.4), and soy (whole beans and soy products) are China's third most valuable import.

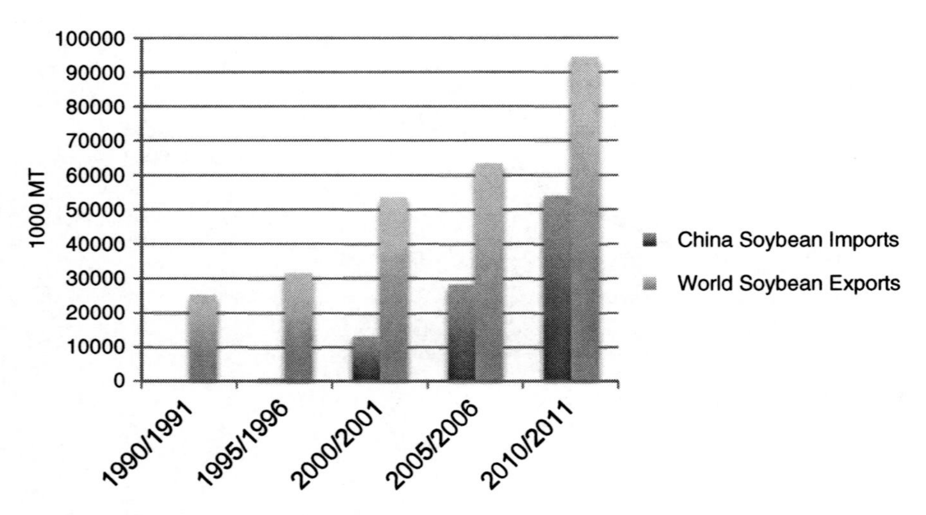

Fig. 10.4 Soybean imports and exports, China/world (Source: USDA FAS (2011))

As soy becomes an increasingly important commodity import for China, Brazil becomes an increasingly important trading partner. In 2010, the US, Brazil, and Argentina together account for 88% of the world's soybean exports (USDA FAS 2011). Since Argentina taxes the export of whole beans to promote domestic processing, the US and Brazil alone contributed 78% of the world's whole soybean exports. China also wants to encourage domestic soybean processing, and so imports more whole beans than soybean products. Figure 10.5 shows the concurrent rise in whole bean exports from Brazil and soybean crushing in China. While crushing in Brazil and production and China have remained relatively flat, the trend of crushing in China has closely followed the production trend in Brazil.

It is not surprising to find, then, that China has become Brazil's most important trading partner. Between 1990 and 2010, the share of revenue from Brazil's international trade of soybeans, oil and meal coming from China increased from four to approximately 50%, whereas the share from the EU during the same period declined (Aprosoja 2010). In overall trade, China supplanted the US as Brazil's most important trading partner in 2009 (Moore 2009). In the soy sector, Brazil has become as dependent on the Chinese market as China has become on Brazilian exports.

The picture that emerges here is one of co-dependent national agricultural markets. From the point of view of TNCs, however, the two markets are an integrated commodity complex, because many of the same corporations that export soybeans from Brazil also import them to their own crushing plants in China. While this commodity complex operates across very different political contexts, from an economic perspective the "national" markets are not separate and interacting with one another, but rather successive stages of production along the global protein assembly line that is still largely organized and operated by transnational firms.

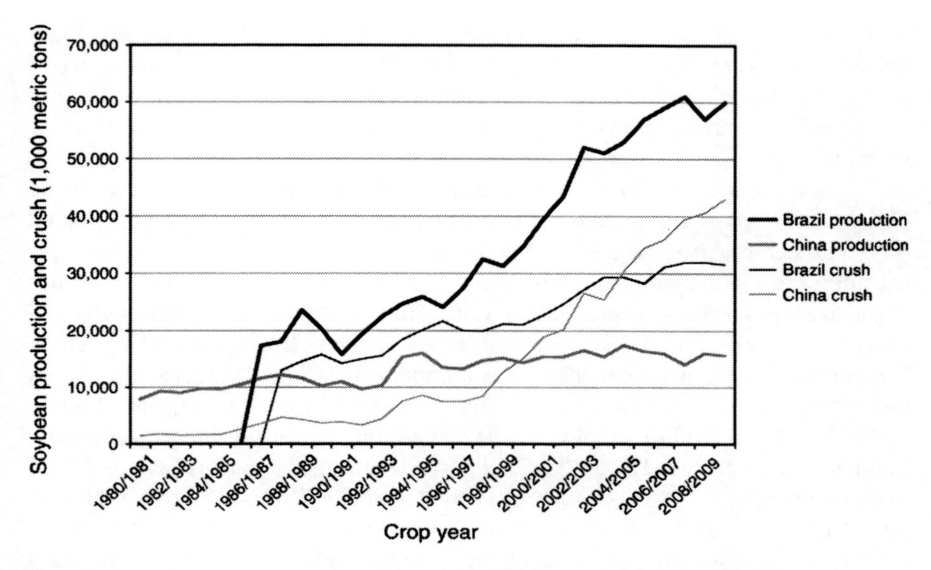

Fig. 10.5 China and Brazil soybean production and crush (Source: USDA FAS (2011))

10.4 Consolidating the Global Soybean Commodity Complex I: Brazil

The Brazilian soybean boom has been widely documented (Peine 2009; Steward 2007; Nepstad et al. 2006; Zancopé and Nasser 2005; Fearnside 2001; Warnken 1999; Hasse 1996), and the role of transnational corporations has not gone unnoticed. In 2006, following a global outcry over deforestation associated with increased soybean cultivation, the primary transnational players in the Brazilian soy sector agreed to a moratorium on buying soybeans grown on recently deforested land in the legally designated Amazon region (Rosenthal 2009; Nepstad et al. 2008; Greenpeace 2006). Environmental activists targeted ADM and Cargill in particular as "American" companies that were directly contributing to the northward march of soy farms that, while not necessarily directly responsible for deforestation, were nonetheless displacing cattle ranchers and pushing those *pecuários* farther and farther into the legal Amazon (Morton et al. 2006). But the reach of TNCs in the Brazilian soy sector is much deeper than simply buying and exporting beans.

The "tradings," as Brazilians call them, have far greater dominance in the soybean sector of Mato Grosso state than in other soy growing regions of Brazil. Until the late 1980s, soybeans were grown almost exclusively in the southern states, but with the advent of a soybean variety x that could grow in the tropical climate of Brazil's vast interior, the states of Mato Grosso, Mato Grosso do Sul, Goiás, and Bahia took over as the country's biggest soy producers. Among those, Mato Grosso is the clear leader, producing 30–40% of Brazil's entire soybean crop.

While most of the soybeans grown in the south are consumed domestically, Mato Grosso's beans are almost exclusively exported. Here, because of the importance of the export market and the control that the big soy TNCs (ADM, Bunge, Cargill, and Dreyfus) exert over that trade, farmers in Mato Grosso are tied to them in multiple ways.

The first and perhaps most important form of control is in the credit market. In the US, farmers have several options to finance planting costs, including publicly funded or guaranteed credit programs. In Mato Grosso in 2005, the amount of federally subsidized credit available to each farmer was only enough to finance about 6% of the average farm's total production costs. The other 94%, at roughly double the subsidized interest rate, came directly from agribusiness (Menegheti 2005). These firms are soy companies, not banks, and so farmer debt is repaid in sacks of soybeans rather than currency. Farmers sign a very loose kind of contract called a Cédula de Produto Rural (Bill of Rural Product) that records the cost of inputs (fertilizers, fungicides, etc.) provided by the TNC. The farmer must pay in sacks of soy delivered to the company at harvest time, thereby guaranteeing the TNC will enjoy low harvest time prices, maximizing the "soy return" on its investment. If the farmer cannot deliver the requisite tonnage, the company enjoys an advance claim on next year's crop (Peine 2009).

Soy companies in Mato Grosso also capitalize on low harvest time prices because farmers have little on-farm drying and storage, so many of the beans (harvested during the rainy season) go directly to huge wood-fired dryers owned by the "tradings", and then on to the company's storage barns. In the US, of course, farmers can hold their crop until months after harvest ends when supplies tighten and prices begin to rebound. Because of the level of concentration of control that the big soy companies hold over credit and infrastructure in Mato Grosso, it is very difficult for farmers truly participate in the market. According to former president of the Mato Grosso Agriculture Federation (FAMATO) Homero Pereira,

> The producer doesn't have any other option than to be bound to the transnationals. We know that it is not the desire of all producers to be in these relationships. The desire of the producer is to get capital from a source of financial resources, and to owe in financial resources as well, rather than in produce. Because the biggest problem that we have with the system here today is not so much the interest rates that you pay to the transnationals, but the market opportunities that you lose. Because when you get financing you tie yourself, you compromise so many tons of grain and so you lose sometimes a market much larger than your own interest rate. And so to be in debt to a financier and to remain in control of your own product is obviously much better (Pereira, H., 2005, personal communication)

The reach of these companies into the Mato Grosso soybean sector, therefore, is both deep and broad. In recent years, they have made clear attempts to extend that influence into the soybean sector of the world's largest consumer as well: China. By sending whole beans from Brazil to be crushed at their own facilities in China, TNCs can take advantage of cheaper raw material prices (in Brazil), lower processing costs (in China), and robust demand for the manufactured product (from Chinese hogs). The ability of these firms to exercise the same sort of market dominance in China that they do in Brazil, however, remains to be seen.

10.5 Consolidating the Global Soybean Commodity Complex II: China

China has long prioritized food self-sufficiency through complex and generous government support for the domestic production and processing of staple food crops, namely corn, rice, and wheat (Gao 2010; Martin 2001). Because of this policy priority, foreign investments in and imports of these commodities have historically been restricted. Soybeans are not considered to be a "grain" and so are not as heavily protected as corn, rice, and wheat, but with the industrialization of pork production, soybeans are becoming an increasingly important (though indirect) aspect of China's food security. Imports of soybeans and processed soy products (meal and oil) are subject to taxes and tariffs, though processed products are subject to higher tariffs as well as quotas from which whole beans are exempt (Provance 2003). A study by the USDA's Economic Research Service concluded that corn is a much more highly protected commodity than soybeans in China, and that the relatively higher profits for corn farmers mean that significant growth in domestic soybean production is unlikely (Gale 2007).

As shown in Fig. 10.5 above, domestic soybean production in China has remained relatively flat while crushing has increased dramatically. Much of this increased crushing capacity was built by foreign firms (ABCD, plus Wilmar International based in Singapore). Until recently, the Chinese government encouraged foreign investment in soybean crushing to help meet rapidly growing demand for livestock feed. Under a 1991 tax law, soybean mills with foreign investment were subject to a 15% income tax, whereas domestically owned mills paid a rate of 33% (INAI 2008). In 2000, foreign investment accounted for just 9% of actual crushing (Petry and O'Rear 2008).

In 2005, however, the profile of the industry changed dramatically. Spring futures prices for the 2004 soy harvest were near all-time highs at almost $10 per bushel, and Chinese soybean crushers rushed to sign contracts with the TNCs in fear that the price would continue to rise. That year saw record-busting harvests in both the US and Brazil, fears of Asian soybean rust in the US failed to materialize, and futures plummeted. By the late summer, prices had dropped by nearly half, and Chinese contract holders were faced with losing billions of dollars paying double the current market price for imported beans. Rather than take the loss, Chinese crushers defaulted on their contracts. Arbitration under the Federation of Oils, Seeds, and Fats Association (FOFSA) found in favor of the TNCs, and as compensation these firms were permitted to buy up capacity from struggling domestic crushers (Cabral, M.T., June 15, 2010, Brazilian embassy, Beijing, China, personal communication; Tuan et al. 2004). When the dust cleared, 80% of Chinese crushing capacity was in foreign hands (Xiang 2009). At the end of 2006, 64 of China's 97 large-scale crushing facilities were foreign-owned or controlled (Yan 2007).

The primary beneficiaries of this ruling were the TNCs that held the defaulted soybean contracts: ADM, Cargill, Bunge, and LDC (Louis-Dreyfus Commodities). Today, ADM has several crushing facilities across China, some wholly owned and some built through joint ventures with Chinese agribusiness giant COFCO and with Singapore-based Wilmar International. ADM also has a trading office in Shanghai.[5] Bunge owns three of the largest crushing facilities in the country, with a total of 20 entities and over 700 employees (Howie 2005; China Business News 2007).[6] Cargill has 5,000 employees and operates 39 wholly-owned and joint venture facilities.[7] Louis-Dreyfus incorporated LDCommodities in Beijing in 2005, becoming the first Wholly Foreign Owned Entity (WFOE) with trading rights in the agricultural sector.[8]

The reliance on foreign capital in a very strategic sector causes unease in China. That unease was translated into policy when, in 2007, the National Development and Reform Commission (NDRC) revised the Catalog for the Guidance of Foreign Investment. This document divides the Chinese economy into sectors where foreign investment is "encouraged", "restricted", or "prohibited". The revision singled out soybean oil processing as a "restricted" activity, mandating that a Chinese-owned enterprise must hold the majority of shares in any joint venture, essentially precluding the establishment of any new WFOE facilities (State Development and Reform Commission 2007).

In 2008, this department released the "Directive on Promoting the Healthy Development of the Soybean Processing Industry" (Petry and O'Rear 2008). This document emphasizes both domestic soy production and processing, and encourages the integration and consolidation of the domestic soybean and animal feed industries while also protecting competition.[9] In the directive, the NDRC identifies three current "problems" with the Chinese soybean processing industry: (1) the overcapacity of oil processing (which leads to low margins), (2) low domestically owned capacity versus foreign capacity, and (3) excess reliance on imported raw materials (Petry and O'Rear 2008, p. 4). According to the USDA, the NDRC's proposed response to these problems suggests deepening government involvement in the sector. For instance, the directive suggests eliminating smaller, less technologically advanced crushing facilities and consolidating larger, more sophisticated operations that also integrate feed production and can compete more effectively with foreign-owned plants. The directive also calls for structural changes to the industry:

> Compress the total soy oil processing capacity. Encourage the merger and reorganization of domestic enterprises to facilitate industrial consolidation. Reasonably deploy the soybean producing across the country ... with each area having its own focus (p. 7).

The directive, therefore, points toward a robust government policy to restructure the domestic soybean industry to both mirror the integrated industrial model imported to China by the TNCs, and to more effectively compete with those firms.

---

[5] See http://www.adm.com/en-US/worldwide/china.

[6] See http://www.bunge.com.cn/en/bgchina.php.

[7] See http://www.cargill.com.cn/china.

[8] See http://www.louisdreyfus.com.cn/enbusiness.htm.

[9] The directive stipulates that if a single firm's soybean oil production reaches 15% of the national total, that firm shall be prohibited from further expanding capacity.

Thought the directive emphasizes the domestication of the industrial side of the soy sector, there is mention of domesticating the supply of raw materials as well. As mentioned above, the heavy reliance on imported beans is of concern to the NDRC. One directive states that "Greater efforts should be made to expand domestic soybean production to make the raw material supply more independent" (Petry and O'Rear 2008, p. 6) In addition to encouraging domestic soybean production, the NDRC also advocates direct investment in the Brazilian soy sector in order to achieve greater independence in the soybean supply chain.

10.6 Chinese Investment in Brazilian Soy: Another Kind of "Self-Sufficiency"

The NDRC directive includes a special section advocating Chinese investment in the foreign soybean supply chain: Section 6.4 Policy Measures—Encourage and guide enterprises to "go out" and develop international resources, which states:

> Encourage domestic enterprises to establish a stable soybean import system. The proposal is to: target soybean-export countries to purchase soybean locally, and then rent port terminal, establish warehouse and transportation system, or purchase stakes of local agricultural enterprises and rent land to grow crops. Encourage domestic enterprises to build soybean processing plants in foreign countries.
>
> Guide, arrange, organize and coordinate external purchases, while gradually improving domestic enterprises' international influence and bargaining power and reduce the cost of purchasing (Petry and O'Rear 2008, p. 11).

What this suggests is that Chinese interests are looking to build an international soybean infrastructure to rival (and replace, or at least circumvent) that already established by TNCs. The directive appears to mirror three primary TNC strategies in the sector: (1) vertical integration of commodity chain; (2) horizontal integration in the processing sector to capture economies of scale and; (3) capture of the raw material through contracts, financing, storage, and transportation. Considering the overwhelming success of the TNC model, it not surprising that well-financed Chinese interests would pursue a similar strategy. However, these relationships are only now being forged and it remains to be seen whether the Chinese model is a structural alternative to the existing market. The question remains open as to whether this investment would meaningfully increase competition in the sector, and whether it would result in real alternatives for Brazilian soybean farmers. However, Chinese interests are currently taking concrete steps to construct the foundation for this alternative market in Brazil.

Since 2008, the NDRC directive has manifested in several moves by Chinese agribusiness to buy farmland or otherwise invest in Brazilian soybean production. In 2010 *The Financial Times* reported that the Chongqing Grain Group planned to purchase 100,000 ha of land in the state of Bahia to produce soybeans. The Chinese Development Bank would fund 60% of the project, with the company responsible for the other 40% (Tepfer 2010). Since then, the Brazilian government has tightened the regulations on foreign ownership of land (Barrionuevo 2011), and so Chongqing is investing in the state of Bahia instead, building a soy crushing plant, a textile mill, rail terminal, storage facilities, and a private port to facilitate its soy purchases and provide some of the infrastructural support for which Brazilian farmers are currently largely dependent on the multinationals. China is exploring other ways to "improv[e] domestic enterprises' international influence" as well, including a 7.5 billion (USD) project funded by the Chinese state-owned company Sanhe Hopeful in the Brazilian state of Goias. The proposal aims to lock in purchases of 6 million tons of soybeans (estimated to be the equivalent of the state's entire harvest) directly from farmer cooperatives, thereby cutting the big traders out of the deal (Merco Press 2011).

These activities are particularly important in the context of the global uptick in "land grabbing," or foreign investment in direct purchases or acquisitions of farmland. Recurrent food crises have shaken countries' faith in the market mechanism to provide food security, and so cash-rich but land-poor countries like the Gulf states and China have begun acquiring land abroad to grow crops exclusively for domestic consumption. Aside from the important implications that this trend has for the hegemony of neoliberal ideology, many countries already dependent on food aid are seeing their farmland base sold to into foreign ownership (GRAIN 2008).[10]

10.7 Conclusion

The case of the Brazil-China-soy-pork commodity complex offers a new twist on the question of whether there is "adequate competition" in the global soybean industry. The implications of emerging trade patterns, investment initiatives, and political alliances for the competitiveness of the sector depend on where you stand. At the farmer level, US soybean growers are in a better position than their Brazilian counterparts to take advantage of market opportunities, as Homero Pereira's statement above indicates. Farmers in the US are far more likely to have on-farm storage, independent (and often government-backed) financing, cheaper credit, and more marketing options. Whether Chinese involvement in the Brazilian soy industry will provide more diverse market opportunities, autonomy, sources of credit, and infrastructure for Brazilian producers remains to be seen. However, it is clear that both Chinese buyers and Brazilian farmers are interested in the possibilities offered by an end-run around the market control wielded by the big "tradings."

[10]An international conference in 2011 sponsored by the Land Deals Politics Initiative in collaboration with the *Journal of Peasant Studies* and hosted by the Future Agricultures Consortium at the University of Sussex included 89 academic papers analyzing the wave of global land grabbing. Full conference proceedings can be found at http://www.future-agricultures.org/index.php?option=com_content&view=category&layout=blog&id=1547&Itemid=978.

At the state level, the "competition" between TNCs and state-owned enterprises in China suggests yet another twist on the question. Because of the size and market dominance of TNCs, they have the ability to wield power relative to governments. The self-sufficiency imperative of Chinese agricultural policy has been compromised in the soy sector, and the state is now looking for ways to leverage power against the economic dominance of foreign companies, primarily by cultivating supplies of soybeans outside the international market. The decision to look to Brazil is easy to understand.

In China, domestically produced beans are simply much more expensive than those imported from the US and South America (Niu 2008; Lan 2010). Crushing margins are low, because the government caps the price of cooking oil to support food security and as mentioned above, many crushers are already idling up to 50% of capacity. This means that Chinese crushers, following the government's directive to source beans domestically, are at a distinct economic disadvantage. These market imbalances combined with the self-sufficiency policies of the Chinese state and concerns about foreign ownership are prompting dramatic state intervention in the market. As China shows signs of moving toward a centrally-planned soybean supply chain, the consequences for the TNCs—and for Brazilian soybean farmers and the Brazilian Amazon and *cerrado* ecosystems—remain unknown. Will these policies serve to enhance the competitiveness of domestic processing in a way that meaningfully diversifies the global market? Or is the Chinese model simply supplanting one oligopolistic market structure with another?

What is clear is that TNCs are facing a new kind of political landscape in China, and interesting new patterns in the industry are emerging, including more independent connections between Chinese soy consumers and Brazilian growers. However, at this point, these relationships seem to simply mirror the industry structure established by the TNCs—namely big growers forming cooperatives to sell to big consumers adopting the technology and production systems introduced by the TNCs. For consumers of cheap pork in Chinese cities, competition in the soybean industry might not be a top concern. But to soy growers in both Brazil and China who feed the global protein complex, the market is certainly not "free."

As mentioned in the introduction, the Brazilian soybean boom also has serious environmental implications. There is significant controversy over the culpability of the soybean in causing record levels of Amazonian deforestation during the 2000s, since many analysis argue that cattle ranchers are actually responsible for more direct deforestation. However, the movement of pasture to the north is an indirect result of the expansion of soy production to feed the world's confinement livestock. The broader implications of this commodity network and the kind of food system in which it is situated must be addressed. Inadequate competition in the soybean industry is not only bad for the soybean growers—large and small—for whom the "free market" is a Smithian fantasy. It also precludes alternative arrangements of the food system that could be based on decentralized production, crop biodiversity, low-input and low-carbon production processes, and land reform rather than high-carbon, high-input, high-capital, centralized production processes. As long as policy and production systems drive and mutually reinforce one another, the level of competition in the soybean industry is unlikely to improve. With that, an ethical farm economy that is healthy for growers and for the environment faces serious challenges.

Acknowledgement The author would like to thank Mindi Schneider for her help researching this chapter. Without her expertise in the politics of the Chinese pork industry, her generous collaboration, and her hospitality in Chengdu, China, this chapter would never have been possible. This research was conducted with support from the Trimble Foundation at the University of Puget Sound.

References

Aprosoja. 2010. *Outlook for internal and port infrastructure growth in Brazil*. Cuiaba: Mato Grosso Soybean and Corn Growers Association (Aprosoja).

Arce, L. 2009. Brazil, China deals challenge US position in Latin America. *World Socialist Web Site*. http://www.wsws.org/articles/2009/jun2009/braz-j06.shtml. Accessed 1 July 2011.

Barbier, E. 2003. Explaining agricultural expansion, resource booms, and growth in Latin America. *Environment, Development and Sustainability* 5(3–4): 437–458.

Barrionuevo, A. 2011. China's interest in farmland makes Brazil uneasy. *The New York Times*, May 27, A1.

Bello, W. 2009. *The food wars*. London: Verso Press.

China Business News. 2007. Bunge enters china vegetable oil retail market. *China Business News*, January 5.

Conceicao, P., and R.U. Mendoza. 2009. Anatomy of the global food crisis. *Third World Quarterly* 30(6): 1159–1182.

Eriksen, P., P. Thornton, A. Notenbaert, L. Cramer, P. Jones, and M. Herrero. 2011. Mapping hotspots of climate change and food insecurity in the global south. CCAFS Report No. 5. Washington, DC: Consultative Group on International Agricultural Research.

Fearnside, P.M. 2001. Soybean cultivation as a threat to the environment in Brazil. *Environmental Conservation* 28: 23–38.

Gale, F. 2007. A tale of two commodities: China's trade in corn and soybeans. *International agricultural trade consortium meeting*, Beijing.

Gallagher, K., and R. Porzecanski. 2010. *The dragon in the room: China and the future of Latin American industrialization*. Stanford: Stanford University Press.

Gao, S. 2010. Discussion on issues of food security based on basic domestic self-sufficiency. *Asian Social Science* 6(11): 42–46.

GRAIN. 2008. *Seized! the 2008 land grab for food and financial security*. Barcelona: GRAIN.

Greenpeace. 2006. Eating up the Amazon. http://www.greenpeace.org/international/en/publications/reports/eating-up-the-amazon/. Accessed 7 Mar 2009.

Halper, S. 2010. Beijing's coalition of the willing. *Foreign Policy* 180: 100–102.

Harris, J. 2005. Emerging third world powers: China, India and Brazil. *Race & Class* 46(3): 7–27.

Hasse, H. 1996. *O brasil da soja: Abrindo fronteiras, semeando cidades*. Porto Alegre: Ceval Alimentos/L & PM Editores S.A.

Howie, M. 2005. Bunge expands into China. *Feedstuffs* 77(30), July 25, 7.

INAI. 2008. *The China soybean industry policy*. Buenos Aires: Instituto para las Negociaciones Agrícolas Internacionales.

Jilberto, A.E.F., and B. Hogenboom. 2010. *Latin America facing China: South-south relations beyond the Washington consensus*. New York: Berghahn Books.

Kennedy, S. 2010. The myth of the Beijing consensus. *Journal of Contemporary China* 19(65): 461–477.

Lan, L. 2010. Battle of the beans. *China Daily*, August 23. http://www.chinadaily.com.cn/business/2010-08/23/content_11189082.htm. Accessed 2 May 2011.

Martin, W. 2001. Implications of reform and WTO accession for China's agricultural policies. *The Economics of Transition* 9(3): 717–726.

Masuda, T., and P.D. Goldsmith. 2009. World soybean production: Area harvested, yield, and long-term projections. *International Food and Agribusiness Management Review* 12(4): 143–162.

McMichael, P. 2009a. The agro-fuels project at large. *Critical Sociology* 35(6): 825–839.

McMichael, P. 2009b. A food regime genealogy. *Journal of Peasant Studies* 36(1): 139–169.

McMichael, P. 2009c. The world food crisis in historical perspective. *Monthly Review* 61(3): 32–47.

Menegheti, G. 2005. E agora, valcir? *Produtor Rural* 149: 245–313.

Merco Press. 2006. China, Brazil, and Argentina seeking soy axis. *Merco Press*, April 17. http://en.mercopress.com/2006/04/17/china-brazil-and-argentina-seeking-soy-axis. Accessed 10 June 2011.

Merco Press. 2011. China plans to invest 10 billion USD in soy production and processing in Brazil. *Merco Press*, June 1. http://en.mercopress.com/2011/04/11/china-plans-to-invest-10-billion-usd-in-soy-production-and-processing-in-brazil. Accessed 10 June 2011.

Moore, M. 2009. China overtakes the US as Brazil's largest trading partner. *The Telegraph*, May 9. http://www.telegraph.co.uk/finance/economics/5296515/China-overtakes-the-US-as-Brazils-largest-trading-partner.html. Accessed 15 June 2011.

Morton, D.C., R.S. DeFries, Y.E. Shimabukuro, L.O. Anderson, E. Arai, F.D.B. Espirito-Santo, R. Freitas, and J. Morisette. 2006. Cropland expansion changes deforestation dynamics in the southern Brazilian Amazon. *Proceedings of the National Academy of Sciences* 103(39): 14637–14641.

Narlikar, A. 2010. New powers in the club: The challenges of global trade governance. *International Affairs* 86(3): 717–728.

Nepstad, D.C., C.M. Stickler, and O.T. Almeida. 2006. Globalization of the Amazon soy and beef industries: Opportunities for conservation. *Conservation Biology: The Journal of the Society for Conservation Biology* 20(6): 1595–1603.

Nepstad, D.C., C.M. Stickler, B. Soares-Filho, and F. Merry. 2008. Interactions among Amazon land use, forests and climate: Prospects for a near-term forest tipping point. *Philosophical Transactions of the Royal Society*. doi:10.1098/rstb.2007.0036.

Niu, S. 2008. China seeks to calm anger over soy imports. *Reuters*, December 11. http://www.reuters.com/article/2008/12/11/china-farmers-soy-idUSPEK218720081211. Accessed 2 May 2011.

Peine, E. 2009. The private state of agribusiness: Brazilian soy on the frontier of a new food regime (Unpublished Ph.D.). Ithaca: Department of Development Sociology, Cornell University.

Petry, M., and J. O'Rear. 2008. China, Peoples Republic of agricultural situation new oilseed industrial policy 2008. No. CH8084. Washington, DC: Foreign Agricultural Service, USDA.

Provance, P. 2003. China: Soy producers face shifting internal policies and world markets. Washington, DC: Production Estimates and Crop Assessment Division, Foreign Agricultural Service, USDA.

Ramo, J.C. 2004. *Beijing consensus: Notes on the new physics of Chinese power*. London: Foreign Policy Center.

Rosenthal, E. 2009. In Brazil, paying farmers to let the trees stand. *The New York Times*, August 22. http://www.nytimes.com/2009/08/22/science/earth/22degrees.html?pagewanted=all. Accessed 30 Oct 2010.

Schneider, M. 2011. *Feeding China's pigs: Implications for the environment, China's smallholder farmers and food security*. Minneapolis: Institute for Agriculture and Trade Policy.

State Development and Reform Commission. 2007. Catalog for the guidance of foreign investment industries (Amended 2007). http://www.fdi.gov.cn/pub/FDI_EN/Laws/law_en_info.jsp?docid=87372. Accessed 3 June 2010.

Steward, C. 2007. From colonization to "environmental soy": A case study of environmental and socio-economic valuation in the Amazon frontier. *Agriculture and Human Values* 24(1): 107–122.

Tepfer, D. 2010. China Chongqing Grain Group plans to produce soy in Brazil—report. *AE Brazil Newswire*, April 22. http://www.accessmylibrary.com/article-1G1-224690585/china-chongqing-grain-group.html. Accessed 17 Jan 2012.

Tuan, F.C., C. Fang, and Z. Cao. 2004. China's soybean imports expected to grow despite short-term disruptions. No. OCS-04J-01. Washington, DC: Economic Research Service, USDA.

UNCTAD. 2009. World investment report 2009: Transnational corporations, agricultural production and development. Geneva: United Nations Conference on Trade and Development.

US Department of Agriculture (USDA) Foreign Agricultural Service (FAS). 2011. Production, supply and distribution online. http://www.fas.usda.gov/psdonline/. Accessed 2 June 2011.

Warnken, P.F. 1999. *The development and growth of the soybean industry in Brazil*. Ames: Iowa State University Press.

Weis, T. 2007. *The global food economy: The battle for the future of farming*. London: Zed Books.

Wilkinson, J. 2009. The globalization of agribusiness and developing world food systems. *The Monthly Review* 61(4): 38–50, September.

Xiang, L. 2009. No end to soybean wars. *China Business Weekly*, April 20. http://www.chinadaily.com.cn/business/2009-04/20/content_7693989.htm. Accessed 10 June 2011.

Xiaokun, L., A. Yang, and B. Chang. 2011. China vows new Brazil trade ties. *China Daily*, April 13. http://www.chinadaily.com.cn/bizchina/2011-04/13/content_12316309.htm. Accessed 2 May 2011.

Yan, Q. 2007. The influence of trade policy changes on China's soybean market. *IATRC symposium*, July 8–9. Beijing: International Agricultural Trade Research Consortium.

Zancope, G., and J.M. Nasser. 2005. *O brasil que deu certo: A saga da soja brasileira*. Curitiba: Tríade.

Chapter 11
Who's Got the Power? An Evaluation of Power Distribution in the German Agribusiness Industry

Jon H. Hanf, Vera Belaya, and Erik Schweickert

Abstract Retail chains have increased in importance during the past several decades. Currently, only a handful of retailers dominate the major food markets. The resulting market shares are generally viewed as the major source of market power for these firms. We consider market power in the German agrifood industry using the framework developed by French and Raven, who identify five sources of power—legitimate, coercive, reward, expert, and referent power. Although each source is equally important, power is hard to measure and cannot be identified with a single measure. With this context, we analyze the transcripts of a public hearing of the 18th meeting of the German Bundestag, Committee on Food, Agriculture and Consumer Protection, that dealt with the topic "Supply and demand power of retailers and its consequences for consumers." As representatives from all relevant food chain participants were heard, the transcripts provide insights on the power that food retailers have in Germany.

11.1 Introduction

At the beginning of a series of government sponsored public workshops on agrifood competition in the United States in 2010, U.S. Attorney General Eric Holder posed the following question: "Is today's agriculture industry suffering from a lack of

J.H. Hanf, Ph.D. (✉) • E. Schweickert, Ph.D.
University of Geisenheim, Von-Lade-Str. 1, D-65366 Geisenheim, Germany
e-mail: jon.hanf@hs-gm.de

V. Belaya, Ph.D.
Federal Research Institute for Rural Areas, Forestry and Fisheries, Johann Heinrich von Thünen-Institute, Bundesallee 50, 38116 Braunschweig, Germany

H.S. James Jr. (ed.), *The Ethics and Economics of Agrifood Competition*,
The International Library of Environmental, Agricultural and Food Ethics 20,
DOI 10.1007/978-94-007-6274-9_11,

free and fair competition in the marketplace? That's the central question" (USDA-DOJ 2010, p. 11). This question was also the central theme of the meeting of the "Committee on the Internal Market and Consumer Protection" of the European Parliament on June 1, 2011 (see Corazza Bildt 2011), as well as of the meeting of the "Committee on Food, Agriculture and Consumer Protection" of the German Parliament on July 5, 2010 (see Goldmann 2010). This co-incidence suggests that the question is important and relevant in many countries.

In Germany today, the top 10 retail chains have a roughly 90% market share at the national level, while at the regional level some retail chains have even higher shares, which could be an indication of their possessing strong market power. That is, due to their size, these retailers could influence the decisions and actions of their suppliers or buyers. To put it more straightforwardly, retailers with this much market share might be able to tell their suppliers and buyers what they should do, maybe even to the suppliers' and buyers' disadvantage. This view assumes that power asymmetries exist, and it assumes further that suppliers and buyers do not have equal influence. However, a careful review of the processing industry shows that there are a number of processors with similarly large market shares within their more specialized sectors, suggesting that a pure comparison of market share in either the German food processing or food retail industries might not be adequate in discussions of power and power asymmetries.

As an example, consider the case of the evolution of branding in Germany. For years brands have been discussed solely in the context of strong national and manufacturer brands. However, over the past two decades, retailers' private brands have increased in importance. Today the majority of German retailers have a private "umbrella" brand that also consists of sub brands (such as low price and premium). At the same time as they established private brands, retailers also started using scanner data (data generated from electronic records of consumer purchases). This data provides retailers with substantial information about consumer behavior, often allowing them to outperform processors who must rely on purchasing data they receive from the retailers. Furthermore, consumers increasingly perceive retailer brands to be on the same footing as national and manufacturer brands. We claim that this suggests there is no longer a large difference between retailer and national brands, at least from the perspective of consumers.

As the distinction between retailer and producer blurs, consumers as well as policymakers will begin to attribute the same responsibilities to retailers as they do to processors. One area which is affected by this change in perception is the responsibility for safe and secure food quality along the whole value added food supply chain. Because of the success of private label retail branded products and the public's perception about retailer's responsibilities for food safety, retailers are now seen as liable for the total chain regardless of firm boundaries. This means that in the context of vertical coordination, retailers today have to build long term relationships with their suppliers. Excessive and anti-competitive power usage by retailers against food processors could hamper the establishment and the continuation of tighter vertical relationships. For this reason, at a recent annual meeting of the Efficient

Consumer Response initiative, retailers emphasized their efforts to build reliable relationships with their suppliers and customers.[1]

Although the market power of retailers might give them incentives to exercise inappropriate economic influence on their suppliers as well as to overcharge their customers, the discussion of retail branding above suggests that in the agrifood sector, concepts such as competition and power are complicated. Power is a multi-dimensional concept. In order to understand power use or misuse, we must first examine the different meanings and sources of power. Only then can we obtain a more balanced perspective of power in the context of the German agrifood industry. In this chapter we argue that power distribution does not reside unilaterally with retailers because processors possess countervailing power along different dimensions and types of power. Moreover, German consumers have some of the lowest food prices in Europe, and the quantity and quality of food products are good. Hence, we argue for moderation in the debate regarding retail power for these reasons: Either retailers are not prone to misuse their market power or they do not possess the market power that often is ascribed with them.

We begin this chapter by presenting a review of power and power asymmetries from the literature. In this review we also discuss how to measure power in marketing channel relationships. Based on the power concept of French and Raven (1959), we present an analysis of German agribusiness in order to answer to the questions "Who has power?" and "What are the resulting consequences?" The focus of our analysis is on the retailer-first tier supplier relation, although we will also address briefly consumers as well as farmers. Our analysis is based on a review of transcripts of a public hearing of the German Parliament, from which we argue that there are important lessons not only for the German agrifood industry but also for understanding the nature of agrifood competition generally.

11.2 Power in Marketing Channels

Several studies on marketing channels have shown that channel power has a significant impact on the buyer–supplier relationship and performance (Liu and Wang 2000; Lee 2001; Hingley 2005; Leonidou et al. 2008; Zhao et al. 2008; Yeung et al. 2009; Sheu and Hu 2009). The power relationship also has implications in the development of partnerships, as does the structure of the power-dependence relationship (Kumar 2005). Power is central not only in understanding the nature of the supply network and the power structures that exist within it, but also in implementing procurement and supply chain strategies (Cox 2001; Crook and

[1]Efficient Consumer Response (ECR) is a European food retailer industry group whose purpose is "to make the grocery sector as a whole more responsive to consumer demand and promote the removal of unnecessary costs from the supply chain" (ECR 2011). The annual meeting mentioned here was held in Berlin, Germany, on September 21–22, 2011. The organization was founded in 1994 and has its headquarters in Brussels.

Combs 2007; Ireland and Webb 2007; Flynn et al. 2008; Ganesan et al. 2009; Sheu and Hu 2009). Research has shown that the exercise of power in supply chains can impede cooperation through its interactions with other elements of the relationship (Cox 2001; Caldwell 2003; Watson et al. 2003; Corsten and Kumar 2005; Tokatli 2007; Yaqub 2009). That said, not all scholars agree on the effect of power in supply chain relationships or view power in supply chains as a negative force (Chung and Kim 2003; Hingley 2005; Maloni and Benton 2000; Sodano 2006).

There is little agreement within the literature about an exact definition of power, however. In fact, the problem of defining "power" is that it has many definitions and conceptualizations (Dahl 1957). Authors who have focused on this problem agree that power is an extremely troublesome, elusive, notoriously evanescent and subjective concept (Bierstedt 1950; Bachrach and Baratz 1962; Ramsay 1996); a vague, poorly defined "primitive" term (Hage 1972); and a difficult idea to pin down (Clegg et al. 2006). After reviewing roughly 250 definitions of power from the fields of sociology, psychology, political science, economics, management, marketing and chain and network science, we agree with Cartwright (1965) who points out that many authors "invent" their own definitions in order to suit their needs. Following the advice of Bacharach and Lawler (1980, p. 14), who state that "when doing research in order to capture the term of power we must identify a more concrete phenomenon or idea to which the primitive term points," we concentrate on definitions presented in the field of supply-chain and marketing-channel literature.

El-Ansary and Stern (1972, p. 47) define power as "the ability of a channel member to control the decision variables in the marketing strategy of another member in a given channel at a different level of distribution." Cox et al. (2002, p. 3) define power in supply chains as "the ability of a firm to own and control critical assets in markets and supply chains that allow it to sustain its ability to appropriate and accumulate value for itself by constantly leveraging its customers, competitors and suppliers." Hu and Sheu (2005) view power in terms of a strategy-influencing source that is oriented from one channel member to another. Other literature on power in supply chains and marketing channels uses similar definitions, such as the ability to influence other firms to act in a desired manner for economic gains (Ireland and Webb 2007) or to get them do things that they would not normally do (Reid and Bojani 2009). This review leads us to conclude that power generally refers to the ability, capacity or potential to get others to do something; to command, influence, determine or control the behaviors, intentions, decisions or actions of others in the pursuit of one's own goals or interests against their will; as well as to induce changes, to mobilize resources, or to restructure situations, among other things. All definitions of power seem to use similar terms and have a common theme.

French and Raven (1959) identified five types or channels of power, each based on its source or origin: coercive, reward, expert, legitimate, and referent power. *Coercive power* enables an individual to punish others. In the supply chain network context, it reflects a supplier's fear that it will be punished if it fails to comply with the requirements of the retail company. *Reward power* depends on the ability of the power holder to offer rewards to others. If a company has access to resources which are valuable to other firms, it can use them to influence the behavior of the other firms. *Expert power* is derived from the skills or special knowledge of a particular subject. Within a supply chain, a retailer possesses expert power if its suppliers believe that the retailer possesses a special knowledge which is valuable to them (the suppliers). *Legitimate power* stems from a legitimate right to influence and an obligation to accept this influence. For example, a formal supply contract might grant certain rights to the retailer or supplier to make specific decisions in certain circumstances. Legitimate power can also arise from one's position in a network. *Referent power* is the ability to be attractive to others and depends on the charisma and interpersonal skills of the power holder. Referent power can arise when a party possesses unique or important knowledge. Within the supply chain, this power is manifested when firms want to join the procurement network of a specific retailer and when a retailer learns information about the production process of goods the retailer sells.

If power is the ability to get others to do something in the pursuit of one's own goals, even if it is against interests of others, then in the end it does not matter which source or type of power enables one to achieve the result. Power will be visible by its results. Hence, no source or type of power is more important than the other, even though some sources, such as coercion, might seem more potent.[2] What this means is that in our analysis of market power in the German agrifood industry, we consider all sources and types of power. Retailers possessing one type of power may face countervailing power possessed by food processors that is not directly tied to measures of market share.

11.3 Power Measurement

Recognizing that there are five types of power usage in marketing channel relationships, our objective is to apply them to the question of power asymmetry in the German agrifood industry. Ideally we want to measure or quantify power relations. To do so we must first define a standard for its measurement. When measuring weight, we apply kilograms, pounds or tons. The measurement of distance is expressed in meters, yards or miles. Unfortunately, as demonstrated below, there is no standard dimension for the measurement of power, which makes an objective assessment difficult if not impossible.

According to Dahl (1957) power can be estimated by measuring the amount of change induced in the actions of others. He conceptualized power as the probability that the respondent does what the actor requests minus the probability that the respondent would have done it in the absence of the request, a quantity ranging from minus one to plus one. In order to quantify power Dahl estimated conditional probabilities and calculated the difference between them. Van den Brink et al. (2005)

[2]This perception might derive from the idea that coercion is the dark side of power, in contrast to the other types of power (Craig and Gabler 1963).

introduced the idea of a cooperative transferable utility game within a symmetric network of players. They measured the power of each coalition of positions within the network by assigning them a β-value, where each position in the network has an initial weight equal to one, and measuring power is seen as redistributing this weight to all its neighbors. This measure fits well with power dependence theory developed by Emerson (1962), since the power value of a position decreases when the number of its neighbors increases.

Many studies have centered their attempts to measure power on the concept of dependence, stating that the power of *A* over *B* is equal to, and based upon, the dependence of *B* upon *A* (see El-Ansary and Stern 1972; Spekman 1979; Frazier 1983). A number of attempts have been made to measure power in marketing channels as a function of the sources of power based on the French and Raven taxonomy mentioned above (e.g., Johnson et al. 1993; Greene and Podsakoff 1981; Cobb 1980; Busch 1980). In some studies specific attention is paid to the measurement of informational power (Nermin 1991; Johnson et al. 1985), legitimate power (Ketilson 1991) and even to the additional power sources added to the typology of French and Raven (1959), such as incremental power (Ivancevich 1970) and upward influence (Greene and Podsakoff 1981). Some researchers differentiated specifically among coercive and noncoercive power sources (Hunt and Nevin 1974; Lusch 1976; Frazier and Summers 1984). Etgar et al. (1978) consider whether economic or non-economic-based power sources are more effective in enhancing channel control.

Cool and Henderson (1998) operationalized supplier/buyer power by differentiating among structural power (the number of potential suppliers/buyers and supplier/buyer concentration), dependence power (impact on seller's cost, impact on seller's differentiation and switching cost), attribution power (capacity of suppliers/buyers to bargain and the cost to switch suppliers/buyers), and integration power (the incidence of forward integration from suppliers/buyers). Their results indicate that buyer power has a much larger effect on seller profitability than supplier power. Porter (1974) attempted to model the retailer power of convenience stores and non-convenience stores. He argued that small non-convenience stores could be relatively more influential in sales than larger stores. The reason has to do with the effect of product differentiation. When the retailer is more influential in product differentiation, retailer bargaining power increases, suggesting that the size of firms can be inversely related to dealer bargaining power in contrast to popular perception (because smaller stores sell specialized lines, hence, having a greater contribution to differentiation).

Our discussion on power measurement has demonstrated a number of important insights. First, there is not one measurement or measurement system that is capable of including all relevant aspects of power. Second, power is complex and highly multidimensional. Third, power is best understood by considering each bilateral relationship among players within the network separately. Given these insights, we seek to assess the multi-facetted nature of power within the German agrifood sector by examining the perspectives of a wide variety of individual and specific stakeholders. To do this we examine the transcripts of a public hearing of the Committee on Food, Agriculture and Consumer Protection of the German

Parliament on the topic of market power, conducted in July of 2010. Spokesmen from relevant stakeholder groups were included in the hearing.[3] Thus, in addition to parliamentarians of all German parties that form the Committee, representatives of German farmers, manufacturers, retailers as well as consumers were present. Furthermore, as part of their participation in the hearings, the participants were given a questionnaire with more than twenty items asking for their perceptions on the different aspects of power. In order to analyze the different types of power and their effects we studied all transcripts and attempted to document evidence of the different sources of power (coercive, reward, expert, legitimate, and referent). Our objective is to determine if food retailers possess significant market power, given that the top 10 retail chains have roughly 90% of the retail market, through a qualitative assessment of representative comments. We present below our assessment of these transcripts and what we believe they mean in terms of power within the German agrifood industry.

11.4 German Agribusiness: Analysis of the Power Structure

11.4.1 Background Information on the German Agrifood Industry

In Germany consumers, numbering roughly 80 million inhabitants plus several million tourists per year, have many options for buying food products. A comparative study of food prices of different European countries has shown that German food prices are some of the lowest in the European Union (Lademann and Associates 2010).[4] Jürgen Abraham (Goldmann 2010, p. 8) of the food processor organization

[3]Different institutions were asked to give their opinion on the nature of competition and to send one or two representatives who delivered prepared remarks and answered questions asked by the parliamentarians at the meeting of the Committee on Food, Agriculture and Consumer Protection of the German Bundestag, 5 July 2010, in Berlin, Germany. The given remarks and comments of the participants were recorded and transcribed in the same document. We analyzed this transcript of the as well as the written comments of the invited participants. Participants and their representatives included the following: Federation of the German Food Processors (BVE 2010) represented by Jürgen Abraham; Federation of the German Retailers (HDE 2010) represented by Stefan Genth; Federation of the German Farmers (DBV 2010) represented by Dr. Helmut Born and Reinhard Schoch; Retail Chain "tegut... (2010) represented by Wolfgang Gutberlet; Lademann & Associates represented by Prof. Dr. Rainer Lademann; labor union Food Consumption Gastronomy (NGG 2010) represented by Franz-Josef Möllenberg; Consumer Advice Centre Hamburg (Verbraucherzentrale Hamburg 2010) represented by Armin Valet; the non-governmental organization Oxfam (2010) represented by Marita Wiggerthale; and Parliament Member Erik Schweickert.

[4]The study included Belgium, Denmark, Germany, Spain, France, Italy, the Netherlands, Austria, and United Kingdom for which Eurostat data of the period summer 2009 to summer 2010 had been analyzed.

BVE pointed out that because of relatively strong price competition, German consumers were at an advantage compared with consumers from other countries.[5] Only 11% of expenditures by German consumers are on food products (BVE 2010). Furthermore, consumers can select from a wide assortment of food and non-food products. For example, an average of 50,000 items are offered for sale in department stores, 10,000 items in traditional supermarkets and 2,000–3,000 items in discounters. The most important marketing channels available to consumers are retailers, direct selling by processors or farmers, and restaurants and bars. Among these, retail is the most important channel.

The German retail sector has changed dramatically since the end of World War II. In the 1950s, the first larger retailers (e.g. Tengelmann, EDEKA, REWE) were established. Today the five largest retailers have about 60–70% market share (Trade Dimension 2009); the largest ten retailers account for roughly 90% of the market share. However, a comparison of the Herfindahl-Hirschman indexes of different European countries shows that Germany is in the middle with a value of 1,900, whereas Switzerland has the most concentrated industry with over a value of 3,500 points.[6] The EU commission considers these results as high but not critical (Lademann and Associates 2010). Whereas the retail sector is dominated by a number of large firms, the processing sector is much more heterogeneous. For the last 20 years there have been roughly 5,000 processing firms in Germany. However, only 10% of them generate between 80 and 85% of all inland sales, with an average sales volume of 230–250 million Euros. The other 4,500 firms have an average sales volume of between 5 and 7 million Euros. These processors have limited production and marketing capacity and knowledge. Lademann (Goldmann 2010, p. 15) concluded that because many of these small processors are not capable of delivering to large retailers, the processors that supply retailers are relatively large. That said, a typical retailer has between 1,500 and 2,500 German suppliers on average.

A comparison of the average profits of retailers and processors is interesting since profits at the retail level are lower than at the processing level. Sales profitability before taxes on the retailing level decreased from between 0.6 and 1.6% in 2003 to between 0.3 and 0.9% in 2006. However, the same performance indicator on processing level increased in the period 1997–2007 from 2.1 to 3% (Statisches Bundesamt, various years). As an alternative to selling their products via retailers, food processors also have the option of marketing their products directly via specialized retailers, online retailers, restaurants, bars and catering firms and export. The existence of these alternatives is one of the reasons why such a high number

[5]Written opinions by the invited organizations are cited in the reference section (e.g., Lademann & Associates). Comments by organization representatives (e.g., Abraham) are taken from the Goldmann (2010) transcript with corresponding page number from the document.

[6]The Herfindahl-Hirschman Index (HHI) is a measure of the size of firms in relation to the industry and an indicator of the amount of competition among them. It is defined as the sum of the squares of the market shares of the firms within the industry, where the market shares are expressed as fractions. The HHI ranges from 1/N to 1, where N is the number of firms in the market.

of processors still exist. Besides industrial processors, there are approximately 30,000 food trade businesses. On the farm level there are around 360,000 farmers, although their numbers are declining. Dr. Helmut Born, representing the Federation of German Farmers DBV (Goldman 2010, p. 9) says that 2–4% of farmers leave the sector annually, due in part because of an overcapacity created by market interventions of the EU.

Because there are substantially more food processors and an even greater number of farmers, there is likely a significant degree of power asymmetry in the German agrifood sector. However, as Lademann (Goldmann 2010, p. 33) emphasized, power is a bilateral construct and thus should be examined separately in each buyer–supplier relationship. Broad-stroke assessments of market power or power asymmetry based solely on market shares or the number of participants can be misleading, in part because there is no single measurement of power, as stated above. Determining objective indicators is difficult because the information needed for generating them is usually not available (e.g., a determination of buyer power may require an assessment of purchase pricing below marginal cost, which requires access to private information on real costs). Because of the difficulty of working with objective measures, we consider a more qualitative analysis of power and power asymmetries by separately discussing all five sources of power (coercive, reward, expert, legitimate, and referent power) identified by French and Raven (1959).

11.4.2 Stakeholder Analysis and Sources of Power

Participants of the public hearings of the Committee on Food, Agriculture and Consumer Protection generally agreed that legitimate or position power is the most common type considered when discussing power in the food chain. Wolfgang Gutberlet (Goldmann 2010, p. 12) of the retailer "tegut..." stated that retailers are fundamentally important in the marketing channel for German agribusiness, because to reach mass markets, a supplier cannot fully avoid retailers. Since there are a limited number of nation-wide distributing retailers, such retail firms possess legitimate power. Stefan Genth (Goldmann 2010, p. 11) of the retailer federation HDE argued that while suppliers still have some alternatives, such as exporting the goods, medium-sized processors have to accept the position power of retailers. Genth also noted, however, that this can sometimes work to their advantage, since retailers often look to medium-sized processors to produce retail brands. For processors that specialize in the production of retail brands, such agreements can be very profitable as they do not have to spend any money on end-consumer marketing.

Lademann (p. 14) as well as Genth (p. 10) pointed out that in contrast to the large number of small and medium sized producers, the top 500 processors are often in a favorable position themselves, particularly if they own a "must-have" or dominant brand. In the case of such brands, consumers are willing to change their shopping outlet if their preferred on does not carry the product or brand, which suggests that the brand-owning food processor possesses countervailing position power. Furthermore, Genth (p. 27) showed, and Abraham (p. 30) admitted, that in some segments of the food market only a handful of processors operate, so that these processors can have legitimate power. However, there can be exceptions here. For example, within the dairy industry, even though there are only a few dominant dairy companies, they do not possess significant position power because too much milk is produced by dairy farmers. Thus, regarding position power, retailers are often able to influence the decisions of their suppliers. However, in the case of large, well branded producers, the relationships are more power symmetric or even a bit asymmetrically distributed in favor of the processors.

Coercive power can evolve from asymmetries in position power. If a retailer is in a favorable position, it is also capable of punishing its suppliers if they are unwilling to make desired concessions. Small and medium sized processors often fear the potential of being delisted or having prices received cut by large retailers. As one Member of Parliament said (Goldmann 2010), "if you go – as a small family business – to a retailer for your annual meeting and there is the word delisting in the room it could be that you accept some terms that you would normally not accept." Virtually all experts commenting at the public hearing indicated that retailers use coercive power. However, large processers of top-selling brands also use coercive power, if less frequently than dominant retailers. On some occasions, processors withheld supply of some branded products to retailers in retaliation to retailer behavior. Coercive power, when applied too frequently, can create an atmosphere of distrust and suspicion between food processors and retailers, resulting in frequent re-negotiations of contracting conditions and terms (Lademann and Associates 2010).

The exercise of reward power does not seem to be too evident from retailers. However, processors frequently use rewards and incentives to influence the buying decisions of retailers. There is some concern that reward power can be used in the form of bribery. For example, Lademann (p. 14) stated that all German retailers have rules that prohibit managers from accepting any gifts from their suppliers; even product samples have to be reported. Thus, reward power appears to reside primarily in the hands of suppliers.

Both expert power and referent power are rooted in brand management. Traditionally, the marketing knowledge of processors gave them expert power over retailers. Through careful marketing studies, processors knew what consumers wanted, and so they produced the products that they believed would generate the greatest demand. Retailers acted merely as the fulfilling agents of processors. However, as producers outsourced their marketing research to external service providers, such as Nielson[7] and GFK,[8] they started to lose their relative expertise in the consumer psyche because retailers could purchase marketing data from the third party external providers. Today, Abraham (p. 32) conceded that retailers often have

[7] See http://www.nielsen.com/us/en/measurement/retail-measurement.html.

[8] See http://www.gfk.com/gfkcr/.

superior customer knowledge because of their access to and analysis of point-of-sale scanner data. Small and medium sized processors are often dependent on marketing information they can receive only from retailers. Thus, over time there has been a shift of expert power from processors to retailers, which has been a function largely of technology rather than firm size or market share. However, this is only partly true in the case of popular and well-established brands. Genth (p. 29) stated that producers of "must-have" brands still utilize their own marketing studies and thus have excellent consumer knowledge.

In the context of well-known brands, referent power is also evident. For example, processors possess referent power when retailers use "big name" brands as a way to attract consumers to their stores. This is especially true for many discount retailers. However, as Lademann (p. 41) and Abraham (p. 37) observed, retailers that have private label brands can acquire and use referent power over processors. Working together with suppliers of their own private brands, retailers can learn a lot about the input markets of their supplier. Because of the number and variety of private label brands some retailers operate, retailers can sometimes have better knowledge about input prices and product development and production costs than the processors themselves. In some cases, retailers use this knowledge to establish cost-saving procedures with their retail brand suppliers in order to improve working relationships and to better coordinate the vertical product flow. Thus, the rise in private label brands seems to have increased the retailers' referent power while simultaneously decreasing it on processor side. That said, to the extent that producers of popular "must-have" brands and other processors have superior knowledge about production and development, that can enable them to influence the retailers' decisions, thus allowing some referent power to remain with processors, although it seems to be most utilized by producers of the most well-known and well-branded products.

Table 11.1 summarizes our analysis of sources of market power in the retailer and processor (supplier) relationship.

Even though the focus of our analysis has been on the retailer-processor relationship, Born (Goldmann 2010, p. 30) noted that farmers are also affected by the downstream power shifts. The vast majority of farm produce is marketed as unbranded bulk products. Furthermore, German farmers often lack customer insights so that farmers do not know which information is of high relevance to their customers. Lacking these insights, farm suppliers such as BASF or Bayer Cropscience are stepping in the position to be the knowledge broker giving them the chance to act as a system supplier for the retailers. This means that these agriculture input providers increased their expert power on the farm level. This development might result in a situation in which farmers are placed at a power disadvantage relative to the input providers.

All things considered, we conclude that power asymmetries dominate the agrifood industry, but not fully in favor of the large retailers. Retailers and food processors of well-known "must-have" brands, as well as some knowledge specialists, can have relatively symmetrical power relationships. However, the vast majority of food processors are small to medium sized processors, and most of

Table 11.1 Summary of types of power and power asymmetries in the retailer and processor (supplier) relationship

Type of power	Retailers	Food processors
Legitimate or position	Favors large retailers due to relatively larger number of food processors	Favors large processors that have popular brands Favors medium-sized processors that produce private label brands for retailers
Coercive	Dominant firms can force concessions from processors, especially small and medium-sized ones	Large processors with branded products can threaten to withhold supply
Reward	Rarely evident or used by retailers	Processors use rewards to influence retailer behavior Potential for bribery
Expert	Point-of-sale scanner data can give retailers an advantage	Marketing knowledge of branded products, though marketing studies by third parties can weaken processor advantages
Referent	Private label brands gives retailers access to production and development information and greater control over some vertical supply chains	Popular brands as sale leaders, as well as production knowledge, gives an advantage to processors

Note: Summary of examination of participant comments from July 2010 public meeting of the committee on food, agriculture and consumer protection of the German parliament.

these have weak brands and are not able to exert meaningful economic power against the retailers. Because they are small they are not able to achieve position power, and without position power and resulting (financial) capability, they also do not hold coercive or reward power. These producers also generally do not have sufficient expert knowledge of their customers or referent power to balance the power asymmetries they face elsewhere.

In contrast, small or medium sized processors that are able to establish a unique niche brand are also able to withstand competitive pressures from retailers. The reason is that niche branding allows the firms to gain specialized consumer knowledge in their segment and thus obtain expert and other types of power associated with a successful brand. Indeed, if there is one major implication of our analysis of power in the German agrifood industry, it is that consumer knowledge and professional brand management are the most valuable resource for successfully mastering the (future) competition because with these capabilities small and medium sized companies are capable of leveraging their expert power against the power asymmetries resulting from the legitimate power of large retail chains.

11.5 Summary

The trend toward concentration within the agrifood industry is being watched carefully by politicians, consumer protecting institutions, and researchers all over the world. The evolving multinationals (retail chains and food processors) have reached the economic magnitude of small countries,[9] so that the term "powerful" can be attributed to them. This claim is supported by the fact that these companies also often have huge market shares. Undoubtedly power results from possessing such market shares. However, our review of the literature has led to three observations. First, power is a multifaceted construct, emerging from different sources, and position is only one of them. Second, there is no single measure that combines all sources of power, so that a differentiated analysis of power and its sources must be used to answer the question of whether a retailer is exerting power over a supplier. Third, power is a construct that can only be analyzed in a concrete situation of two players, as it is a bilateral construct; hence, concentration ratios on the industry level have only very limited usage. For these reasons we analyzed German agribusiness, focusing on the retailer-processor relation, considering all five power sources identified by French and Raven (1959): legitimate, coercive, expert, reward, and referent power. We did this by studying the verbatim transcripts of the 18th Meeting of the "Committee on Food, Agriculture and Consumer Protection" of the German Parliament on July 5, 2010. Within the meeting representatives from all stages of the food chain commented on the power situation within the agrifood sector from their perspective. The controversial opinions provided by meeting participants enabled us to study the complex nature of power.

Our analysis of the transcripts showed that the position power of retailers, derived primarily from their market share, is of key importance. However, large processors and processors with popular brands or who produce private label products for retailers also possessed some countervailing position power. The transcripts also showed that retailers would use coercive power to discipline their suppliers, but the threat of withholding supply of popular products could give processors coercive power, but less frequently. Reward power is rarely used by retailers, but it is often used by producers. With respect to expert power, popular, strongly branded processors dominate in consumer knowledge, but retailer access to scanner data and customer buying behavior helped shift some power from processors to retailers. Referent power is generally possessed by producers, who use it, although the marketing of private labels provides some power benefit to retailers.

Overall, we conclude that power is asymmetrically distributed in the German agrifood industry, but not uniformly and not fully in favor of large retailers. Instead, large and well-branded processors possess and use some power sources and hence

---

[9] For example, the world largest retailer Wal-Mart had total food sales of roughly 255 billion USD in 2010, whereas Luxemburg had a gross domestic product of 41 billion USD. The largest German retailer the Schwarz-Group had total food sales of 72 billion in 2010, whereas Cyprus had a GDP of 23 billion.

are not always affected by them. This leads to the situation that the "power game" is being played very intensively among food chain participants in Germany, generally to the benefit of German consumers. The lessons here ought to apply in other countries where there are concerns about dominating retailers and food processors.

References

Bacharach, P., and M.S. Lawler. 1980. *Power and politics in organizations*. San Francisco: Jossey-Bass.

Bachrach, P., and M. Baratz. 1962. The two faces of power. *American Political Science Review* 56: 947–952.

Bierstedt, R. 1950. An analysis of social power. *American Sociological Review* 15: 730–738.

Busch, P. 1980. The sales manager's bases of social power and influence upon the sales force. *Journal of Marketing* 44(3): 91–101.

BVE. 2010. Comments of the Federation of German Food Processors, German Bundestag: Committee on food, agriculture and consumer protection, 5 July 2010, Ausschussdrucksache 17(10)201-D, Berlin.

Caldwell, N. 2003. The treatment of power in supply chains: Power, method and ontology. *12th international IPSERA conference*, Budapest, 501–512.

Cartwright, D. 1965. Influence, leadership and control. In *Handbook of organizations*, ed. J.G. March, 1–47. Chicago: Rand McNally.

Chung, S.A., and G.M. Kim. 2003. Performance effects of partnership between manufacturers and suppliers for new product development: The supplier's standpoint. *Research Policy* 32(4): 587–603.

Clegg, S., D. Courpasson, and N. Phillips. 2006. *Power and organizations*. London: Sage Publication.

Cobb, A.T. 1980. Informal influence in the formal organization: Perceived sources of power among work unit peers. *Academy of Management Journal* 23(1): 155–161.

Cool, K., and J. Henderson. 1998. Power and firm profitability in supply chains: French manufacturing industry in 1993. *Strategic Management Journal* 19(10): 909–926.

Corazza Bildt, A.M. 2011. Report of the plenary session of the committee on the internal market and consumer protection of the European Parliament, 1 June 2011, Brussels.

Corsten, D., and N. Kumar. 2005. Do suppliers benefit from collaborative relationships with large retailers? An empirical investigation of efficient consumer response adoption. *Journal of Marketing* 69(3): 80–94.

Cox, A. 2001. Understanding buyer and supplier power: A framework for procurement and supply competence. *Journal of Supply Chain Management* 37(2): 8–15.

Cox, A., P. Ireland, C. Lonsdale, J. Sanderson, and G. Watson. 2002. *Supply chains, markets and power: Mapping buyer and supplier power regimes*. New York: Routledge.

Craig, D.R., and W.K. Gabler. 1963. The competitive struggle for market control. In *Readings in marketing*, ed. J.E. Westing. Englewood Cliffs: Prentice Hall.

Crook, T.R., and J.G. Combs. 2007. Sources and consequences of bargaining power in supply chains. *Journal of Operations Management* 25(2): 546–555.

Dahl, R.A. 1957. The concept of power. *Behavioral Science* 2(3): 201–215.

DBV. 2010. Comments of the Federation of German Farmers, German Bundestag: Committee on Food, Agriculture and Consumer Protection. 5 July 2010, Ausschussdrucksache 17(10)201-G, Berlin.

Efficient Consumer Response (ECR). 2011. Organization and principles. http://ecr-all.org/about-ecr-europe/organisation-and-principles/. Accessed 19 Dec 2011.

El-Ansary, A.I., and L.W. Stern. 1972. Power measurement in the distribution channel. *Journal of Marketing Research* 9(1): 47–52.

Emerson, R.M. 1962. Power-dependence relations. *American Sociological Review* 27: 31–41, February.

Etgar, M., E.R. Cadotte, and L.M. Robinson. 1978. Selection of an effective channel control mix. *Journal of Marketing* 42(3): 53–58.

Flynn, B.B., X. Zhao, B. Huo, and J.H.Y. Yeung. 2008. We've got the power! How customer power affects supply chain relationships. *Business Horizons* 51: 169–174.

Frazier, G.L. 1983. On the measurement of interfirm power in channels of distribution. *Journal of Marketing Research* 20(2): 158–166.

Frazier, G., and J.O. Summers. 1984. Interfirm influence strategies and their application within distribution channels. *Journal of Marketing* 48(3): 43–55.

French, J.R.P., and B. Raven. 1959. The bases of social power. In *Studies in social power*, ed. D. Cartwright, 150–167. Ann Arbor: University of Michigan Press.

Ganesan, S., M. George, S. Jap, R.W. Palmatier, and B. Weitz. 2009. Supply chain management and retailer performance. Emerging trends, issues, and implications for research and practice. *Journal of Retailing* 85(1): 84–94.

Goldmann, H.-M. 2010. Transcript of the Speeches; German Bundestag: Committee on Food, Agriculture and Consumer Protection, 5 July 2010, Berlin.

Greene, Ch N., and P.M. Podsakoff. 1981. Effects of withdrawal of a performance-contingent reward on supervisory influence and power. *Academy of Management Journal* 24(3): 527–542.

Hage, J. 1972. *Techniques and problems of theory construction in sociology*. New York: Wiley.

HDE. 2010. Comments of the Federation of the German Retailers, German Bundestag: Committee on Food, Agriculture and Consumer Protection. 5 July 2010, Ausschussdrucksache 17(10)201-B, Berlin.

Hingley, M. 2005. Power to all our friends? Learning to live with imbalance in UK supplier-retailer relationships. *Industrial Marketing Management* 34(8): 848–858.

Hu, T.-L., and J.-B. Sheu. 2005. Relationships of channel power, noncoercive influencing strategies, climate, and solidarity: A real case study of the Taiwanese PDA industry. *Industrial Marketing Management* 34(5): 447–461.

Hunt, S.D., and J.R. Nevin. 1974. Power in a channel of distribution: Sources and consequences. *Journal of Marketing Research* 11(2): 186–193.

Ireland, R.D., and J.W. Webb. 2007. A multi-theoretic perspective on trust and power in strategic supply chains. *Industrial Marketing Management* 25(2): 482–497.

Ivancevich, J.M. 1970. An analysis of control, bases of control, and satisfaction in an organizational setting. *Academy of Management Journal* 13(4): 427–436.

Johnson, J.L., H.F. Koenig, and J.R. Brown. 1985. The bases of marketing channel power: An exploration and confirmation of their underlying dimensions. In *AMA educators' proceedings*, ed. R. Lusch et al., 160–165. Chicago: American Marketing Association.

Johnson, J.L., T. Sakano, J.A. Cote, and N. Onzo. 1993. The exercise of interfirm power and its repercussions in U.S.-Japanese channel relationships. *Journal of Marketing* 57(2): 1–10.

Ketilson, L.H. 1991. An examination of the use of legitimate power in marketing channels. *International Review of Retail, Distribution and Consumer Research* 1(5): 527–548.

Kumar, N. 2005. The power of power in supplier–retailer relationships. *Industrial Marketing Management* 34: 863–866.

Lademann & Associates. 2010. Comments, German Bundestag: Committee on Food, Agriculture and Consumer Protection, 5 July 2010, Ausschussdrucksache 17(10)201-F neu, Berlin.

Lee, D.Y. 2001. Power, conflict, and satisfaction in IJV supplier-Chinese distributor channels. *Journal of Business Research* 52: 149–160.

Leonidou, L.C., M.A. Talias, and C.N. Leonidou. 2008. Exercised power as a driver of trust and commitment in cross-border industrial buyer–seller relationships. *Industrial Marketing Management* 37: 92–103.

Liu, H., and Y.P. Wang. 2000. Interfirm channel relationships, influence strategies and performance in China: An empirical examination. *Journal of Transportation Management* 4(3–4): 135–152.

Lusch, R.F. 1976. Sources of power: Their impact on intrachannel conflict. *Journal of Marketing Research* 13(4): 382–390.

Maloni, M.J., and W.C. Benton. 2000. Power influences in the supply chain. *Journal of Business Logistics* 21(1): 49–73.

Nermin, E. 1991. Informational power: A means for increased control in channels of distribution. *Psychology and Marketing* 8(3): 197–213.

NGG. 2010. Comments of the Labor Union Food Consumption Gastronomy, German Bundestag: Committee on Food, Agriculture and Consumer Protection. 5 July 2010, Ausschussdrucksache 17(10)201-H, Berlin.

Oxfam. 2010. Comments of the NGO Oxfam Deutschland, German Bundestag: Committee on Food, Agriculture and Consumer Protection. 5 July 2010, Ausschussdrucksache 17(10)201-A neu, Berlin.

Porter, M.E. 1974. Consumer behavior, retailer power and market performance in consumer goods industries. *The Review of Economics and Statistics* 56(4): 419–436.

Ramsay, J. 1996. Power measurement. *European Journal of Purchasing & Supply Management* 2(2–3): 129–143.

Reid, R.D., and D.C. Bojanic. 2009. *Hospitality marketing management*, 5th ed. Hoboken: Wiley.

Sheu, J.-B., and T.-L. Hu. 2009. Channel power, commitment and performance toward sustainable channel relationship. *Industrial Marketing Management* 38(1): 17–31.

Sodano, V. 2006. A power-based approach to the analysis of the food system. In *International agri-food chains and networks*, ed. J. Bijman, S.W.F. Omta, and J.H. Trienekens, 199–215. Wageningen: Wageningen Academic Publishers.

Spekman, R.E. 1979. Influence and information: An exploratory investigation of the boundary role person's basis of power. *Academy of Management Journal* 22(1): 104–117.

Statisches Bundesamt. Various years. Kostenstrukturstatistik. Report of the German Federal Statistics Office, Wiesbaden.

tegut... 2010. Comments of the retailer "tegut...", German Bundestag: Committee on Food, Agriculture and Consumer Protection. 5 July 2010, Ausschussdrucksache 17(10)201-C neu, Berlin.

Tokatli, N. 2007. Asymmetrical power relations and upgrading among suppliers of global clothing brands: Hugo Boss in Turkey. *Journal of Economic Geography* 7: 67–92.

Trade Dimensions. 2009. Top-firmen 2010, Der lebensmittelhandel in Deutschland, Food/Nonfood. Frankfurt: Trade Dimensions.

US Department of Agriculture/Department of Justice (USDA-DOJ). 2010. Agriculture and antitrust enforcement issues in our 21st century economy. Washington, DC: US Department of Agriculture & US Department of Justice. http://www.justice.gov/atr/public/workshops/ag2010/index.html. Accessed 1 Dec 2011.

Van den Brink, R., P. Borm, R. Hendrickx, and G. Owen. 2005. Characterizations of network power measures. Tinbergen Institute Discussion Paper TI 2005-061/1.

Verbraucherzentrale Hamburg. 2010. Comments of the consumer advice centre Hamburg, German Bundestag: Committee on food, agriculture and consumer protection. 5 July 2010, Ausschuss-drucksache 17(10)201-E neu, Berlin.

Watson, G., C. Lonsdale, A. Cox, and D. Chicksand. 2003. Effective demand management in the NHS. *12th international IPSERA conference*, Budapest, 1113–1125.

Yaqub, M.Z. 2009. Antecedents, consequences and control of opportunistic behavior in strategic networks. *Journal of Business & Economics Research* 7(2): 15–32.

Yeung, J.H.Y., W. Selen, M. Zhang, and B. Huo. 2009. The effects of trust and coercive power on supplier integration. *International Journal of Production Economics* 120(1): 66–78, Special Issue on Operations Strategy and Supply Chains Management.

Zhao, X., B. Huo, B.B. Flynn, and J.H.Y. Yeung. 2008. The impact of power and relationship commitment on the integration between manufacturers and customers in a supply chain. *Journal of Operations Management* 26: 368–388.

Chapter 12
Local Foods and Food Cooperatives: Ethics, Economics and Competition Issues

Ani L. Katchova and Timothy A. Woods

Abstract Consumer interest in locally produced foods marketed through local food networks has been increasing. Local food networks utilize local supply chains such as direct market sales to consumers through CSAs, farmers markets, farm stands, and other alternative outlets. Our goal is to examine the role of food cooperatives in strengthening the local food networks and distributing locally produced products. We utilize data from a national study which includes case studies with three leading food co-ops and a national survey of the general managers of food co-ops. We focus on analyzing the business strategies and competitive advantages of food co-ops sourcing local foods from local producers and marketing these local foods to consumers. We identify the emerging business practices, ethics principles, and competition issues for food co-ops with respect to sourcing and marketing of local products. Specifically, we provide a literature review on local food systems, examine local food definitions and recent trends for food co-ops, examine the business models and ethics principles for food co-ops, discuss the business strategies in sourcing and marketing of local foods by food co-ops, and examine the frequency and effectiveness of these business strategies to source and promote local foods. We show that when compared to other grocers, food co-ops have competitive advantages in working with local producers and often play a key role in the local producers' business viability.

A.L. Katchova, Ph.D. (✉)
Department of Agricultural Economics, University of Kentucky,
320 Barnhart Bldg, Lexington, KY 40546, USA
e-mail: akatchova@uky.edu

T.A. Woods, Ph.D.
Department of Agricultural Economics, University of Kentucky,
402 Barnhart Bldg, Lexington, KY 40546, USA

H.S. James Jr. (ed.), *The Ethics and Economics of Agrifood Competition*,
The International Library of Environmental, Agricultural and Food Ethics 20,
DOI 10.1007/978-94-007-6274-9_12,

12.1 Introduction

The U.S. food system is characterized by two polarizing systems: the global corporate model and the local/regional food network. Under the global corporate model, the food retail sector has become increasingly concentrated with mainstream supply chains separating producers and consumers through a chain of processors/manufacturers, shippers, and retailers. On the other hand, local/regional food networks utilize "shorter" or local supply chains, particularly direct market sales to consumers through community supported agriculture (CSA), farmers markets, farm stands, and other alternative outlets.

Local/regional food networks are a collaborative effort to build more locally-based, self-reliant food economies. These local food networks emphasize sustainable food production, processing, distribution, and consumption that are integrated to enhance the economic, environmental and social health in a particular location and are considered to be part of the more global sustainability movement. On the other hand, Lusk and Norwood (2011) have expressed some concerns about the economic viability of local supply chains as a sustainable business model, mostly because they violate the economic principle of comparative advantage (food should be grown in a location that is most productive and cheapest). Yet retail grocers, from the smallest to the largest, continue to seek various means to respond to a growing consumer demand for local products (NGA 2011). Food cooperatives, a small but active retailer segment with a highly localized consumer base, represent a unique class of retail grocers that present their own motivations and strategies for sourcing locally.

We present an economic analysis of how food cooperatives source and promote local foods based on a comprehensive study funded by a USDA-Rural Development (Katchova and Woods 2011). We conducted phone interviews with general managers of ten food co-ops across the U.S. and visited with general managers, staff, and local suppliers of three leading food co-ops (Good Foods Co-op in Lexington, KY, Hanover Co-op in Hanover, NH, and La Montanita in Albuquerque, NM). We conducted a national survey of general managers for food co-ops to learn more about business strategies and competitive advantages related to sourcing and marketing of local foods. General managers discussed various strategies for procurement of local foods and building long-term supplier relationships with farmers. We further examined supply chain strategies food co-ops used to manage and assist farmers with production and planning activities and the subsequent competitive advantages/disadvantages of working with local farmers relative to other grocers in the same market area. We examined various merchandising approaches used by food co-ops as they sought to convey the messages about local foods to their buyer members and patrons, including advertising via labels, farmer photos and stories as well as organizing farmer-led sampling, on-site festivals, deli features, etc. The survey was mailed to 350 food co-ops across the U.S. in November 2010.

Our goal in this chapter is to identify the emerging business practices, ethics principles, and competition issues for food co-ops in relation to sourcing and marketing of local products. The specific objectives are (1) to provide a literature review on local food networks, (2) to examine local food definitions and recent trends for food co-ops, (3) to examine the business models and ethics principles for food co-ops, (4) to examine competition in sourcing and marketing of local foods by food co-ops, and (5) to examine the frequency and effectiveness of business strategies to source and promote local foods, analyzing whether food co-ops perceive themselves as having competitive advantages over other grocery stores. We show that when compared to other grocers, food co-ops have competitive advantages in working with local producers and often play a key role in the local producers' business viability.

12.2 Literature Review on Local Food Systems

Consumer interest in locally produced foods has been increasing in the U.S. The popular press has frequently published articles on local foods. In addition, two recent best-selling books, *Animal, Vegetable, Miracle* (Kingsolver et al. 2007) and *In Defense of Food* (Pollan 2008), show the growing interest in sourcing local food products by making the case for going "local." According to a nation-wide survey by the Hartman Group (2008), many consumers define local in terms of distance from their home with 50% define local as made or produced within 100 miles, while 37% of consumers understood local to mean made or produced in their state. The survey also indicates that consumer interest in locally produced foods was driven primarily by their belief that these products are healthier.

Two reports provide overviews of local food systems and compare them with the mainstream food supply chains. Martinez et al. (2010) explore alternative definitions of local food, estimate the market size and reach, describe the characteristics of local consumers and producers, and examine the benefits of local food markets in terms of economic development, health and nutrition, and food security. King et al. (2010) describe several case studies that compare the structure, size, and performance of local food supply chains with those of mainstream supply chains. For each of their cases, they consider degree of product differentiation, diversification of marketing outlets, and information regarding product origins and how they differ under the two supply chains.

The literature on consumer preferences for locally produced food is small but growing. Darby et al. (2008) analyzed stated preference data for locally produced foods among consumers in Ohio. They concluded that demand for local products exists and that the value consumers place on local production is separate from other factors such as farm size and product freshness. Hu et al. (2009) examined consumer acceptance and willingness to pay for three nonconventional attributes associated with various value-added blueberry products, including whether the product was produced locally. Their results show that consumers have a positive willingness to pay for local even more than organic formulations across all products, clearly showing consumers' preference toward locally produced products. A subsequent study identified a local premium for a prototypical processed product (blackberry jam) and also identified differences in consumer preferences for local products associated with various types of products (Hu et al. 2012). Nurse et al. (2010) used an attitude-behavior framework to explore the predictive ability of psychological concepts of willingness to pay for different attributes (including local and organic) associated with sustainable foods.

Other studies analyze how local food networks source and market local products. Two elements of the local food networks have been studied previously: farmers markets and CSAs. Farmers markets consist of individual vendors (mostly farmers) who set up booths, tables or stands outdoors or indoors to sell produce, meat products, fruits, and other prepared foods. CSAs consist of individuals who purchase shares of a farm operation with weekly delivery or pick-up of produce, where the growers and consumers share the risks and benefits of food production. Hardesty (2008) and Brown and Miller (2008) have considered the economic impacts that farmers markets and CSAs have on the communities, consumers, and producers. Using case studies of farmers markets in both rural and urban areas, and in three states from the east to west coasts, Gillespie et al. (2007) found that farmers markets play an important role in building local food networks.

The role of food co-ops to supply locally produced products has only recently been examined. Liang and Michahelles (2010) survey 67 consumer co-ops in 13 Northeastern states to identify the strongest reasons for sourcing locally (environmental concerns, relationship with producers, ethical reasons, and aiding local economy), and the strongest barriers for sourcing locally (limited supply of local goods, complicated vendor relationships, and distribution and logistics). Katchova and Woods (2011) use a national survey of food co-ops to identify how food co-ops group into clusters based on their competitive advantages for sourcing local foods.

Our goal is to examine the role of food co-ops in strengthening the local food networks and marketing locally produced products. Food co-ops serve as important business organizations that contribute to the increase in the density of local food networks and relations. Food co-ops also expand the reach of local food markets to a variety of consumers including core, mid-level, and periphery consumers. The economic interactions that take place at food co-ops are combined with social interactions that make them valued community institutions.

12.3 Ethics Principles and Business Models for Food Cooperatives

Local food networks include organizations that produce, distribute, and promote locally produced products. While regional chain grocery retailers and restaurants may include locally produced products, it is food consumer co-ops, CSAs, and farmers markets that are uniquely positioned in the local food networks and capable of placing greater emphasis on locally produced products, primarily by virtue of their smaller scale and focus on a limited geographic market. One of the key aspects to a "local" marketing program is the emphasis on "local sourcing," which is defined as the consumers' preference to buy locally produced goods and services.

Local food networks are an alternative business model to the global corporate models where producers and consumers are separated through a chain of processors, manufacturers, shippers and retailers. As the length of the food supply chain increases, consumers' cost of assessing the quality of food may increase. Conversely, local food networks have re-established a direct relationship between producers and consumers to increase the perceived quality characteristics of the products which include freshness and durability but also include characteristics such as the method and location of producing. Traditional grocery retailers are also responding to high demand for local products, but there is a potential for food co-ops to have a competitive advantage in scale, customer focus, and credible community orientation for locally produced products. Further, these local food supplier relationships tend to be developed over a long term and are management intensive to both build and maintain.

Food co-ops that operate retail stores are predominantly single-store operations and several of them have expanded into non-grocery businesses such as restaurants and delis. The store-based food co-ops are usually characterized by their strong support for natural and organic foods, community activities, environmental sustainability, and local food systems.

A food cooperative is a grocery store organized as a cooperative. Food co-ops are typically consumer cooperatives, meaning they are owned by their members and typically feature natural and/or organic foods. Food co-ops adhere to the seven Cooperative Principles: (1) open, voluntary membership, (2) democratic governance, (3) limited return on equity, (4) surplus belongs to members, (5) education of members and public in cooperative principles, (6) cooperation between cooperatives, and (7) concern for community (Wikipedia, Rochdale Principles).

According to Deller et al. (2009), food co-ops have a distinctly different business organization than the more traditional grocery stores. Most food co-ops require a relatively small investment in an initial membership share, and an additional financial contribution, such as an annual membership fee. Investment in membership shares is considered a contribution to equity, while membership fees are usually treated as income. Consumer cooperatives are not required to pay income taxes on member-based income if they distribute that income back to members either as cash or as allocated patronage. However, they will be required to pay income taxes on non-member income and unallocated member income. Food cooperative members vote on a one-member-has-one-vote basis and elect a board of directors from its members. Many of the current store-based food co-ops originally encouraged members to work voluntarily in the store in return for a member discount, but more recently, most food co-ops hire professional management and paid staff.

Several key characteristics were revealed in our case studies conducted with general managers and other staff members in three leading food co-ops (Good Foods Co-op in Lexington, KY, Hanover Co-op in Hanover, NH, and La Montanita in

Albuquerque, NM). Food co-ops have deeply ingrained within their membership and management a values-driven rationale for their commitment to build long-term local supplier relationships. Food co-ops claim to have an "authentic" commitment to local, meaning that they have always sourced and marketed local products, while this is a relatively recent trend for other food retailers. In addition, supporting the local community (especially local agriculture) is one of the seven principles and an end policy for food co-ops. Communities benefit from the multiplier effect when co-op members spend money on local products and keep them in the community. Other ways in which food co-ops are involved in the community include their support of farmers' markets and local fairs. Food co-ops are differentiated as businesses from other grocery stores through their local programs which have sustainable business models to sourcing local products. One fact that helps food co-ops to source local foods is the proximity of administration and ease of making decisions – department managers have the authority to make decisions and work directly with local producers. Another advantage that food co-ops have is that they are relatively small in size compared to other grocery stores, therefore, they have the ability to work with small producers; department managers are in frequent contact with a number of small producers and some co-ops even organize annual meetings for producers. Finally, food co-ops have a commitment to serve their members considering themselves as buying local products for their members, rather than selling local products to them.

Consumer cooperatives, and in particular food consumer cooperatives, have increased in importance. Over the past decade, it is estimated that about 350 food co-op stores have been operating in the U.S.; these food co-ops have been serving nearly 150,000 households throughout the U.S. (Deller et al. 2009). The National Cooperative Grocers Association (NCGA) is a cooperative federation that includes 146 food co-ops.

Most of the food co-ops are relatively small compared to the chain grocers and supercenters, but they have been growing even through a recent difficult economic period. The median sales weekly sales were $466,011 per supermarket in 2010, which is equivalent to $24.2 million in annual sales per supermarket (Food Market Institute 2011). Katchova and Woods (2011) provide additional statistics on food co-ops with respect to recent sales, employment, and geographic distribution. On average, food co-ops are much smaller than the traditional grocery stores with $8,582,122 in annual gross sales and 39% of the sales to non-members. The annual gross sales for food co-ops have been increasing, reporting $6.7 million in 2007, $7.3 million in 2008, $7.8 million in 2009, and $8.6 million in 2010. The average number of employees and management full-time employees were 62 and the average number of members was 4,879 members in 2010. Most of the food co-ops are located in the Midwest (42%), the Atlantic region (31%), and the West region (15%) with a limited number of co-ops in the South and Plain regions.

12.4 Local Food Definitions and Recent Trends for Food Cooperatives

The term "local foods" has a geographic connotation but there is no consensus on the definition in terms of the maximum distance between consumers and producers in order for a product to be considered local. Definitions also vary based on the geographic region, organizations, consumers, and specific local markets. According to the 2008 Food, Conservation, and Energy Act (2008 Farm Act), local products are defined in two different ways: (1) by the locality or region in which the final product is marketed, so that the total distance that the product is transported is less than 400 miles from the origin of the product, or (2) by the state in which the product is produced. The concept of "local" is also often seen in terms of ecology – a foodshed, which is an area where food is grown and eaten. Generally, marketers have used the term liberally, causing some frustrations among consumers that rarely have the ability to understand the story behind the supplier.

Our national survey shows how food co-ops define local (Katchova and Woods 2011). While there is some variation across different parts of the country, general managers of food co-ops consider local products to be produced within 100 miles (the median of all responses) or 125 miles (the average). Also, 44% of the co-ops consider local to be produced in the state and additional 39% consider local to be produced in the region including neighboring states. In general, there is a considerable flexibility in defining the term "local," even among the food co-ops themselves.

The percent of annual gross sales that comes from local products varies depending on the department (Table 12.1). For example, the meat department has the highest percent of annual sales from local products (42%) whereas health/nutrition/cosmetics have the lowest (6%). Dairy products, fresh produce, and deli departments have about 30% of the annual sales from local products. About 21% of the annual gross sales for food co-ops are from local products store-wide. On average, food co-ops work with 8 dairy farmers, 22 fresh produce farmers, and 5 meat producers, although these numbers vary considerable among co-ops (Table 12.2). The average for the number of local producers that food co-ops work with is 68. One of the major competitive advantages of food co-ops is their ability to work with a relatively high number of local producers when compared to other grocery stores.

The demand for local foods within food co-ops was noted to have been increasing over the last few years. About three-quarters of food co-ops indicate that there is a net increase in the share of local foods sold at their stores for meat, dairy, and fresh produce categories (Table 12.3). Over a half of food co-ops report that there is an increase in the percentage of locally-produced packaged goods and health/nutrition/cosmetics products.

Table 12.1 Percent annual gross sales from local products for food co-ops

Category	Mean	Standard deviation	25% percentile	50% percentile	75% percentile
Meat	42.0	28.9	17.2	44.7	62.3
Deli	33.8	37.3	1.9	15.0	75.0
Dairy products	27.6	25.3	5.1	17.5	50.0
Fresh produce	27.2	20.6	11.2	21.0	34.8
Bulk	11.8	12.3	2.0	10.0	18.0
Packaged goods	10.0	11.9	4.2	5.0	12.0
General merchandise	9.1	14.2	1.9	5.0	10.0
Health/nutrition/cosmetics	6.0	5.4	2.0	5.0	8.1
Average for the store(s)	20.3	12.3	11.2	20.0	25.0

Table 12.2 Number of local grower-vendors working with food co-ops

Category	Mean	Minimum	Maximum	Standard deviation
Dairy products	8.3	0.0	35.0	7.7
Fresh produce	22.4	4.0	75.0	15.8
Meats	5.3	0.0	20.0	4.4
Total all products	68.1	7.0	350.0	72.5

Table 12.3 Percent change in local products sold within the various categories over the last 2 years relative to other products in the category

Category	Declined substantially	Declined somewhat	Stayed about the same	Increased somewhat	Increased substantially	Don't know	Net increase[a]
Meats	3.8	0.0	17.3	36.5	42.3	0.0	75.0
Fresh produce	1.6	1.6	15.2	45.7	35.5	0.0	77.9
Dairy products	0.0	1.7	22.4	43.1	32.7	0.0	74.1
Packaged goods	0.0	3.4	37.9	51.7	6.9	0.0	55.1
Health/nutrition/cosmetics	1.7	3.4	32.7	60.3	0.0	1.7	55.1

[a]The net increase is the sum of the percentages for increased somewhat and increased substantially minus the sum of percentages for declined substantially and declined somewhat

12.5 Competition in Sourcing and Marketing Local Products

There are two types of competition that arise when sourcing and marketing local foods. The first type of competition is among farmers to introduce new local products into the existing local food networks. The second type of competition is among food co-ops, other area grocers, and local food networks (CSAs, farmers markets, etc.) to introduce and market local products to consumers.

There are several barriers facing producers choosing to enter local food markets and establish a sustainable farm business (Martinez et al. 2010). Typically, there are capacity constraints for small farm businesses and lack of a distribution system for marketing local products through mainstream supply chains. Farmers also may have

Table 12.4 Perception of food co-op managers of how difficult it is for a farmer to introduce new local products, percent indicating level of difficulty

Category	None or minor	Some but stable	Increasing but not significant	Significant	Don't know
Fresh produce	11.6	13.3	38.3	33.3	3.3
Meat	28.5	23.2	28.5	16.0	3.5
Grocery	36.6	40.0	13.3	6.6	3.3
Dairy	22.8	35.0	33.3	5.2	3.5

limited education and training in growing and marketing a variety of local foods. There may also be uncertainties with respect to regulations that may affect local food production such as food safety requirements. Interviews with local farmers delivering to food co-ops show that co-ops play an instrumental role in farm business start-up and/or its financial viability (Katchova and Woods 2011).

Food co-ops report the degree of competition when farmers plan on introducing new local products by different category of products: fresh produce, meat, dairy, and grocery products (Table 12.4). The degree of competition reported is the perception of food co-op managers of how difficult it is for a farmer to break into the local food supply network. Only 11.6% of the food co-ops state that there is none or minor competition among farmers to introduce new local products for fresh produce, 28.5% report lack of competition for new local meat products, 22.8% for local dairy products, and 36.6% for local groceries. On the other hand, 33.3% of the food co-ops report significant competition among farmers to introduce new local products for fresh produce, 16% report significant farmer competition for local meat products, 5.2% for local dairy products, and 7% for grocery products. Therefore, the most significant competition among farmers is for introducing local fresh produce, while meat, dairy, and grocery producers face much lower competition to supply local products to food co-ops.

Food co-ops participate in local food networks together with farmers' markets, CSAs, and other retailers. Our interviews with general managers of several food co-ops across the U.S. and a focus group with members of the Good Foods Co-op in Lexington reveal that competition in the local food networks is viewed in a complex way. Typically, farmers' markets and CSAs are not viewed as competing but rather complementary outlets for providing more diverse local products. Because food co-ops follow the principle of supporting the local community, they often facilitate and support farmers' markets in their area. Retail stores (especially Whole Foods) are generally viewed as a competitors, mostly for total food dollars but less so for local foods. There is a general agreement among co-op members that the origin and quality of local products marketed by other groceries are less trusted.

Food co-op managers also reported their perception of how competitive their food co-ops are when competing with other grocery stores to introduce new local products. About 37.2% of the food co-ops identify significant competition from other area grocers for marketing fresh produce, 17.2% for meat, 16.9% for dairy and 11.6% for grocery items (Table 12.5). Overall, two-thirds to three-quarters of

Table 12.5 Perception of food co-op managers of how competitive their co-ops are relative to competition from other area grocers when introducing new local products, percent indicating level of difficulty

Category	None or minor	Some but stable	Increasing but not significant	Significant	Don't know
Fresh produce	25.4	8.4	23.7	37.2	5.0
Meat	34.4	10.3	27.5	17.2	10.3
Dairy	30.5	13.5	33.9	16.9	5.0
Grocery	36.6	15.0	30.0	11.6	6.6

food co-ops view grocery stores as providing somewhat to significant competition to introduce new local products; the rest of the co-ops perceive none or minor competition from other grocery stores in the area to introduce new local products.

12.6 Business Strategies and Competitive Advantages: Definitions and Concepts

The concept of competitive advantage is important in understanding business strategies and firm performance. Porter (1998) examines two basic types of competitive advantage: cost advantage and differentiation advantage. A *competitive advantage* is defined as an advantage a firm has over competitors by offering its consumers greater value, either by selling products at lower prices (cost advantage) or by providing greater benefits and service justifying higher prices (differentiation advantage). The goal of a business strategy is to achieve a sustainable long-run competitive advantage over its competitors and to enable the firm to create a greater value for its customers and superior profits for itself.

There are four general business strategies that firms can adopt in order to gain competitive advantage. These strategies are based on whether or not the scope of the business activities is focused or broad and also on whether or not the business aims to differentiate its products or concentrate on cost reduction. Differentiation and cost leadership strategies pursue competitive advantage in a broad market. On the other hand, differentiation focus and cost focus strategies are targeted in a narrow market (niche market).

More specifically, the *differentiation strategy* involves one or more criteria that consumers in the market demand, positioning the business to uniquely meet those needs. This strategy is usually associated with delivering a differentiated product and charging a premium for the product, often because of either higher production costs or value-added features provided for consumers. The *differentiation focus strategy* aims to differentiate firm's products in a relatively small market segment. The special customer needs in a given market segment implies that there are opportunities for the business to provide products that are clearly differentiated from competitors who may be targeting a broader group of customers. The main issue for businesses adopting this strategy is to ensure that customers have specific and different needs and preferences and that the existing competitors are not meeting these needs and preferences. This differentiation focus strategy is the strategy typically pursued by food co-ops seeking to differentiate their products as healthy, organic, natural, local, etc. and market them to a select market segment of consumers who seek such attributes. Unlike healthy or organic products which can be produced anywhere, local products may be easier to differentiate because they need to be produced in a "local" area. Therefore, the "local" attribute of products may not be easily replicable by producers in "distant" areas.

On the other hand, the *cost leadership strategy* involves becoming the lowest-cost producer in the market. The main emphasis is placed on minimizing costs along the supply chain. If the prices charged for products are similar, then the best profits will be realized by businesses with lowest costs. This strategy is usually adopted by large-scale businesses (like Wal-Mart and other major retailers) that are offering "standard" products with relatively little differentiation at the lowest possible price. The *cost focus strategy* is implemented by businesses seeking a lower cost advantage in a small number of segments.

12.7 Business Strategies and Competitive Advantages for Sourcing Local Foods

Food co-ops primarily use differentiation focus business strategies to differentiate their products and market them to a specific segment of consumers. Specifically, food co-ops routinely pursue opportunities to build on differentiation strategies through their unique ability to maintain close working relationships with local producers. Food co-ops are able to implement these business strategies for several reasons: (1) food co-ops are smaller when compared to other grocers, (2) food co-ops make decisions locally at their store rather than at remote headquarters, (3) their business model allows for department managers to make decisions and maintain frequent contact with a large number of small producers, and (4) food co-ops have long-term experience working with local producers.

One set of business strategies that food co-ops use includes price negotiation, lower margins for local, quality negotiations, delivery/logistics coordination, and local merchandising material design. About 40–50% of food co-op general managers report frequent or extensive use of these business strategies and about the same percentages report competitive advantages using these strategies over non-cooperative grocers (Table 12.6). One explanation is that many food co-ops are willing to use lower margins for local products or price negotiations, but in general other grocery stores are better positioned to compete on most cost minimization strategies than food co-ops who frequently use differentiation strategies. Fewer food co-ops report competitive advantages with respect to volume planning, packaging design, and food safety/quality assurance.

Another set of business strategies include promotional set of activities for farmers such as planning merchandising events and in-store farmer sampling. A third of the

Table 12.6 Business strategies for food cooperatives working with local producers: frequency of use and competitive advantages as compared to other grocers

Business strategy	Frequency of use[a] Percent co-ops reporting intensive use	Rank[c]	Competitive advantages[b] Percent of co-ops reporting advantages	Rank[c]
Price negotiation	39.0	7	45.8	10
Lower margin for local	49.2	2	36.8	12
Quality negotiation	49.1	3	50.8	8
Delivery/logistics coordination	53.4	1	57.6	4
Local merchandising material design	39.7	5	51.7	7
Volume planning	39.7	6	35.1	14
Packaging design	6.8	16	21.1	18
Food safety/quality assurance	35.6	8	33.9	15
Planning merchandising events	40.7	4	63.2	3
In-store farmer sampling	33.9	9	70.7	1
Local producer rights advocacy	12.1	13	54.7	6
New product development	8.8	15	35.7	13
Assistance with farmer loans	0.0	18	27.3	16
Farm production planning	23.7	11	46.4	9
Annual producer group meetings	17.9	12	57.1	5
Farmer co-op development	1.8	17	70.7	2
Vendor managed inventory	9.4	14	43.4	11
Farm visits	28.8	10	22.6	17

[a]Food co-op managers reported the frequency of use for various business strategies: minimal, occasional, frequent, and extensive. Intensive use is defined as the sum for the categories frequent and extensive

[b]Food co-op managers reported the competitive advantages (five categories: major disadvantage, slight disadvantage, no difference, slight advantage, major advantage) they perceive they have over other grocers when using these business strategies. Competitive advantage is the sum of slight advantage and major advantage categories

[c]Rank was assigned after sorting the strategies from most to least in terms of frequency or competitive advantage and assigning ranks

food co-ops report frequent or extensive use of these strategies while two-thirds of them report having a competitive advantage when compared to other grocery stores (Table 12.6). Food co-ops perceive these two strategies, planning merchandizing events and in-store farmer sampling, as their biggest competitive advantages over other grocers (as shown by the ranking of strategies in Table 12.6).

A third set of business strategies include working directly with local producers on the farm production process, farmer assistance, and production planning. While these strategies are not as frequently used by food co-ops, many of the co-ops perceive that they have competitive advantages using them. Interviews with select local producers working with food co-ops indicate that food co-ops play an important role in helping them establish their businesses and making it sustainable and successful. Food co-op's support and promotion is essential for small producers who often struggle to compete with large producers because of economies of scale for conventional production. Food co-ops often educate new farmers about packaging of products, quality standards, food safety regulations, etc. Food co-ops are also involved with planning annual producer group meetings and organizing farm visits to gather information and coordinate logistics.

Overall, food co-ops state that they have a competitive advantage over non-cooperative grocery stores for sourcing local products and working with local farmers. The business strategies that also work well for their competitors include providing lower margin for local, volume planning, packaging design, assistance with farmer loans, and maintaining a vendor managed inventory. These competitive advantages are also found to differ based on food co-op size: smaller food co-ops tend to have more disadvantages while large food co-ops tend to have more competitive advantages in sourcing local products.

12.8 Business Strategies for Marketing Local Foods to Consumers

Marketing is the process which connects producers and consumers. Food marketing has four components, called the "four Ps" of marketing mix: product, price, promotion and place. When retailers decide what type of new foods to introduce to consumers, they develop either new food products or extend an existing food product. For products, brand loyalty and product attributes play an important role in consumer demand. Price is also an important component of marketing as retailers have some flexibility in charging variable price margins for different products. Promotion can be done in store, out of store, and on the package. Place refers to where products are located in the store, including end caps, top or bottom shelf, etc. Place is especially important in promoting products in the store.

Marketing strategies allow businesses to concentrate their limited resources on the greatest opportunities to increase their sales and achieve a sustainable competitive advantage over their competitors. Food co-ops use several marketing strategies to promote local products, including farmer photos and stories, food sampling, newsletters and social media, etc. The most frequently used promotion strategies include newsletters, social media/Facebook, and websites to disseminate information about local products, with over half of the food co-ops reporting frequent or extensive use of these strategies (Table 12.7). Co-ops also provide staff training on local products, samplings, annual merchandising features, sponsorship of off-site local food events, on-site festivals, and deli features to increase consumer awareness of local foods. Other less frequently used strategies include point-of-purchase (POP)

Table 12.7 Business strategies food co-ops use to promote local products to consumers

	Frequency of use[a]	
	Percent co-ops reporting intensive use	Rank[b]
POP farmer photos	41.7	6
POP farmer stories	36.7	8
POP farm brands	31.0	11
End caps or special displays	30.0	12
Samplings	55.0	3
Annual merchandising features	39.7	7
Cross merchandising	33.3	10
Farmer-led sampling	20.0	15
Newsletters	80.0	1
Social media/Facebook etc.	56.7	2
Website	48.3	5
On-site festivals	28.8	13
Deli features	28.6	14
Sponsorship of off-site local food events	36.7	9
Staff training on local products	50.0	4
Blogs	17.9	16

[a]Food co-op managers reported the frequency of use for various business strategies: minimal, occasional, frequent, and extensive. Intensive use is defined as the sum for the categories frequent and extensive

[b]Rank was assigned after sorting the strategies from most to least in terms of frequency of use and assigning ranks

farmer photos, POP farmer stories, POP farm brands, and end caps or special displays. Overall, most food co-ops use these strategies to increase consumer awareness of local products and effectively promote them to consumers.

Selected general managers also provided additional insights on member preferences for local foods and the effectiveness of various promotion strategies. Consumers shopping at food co-ops are typically more educated and with higher income. They typically show concern about the origin and quality of food and are willing to pay a premium for these attributes. They have a greater social and community awareness and activism and desire to support local agriculture and community. Finally, the co-op members show loyalty to their food co-ops and provide feedback to food co-ops about their preferences.

12.9 Concluding Comments

The ability of food co-ops to competitively supply locally produced products has only recently been examined even though the popularity of food co-ops has been increasing over time (Katchova and Woods 2011). Food co-ops are important business organizations that contribute to the increase in the density of local food networks and relations. Food co-ops also expand the reach of local food markets to a variety of consumers. The economic interactions that take place at food co-ops are combined with social interactions that make them valued community institutions.

We identify the emerging business practices, ethics principles, and competition issues for food co-ops in relation to local sourcing and marketing of products. We provide a literature review on local food systems, examine local food definitions and recent trends for food co-ops, examine the business models and ethics principles for food co-ops, analyze food co-ops' business strategies in terms of frequency of use and effectiveness in sourcing and marketing of local foods.

The findings help food co-ops identify the business strategies that are typically most successful and have a competitive advantage in the procurement and promotion of local foods. As a result, food co-ops will be able to develop better supply chain management and new cooperatives will be better aware of viable business models based on the characteristics of their local food networks. We show the key role that food co-ops play in the local food networks and the business strategies that are most successful in connecting local producers with consumers using the food co-op business model. We show that when compared to other grocers, food co-ops perceive to have competitive advantages in creating and promoting their relationships with local producers and often play a key role in the producers' business viability.

Our research contributes to the ongoing discussion about whether there is an adequate competition in the agrifood sector. We focus here on an under-studied player in the local food networks – food cooperatives – and how they perceive competition in the local food networks. Our findings show that there is an adequate competition along two dimensions: sourcing local products from farmers and competing with other retailers to market these products to consumers. Food co-ops report somewhat to significant competition among farmers to introduce new local products, particularly for fresh produce, meat, and dairy. Farmers generally do not feel locked out of alternative outlets for their production, but food cooperatives play an important role in their business' viability and success. In addition, food co-ops report somewhat to significant competition with other area grocers to introduce and market new local products to consumers, showing an adequate competition among retailers. We conclude that in the local food systems there is an adequate competition mostly along niche, highly differentiated markets and local supply chains.

Acknowledgements The authors would like to thank Alan Borst, Matt Ernst, Sierra Enlow, and Sara Williamson for their assistance with this project. The authors gratefully acknowledge the funding received from USDA-Rural Development.

References

Brown, C., and S. Miller. 2008. The impacts of local markets: A review of research on farmers markets and Community Supported Agriculture (CSA). *American Journal of Agricultural Economics* 90: 1296–1302.

Darby, K., M.T. Batte, S. Ernst, and B. Roe. 2008. Decomposing local: A conjoint analysis of locally produced foods. *American Journal of Agricultural Economics* 90: 476–486.

Deller, S., A. Hoyt, B. Hueth, and R. Sundaram-Stukel. 2009. *Research on the economic impact of cooperatives*. Madison: University of Wisconsin Center for Cooperatives. http://reic.uwcc.wisc.edu/. Accessed 1 Sept 2011.

Food Market Institute. 2011. Supermarket facts. http://www.fmi.org/research-resources/supermarket-facts. Accessed 5 Oct 2011.

Gillespie, G., D.L. Hilchey, C.C. Hinrichs, and G. Feenstra. 2007. Farmers markets as keystones in rebuilding local and regional food systems. In *Remaking the North American food system: Strategies for sustainability*, ed. C.C. Hinrichs and T.A. Lyson, 65–83. Lincoln: University of Nebraska Press.

Hardesty, S.D. 2008. The growing role of local food markets. *American Journal of Agricultural Economics* 90: 1289–1295.

Hartman Group. 2008. Pulse report: Consumer understanding of buying local. The Hartman Group, Inc. Bellevue, WA.

Hu, W., T. Woods, and S. Bastin. 2009. Consumer acceptance and willingness to pay for blueberry products with nonconventional attributes. *Journal of Agricultural and Applied Economics* 41: 47–60.

Hu, W., M. Batte, T. Woods, and S. Ernst. 2012. Consumer preferences for local production and other value added label claims for a processed food product. *European Review of Agricultural Economics* 39: 489–510.

Katchova, A.L., and T.A. Woods. 2011. *The effectiveness of local food marketing strategies of food cooperatives*. Selected paper, Agricultural and Applied Economics Association Meeting, Pittsburgh, 24–26 July.

King, R., M.S. Hand, G. DiGiacomo, K. Clancy, M.I. Gomez, S.D. Hardesty, L. Lev, and E.W. McLaughlin. 2010. *Comparing the structure, size, and performance of local and mainstream food supply chains*. Economic Research Report ERR-99. Washington, DC: Economic Research Service, U.S. Department of Agriculture.

Kingsolver, B., S.L. Hopp, and C. Kingsolver. 2007. *Animal, vegetable, miracle*. New York: Harper-Collins Publishers.

Liang, K., and M. Michahelles. 2010. *Exploring the consumer co-op as an innovative local food distribution method: The case of the Northeast*. Selected poster, NAREA Workshop "The Economics of Local Food Markets," Atlantic City, 15–16 June.

Lusk, J.L., and F.B. Norwood. 2011. The Locavore's Dilemma: Why pineapples shouldn't be grown in North Dakota. Library of Economics and Liberty. http://www.econlib.org/library/Columns/y2011/LuskNorwoodlocavore.html. Accessed 1 Sept 2011.

Martinez, S., M. Hand, M. Da Pra, S. Pollack, K. Ralston, T. Smith, S. Vogel, S. Clark, L. Lohr, S. Low, and C. Newman. 2010. *Local food systems: Concepts, impacts, and issues*. Economic Research Report ERR 97. Washington, DC: Economic Research Service, U.S. Department of Agriculture.

National Grocers Association (NGA). 2011. 2011 consumer survey report. http://www.supermarketguru.com. Accessed 23 Sept 2011.

Nurse, G., Y. Onozaka, and D.D. Thilmany. 2010. *Understanding the connections between consumer motivations and buying behavior: The case of the local food system movement*. Selected paper, Southern Agricultural Economics Association Annual Meeting, Orlando, 6–9 February.

Pollan, M. 2008. *In defense of food*. New York: Penguin.

Porter, M.E. 1998. *Competitive advantage: Creating and sustaining superior performance*, 1st ed. New York: The Free Press.

Chapter 13
Price Transparency as a Prerequisite for Fair Competition: The Case of the European Food Prices Monitoring Tool

Adrienn Molnár, Katrien Van Lembergen, Federico Tarantini, Aimé Heene, and Xavier Gellynck

Abstract In this chapter we examine the European Food Prices Monitoring Tool as a case study to improve price transparency and, as a result, competitiveness in the European food system. We first analyze the relation between price transparency and fair competition from a theoretical point of view. We then investigate agricultural and food prices evolution in the EU over the last decade, with a specific focus on the price transmission along the food supply chain. We follow with an assessment of the rationale for the price monitoring tool and analyze its functioning as a case study. We conclude with a few comments on how this tool can contribute to fair competition through an increase in price transparency.

13.1 Introduction

Because the European food system is active on both domestic and international markets, innovation in food markets is a necessary precursor to competiveness, growth, welfare and well-being. A well-functioning European food supply chain

A. Molnár, Ph.D. • X. Gellynck, Ph.D.
Department of Agricultural Economics, Ghent University, Coupure Links 653, Ghent 9000, Belgium

K. Van Lembergen, M.Sc. (✉)
Bio- and Food Sciences Department, Faculty of Science and Technology, University College Ghent, Brusselsesteenweg 161, Melle 9090, Belgium
e-mail: katrien.vanlembergen@hogent.be

F. Tarantini, M.A.
European Economic Integration and Business Programme, College of Europe, Dijver 9-11, Bruges 8000, Belgium

A. Heene, Ph.D.
Department of Management, Ghent University, Tweekerkenstraat 2, Ghent 9000, Belgium

H.S. James Jr. (ed.), *The Ethics and Economics of Agrifood Competition*, The International Library of Environmental, Agricultural and Food Ethics 20,
DOI 10.1007/978-94-007-6274-9_13,

requires both adequate and fair competition. Price transparency is a prerequisite for these. Therefore, in this chapter we examine the European Food Prices Monitoring Tool as a case study to improve price transparency and, ideally, competitiveness in the European food system.

The European Food Prices Monitoring Tool (EFPMT), available to the public, brings together European data on price developments at different levels of selected food supply chains (e.g., farmer, food processer and retailer). This tool was introduced by the European Commission as a result of variable agricultural commodity prices and steadily increasing producer and consumer prices during the previous two decades. Its intent is to increase transparency for price transmission in the food supply chain and to facilitate comparisons across the European Member States (EC-Eurostat 2009).

First, we analyze the relation between price transparency and fair competition from a theoretical point of view. Second, we investigate agricultural and food prices evolution in the EU over the last decade, with a specific focus on the price transmission along the food supply chain. Third, we assess the rationale for the EFPMT and analyze its functioning as a case study. Finally, we draw conclusions on how this tool can contribute to fair competition through an increase in price transparency.

13.2 Link Between Price Transparency and Fair Competition

13.2.1 Competition Between Firms

Competition is the process through which entities, such as people, organizations or nations, try to acquire or employ resources that are desired by them, but that are not freely available to meet their demand. Resources are defined as anything that the entities can use to achieve their objectives (Sanchez and Heene 2004). Because resources are scarce, firms' efforts to access and control resources contribute to the competitive capacity of firms. In other words, competition exists when the acquisition or access of resources by one firm prevents other firms from acquiring or accessing these resources due to the scarceness of the resources.

Economic theory considers competition as a major and necessary driver of economic improvement, growth and social welfare. Economies are said to improve when they generate and offer more products and services that more effectively satisfy client's needs and preferences while at the same time consuming a decreasing quantity of resources. The intensity of competition has implications for the profits that companies can earn. Competition drives down prices, margins, and reduces opportunities for gaining financial profit. "Perfect competition" results in zero margins and thus zero profits for all competitors.

13.2.2 Fair Competition

Economists and regulators (such as governmental authorities) consider competition to be “fair” when firms “compete on the merits,” meaning that firms can engage in conduct that results in rivals being forced to exit or discouraged from entering the market, as long as such behavior does not violate specific standards or “tests,” such as the profit sacrifice test or the equally efficient firm test (OECD 2006).[1] Unfair competition prevents competitors from taking similar or compensating actions. According to EU competition law, unfair competition exists under many forms including: abuse of a dominant position, state aid that gives competitors an advantage that cannot be gained by others, collusive behavior (EU 2008, Title VII, chapter 1), infringement of intellectual property rights (EPC 2004), misleading communication and advertising (EPC 1997, 2005).

13.2.3 Price Transparency and Fair Competition

According to microeconomic theory, perfect information on price and quality of products and services is one of the fundamental conditions required for a “perfectly competitive” market. Perfect information on prices minimizes search costs, such as the time and money spent to discover best prices, and contributes to perfect competition. According to Sanchez and Heene (2004, p. 14): “Having full information about prices of goods, buyers will only buy at the lowest price available in the market, and only when the utility they will derive from use of a good exceeds the market price of the good. Sellers, in turn, will allocate their available resources to producing goods that would bring them the greatest surplus of price over costs available in the market.” Hence, price transparency contributes to the availability, completeness, and perfectness of information and resources available to buyers and sellers and in this sense contributes to competition.

Price transparency means that sellers and buyers are able to obtain valid and reliable information on prices in a fast, cheap, and simple way. It is generally accepted that price transparency can signal the existence of unfair or inadequate competition. This is illustrated by the statement of European Commission Vice-President Antonio Tajani, on the occasion of the EU enforcement of price transparency in the European airline industry: “Fair competition is the key to success: with price transparency, passengers will know in advance how much they are going to pay and will be able to make informed choices” (New Europe 2008). When prices are transparent, buyers and sellers are in a position to make the best and most informed consumption and production decisions.

[1] The profit sacrifice test, also known as the no economic sense test, states that firms should not engage in activities that irrationally results in a loss of profits or that make no economic sense, except for a tendency to eliminate or lessen competition. The equally efficient firm test states that firms should not engage in activities that exclude rivals who are as efficient as the firm in question.

However, the effect of price transparency on competition varies according to the structure of the market in which price transparency is enhanced because price transparency is a "two-edged sword" (OECD 2001); it can both impede as well as promote competition. On the one hand, price transparency contributes to an economically sound allocation of resources, thus promoting competition. On the other hand, in concentrated markets supplying homogeneous products, an increase in price transparency might harm fair competition. In this kind of market, a high level of price transparency can increase the risk of tacit collusion among producers or the stability of a "classic" cartel: if a firm deviates from the agreed pricing behavior the other cartel participants could easily spot this behavior and "punish" the firm. If one assumes firms to be forward looking, cartel participants should have a lower incentive to "cheat" on the other participants. In addition, Mollgaard and Overgaard (2001) suggest another (indirect) effect: if a firm "cheats" on the other cartel participants their punishment would be – *ceteris paribus* – "more severe since consumers become more sensitive to perceived differences in the mix of price and characteristics across products."[2] In any case, these drawbacks of higher price transparency are valid for markets which are already at risk of collusion, and it is highly unlikely that an increase in price transparency would *per se* hamper fair competition in markets where the risk of collusive behavior is low.[3] Thus, an increase in price transparency is generally beneficial for competition unless it takes place in markets at risk of collusion. In the latter case, the potential downsides can be reduced by disclosing sufficiently aggregated and historical data, as commonly agreed under EU competition law (EU 2011, para. 89–90).

13.3 Transmission and Developments of Agricultural and Food Prices in Europe

The food supply chain can be divided in three main sectors or levels: agricultural production, food processing, and distribution. Therefore, price developments along the food supply chain can be analyzed by looking at the evolution of (1) agricultural commodity prices at the agricultural production level, (2) food producer prices at the food processing level, and (3) consumer prices at the distribution and retail level.

The most relevant issue when analyzing price developments along a food supply chain is the price transmission – or pass-through – of a price change among the different levels of the food supply chain (e.g., from agricultural commodities

[2]However, a high price transparency would also increase the "one-time" benefit of deviating from the agreed cartel price; the net effect would depend on the specific characteristics of the market and the cartel.

[3]Notably those are characterized by: "low levels of concentration; large number of sellers; low barriers to entry; low transparency as to prices, quantities transacted and marketing strategies; asymmetries among sellers and product offerings; rapidly changing demand and cost conditions; lumpy purchasing patterns; and the presence of one or more maverick competitors" (OECD 2001).

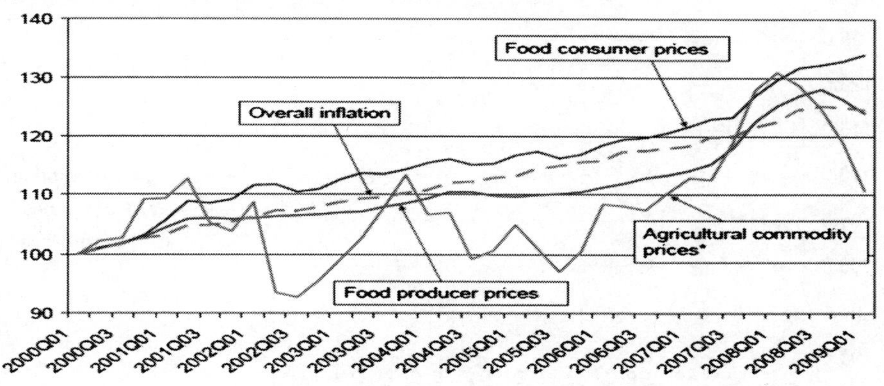

Fig. 13.1 Long term prices evolution within the EU food supply chain (Source: EC 2009a)

to food processing, and from food processing to consumers). Taking inspiration from Bukeviciute et al. (2009a), at least three different aspects of price transmission should be considered: the *magnitude*, the *speed* and the *symmetry* of price transmissions.

The *magnitude* shows how much of the price change at one step of a supply chain is transmitted downward to the next step. It ranges between 0%, when an increase (decrease) in the upstream output price has no impact on the downstream output price, and 100%, when a given percentage increase or decrease in the upstream output price entails the same percentage change in the downstream output price. The *speed of the pass-through* refers to the time lag required for the price transmission to happen (the time between the variation in the upstream output price and the related change in the downstream output price). The *symmetry of the price transmission* concerns the differences in pass-through – both in terms of magnitude and speed – depending on whether the upstream output price variation is positive or negative. The more the speed and the magnitude of the pass-through differ depending on the sign of the initial price variation, the less the price transmission is symmetric.

As shown in Fig. 13.1, a first look at the European food supply chain in the last decade shows a variable evolution of the agricultural commodity prices while food producer and consumer prices increase "slowly and surely" over time.

The high volatility of agricultural commodity prices is generally absorbed in the downstream sectors. This is mainly due to the low (and decreasing) value share of the agricultural commodities (farm value), and the high (and increasing) value share of transforming raw food into consumer goods (marketing bill), in the value of the food products at retail level (food expenditures). The "ever-increasing margin between agricultural market price for bread making wheat (0.13 EUR/kg in April 2009) from retail consumer prices for baguette (3.35 EUR/kg in April 2009) in France" well-illustrates this development (EC 2009a, p. 16).

However, despite the smoothing role played by the downstream levels on agricultural commodity price fluctuations over the medium run, in the long run

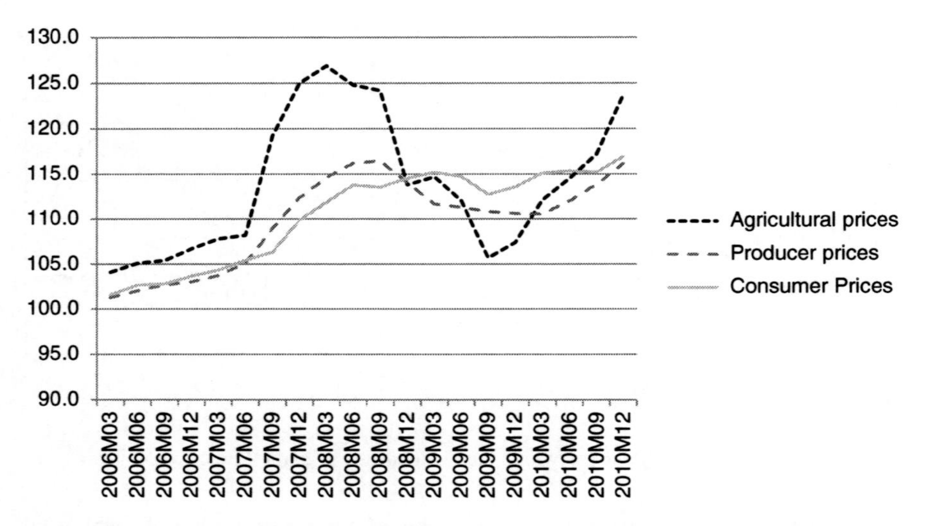

Fig. 13.2 Recent prices evolution within the EU food supply chain (2005 Q1 = 100) (Source: Own work, based on Eurostat 2011)

the price difference between agricultural commodities and food products has been widening. This trend is reinforcing the striking gap between the value of agricultural commodities and the value of the food products at retail level.

The period 2007–2009 has been characterized by an exceptional variation in agricultural commodity prices: raw food prices increased dramatically from May 2007 to February 2008 before returning to the initial price level in March 2009 (see Fig. 13.2).[4] During this period, the pass-through along the food supply chain has been interesting. The main insight is the asymmetric nature of the price transmission: while the surge in agricultural commodity prices (16% increase between May 2007 and February 2008) entailed a fast and important pass-through to the producers and consumer prices (respectively 9 and 5% over the same period), the decrease in agricultural commodity prices led only to small producer and consumer prices reductions. Moreover, these reductions took place with significant time lags (EC 2009a).

13.3.1 Price Transmission from the Agricultural Sector to the Food Processing Sector

Over the previous decade, the link between price fluctuations in agricultural commodity prices and food producer prices seems (at best) very weak. According

[4]Between the end of 2010 and the beginning of 2011, the last available data at the time the authors are writing, agricultural price levels are increasing at the peak reached during the 2007–2008 crisis.

to European Commission calculations, the pass-through from the agricultural sector to the food processing industry has a magnitude of 4%. With regard to the speed, the price transmission reaches its full magnitude within a 3-month lag. If one takes into account only the period 2007–2009, the magnitude is much higher while the speed is lower: an increase in raw food prices has been passed-through by one third within 6 months (EC 2009a).

13.3.2 Price Transmission from the Food Processing Sector to the Retail Sector

The pass-through from food processor to the distribution industry has considerably higher magnitude and speed values compared to the previously discussed pass-through. Over the period 2000–2009, an increase in the price of processed food products is transmitted to the consumer by 51% (31% immediately and 20% after 1 month) (EC 2009a). As in the previous case, the data for the window 2007–2009 shows a price transmission characterized by a higher magnitude (70%) and a lower speed (6 months).

13.3.3 Price Transmission Differences Across EU Member States

The above-mentioned price transmission figures refer to the whole EU. By analyzing price evolutions along different Member States, one major *cleavage* appears: new Member States are characterized by a pass-through with higher magnitude (for both raw food price increases and decreases) and faster speed (Bukeviciute et al. 2009a). This may be due to the greater share of raw food in the value of consumer food products for Member States characterised by low price levels. The other reasons, such as VAT and energy price increases, arbitrage within the EU, and new Member States' catching-up (see Bukeviciute et al. 2009b), do not adequately explain the stronger and faster pass-through due to agricultural commodity price reductions.

13.3.4 Bottom Line

Although the analysis of the European-wide food price developments over the long run does not raise specific issues, the asymmetric nature of price transmission within the food supply chain, especially since 2007, can be seen as a cause of concern. Coupled with the large and increasing spread between agricultural commodity prices and retail food prices and continuing agricultural commodity price increases, this suggests that retail food prices will remain high or even increase in the future.[5]

This trend implies a need for greater attention in ensuring an adequate level of fair competition within the European food supply chain in order to avoid inefficiencies. Higher prices for food would be harmful to European consumers and will undermine the competitiveness of the European food industry. Monitoring food price evolutions will not only increase price transparency, but also shed light on the level of integration of the European market for food. Significant differences in food product prices among Member States could signal an incomplete Internal Market for food,[6] because in a single market, significant price differences should be reduced over time by arbitrage activity. If not, then the persistence of significant price differences could imply the presence of obstacles and practices that fragment the European Internal Market and reduce the competition in it (EC 2008).

13.4 The European Food Prices Monitoring Tool

In order to investigate price transparency as a prerequisite for fair competition, we analyze the functioning of the European Food Prices Monitoring Tool (EFPMT) as a case study. Case studies allow researchers to explore and understand complex issues within a specific context. In a case study, a few subjects are investigated in-depth through detailed contextual analysis (Zainal 2007). In the case of the EFPMT, one interview was conducted with one national expert and two representatives of Unit G-6 Price Statistics (Purchasing Power Parities) of Eurostat in January, 2011, in Luxembourg. Since the existence of clearly defined goals for transparency practices (i.e., clear statements of what the installed transparency system intends to achieve) is regarded as the first and most important step in evaluating transparency performance (Kaplan 1983), the first part of the interview focused on the identification of the transparency goal. In the second part of the interview, the respondents were asked to prepare a general flow diagram of the food supply chains with the indication of the different stakeholders. The third part targeted the analysis of the information flow between the stakeholders: the transparency needs and preferences, the current status of transparency and the information quality. In the last part, the transparency performance was evaluated based on a set of direct and indirect performance indicators, which required the measurement of the goal achievement (Kaplan 1983). Additional insights were gained from publications of the European

[5]This evolution finds additional grounding at the time this chapter has been finalized: a recent article on the *Financial Times* illustrates the outcome of a global survey conducted by Grant Thornton on 11,000 food producers across 39 countries, showing that 41% of the respondents will increase their prices in the following 12 months (Lucas 2011).

[6]The "incompleteness" of the internal market refers to the degree of barriers to the free cross-border flow of goods, services, capital, and people (Ilzkovitz et al. 2007).

Commission (Eurostat) and feedback of local policy makers.[7] Moreover, opinions and recommendations of European Food Associations and Federations, which are (were) published on the internet, were considered (CIAA 2009; EDA 2010; EUCOLAIT 2010).

13.4.1 Background

In the second half of 2007, there was a sudden and significant increase in agricultural commodity prices, reversing a 30-years-long trend of declining agricultural commodity prices in real terms. Although unexpected, it is important to note that agricultural commodity prices are expected to eventually increase in the long run because of increasing global demand (due, among other things, to the emergence of alternative market outlets as the biofuels market), rising energy prices, changing world demographic patterns, declining food crop productivity growth, and changing climate conditions (Abbott 2009).

Concerns within the EU were growing regarding the striking difference between agricultural price levels and food price levels in the retail sector. These concerns were sharpened by the fact that the decrease in commodity prices following the price spike in 2007 did not result in a rapid or significant reduction in food prices at the retail level. Moreover, persistent differences in food product prices among Member States were believed to signal the presence of barriers to cross-border flows of goods and services, indicating an incomplete Internal Market for food, as argued above.

Because of the spike in food and commodity prices, combined with the fact that the food sector is a significant part of the European economy (5% of EU value added, 7% of EU employment) and food purchases comprise a significant share of consumer expenditures (16% of EU household expenditure) (EC 2009b), there was a *momentum* for a reflection on the functioning of the European food supply chain. A number of European Commission communications on this issue started to emerge between 2008 and 2009, culminating with the communication "A better functioning food supply in Europe," published on October 28, 2009 (EC 2009b). The increase in food price transparency is one of the four main objectives defined by the document in order to improve the soundness of the European food supply chain: "The Commission will also contribute to increase the transparency on prices in the food supply chain. It has set up a food prices monitoring tool, available to the public, which will enable to follow price developments of food at each step of the food supply chain. It will then be easier to identify, for example, when the food consumer prices do not decrease fast enough" (EC 2009c, p. 2).

[7] See Eurostat homepage online at http://epp.eurostat.ec.europa.eu/portal/page/portal/eurostat/home/

The need for more price transparency has been recognized at both the supply and demand sides of the food supply chain. On the supply side, agricultural commodity prices have been characterized by a strong volatility during the past decade, which weakens price predictability. At the same time, after the deregulatory process on commodity markets in the mid-1990s, the last decade has also seen a strong growth of financial market activities for agricultural commodities, both in terms of exchange platforms and of financial products offered, such as derivatives. This development can reduce uncertainty by facilitating risk management and price discovery, but it can also create the risk of speculative bubbles that can exacerbate price volatility (EC 2008, 2009d). A recent article in the *Guardian* reports several declarations by bankers and traders admitting that speculation played a non-negligible role in the 2007–2009 food price crisis (Vidal 2011).

On the demand side of the food supply chain, an increase in food retail price transparency is crucial to reduce search costs for consumers and stimulate competition in the distribution sector. According to a survey accompanying the communication "A better functioning food supply in Europe," most EU consumers find it easy to compare prices of products at their retailer and are satisfied with the price transparency. The major problem seems to be the comparability of prices among different retailers (EC 2009e).

In order to address the problem in the upstream market, the European Commission intends to improve "the oversight and overall transparency of agricultural commodity derivatives markets" EC (2009b, p. 9) in order to increase confidence for commercial actors while reducing the risk of speculative bubbles. With regard to food retail price transparency and comparability, the Commission suggests the development of price comparison tools (i.e., websites) at the national level. In addition, a comprehensive initiative covering the whole food supply chain has been developed as the EFPMT. According to the European Commission, the purpose of this tool is to contribute in ensuring competition in the food sector through two channels. First, by tracking consumer price levels of comparable food products across Member States, it allows European regulators to assess the level of integration of the internal market for retail food as it is believed that price differences between Member States for comparable food products signal the level of fragmentation within the Internal Market. Second, by tracking (selected) food price developments at each level of the food supply chain for each Member State, it improves transparency of food prices (EC 2009b).

13.4.2 Description

The EFPMT intends to increase price transparency by facilitating comparisons of price developments at the agricultural commodity, food processing and retail levels of the food supply chain across the European Member States. Since it is impossible to give a full description of all food supply chains in Europe and to show the

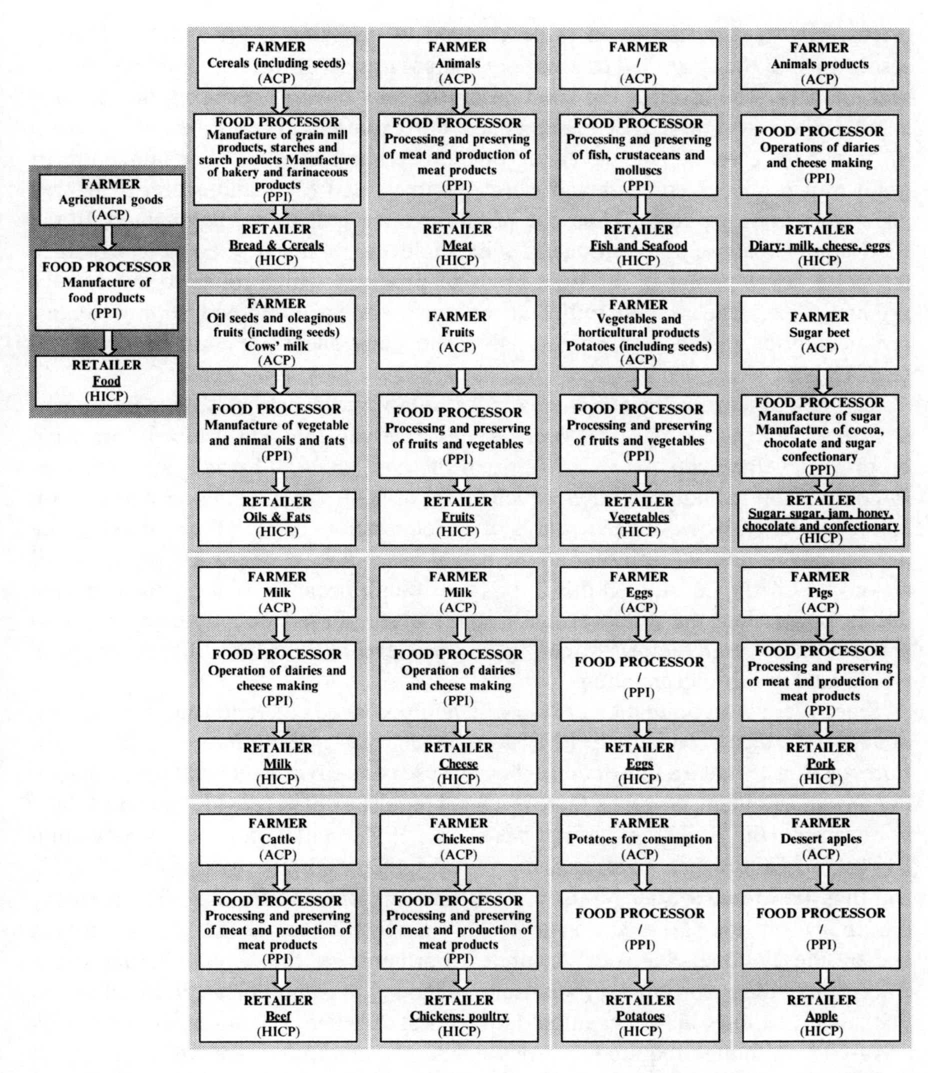

Fig. 13.3 Flow diagram of the 17 food supply chains in the European Food Prices Monitoring Tool. Note: *ACP* agricultural commodity price index, *PPI* producer price index, *HICP* harmonized index of consumer prices

complete price transmission process, only some parts of selected food supply chains are included in the EFPMT. The 17 selected food supply chains, together with their involved stakeholders and their activities, are shown in Fig. 13.3.

For each of these food supply chains, the agricultural commodity price index (ACP), the producer price index (PPI) and the harmonized index of consumer prices (HICP) (i.e., the retail price charged to consumers) are presented. As a result, each of the described food supply chains consists of farmers, food processors and retailers. The level of the food processor may cover, depending on the food supply chain, several stages of the chain. For example, in the food supply chain of "bread & cereals," the level of food processor includes (1) manufacture of grain mill products, starches and starch products and (2) manufacture of bakery and farinaceous products. Thus, the producer price indices are aggregated. In the food supply chain of dairy products for example, the producer price indices include the price development in different kinds of products which relate to these dairy products (e.g., cheese and milk). In contrast, for specific food supply chains, producer price indices are not available and consequently cannot be displayed (e.g., eggs).

The EFPMT exclusively includes index numbers; the statistics have no dimension (e.g., euro per kilogram). Price indices give valuable and useful information on price developments over time (e.g., in the beef chain, all prices are expresses in comparison to the year 2005 which is set at 100). This avoids problems with incomparability. However, Eurostat is often requested to expand the tool to include dimensions of prices (representing the actual price, e.g., euro per kilogram). Until recently, Eurostat considered this to be too difficult because food products change during processing: the products that farmers make are not directly comparable to products in the retail sector. Presenting the price level of these two different products would lead to misinterpretation.

Since there is no regulation or rule which imposes the collection and comparison of data at the chain level, the EFPMT goes beyond the legal minimum requirements. Eurostat tries to make a more comprehensive use of statistical data that are available. For the stakeholders, however, there is a legal requirement to provide statistical data. For example, the HICP is produced based on a 1995 regulation (Council regulation 2494/95 of EC), which states that the European Commission will produce HICPs and that the Member States must provide data on prices to Eurostat for preparing the HICPs following all rules that are established by the Member States, by Eurostat and by the National Statistical Institutes. Furthermore, the regulation states that enterprises selling consumer products are obligated to communicate to the National Statistical Institutes all information they request. Similar regulations exist for PPIs and ACPs. Although required to provide data, the enterprises are willing to report the necessary information because the National Statistical Institutes guarantee the secrecy of the individual data of the individual enterprises. Moreover, the enterprises understand the necessity of having the statistics, but they do not want to lose time and money on calculating these statistics themselves if their competitors would not participate in the surveys.

For consumer prices there is a regulation on time coverage for data measurement, which is particularly important for vegetables and fruits, and other products that have volatile prices. Here, prices must be collected in the country during at least 3 weeks of the month. Member States report the collected consumer prices monthly to Eurostat and the results are published within 2 weeks after the reporting

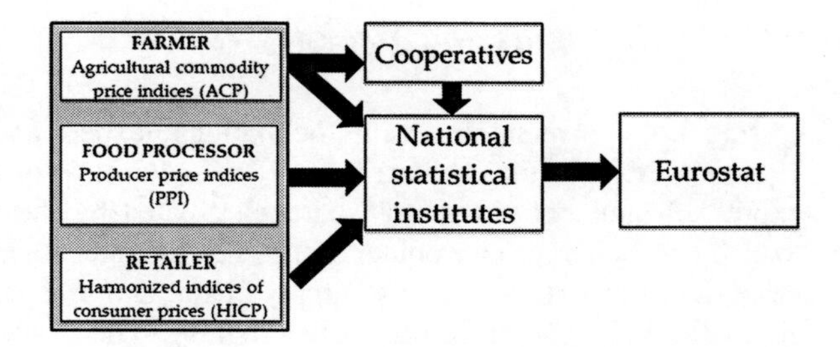

Fig. 13.4 Information flow in the food supply chains of the European Food Prices Monitoring Tool

month. This means that consumer prices are available monthly. Producer prices are collected and reported monthly, and published around 1 month later. Agricultural commodity prices are collected and reported quarterly (budget constraints). Eurostat has so far solved this problem in the tables by attributing the quarterly data to each month of the quarter.

The retailers and food processors report respectively the consumer price indices and the producer price indices to the National Statistical Institutes. For the ACPs, farmers report directly to National Statistical Institutes or to cooperatives that represent farmers and then the cooperatives report to the National Statistical Institutes. This means that there is no price information flow in the food supply chains between the different stakeholders; there is a third party (Eurostat) that aggregates the data (Fig. 13.4).

Before 1996, all countries had their own consumer price index and used their own methods for data collection. When Eurostat started to collect European prices, they harmonized an important part of the process, focused on collecting price indices of comparable products, and agreed on certain aspects of the methods used. However, the primary focus lies in harmonizing the output of the statistics to make the output comparable and it is the task of the National Statistical Institutes to define the process and collect the data. Here it should be mentioned that there can be a difference in the process for different statistics (e.g., there is a different approach for collecting consumer prices, regional prices, producer prices, commodity prices). Currently, the emphasis is shifting towards harmonizing the process because it is believed that it would be more advisable to have one system that is applied to all countries.

Eurostat performs regularly monitoring visits to the European Member States, where they discuss the methodology behind the process of price collection and price processing. In this way, Eurostat ensures that all Member States follow the regulations and interpret the regulations consistently so that Eurostat is able to report comparable statistics. It may happen that, during such visits, Eurostat encounters interesting methodology problems (e.g., how to classify new consumer products in the COICOP, or Classification of Individual Consumption According to Purpose). In these cases, Eurostat works out a solution for these problems based on agreements with all Member States.

13.4.3 Strengths and Weaknesses

During our conversations with the national expert and two representatives of Unit G-6 Price Statistics (Purchasing Power Parities) of Eurostat, the respondents expressed their belief that transparency created by the EFPMT is important (1) to achieve better price comparability, (2) to understand price transmission and price developments in the food supply chain, and as a result (3) to identify unfair competition, and (4) to inform policy making. The Confederation of the Food and Drink Industries of the EU (CIAA) supports the EFPMT that aims to report price developments and differences between Member States and sub-sectors in order to increase price transparency throughout the food supply chain. They acknowledge the importance of (1) improving the competitiveness along the food supply chain and (2) ensuring fair and market-based prices by providing better information to consumers, public authorities and market operators (CIAA 2009). Furthermore, the European Parliament is pleased with the tool in the context of rising food prices (Lyon and Reimers 2011). The European Dairy Association (EDA) believes that the EFPMT will improve information on the production of milk and milk products, which could help better adjust supply to demand (and consequently contribute to perfect competition) (EDA 2010).

In the EFPMT, price indices of agricultural products are compared along the food supply chain to evaluate price transmission. Agricultural products are only one of the inputs in the production process, however. Inputs such as labor, energy and transport – which significantly contribute to the added value of the final product – are not considered in the tool. Furthermore, not only can different sets of inputs be used to produce specific final products, but also one specific input (agricultural commodity) can result in different kinds of final products, thus weakening price comparisons. For example, beef from cattle can end up in steak and in minced meat, each with different prices.

In addition, there can be differences between the production processes and products covered across Member States. Because of a high level of aggregation, the data of the tool represents broad categories of selected food products (e.g., bread and cereals) and not all production processes and products per Member State. For example, the retail price index for bread and cereals will include different products in Bulgaria as compared to Finland or Spain. As a result, the National Statistical Institutes attempt to identify representative samples of retail products within a certain core group to reflect specific national circumstances. The selection of sampled products may depend on consumption patterns within the country, and the selected products can differ between two shops depending on the assortment of produces within the shops. The retail prices are translated into price indices before they are aggregated and sent to Eurostat. As these are all products within the same core group and as the prices are expressed as indices, the retail prices become comparable. Moreover, the three main statistics (agricultural commodity price indices, producer price indices, harmonized indices of consumer prices) are not always available for all food products of all Member States, because in some countries particular food products are not produced and consequently data cannot be provided.

International trade is not reported because it is difficult to select the relevant trade flows and to have comparable data on price developments for trade of food products (EC 2009b). Eurostat acknowledges the importance of these international trade data. Therefore, Eurostat is currently investigating which international trade figures they can include (by using import price indices or by using Unit Value Indices based on detailed international trade data) and in which food supply chains, because all food supply chains are different and each situation may be different between countries.

Besides the EFPMT, other price monitoring initiatives exist, such as the Price Monitoring Tool of the Food and Agricultural Organization (FAO), and the Quarterly Food Price Monitor of the National Agricultural Marketing Council of South Africa (NAMC). FAO published the Price Monitoring Tool, which can be used to monitor developments in market prices by including monthly data for at least 7 years on nominal market prices and consumer price indices. This tool is applicable for every type of food commodity and stage in the food supply chain (e.g., farmer, wholesaler, retailer). The output is a graph that indicates past trends in prices and future benchmark price developments (Dawe and Doroudian 2011). NAMC aims "to provide service of excellence to the Minister, Department of Agriculture and Directly Affected Group's (DAGs) on the strategic positioning of South African Agriculture in dynamic global markets." The Quarterly Food Price Monitoring Report is one of the publications of NAMC, which describes overall inflation and food inflation rates for South Africa and other selected countries, urban and rural food price trends, international food/commodity prices and trends. The reported data are obtained from Statistics South Africa (urban food prices and consumer price indices), AC Nielsen (urban food prices), Adcheck (retail prices) and FAO (food price indices on a monthly basis) (NAMC 2011). These initiatives indicate that there is a large interest in price developments. However, the EFPMT goes even further by aiming to display price transmissions.

13.5 Contribution to Fair Competition

In principle, price transparency should contribute to fair competition. By increasing the visibility of food price developments and price transmission, customers (food processors, retailers and consumers) become more price sensitive (demand elasticity should increase), which in turn should enhance competition among food processors and retailers.[8] This is particularly true when customers can compare price

[8]For example, in the case of water demand, Gaudin (2006) shows that when consumers are given information about the price of water on their water bills, their price elasticity for water increases by 30%.

developments of substitute goods, since price transparency improvements would cover in detail a wider part of the relevant market, if not the whole relevant market. In this respect, the tool can be more effective in product areas where there is a clear distinction among product types (e.g., beef/pork/poultry meat, in contrast to oils and fats which are considered together). However, this effect depends largely on the visibility the tool will get. Since food processors and retailers are more concerned than consumers with input prices, it seems reasonable that food processors and retailers will use it more than consumers will. In this regard, the possibility of processors and retailers comparing price variations among Member States can serve the purpose of the tool: if price differences among EU countries are high enough to offset transportation costs (and if one assumes national and foreign products to be homogeneous), producers might decide to switch suppliers from one country to another, thus enhancing the internal market for food products and the merits-based competition in it.

Nevertheless, the link between price transmission and fair competition need not be direct or automatic. On the one hand, imperfect price transmission can be compatible with fair competition, if, for instance, the imperfection is due to menu or reputational costs (EC 2009a) or the perishable nature of some food products (Ward 1982). On the other hand, a sound pass-through of prices does not guarantee a perfect functioning of the food supply chain because it does not preclude the possibility of rent extraction in case of monopsony power.

However, one could question whether the EFPMT is an effective way of creating transparency and thus fair competition. First, there is no transfer of actual price information between the different levels of the food supply chain. Rather, a third party (Eurostat) aggregates the data and makes them transparent. But aggregation at a national level and among specific products (cheese, milk, oils and fats etc.) might attenuate the ability of price signals to foster competition among specific products, especially if consumers are not interested in monitoring the tool on a regular basis. It is possible that other initiatives could better target these buyers, given the lack of comparability among retailers (EC 2009e), which is why the EC suggests internet tools at national levels to compare prices among retailers (EC 2009b).

Second, an improvement in price transparency could increase the risk of collusion among suppliers. The tool could harm fair competition if any of the product groups is characterized by a very "tight and stable oligopoly" (EU 2011, para. 89) in one of the three main levels of the food supply chain, especially in the last two levels (food processors and retailers), because of the more frequent data release. For this reason, the tool does not contain current price information (it is usually 45 days to 6 months), thus lowering the risk of collusive practices among food processors but also weakening its relevance (because prices information is not current).

Third, the tool displays a very simplified image of the reality, where price transmission is studied by comparing agricultural commodity, producer and consumer price indices, even though the correlations among these indices are not well understood. As stated above, the correlation between agricultural commodity and food producer prices is weaker than the correlation between food producer and retail prices. This might suggest that the agricultural sector is the weaker link in the food supply chain. However, since more value is created throughout the food supply chain by transformation activities, such as the processing of agricultural commodities into food products, rather than through transportation from processor to retailer, it is reasonable to expect that the three price indices do not present similar pictures.

In spite of these drawbacks, the EFPMT creates experience in price transparency and thus can contribute to debates regarding fair competition. Therefore, it will be important, but also difficult, to find the right balance between details (complexity) and understandability (transparency), as well as between potential positive and negative effects. Hence, there is a case for different levels of disclosure according to different market structures to maximize the positive effect of price transparency on fair competition.

Acknowledgment This chapter was prepared under the framework of the Transparent_Food (Quality and Integrity in Food: A Challenge for Chain Communication and Transparency Research) project. Transparent_Food is an integrated project financed by the European Commission under the 7th Framework Programme (FP7/2007-2013, grant agreement no. 24500). The information in this document reflects only the authors' views and the Community is not liable for any use that may be made of the information contained therein. The authors are grateful for the consortium members for their contributions.

References

Abbott, P. 2009. *Development dimensions of high food prices*. OECD Food, Agriculture and Fisheries Working Papers No. 18. doi: 10.1787/222521043712.

Bukeviciute, L., A. Dierx, F. Ilzkovitz, and G. Roty. 2009a. *Price transmission along the food supply chain in the European Union*. 113th EAAE Seminar, "A resilient European food industry and food chain in a challenging world," 3–6 September 2009, Chania, Crete, Greece, 17. http://ageconsearch.umn.edu/bitstream/57987/2/Bukeviciute.pdf. Accessed 1 Sept 2012.

Bukeviciute, L., A. Dierx, and F. Ilzkovitz. 2009b. *The functioning of the food supply chain and its effect on food prices in the European Union*. European Commission, Economic and Financial Affairs, Occasional Papers 47, May. http://ec.europa.eu/economy_finance/publications/publication15234_en.pdf. Accessed 1 Sept 2012.

CIAA. 2009. CIAA comments and reaction on the European Commission's Communication "Food Prices in Europe" – COM (2008) 821/4. *Confederation of the Food and Drink Industries of the EU*. http://www.ciaa.be/documents/positions/pos_20090218-001.pdf. Accessed 17 June 2011.

Dawe, D., and A. Doroudian. 2011. A simple monitoring tool to assess monthly changes in food prices. *Food and Agriculture Organization*. http://www.fao.org/docrep/013/am241e/am241e00.pdf. Accessed 17 June 2011.

EC. 2008. *Food prices in Europe*. COM(2008) 821/4. Brussels: Commission of the European Communities. http://ec.europa.eu/economy_finance/publications/publication13571_en.pdf. Accessed 17 Jan 2012.

EC. 2009a. *Analysis of price transmission along the food supply chain in the EU*. SEC(2009) 1450. Brussels: Commission of the European Communities. http://ec.europa.eu/economy_finance/publications/publication16067_en.pdf. Accessed 17 Jan 2012.

EC. 2009b. *A better functioning food supply chain in Europe*. COM(2009) 591. Brussels: Commission of the European Communities. http://ec.europa.eu/economy_finance/publications/publication16061_en.pdf. 17 Jan 2012.

EC. 2009c. *A better functioning food supply chain in Europe*. Press Release, MEMO/09/483. Brussels: Commission of the European Communities. http://europa.eu/rapid/pressReleasesAction.do?reference=MEMO/09/483&format=HTML&aged=0&language=EN&guiLanguage=en. Accessed 17 Jan 2012.

EC. 2009d. *Agricultural commodity derivative markets: The way ahead*. SEC(2009) 1447. Brussels: Commission of the European Communities. http://ec.europa.eu/economy_finance/publications/publication16071_en.pdf. Accessed 17 Jan 2012.

EC. 2009e. *Improving price transparency along the food supply chain for consumers and policy makers*. SEC(2009) 1446. Brussels: Commission of the European Communities. http://ec.europa.eu/economy_finance/publications/publication16073_en.pdf. Accessed 17 Jan 2012.

EC-Eurostat. 2009. A European food prices monitoring tool: A first design. http://epp.eurostat.ec.europa.eu/portal/page/portal/hicp/documents/Tab/Tab/European%20Food%20Prices.pdf. Accessed 17 June 2011.

EU. 2008. Consolidated version of the treaty on the functioning of the European Union. *Official Journal of the European Union* 9.5.2008, C115/47–C115/199. http://eur-lex.europa.eu/LexUriServ/LexUriServ.do?uri=OJ:C:2008:115:0047:0199:en:PDF. Accessed 17 Jan 2012.

EU. 2011. Guidelines on the applicability of Article 101 of the Treaty on the Functioning of the European Union to horizontal co-operation agreements. *Official Journal of the European Union* 14.1.2011, C 11/1–C 11/72. http://eur-lex.europa.eu/LexUriServ/LexUriServ.do?uri=OJ:C:2011:011:0001:0072:EN:PDF. Accessed 17 Jan 2012.

EUCOLAIT. 2010. EUCOLAIT comments on the recommendations of the High Level Experts Group on Milk. *European Association of Dairy Trade*. http://www.eucolait.be/positions. Accessed 17 June 2011.

European Dairy Association (EDA). 2010. Position paper: EDA's position on High Level Expert Group on milk recommendations. *European Dairy Association*. http://www.euromilk.org/upload/docs/EDA/100615_EDA%20Position%20on%20HLEG%20Recommendations.pdf. Accessed 17 June 2011.

European Parliament and Council (EPC). 1997. Directive concerning misleading advertisings so as to include comparative advertising. Directive 97/55/EC. http://eur-lex.europa.eu/LexUriServ/LexUriServ.do?uri=CELEX:31997L0055:EN:NOT. Accessed 17 Jan 2012.

European Parliament and Council (EPC). 2004. Directive on the enforcement of intellectual property rights. Directive 2004/48/EC. http://eur-lex.europa.eu/LexUriServ/LexUriServ.do?uri=CELEX:32004L0048:EN:NOT. Accessed 17 Jan 2012.

European Parliament and Council (EPC). 2005. Directive concerning unfair business-to-consumer commercial practices in the internal market. Directive 2005/29/EC. http://eur-lex.europa.eu/LexUriServ/LexUriServ.do?uri=CELEX:32005L0029:EN:NOT. Accessed 17 Jan 2012.

Gaudin, S. 2006. Effect of price information on residential water demand. *Applied Economics* 38(4): 383–393.

Ilzkovitz, F., A. Dierx, V. Kovacs, and N. Sousa. 2007. *Steps towards a deeper economic integration: The internal market in the 21st century*. European Economy, European Commission, Directorate-General for Economic and Financial Affairs, Economic Papers, No. 271, January 1988.

Kaplan, R.S. 1983. Measuring manufacturing performance: A new challenge for managerial accounting research. *The Accounting Review* 58(4): 686.

Lucas, L. 2011. Food producers plan price increases. *Financial Times,* November 24.

Lyon, G., and B. Reimers. 2011. Motion for a resolution. *European Parliament*. http://www.europarl.europa.eu/sides/getDoc.do?type=MOTION&reference=B7-2011-0116&language=EN. Accessed 17 June 2011.

Mollgaard, H.P., and P.B. Overgaard. 2001. Market transparency and competition policy. *Rivista di Politica Economica* 91(4–5): 11–58.

NAMC. 2011. Food price monitoring. *National Agricultural Marketing Council*. http://www.namc.co.za/dnn/PublishedReports/FoodPriceMonitoring.aspx. Accessed 17 June 2011.

New Europe. 2008. EU enforces transparency in air travel sector. http://www.neurope.eu/print.php?id=90396. Accessed 17 June 2011.

OECD. 2001. Price transparency. Directorate for Financial, Fiscal and Enterprise Affairs/Committee on Competition Law and Policy. http://www.oecd.org/dataoecd/52/63/2535975.pdf. Accessed 17 June 2011.

OECD. 2006. Policy brief: What is competition on the merits? http://www.oecd.org/dataoecd/10/27/37082099.pdf. Accessed 17 June 2011.

Sanchez, R., and A. Heene. 2004. *The new strategic management: Organization, competition, and competences*. New York: Wiley.

Vidal, J. 2011. Food speculation: "People die from hunger while banks make a killing on food." *Guardian*, January 23. http://www.guardian.co.uk/global-development/2011/jan/23/food-speculation-banks-hunger-poverty. Accessed 17 June 2011.

Ward, R.W. 1982. Asymmetry in retail, wholesale, and shipping point pricing for fresh vegetables. *American Journal of Agricultural Economics* 62: 205–212.

Zainal, Z. 2007. Case study as a research method. *Jurnal Kemanusiaan* 9: 6.

Index

H.S. James Jr. (ed.), *The Ethics and Economics of Agrifood Competition*, The International Library of Environmental, Agricultural and Food Ethics 20, DOI 10.1007/978-94-007-6274-9, © Springer Science+Business Media Dordrecht. 2013

CPSIA information can be obtained at www.ICGtesting.com
Printed in the USA
LVOW071438030413

327443LV00008B/218/P